Contemporary Trends in Conflict and Communication

Emerging Trends in Conflict Management

Editor-in-Chief
Helena Desivilya Syna

Volume 1

Contemporary Trends in Conflict and Communication

Technology and Social Media

Edited by
Jessica Katz Jameson and Missy F. Hannah

DE GRUYTER

ISBN 978-3-11-068721-7
e-ISBN (PDF) 978-3-11-068726-2
e-ISBN (EPUB) 978-3-11-068732-3

Library of Congress Control Number: 2022932637

Bibliographic information published by the Deutsche Nationalbibliothek
The Deutsche Nationalbibliothek lists this publication in the Deutsche Nationalbibliografie; detailed bibliographic data are available on the internet at http://dnb.dnb.de.

Cover image: Gettyimages/ngupakarti
Typesetting: Integra Software Services Pvt. Ltd.
Printing and binding: CPI books GmbH, Leck

www.degruyter.com

MIX
Papier aus verantwortungsvollen Quellen
FSC® C083411

The editors wish to dedicate this book to our partners in life, Brian Jameson and Tom Hannah, and family members, for their endless patience as we practice our conflict management skills with them.

Foreword

Over the course of 2019, I contemplated and ultimately engaged in planning the multi-volume series *Emerging Trends in Conflict Management*. Conflict constitutes a ubiquitous phenomenon reflected in human interactions at the interpersonal, intragroup, intergroup, and societal levels. Notwithstanding the omnipresence of conflicts, the approaches, strategies, and tactics for engaging discord manifests in wide variations due to global and local developments and specific contextual adaptations.

The impetus for embarking on this project stemmed from vivid, vicarious, and lived experiences of mounting diversification of organizations and communities in most parts of the world as a result of globalization and migration trends. These developments have led to an exacerbation of existing or emerging intergroup tensions and social divisions. Diversity and intergroup tensions enhance the scope and depth of societal, organizational, and community conflicts. Adding to these intricate transitions are unprecedented developments in technology and the prevailing use of social media that have turned conflict management at the societal, organizational, and community levels into a highly perplexing endeavor.

Hence, I was delighted that Jessica Katz Jameson, an accomplished and highly engaged scholar and practitioner of conflict and communication, accepted my invitation to edit a volume she titled *Contemporary Trends in Conflict and Communication: Technology and Social Media*. Missy F. Hannah, a specialist in social media marketing, rhetoric, and activism, later joined as co-editor.

The first volume *of Emerging Trends in Conflict Management* addresses the interface of conflict with technology and social media, and engages with the precarious developments of increased polarization, impeding the capacity of diverse parties to maintain constructive conflict communication. The designated culprits exacerbating this intricacy were those using digital technology, especially social media. At the same time, the latter has also advanced platforms that are potentially capable of promoting communication and advance cooperation in a variety of family, organizational, and community contexts. Jameson, Hannah, and the authors who have contributed to *Contemporary Trends in Conflict and Communication: Technology and Social Media* explore such a duality through their research and practical experiences.

As relayed in the introduction, shortly after sending the call for chapters, the book editors along with most of the world faced the outbreak of COVID-19, where we consequently shifted primarily to online communication to engage with disputes, while retaining some of its components "offline." Thus, conflict management has gradually moved to "hybrid" frameworks – a mixture of online and physical, face-to-face interactions. The book chapters present and discuss the emerging insights and practical lessons with regard to such continuing transformations in conflict resolution training, practice, and future theoretical development. Jameson, Hannah, and the authors also share their online experiences with current events (such as increased social protests around the globe).

https://doi.org/10.1515/9783110687262-202

In sum, *Contemporary Trends in Conflict and Communication: Technology and Social Media* provides a cutting-edge, contemporary collection of chapters, organized into three sections, explicating researchers' and practitioners' reflections and experiences with: ways of creating spaces for dialogue and fostering cooperation by means of technology, thereby attempting to counteract mounting polarization; patterns of conflict communication through social media platforms; and the use of online dispute resolution (ODR) in education and training contexts.

I wish to congratulate the book editors – Jessica Katz Jameson and Missy F. Hannah – for assembling and presenting such a diverse mix of contributions, all engaging with the crossroads of conflict and communication, thus illuminating the current and emerging developments in dispute resolution using technology and social media. I also thank all the authors for sharing their enlightening work. This first volume of *Emerging Trends in Conflict Management* will undoubtedly nourish and enrich readers with novel insights regarding conflict in hybrid spaces of communication.

Helena Desivilya Syna,
Editor-in-Chef, *Emerging Trends in Conflict Management*
Editor-in- Chief, *Conflict Resolution Quarterly*
Professor of Social/Organizational Psychology & Diversity/Conflict Management
The Max Stern Yezreel Valley College
Yezreel Valley, Israel

Acknowledgements

In March of 2019, North Carolina State University's Communication, Rhetoric and Digital Media (CRDM) doctoral program sponsored a symposium titled "Dialog 2.0: Social Movements, Online Communication & Transformation." As Chair of the symposium, Jessica's vision was that this would be a way to engage graduate students and faculty in a discussion of the trends and future of online conflict, with an eye toward promoting dialogue and conflict transformation. As this event was a catalyst for the creation of this volume, our acknowledgements start with the CRDM Symposium committee, which included Missy F. Hannah (co-editor, this volume), Shenita Denson (Symposium co-chair), faculty advisers Dr. David Berube and Dr. Nicole Lee; and committee members Dr. Candice Edrington (contributor, this volume), Beth Greene, Melissa Stone, and CRDM Director, Dr. Nick Taylor. In addition to the faculty and students from around the country who participated, we want to acknowledge the NC State College of Humanities and Social Sciences Research Office, led by Associate Dean Tom Birkland, for awarding us a Lightning Rod grant to support continued conversations and development of publications for dissemination of our work. Dr. Nicole Lee and Jessica previously published a special issue of *Social Media + Society* titled "Dialogue 2.0: New Perspectives, Enduring Challenges, and Promising Directions" (October–December 2020) based on work presented at the Symposium (and supplemented with additional pieces from around the world). We thank editor Dr. Zizi Paparachissi for that opportunity and for serving as keynote speaker for the CRDM Symposium.

Jessica's vision was also to co-edit a book related to the topic of conflict and dialogue in online spaces. It was serendipitous when Dr. Helena Desivilya Syna, Editor-in-Chief of the series in *Emerging Trends in Conflict Management* approached Jessica at the annual conference of the International Association for Conflict Management in Summer of 2019 about editing a book on conflict and technology. That was the very beginning of the planning for this volume, and it is important to acknowledge IACM for connecting Jessica with Helena as well as providing a welcoming, interdisciplinary, and international scholarly community that has supported Jessica's intellectual growth and success since graduate school. We also want to acknowledge SAS Institute where Missy works, for their support and encouragement while she completes the CRDM doctoral program and their enthusiasm for her work on this project. Finally, we want to thank all the contributors to this volume for sharing their ideas, working with us on revisions, and responding to our requests for additional work and information in a timely manner that allowed us to stay on deadline! And of course, thank you to Lucy Jarman and the staff at DeGruyter for their assistance and production support.

https://doi.org/10.1515/9783110687262-203

Contents

Jessica Katz Jameson & Missy F. Hannah

Introduction

We were first invited to compile and edit this volume in 2019. At that time many types of technologies were used in conflict management, and we imagined this book would cover online dispute resolution in various contexts (legal, home, work), the use of online tools for conflict and collaboration among work teams, and conflict and collaboration on social media. By the time we sent out the call for chapter proposals, reports of COVID-19 had emerged, much of the world was on lockdown, and suddenly we were doing nearly all communication online.

We have seen and experienced the myriad ways conflict communication occurs in mediated spaces, whether through social media platforms such as Twitter, Facebook, and Instagram, social enterprise spaces such as Yammer! and proprietary networks, or through formal conflict management and dispute system technologies. Throughout the world, conflicts are increasingly mediated in "hybrid" spaces – intersections among online and physical space. Therefore, learning how to improve mediated communication in these spaces during conflict is an important empirical and practical issue.

Then in the summer of 2020, nationwide protests erupted in the US in response to the murder of George Floyd. In an era of increased polarization, the move to online conflict management became even more challenging as people have often shown a lack of willingness and ability to engage in productive dialogue online. While the use of social media is often implicated in the promulgation of alternative facts, false news, and intimidation, years of experience with social media and formal Online Dispute Resolution (ODR) processes suggest that online spaces also give voice to those who have been historically marginalized and have unique affordances that can be used to enhance and transform conflict communication in family, workplace, and social settings.

As editors, we were living with the stress of these conflicts in our own personal experiences, whether through technologically-mediated meetings or on social media, and it became evident that we and others had theoretical questions about the social consequences of social (physical) distancing, virtual communication, and the proliferation of misinformation as well as practical considerations and best practices for engaging conflict in virtual spaces. We recognized that this book could provide an important vehicle for authors' contributions about the conflicts unfolding on social media platforms.

As chapter proposals started coming in, the influence of the COVID-19 pandemic, increasingly remote work, and ongoing racial and political conflicts were clear in the variety of ways conflict scholars and practitioners were thinking about and using technology and social media. We refined our vision for the book to include sections covering how groups use technology to promote dialogue and collaboration, conflict

https://doi.org/10.1515/9783110687262-001

and dialogue on social media, and online dispute resolution in education and training contexts. These three sections allow us to display contemporary trends in conflict and communication using technology and social media and also showcase cutting-edge research that helps us make sense of the times we are living in. The contributors to this volume also highlight key areas for future research to improve conflict communication, dialogue, and collaboration and propose ideas for using technology to transform and connect rather than polarize and divide. Below we preview the organization of the chapters into three sections with a concluding chapter that synthesizes best practices for developing Online Dispute Resolution systems.

Using Technology to Promote Dialogue and Collaboration

The attention to contentious social issues such as those related to environmental sustainability, health and science communication, and political views and values has inspired many scholars to examine new ways to promote dialogue using digital tools. While social media such as Facebook and Twitter have more often been found to lead to polarization than dialogue (i.e., Matuszewski & Szabo, 2019; Tappin & McKay, 2019; Wolleback et al., 2019) there are also some success stories (Bakshy, Messing, & Adamic, 2015; Haim, Graefe, & Brosius, 2018; Ron, Suleiman, & Maoz, 2020) and several such cases are described in this volume. In a completely different context, much has been written about online collaboration of geographically-dispersed teams. In the pre-COVID-19 era, this work was stimulated by the increasingly global nature of organizations and work teams (Shachaf, 2008), the use of interdisciplinary and cross-sector teams to address complex problems (Janssen et al., 2019), and the proliferation of technological tools to support virtual collaboration (Johnson, Bettenhausen, & Gibbons, 2009; Weber & Kim, 2015).

With social media being one of the most used tools in online conflict and dialogue, more than a billion social media users are communicating with those they know on a personal level every day as well as gaining access to political figures and celebrities. Social media allows users to discuss and debate government policy, share opinions on social and political issues, and reinforce or resist calls to action. In Chapter One of this volume, "*Ways and Means: How Think Tanks Use Social Media to Influence Public Policy,*" Daisung Jang, John Bechara, and William P. Bottom describe how social media allows think tank participants direct access to influencing public policy and societal opinions.

The public nature of social media complicates its use in organizations that must carefully manage the tensions of public and private communication, such as the case of the U.S. Intelligence Community. In Chapter Two, "*AI Platforms and U.S. Intelligence: Opportunities for Collaboration, Dialogue, and Negotiation,*" Kathleen Vogel and Matthew Schmidt discuss the development of the analytic components library (ACL), a platform that would integrate artificial intelligence (AI)-enabled data collection that could then be shared across intelligence agencies to improve collaboration and expedite preparedness and response to security threats. Vogel and Schmidt raise a series of important questions that need to be examined when developing new AI platforms to assist with conflict management and collaboration that extend beyond the world of the intelligence community.

While platforms such as the ACL take years to develop, the COVID-19 pandemic required a rapid shift to online communication for many conflict management practitioners, and Deborah Goldstein describes what she learned in Chapter Three, "*Online Deliberative Dialogue with State Leaders: A North Carolina Case Study.*" In a similar vein, practitioners in community mediation centers had to learn how to maintain their services in light of physical distancing requirements. Jeanne Felicity Zimmer, D.G. Mawn, Lori Dieckman, and Melinda Burrell describe their experience of adapting to online conflict management in Chapter Four, "*Connecting Communities Virtually Through Community Mediation.*" This section shifts from the local to global as Arik Segal and Yotam Keduri describe their innovative analysis of a facilitated program that promoted online discourse between Israeli-Palestinian participants in a Facebook group in Chapter Five, "*Going Hybrid: Using Facebook Groups for People-to-People Dialogue.*"

Continuing the examination of dialogue on social media, Candice Edrington calls our attention to the social issue of race relations and how social media has been used by public figures to organize, inform, and engage productively in Chapter Six, "*Can You Hear Me Now? How #ShareTheMicNow Used Dialogue and Collaboration to Amplify the Voices of Black Women.*"

Conflict Communication on Social Media

In the early days of the internet, scholars speculated on the impact of this new forum for public debate and discourse. Optimists were enthusiastic about the availability of an online town hall that would enable inclusive participation of historically marginalized voices (Papacharissi, 2002), while others expressed a more uncertain or cynical view describing the potential for the technology to lead to the creation of echo chambers and increased polarization (Boyd, 2014; Sunstein, 2002, 2017; Wellman, 1997). Still others proposed that it is not the technology itself, but the interests and goals of the users that influence online communication:

> [T]he Internet functions as an amplifier: It increases our potential for good and productive work as well as for inappropriate and immoral endeavors . . . Ultimately, a technology is only as useful as the intentions of its users. (Banschick & Banschick, 2003, 161)

Intentions of the user notwithstanding, social media is not merely a neutral channel of communication. The second section of the book problematizes the role of social media in conflict, starting with the question of how the affordances of social media impact who is allowed to participate. In juxtaposition to Edrington's study of how famous users can use their voice to promote dialogue, Malaka Friedman presents the case of a public figure who used social media to block dialogue in Chapter Seven, "*The Right to Tweet Freely: Citizen-Government Social Media Conflict.*"

Moving to a micro-level, Ioana Cionea and Amy Johnson present data on the relationship between conflict styles and interpersonal conflict management on Facebook in Chapter Eight, "*Conflict Management on Facebook: Relationships between Conflict Styles, Incivility, Conflict Tactics, and Outcomes.*" This brings us to the specific context of social media conflict about mask wearing during COVID-19, as Tyler Spradley and Elizabeth Spradley examine competing messages on YouTube in Chapter Nine, "*Best Practices for Navigating Escalatory Messages in YouTube Comments: Synthesizing Conflict and Crisis Communication to Address Resistance to Risk Messages.*" The relationship between pandemic communication and the trends of misinformation and disinformation provide a good segway into Ekaterina Bogolometc's discussion of "*Normalizing the New Reality: Newsjacking or Brand Activism?*" in Chapter Ten.

Online Conflict Management in Education, Training, and Practice

Most of this book emphasizes and defines conflict management in the broadest sense of the term: how people interact during instances of conflict in order to manage their interaction and/or try to resolve the conflict. This final section of the book examines conflict in somewhat more formalized contexts, specifically: conflict in K-12 education, conflict in higher education, and the migration of conflict training from face-to-face to the virtual environment. We conclude the volume with a focus on Online Dispute Resolution (ODR), which refers to the ways in which models of alternative dispute resolution, such as mediation and arbitration, have been adapted to the online environment. While ODR was first popularized around 2001 (Katsh & Rifkin, 2001), 2020 saw dramatic changes in ODR training and practice as formats that were traditionally face-to-face shifted online. These natural field experiments allowed scholars and practitioners to compare face-to-face and online training and practice in new ways with useful implications for the future of ODR, especially with respect to mediation.

In Chapter Eleven, "*Resolving Digital Conflicts – Using Community Wisdom for Conflict Resolution Education and Practice in the Digital Era,*" Rachelly Ashwall-Yakar addresses the concerns about the negative effects of online interaction, such as conflict escalation and bullying. Ashwall-Yakar presents the results of the innovative

ODR initiative 'Agree-Online,' which utilized community wisdom to help K-12 students learn to manage conflict in online spaces. From here we move to online conflict in higher education with a chapter that describes student and faculty responses to the quick pivot to distance education required by the COVID-19 pandemic. As instructors and students grappled with adjusting to distance learning, they had to negotiate how to stay engaged. Katie Greenan takes a scholarship of teaching and learning approach to examine her own teaching and present feedback from her students to present practical implications in Chapter Twelve, "*Student Engagement in the Virtual Classroom: Implications for Overcoming Conflict Between Instructors and Students and Creating Collaborative Virtual Workspaces.*"

In Chapter Thirteen, "*Defining the Line: Freedom of Speech and Online Dispute Resolution Best Practices for Higher Education,*" Erica Knotts and Victoria Goodson ask the question: how can universities encourage students to express their freedom of speech while still recognizing and addressing the potential impact to members of the higher education community? The authors provide examples of real university programs to illustrate the best proactive and reactive dispute resolution processes for creating healthy and positive online learning communities for higher education institutions.

The final chapter in this section focuses on how a professional mediation training program managed the shift from traditional, face-to-face training to online training due to COVID-19. Andrea Hartmann-Piraudeau took advantage of this situation to create a natural field experiment that enabled her team to compare the advantages and disadvantages of face-to-face and online training with trainees. One of the most interesting findings was that the biggest advantage of online training – improved time management because participants did not get caught up in conversation at the coffee break – was also its greatest limitation, as participants described networking as the biggest advantage of face-to-face training. The challenges, paradoxes, and opportunities for future training are described in Chapter Fourteen, "*Surprises and New Paths on the Journey to Developing Online Mediation Training.*"

The volume concludes with an in-depth look at the design of online dispute resolution systems in John Zeleznikow's "*Developing User Centric Intelligent Online Dispute Resolution Systems.*" This chapter provides a review of the literature and discussion of best practices that integrates many of the themes throughout this book. We hope that this compilation provides scholars and practitioners with new ideas to try, new questions to ask, and new paths for future research on the trends, challenges, and opportunities associated with contemporary conflict and communication using technology and social media.

References

Bakshy, E., Messing, S., & Adamic, L. A. (2015). Exposure to ideologically diverse news and opinion on Facebook. *Science, 348*(6239), 1130–1132. https://doi.org/10.1126/science.aaa1160.

Banschick, M. R., & Banschick, J. S. (2003). Children in Cyberspace. In L. Shyles (ed.), *Deciphering Cyberspace: Making the Most of Digital Communication Technology* (159–199). Thousand Oaks, CA: Sage Publications.

Boyd, D. (2014). *It's Complicated: The Social Lives of Networked Teens*. New Haven, CT: Yale University Press.

Haim, M., Graefe, & Brosius, H. (2018). Burst of the filter bubble? *Digital Journalism, 6*(3): 330–343. https://doi.org/10.1080/21670811.2017.1338145.

Janssen, A., Robinson, T., Brunner, M., Harnett, P., Museth, K. E., & Shaw, T. (2018). Multidisciplinary teams and ICT: a qualitative study exploring the use of technology and its impact on multidisciplinary team meetings. *BMC health services research, 18*(1): 444. https://doi.org/10.1186/s12913-018-3242-3.

Johnson, S. K., Bettenhausen, K., & Gibbons, E. (2009). Realities of working in virtual teams: Affective and attitudinal outcomes of using computer-mediated communication. *Small Group Research, 40*(6), 623–649. https://doi.org/10.1177/1046496409346448.

Katsh, E., & Rifkin, J. (2001). *Resolving Conflicts in Cyberspace*. San Francisco: Jossey-Bass.

Matuszewski, P., & Szabó, G. (2019). Are echo chambers based on partisanship? Twitter and political polarity in Poland and Hungary. *Social Media + Society, 5*(2): 1–14. https://doi.org/10.1177/2056305119837671.

Papacharissi, Z. (2002). The virtual sphere: The Internet as a public sphere. *New Media & Society, 4*(1): 9–27. https://doi.org/10.1177/14614440222226244.

Ron,Y., Suleiman, C., & Maoz, I. Women for Peace: Promoting Dialogue and Peace through Facebook? *Social Media + Society*. October 2020. https://doi.org/10.1177/2056305120984461.

Shachaf, P. (2008). Cultural diversity and information and communication technology impacts on global virtual teams: An exploratory study. *Information & Management, 45*(2): 131–142. https://doi.org/10.1016/j.im.2007.12.003.

Sunstein, C. R. (2002). The law of group polarization. *The Journal of Political Philosophy, 10*(2): 175–195.

Sunstein, C. R. (2017). *#Republic:: Divided Democracy in the Age of Social Media*. Princeton, NJ: Princeton University Press. Downloaded from ProQuest Ebook Central, http://ebookcentral.proquest.com/lib/ncsu/detail.action?docID=4821064.

Tappin, B. M., & McKay, R. T. (2019). Moral polarization and out-party hostility in the US political context. *Journal of Social and Political Psychology, 7*(1): 213–245. https://doi.org/10.5964/jspp.v7i1.1090

Weber, W. S., & Kim, H. (2015). Virtuality, technology use, and engagement within organizations. *Journal of Applied Communication Research, 43*(4): 385–407. https://doi.org/10.1080/00909882.2015.1083604.

Wellman, B. (1997). The road to utopia and dystopia on the information superhighway. *Contemporary Sociology, 26*(4): 445–449.

Wollebæk, D., Karlsen, R., Steen-Johnsen, K., & Enjolras. B. (2019). Anger, fear, and echo chambers: The emotional basis for online behavior. *Social Media + Society, 5*(2): 1–14. https://doi.org/10.1177/2056305119829859.

Part I: **Using Technology to Promote Dialogue and Collaboration**

Daisung Jang, John Bechara, & William P. Bottom

Chapter 1
Ways and Means: How Think Tanks Use Social Media to Influence Public Policy

Abstract: Think tanks organize at the nexus of business, government, and academia to influence public policy. These organizations take three distinct working forms that utilize different research and communication styles to target different audiences as routes to influence. Traditionally they targeted elite actors such as legislators and executive branch agencies with lengthy scholarly treatises. But with the advent of social media, they can readily extend their reach directly to the voting public. In this chapter, we compare data on the research output and social media footprint of the prototypical organizations that inspired mimesis for each form – the Brookings Institution (a "university without students"), the RAND Corporation (a "contract organization"), and the Heritage Foundation (an "advocacy organization"). We examine their distributions of research output as well as Facebook, Instagram, and Twitter activity. Heritage attracts large numbers of followers for postings across platforms. RAND lagged in timing and frequency of platform use. All three increasingly utilize these media with rapidly expanding reach. Content analysis of tweets using the Linguistic Inquiry Word Count (LIWC) reveals different routes to persuasion. The results are consistent with our hypothesis that the newer forms of advocacy organization rely more on peripheral routes to influence while the two traditional forms stress central routes to persuasion grounded in a logical argument. Systematic differences in social media use indicate the need for additional research directed at fully understanding the impact of emotion-driven communications in facilitating the rapid formation of highly energized social movements (e.g. COVID-19 anti-shutdown protests and Black Lives Matter).

Keywords: public policy, persuasion, research, social media, advocacy

Introduction

Intellectual elites have long sought to influence public policy. To inspire modification of the destructive terms of the Treaty of Versailles, John Maynard Keynes (1919, 1922) published books explaining negotiation mistakes, economic consequences, and necessary reforms. Setting out to roll back the regulatory state, Friedrich Hayek (1944) and Milton Friedman (1962) likewise published lengthy treatises. Friedman (1970) later used the expansive and timely reach afforded by newspaper editorials and television programs. Using those platforms, he persuaded large segments of the public to favor candidates advocating neoliberal ideology (Burgin, 2013).

https://doi.org/10.1515/9783110687262-002

The advent of social media greatly expanded opportunities to influence the voting public about policy issues. Messages quickly reach a global audience providing wide-ranging conversation about topics such as taxes, education, health care, and social justice. In this chapter, we examine how think tanks, non-profit public policy organizations that employ social science, utilize these new media to shape debate over issues while considering implications of their vastly extended reach. We examine both think tank research output as well as the quantity and quality of social media posting to observe differences in how three distinct types of organization fuel conflict on pressing social issues, including the global COVID-19 pandemic and the Black Lives Matter (BLM) movement during the course of 2020.

Social media altered the landscape for influence around public policy debate. Think tanks continue to engage with traditional media, such as newspapers and broadcast news (Groseclose & Milyo, 2005), to convey ideas, evidence, and arguments. But messaging through such channels requires considerable resources. The ability to publish books, op-eds in mass-circulation periodicals, and to program television continues to be reserved for elite actors with financial backing and some credential of expertise (or at least notoriety). For mass-media companies to invest, develop, and deploy their considerable resources to reach audiences, the actor needs to emerge as a viable candidate through a competitive process or have achieved notable status sufficient to assure return on investment (Shoemaker & Vos, 2009). Social media platforms disrupted this dynamic, as there is little upfront cost nor vetting process to engage on these platforms. Social media grants actors a potentially vast audience. Sources report that Facebook has 2.74 billion active users per month, with Instagram reaching 1 billion and Twitter with 330 million active users ("List of Social Platforms with at Least 100 Million Active Users," 2020). The absence of gatekeepers on these platforms opens competition for the attention of the public on any conceivable topic, including government policy.

Social engineers designed early think tanks to use empirical social science methodology to aid the government in making important decisions (Dennison, 1932; Lyons, 1969). Inside the US government, the growing amount of data in the 1920s led to the formation of the Bureau of Agricultural Economics to coordinate research needed to meet the economic needs of farmers (Lyons, 1969). The resulting work legitimized social science as a government function. That decade saw parallel development of non-profit public policy organizations, such as the National Bureau of Economic Research, the Brookings Institution, and the Social Science Research Council, organizations funded by wealthy philanthropic donors to engage in social science research. Think tanks provide a context in which elite actors legitimately favored philosophies (Barros & Taylor, 2020). They also generate ideologies, disseminate agendas, and form coalitions of constituents (Kallick, 2002). A notable recent example is the creation of the 'Green New Deal' by the think tank *New Consensus*, which has sparked numerous policy debates (Meyer, 2019).

Working from archival data and interviews with think tank analysts, Medvetz (2012) noted their 'interstitial' positioning situated between the longer standing fields of business, politics, and the media. He identified academia as a source of personnel, methodology, and legitimacy that enabled think tanks to "become the primary instruments for linking political and intellectual practice in American life" (p. 7). Similarly, think tanks and the government enjoy a symbiotic relationship, becoming a reciprocal source of personnel and resources in a process described as a 'revolving door' (U.S. Department of State, 2002). After beginning her career as an investment banker Elaine Chao, for example, has moved back and forth from leading government agencies like the Department of Transportation and the Peace Corps to working for think tanks like the Hudson Institute and the Heritage Foundation. Because of its unique positioning, changes in the field of think tanks reflect but also cause corresponding changes in the adjoining fields.

Selected examples of the impact of these organizations highlight their influence on the public policy process. Heritage Foundation devised the individual mandate instrumental (Butler, 1990) to the eventual passage of the Affordable Care Act (Jones et al., 2014). More recently, the same organization prepared the list of judges that Donald Trump used for his prolific and lifetime judicial appointments (Restuccia & Bravin, 2020).

Distinct forms of think tanks have emerged at different points in time. They exhibit distinct patterns of research intensity and advocacy activity. Weaver (1989) identified the Brookings Institution, RAND Corporation, and Heritage Foundation as prototypes of think tanks that represent a template that other organizations in the field emulate. The Brookings Institution represents the earliest form – the *University without Students*.[1] These organizations employ scholarly academic researchers using funds from philanthropic foundations and private donors to generate rigorous long-form studies of social problems (Moulton & Pasvolsky, 1932). Founded by dry goods wholesaler Robert S. Brookings in 1927, Brookings targets elite opinion to shape policy decisions.

RAND Corporation represents the *Contract Research* organization. They conduct scientific research but work to specific contract terms with an agency of government to solve a defined problem. The client-agency formulates the research purpose and agenda. A RAND-type think tank generates technical reports, often proprietary, tailored expressly for the client. RAND itself spun off in 1948 from a division of the Douglas Aircraft Corporation sponsored by the Air Force's project RAND (standing for Research and Development). Originally led by Douglas executive Franklin Collbohm, RAND pioneered in the formulation of systems analysis, game theory, organization theory, and military strategy (Augier & March, 2011). RAND published over 500 technical reports under contract with the Defense Department during the

1 Perhaps reflecting this nature, the website of the Brookings Institution uses a .edu domain, usually reserved for educational institutions (https://www.brookings.edu).

Vietnam War. Developing solutions to specific problems on behalf of the government represented a novel extension of the research techniques deployed by the older universities without students.

The Heritage Foundation provided the widely emulated template for *Advocacy* think tanks, which comprise privately funded organizations combining strong ideological positions with aggressive communication strategies. They seek to impact current policy debate in a timely manner. Eschewing original scholarly research, they utilize sophisticated marketing techniques to communicate existing ideas to the broader public in a persuasive manner. Heritage was co-founded in 1973 by political press secretary Paul Weyerich and Edwin Feulner, a Wharton MBA who later completed a Ph.D. in economic history at Edinburgh. They were adamant that:

> Heritage would operate like a business that expected progress from its analysts and results from their policy studies. Heritage would achieve these results by creating timely, concise studies and aggressively marketing them to Congress, policymakers, and the media. This 'briefcase test' concept became a model for other think tanks to follow. (Feulner, n.d.)

The differences between these prototypes and their likely research and social media output create potential for highly asymmetric conflict. The technocratic and empirically focused prototypes of Universities without Students and Contract Research organizations clash with the ideological bent of Advocacy Organizations around pressing social issues. We argue that the advent of social media not only increases the potential reach of these organizations in messaging a larger segment of the public, but also decreases conformity pressures, as activities on social media do not receive screening from gatekeepers such as newspaper or television editorial staff. The context represents a new frontier for conflict over public policy direction.

Social media imposes fewer constraints than traditional media, which should facilitate advocacy think tanks in aggressively pursuing their mission. Representation on traditional media requires adhering to norms of professionalism requiring greater commitment to truth and transparency (Singer, 2007). Arguments and evidence presented in traditional media are ostensibly founded on expertise or empirical data. They may be fact-checked for accuracy either within or outside the reporting organization (Mena, 2019). Social media posts differ qualitatively. They typically carry shorter messages, videos, or images, designed for rapid consumption and sharing with contacts. They are far less subject to screening for rigor. Moreover, the focus on brevity precludes complex or systematic reasoning about issues. With its original focus on producing short, ideologically driven position papers, Heritage would appear ideally placed to capitalize on the properties of the social media context.

Organizations that rely on empirical research cannot easily reduce it to short form communication. While they may produce issues relevant research, they may not communicate it via social media even if there are no gatekeeping forces to limit the volume of messaging.

The distinct modes of operation should result in divergent patterns of research output and media impact. Because of its mission to conduct research, RAND Corporation should produce a greater volume of research output, with less messaging through social media outlets. Advocating predetermined positions, the Heritage Foundation should have the greater tendency to communicate through social media platforms. Brookings likely generates an intermediate level of research and social media output compared to the others. But due to its quasi-academic status, it is likely to be more similar to RAND than Heritage.

Shared ties at the analyst (Medvetz, 2012), board (Burris, 2008; Bechara, Jang, & Bottom, 2021), and founder (Bottom, Jang, & Bechara, 2021) levels facilitate such coordinated action. The pattern of research and messaging we observe from these three prototypes is likely to be reflected across the interconnected network comprising the field. For much of the first decade of this century, John Porter, a long-serving member of congress, worked simultaneously as a director for both RAND and Brookings. Even after Porter retired, the two organizations were not very distant at the board level. Currently, Harvard historian Henry Louis Gates serves as a director for both Brookings and the Aspen Institute. At Aspen Gates works alongside RAND board member Donald Rice and RAND CEO Michael Rich. Corporate board interlocks provide "a mechanism for the rapid diffusion of information and practices and promoting elite cohesion" (Chu & Davis, 2016). In the think tank space, they "enable both information flow in the network, and the establishment of bonding structures that facilitate higher-stakes coordination" (Furnas, 2020).

Heritage formally constructed the State Policy Network, a group of 167 think tanks advocating for neoliberal initiatives (*About State Policy Network*, n.d.). Brookings has been a member of the Policy Action Network, a group of 90 think tanks engaged in policy collaboration and dialogue (*Policy Action Network*, 2002). The research and social media patterns of RAND, Heritage, and Brookings likely align with other closely tied organizations generating the capacity to amplify influence by communicating in a coordinated and systematic way.

In the following sections, we observe the research and social media messaging output of these three prototypical think tanks. Our aim is not only to show differences in operation but also to assess the potential for political polarization that may result. Ideas serve as the basis for social action (Bernini, 2020). In the case of social media, messaging by think tanks can represent a legitimate source of information and thus, form the intellectual capital the public relies upon when engaged in discourse. We first focus on the general research and social media output of the three prototype think tanks. We then narrow the focus on two pressing social issues presenting in 2020, namely the global pandemic caused by COVID-19 and the Black Lives Matter (BLM) movement.

Research and Social Media Output

To examine organizational output, we investigated a number of social media platforms. Research output was tracked using the Altmetrics database, which includes impact metrics. To gauge social media utilization, we examined the number of posts on Facebook, between 2017 and 2019, with data from sproutsocial.com. We downloaded all tweets from the official Twitter account of each think tank and examined the Instagram accounts for activity from each organization. We analyze output generated through the end of 2019. Table 1.1 provides statistics summarizing results from these sources.

RAND generated a high volume of research output but little social media activity. Committed to maintaining a significant research presence, the organization produces a highly respected peer-reviewed journal, *The RAND Journal of Economics*. Neither Brookings nor Heritage do so. Research work generated by RAND authors were cited 4,816 times in 1,387 journals, indicating considerable scholarly impact. This research serves as a topic of public discourse, mentioned 72,246 times on Twitter, 2,701 times on Facebook, 1,574 times on blog posts, and 427 times on Wikipedia. The trend of referencing has been increasing over time. But RAND evinced a low level of social media output and fewer followers than the other organizations.

Table 1.1: Research and Social Media Output.

	Research works produced	**Instagram posts (From account inception)**	**Tweets (From account inception)**	**Facebook posts (2017–2019)**	**Instagram followers in Oct 2020 (000s)**	**Twitter followers in Oct 2020 (000s)**	**Facebook followers in Oct 2020 (000s)**
RAND Corporation	6,310	51	47,118	574	3	209	56
Brookings Institution	656	536	75,889	5,024	24	412	415
Heritage Foundation	27	999	69,542	9,395	108	678	2,107

By comparison, Brookings produced much less research output but a far greater presence on social media. Altmetrics revealed Brookings generated about a tenth of the research work that RAND did. This work was cited 507 times across 250 academic journals. But it was mentioned quite a bit in social media with 8,413 references on Twitter, 329 on Facebook, 393 on blog posts, and 60 on Wikipedia. The trend increases over time. Brookings posted far more on social media than RAND. They also had many more followers across all platforms.

Heritage generated the least research but considerably more social media posting and presence. Heritage research was cited just 11 times in 11 academic journals. This work was mentioned 263 times on Twitter, 5 times on Facebook, 7 times on blog posts, but not at all on Wikipedia. The scant research output is accompanied by far the greatest amount of social media output and visibility. They post often across all platforms. They have many more followers. This pattern aligns with the logic of an *Advocacy* organization reflecting relatively low research output, but with considerable social media presence in pursuit of fixed policy positions.

Analysis of Tweet Content

Having access to the entire corpus of tweets generated by each prototype allowed us to examine the content of the messages these think tanks convey. For this analysis, we examined all tweets from the official accounts of each prototype from account inception to the end of 2019. Figure 1.1 shows the number of tweets from each account over time. Heritage joined Twitter at the earliest and was most prolific in tweeting until 2014. Brookings began a bit later, though they accelerated quickly.

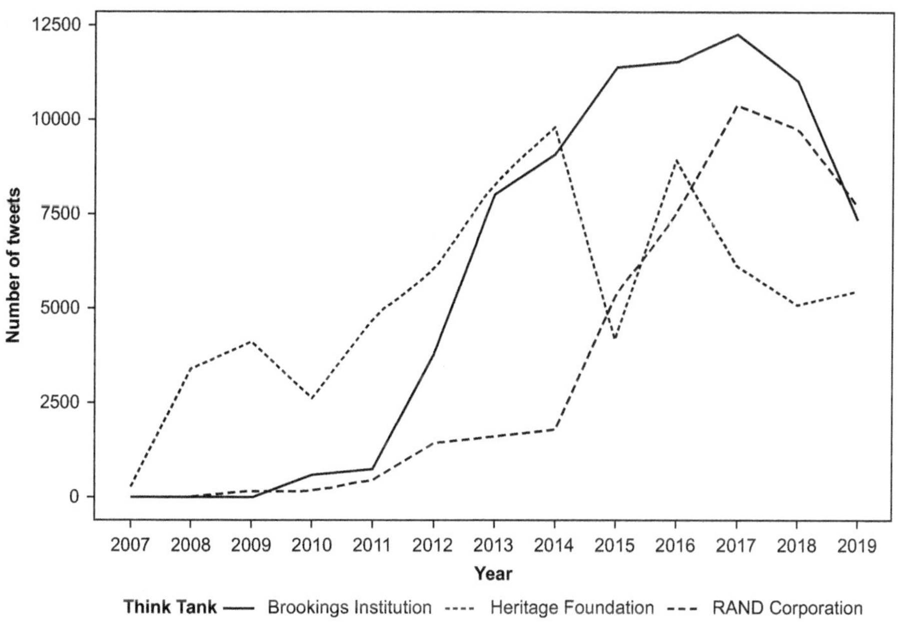

Figure 1.1: Tweets Generated by Think Tanks Across Time.

We analyzed tweet content using the Linguistic Inquiry Word Count program (LIWC; Pennebaker et al., 2007), which counts words that map onto particular psychological concepts. The assumption behind the program is that greater use of words that represent a psychological concept indicates its importance to the actor.

Differences in organizational mission should be reflected in word choice. The elaboration likelihood model (Petty & Cacioppo, 1986) outlines two paths to persuasion that should rely on different types of language. The central route to persuasion requires elaborated thinking about the informational content of a message intended to influence through reasoning and logical argumentation. In contrast, the peripheral route relies on rapid, superficial, heuristic processing of a message. Mood, feelings, liking, and other affective reactions persuade without elaboration or requiring extensive reasoning. The peripheral route demands fewer cognitive resources. It tends to be used when the message recipient has little or no interest in the subject, limited need for cognition, and/or less ability to process the message (Petty & Wegener, 1999). The empirical research focus of RAND and Brookings Institution should necessitate greater use of the central route by providing empirical evidence to analyze problems and potential remedies.

The advocacy mission of the Heritage Foundation may be better met through the peripheral route with messages that appeal to strong emotions rather than complex logic. "Waging and winning the war of ideas" (Feulner, 1986) likely entails greater use of terminology reflecting negative emotions, in particular fear and anger. The latter emotion also requires communication of greater certainty (Ellsworth & Smith, 1988).

To test for this pattern, we examined specific categories of word use tracked by LIWC. The LIWC was created through extensive text analysis and aims to define a list of words that reflect social and psychological states (Pennebaker, Boyd, Jordan, & Blackburn, 2015). For evidence of central routes to persuasion, we examined words in the LIWC categories of insight (e.g., think, know), authenticity (derived from differences between honest vs. deceptive speech), and causality (e.g., because, effect). To find evidence of peripheral routes we examined words in the LIWC categories of affect words (e.g., happy, cried), exclamation marks, and certainty words. Table 1.2 shows the percentage of words used in these categories, aggregated over all tweets.

Table 1.2: Percent Use of Central and Peripheral Route Word Use in Think Tank Tweets.

	Central route word use			Peripheral route word use		
	Insight	**Authentic**	**Cause**	**Affect**	**Exclamation marks**	**Certainty**
RAND Corporation	2.18%	17.83%	2.35%	5.59%	.01%	.59%
Brookings Institution	2.14%	25.75%	2.20%	3.98%	.06%	.49%
Heritage Foundation	1.86%	19.84%	1.86%	6.02%	.80%	1.00%

We then conducted a series of panel regressions to test for differences between the three prototypes, with percentage word use per year as the dependent variable, and dummy variables representing think tanks as the independent variables.

RAND and Brookings used more insightful, authentic, and causal words than Heritage Foundation. There were no significant differences between the prototypes on insight-related words. But Brookings used more authentic communication than RAND ($t = 2.13$, $p = .045$), or Heritage ($t = 1.97$, $p = .06$). RAND Corporation used causal words to a greater extent than Heritage Foundation ($t = 3.91$, $p < .001$). Brookings used causal words marginally more than Heritage ($t = 1.79$, $p = .09$).

Heritage Foundation consistently used more affective terminology, exclamation marks, and certainty. They used affect more often than RAND ($t = 2.16$, $p = .04$) and Brookings ($t = 10.17$, $p < .001$). They also tweeted more exclamation marks than RAND Corporation ($t = 3.36$, $p = .003$) or Brookings ($t = 3.22$, $p = .004$). Heritage expressed words conveying certainty more often than RAND ($t = 7.72$, $p < .001$) or Brookings ($t = 9.50$, $p < .001$).

Overall, these patterns are consistent with the use of central route persuasion by RAND Corporation and Brookings Institution. Their empirical focus is reflected in a recent RAND tweet that links to a longer report: "Where do Americans get their news? What sources do they view as reliable? And how are choices about news consumption linked to demographics or political affiliation? Results from our new national survey provide insights into these questions and more. https://t.co/xmzvVHlgYT" (29 Dec 2019).

A recent tweet from Brookings illustrates a similar focus on empirical analysis to cope with uncertainty: "Young people, less educated workers, men, and Hispanic and black workers will likely be most exposed to disruption from automation https://brook.gs/2HodtAv" (26 Jan 2019). The peripheral route of persuasion taken by Heritage reflects the war of ideas they are attempting to win. A recent tweet illustrates this advocacy pattern: "Who is behind the push for graphic, 'comprehensive' sex education in public schools? Parents? Teachers? Nope! Planned Parenthood. Join us this week to find out how you can fight back and #protectkids" (8 Oct, 2019).

Two organizations use tweets to guide readers to primary research undertaken by the organization. The other tweets emphatic opposition to sex education while imploring the audience to "fight".

This divergent use of routes, coupled with differing bases for argumentation, facilitates an asymmetric conflict between research and emotion. We explore this possibility further by examining social media usage about two pressing issues in 2020: the global pandemic caused by the outbreak of the COVID-19 virus and the BLM movement.

Analysis of COVID-19 Related Output

We examined research output and social media output related to COVID-19 of the prototype think tanks through October 2020. We examined research output in the Altmetrics database and posts on Instagram and Twitter because those platforms allowed examination of the entirety of the posts made by a particular account. We summarize the output from each organization below; statistics appear in Table 1.3.

Both RAND Corporation and Brookings Institution published research papers on the topic, signalling capability to generate in-house expertise and the capacity to disseminate evidence-based knowledge on the topic. In searching for "COVID" or "Coronavirus", and "pandemic" in article titles, we examined the number and content of the articles. In line with Weaver's (1989) expectations, there were differences across prototypes. RAND affiliated authors produced 14 journal articles, mainly in health, medical, and gerontology journals.

Specific topics related to public health, including the pandemic response in Taiwan, resource allocation, emergency risk communication, preparedness in nursing homes, preparedness in home healthcare agencies, testing policy, healthcare design, virtual training, and rationing of healthcare resources. Other topics involved investigations of the impact of COVID on specific populations, including the impact of the virus on users of opioids, adults experiencing homelessness, elderly loneliness, infrastructure, as well as psychological symptoms among frontline healthcare workers. The output speaks to a broad range of topics related to the crisis and reflects a depth of expertise. Brookings Institution affiliated authors had five papers with some in high impact journals (*JAMA: Journal of the American Medical Association, Science*). Specific topics covered included the transparency of COVID epidemiological models, readiness of self-service diagnosis, and changing healthcare models to accommodate pandemics. In contrast to the other organizations, the Heritage Foundation had not published any research work on the topic in peer reviewed journals as of October 2020.

Table 1.3: Research and Social Media Output on COVID-19.

	Research work produced (until October 2020)	Tweets (until October 2020)	Instagram posts (until October 2020)
RAND Corporation	14	6 (27 likes)	12 (668 likes)
Brookings Institution	5	14 (111 likes)	19 (6716 likes)
Heritage Foundation	0	19 (795 likes)	104 (129,684 likes)

We examined messaging on Twitter, narrowing our focus to tweets or hashtags that contained the word 'lockdown' in 2020. Opinion about efforts to contain transmission of the virus through the closure of non-essential businesses and stay at home orders, commonly described as 'lockdown' policies, have been greatly polarized, with voting patterns predicting state pandemic response policies (Makridis & Rothwell, 2020). Such policies have also resulted in protests, with President Trump tweeting in support of protesters against restrictions on activity ("Coronavirus," 2020). We examined the impact the prototype think tanks have had in social media on this topic.

RAND Corporation tweeted six times using the word 'lockdown'. Three tweets outlined how lockdown could lead to unemployed and underemployed people facing homelessness, and three tweets reported on a trend of increasing domestic violence in Europe due to the lockdown. All tweets were accompanied by links to more extensive research reports. Brookings Institution tweeted 14 times using the word 'lockdown'. These tweets referred to health infrastructure, domestic violence, criminal gangs building social capital, regulatory changes to deal with the pandemic, lockdown protest and gun sales, the rights of presidents or governors to enforce lockdowns, the economy in Nigeria, metrics for ending lockdown, and pandemic response in Africa, US, and in France. These tweets are linked to briefs that cite data or the constitution.

The Heritage Foundation tweeted 19 times using the word 'lockdown'. These tweets cast doubt on the processes and the effectiveness of the restrictions, with doubts expressed about the benefits of scientific analysis ("the failures behind the Imperial College Model that spurred unnecessary, widespread #COVID19 lockdowns", June 17, 2020), questioned the value, excessiveness, and effectiveness of lockdowns ("Recent studies, including one by a former Obama administration economic adviser, call into question widely held views on the value of government lockdowns", 3 Oct 2020), and included a positive evaluation of Sweden's comparatively lax response to the crisis ("it has fewer deaths per million population than many Western countries that imposed lockdowns", 22 Oct 2020). The tweets also highlight the harm caused by lockdowns, including the economic effects of lockdown on healthcare providers, the need to revise lockdown strategy, how lockdown affects religious liberty, deaths caused by police enforcement of lockdowns in Africa, and the need to exercise discretion in enforcing lockdown.

We also examined the entirety of Instagram posts from the beginning of the pandemic to the end of October 2020. On this platform, there were vast differences between organizations in their communication. The 12 posts by RAND covered content related to state responses to COVID-19, supporting well-being, alcoholism, secure voting in a pandemic, unemployment, blood donation supplies, as well as remote learning. The 19 posts by Brookings discussed reopening businesses in the context of other international efforts, as well as the economic effects of COVID-19 on rural areas, on Black Americans, essential workers, food insecurity, online learning, voting issues, gun sales, and healthcare. Posts from these think tanks represent a wide array of social concerns about the negative effects of the global pandemic, and attempts to address or call attention to multiple aspects of the crisis.

In contrast, the 104 posts on COVID-19 related topics by the Heritage Foundation expressed skepticism and economic impacts of the pandemic. Posts included encouragement to practice social distancing ("Are you practicing social distancing? Social distancing is one of the primary ways to slow the trajectory of the spread of the coronavirus, reducing the number of active cases at any given time.") early in the crisis (March 15). But as the pandemic progressed, skepticism about public health measures increased. On the 5th of May, Heritage posted a quote from Jordan Peterson, ("It is better to live bravely than cowardly, everyone knows that"). Later posts downplayed the severity of the crisis ("ICYMI: Nearly every state has significant levels of available hospital beds. Visit Heritage.org/Coronavirus to learn more.", June 11; "These results demonstrate how much more deadly the Spanish flu was than COVID-19 has been so far . . ." July 25). Posts also encouraged reopening of business and schools ("A growing list of experts agree: YES, it's safe to send kids back to school . . ." July 27), and greater participation in in-person activities ("The left's national vote-by-mail effort is a really bad idea." August 31).

The organizations' communication diverged more and more as the pandemic progressed. With the sizable social media following that Heritage commands, differing viewpoints on the efficacy of public health measures, such as the closure of businesses and schools, could serve to fuel conflict across many domains of public and private life. Depending on the appropriate course of public health policy, it could influence how sustained the pandemic is across multiple communities.

Analysis of BLM Related Output

The BLM movement seeks to combat violence and discrimination against Black communities. The movement is one of the largest in US history, with 4,700 protests between late May and early July 2020, with an estimated 15 ~ 26 million protesters participating (Buchanan et al., 2020). The movement has been consequential, with one form of impact being the recent removal of public monuments dedicated to the Confederacy ("List of Monuments and Memorials Removed during the George Floyd Protests," 2021). The movement inspired popular countermovements, including the All Lives Matter and Blue Lives Matter movements, and has become a focal point of discussion online, with nearly 47.8 million tweets with the hashtag #BlackLivesMatter sent between late May and early June 2020 (Anderson et al., 2020). We examined research output and social media output related to the Black Lives Matter movement. We also examined research output in the Altmetrics database. We also examined Instagram and Twitter posts for 2020. Statistics appear in Table 1.4.

Both RAND Corporation and Brookings Institution published peer-reviewed research papers on the topic. We searched for the following keywords in article titles: black, African, ethnic, race, equality, police, violence, and law enforcement, between the period of 2014 and 2020 (the inception of the movement to current day). Studies that examined racial equality/disparity and Black people in that period were also included.

Table 1.4: Research and Social Media Output on Black Lives Matter.

	Research works produced (2014 to October 2020)	Tweets (to October 2020)	Instagram posts (to October 2020)
RAND Corporation	120	18 (183 likes)	1 (140 likes)
Brookings Institution	3	19 (456 likes)	9 (1,922 likes)
Heritage Foundation	0	46 (5,179 likes)	48 (165,252 likes)

The RAND Corporation published 120 papers on the topic, with the vast majority of the focus on health and medical studies, and others on psychology, economics, as well as on criminology. Brookings Institution published three papers on the topic, on the topics of income inequality and closing the racial IQ gap. By comparison, the Heritage Foundation produced no research on the topic.

Examining Instagram posts in 2020, there were differences between the prototypes. RAND Corporation's solitary post on the topic on the 4th of June comprised a statement by the president (Michael D. Rich) on the need to recognize the legacy of the passing of George Floyd, Ahmad Arbery, Breonna Taylor, among others. Brookings Institution president (Gen. John R. Allen) also called for efforts to further the cause of racial equity.

Heritage Foundation posted three times in support of racial justice, but also 48 posts justifying stricter law enforcement and patriotism. They also posted questions about the intentions of the Black Lives Matter movement ("Many good intentioned Americans are showing support for #BlackLivesMatter – but do they know the radical goals of the official organization?" July 1).

Twitter posts echoed the pattern observed in Instagram. We examined tweets with hashtags relating to the Black Lives Matter movement in 2020. The RAND Corporation posted 18 tweets with the hashtag #defundthepolice, covering topics on reconsidering the role of law enforcement as well as community support for the strategy. Brookings Institution, using the hashtags #howwerise and #juneteenth tweeted 19 times, suggesting policy solutions to ameliorate systemic racism, and addressing racial justice in the domains of finance, employment, health, and education.

Heritage posted 46 tweets with the hashtags #antifa, #blm, #blacklivesmatter, #defendthepolice, and #fightforamerica. They expressed skepticism about the movement ("Why is a pro-communist China organization with ties to the Chinese Communist Party financially supporting elements of the #BlackLivesMatter movement? @Gundisalvus joined @glennbeck with a story you won't find the mainstream media covering: https://t.co/dkpCiL24nd", September 18), as well as support for law enforcement ("Why are we in a #FightForAmerica? @DHS_Wolf lays out the unprecedented challenges law enforcement are up against every single day – and why they deserve our support: https://t.co/Hyc5czID4x", August 14).

As with messaging on COVID-19, stark differences appeared in relation to the Black Lives Matter movement. Diverging approaches to addressing the topic, via research and via the content of the messaging, signals potential for polarization between those seeking an empirical foundation and those responding emotionally to a pressing social issue.

Conclusions

Through a prescient critique of diplomatic negotiations at the conclusion of the First World War, Keynes (1919) persuasively demonstrated the merits of social scientific influence over public policy-making (Bottom, 2003). Other intellectuals, such as Milton Friedman, relied on lengthy scientific texts, newspaper editorials, and television appearances to influence thinking, working through the organization of public policy think tanks to do so. Using such channels was an innovation that drove public acceptance of neoliberal ideology in public policy (Burgin, 2013). The advent of social media provides a new model for public policy debate, with dramatically lower barriers to communication allowing virtually any actor to engage. Replacing public intellectuals, think tanks have become prominent players in the U.S. public policy arena. While their emergence was in part due to the U.S. government's need for research to buttress and legitimize its work, their role progressively increased over the years.

For example, in the late 1940s, the Marshall Plan – devised by the Committee for Economic Development – completely reconstructed a war-torn Europe (Djelic, 1998; Mizruchi, 2013). In the late 1990s, Project for the New American Century created the blueprint for the disastrous invasion of Iraq. More recently, the Heritage Foundation provided a list of conservative judges which President Trump used to pick nominees who would decisively change the ideological composition of the judiciary. While think tanks continue to wield tremendous influence over governmental policy and public opinion, they work and communicate in very different ways.

We set out to understand how three think tank prototypes communicate by revealing differences in their channel choice: *scholarly*, based on research output and *network*, based on social media output. Our results reveal an important and interesting way in which the Brookings Institution ("university without students" form), the RAND Corporation ("contract organization" form), and the Heritage Foundation ("advocacy" form) communicate and conflict with each other over important issues (e.g., COVID-19 and BLM). When it comes to research, RAND produces by far the most scientific work. As the only think tank with its own scholarly journal, RAND advances its goal of developing and applying research to solve specific government problems. In contrast, the Heritage Foundation produced the fewest scholarly articles electing to focus on direct advocacy channels to communicate ideas, fulfilling its conservative mission. Brookings blended some scientific output with greater use of social media platforms striking a position intermediate between RAND Corporation and Heritage Foundation.

Boasting the most Facebook and Instagram followers, the Heritage Foundation relied on peripheral routes to persuasion using more affect-related words expressing greater certainty than the other organizations. They often punctuated the message with exclamation points to drive home the message. RAND attracted the least number of followers across all three social media platforms. They relied on a central route to persuasion using the information content of messages to send viewers to lengthier reports that elaborate logical arguments and empirical evidence supporting claims. Brookings also utilized the central route to persuasion with links to longer explanations of research. After initially lagging Heritage in joining the platform, Brookings eventually became the most active in tweeting of the three.

While these findings reveal differences across think tanks, a deeper examination of the COVID-19 and BLM debates reveal conflict among those think tanks. In the case of COVID-19, the RAND Corporation and the Brookings Institution stood in stark contrast to the Heritage Foundation when it came to addressing the spread of the virus. While the former think tanks supported mitigating measures to reduce the spread including social distancing, school and business closures, the latter simply cast doubt on the effectiveness of those measures and downplayed the impact of the disease.

A similar conflictual pattern appeared in the case of BLM. RAND Corporation and the Brookings Institution supported the BLM movement and highlighted the importance of reducing racial inequality by reducing systemic racism. In contrast, the Heritage Foundation questioned the role of the BLM movement and was more concerned with justifying stricter law enforcement measures. Engagement in such issues also highlights the changing nature of the audiences think tanks now engage with and the kind of influence they seek to exert. Instead of targeting elite influence, advocacy think tanks may also expand their reach into influencing the public. Casting doubt on the election process, the Heritage Foundation questioned the integrity of the process ("Absentee ballots are the only ballots voted outside the supervision of election officials . . . making them particularly susceptible to fraud, forgery, theft, and other problems we've seen in the latest election." December 8). Such messaging may have fueled members of the public storming the Capitol building in January 2021.

Overall, our chapter represents an initial step toward understanding the role and influence of think tanks across two channels of communication – *scholarly* based on their research output and *network* based on their social media output. Future research could broaden the scope of think tanks by analyzing the entire field – not just the three prototypes. Broadening the scope of think tanks will provide a much richer understanding of the ways in which other think tanks use similar or different approaches in those channels of communication and the extent to which they might have not simply adapted those approaches but also enlarged the repertoire of approaches. This will also provide a better understanding of the network of think tanks (e.g. Progressive vs. Conservative networks of think tanks) that operate in concert to shape policy debates (see Jacques et al., 2008 for the role of conservative think tanks in casting doubt on climate change; and see Ness & Gándara (2014) for the role of both networks in higher education policy).

Future research should also examine other communication channels including talk radio, print media, cable television, and congressional testimony. Our preliminary examination of the transcripts from the Rush Limbaugh radio program widely syndicated by Clear Channel Communication (https://www.rushlimbaugh.com/daily/category/transcripts/) revealed 431 references to the Heritage Foundation between 2002 and 2012. By comparison Limbaugh mentioned Brookings 55 times and RAND just four times over that decade. Limbaugh's daily program reaches an audience of more than 15 million listeners (Wheeler, 2012) providing a powerful means for transmitting ideas or talking points generated by conservative think tanks like Heritage to many prospective voters. Further work analyzing this supply chain of influence will be needed.

This increase in scope will provide a much better understanding of the approaches think tanks use to shape the views of two important audiences: civic society and the legislative branch of the government. This will also provide a better understanding of how think tanks use more established media channels which require more resources and have gatekeepers mediating their access and visibility, versus social media which require very few resources and provide direct unfettered access to their audiences.

Finally, future research could explore the characteristics of think tanks that contribute to their visibility and influence across various channels of communication. For example, think tanks' political ideologies, positions in the board interlock social structure, or their funding sources, could contribute not simply to the content of their messaging but also their choice of communication channels.

In sum, think tanks shape our views about public policy whether we are aware of it or not. Experts housed in such institutions have long played a role in shaping not only our capacity to think about public policy questions and debates but also our policy responses and the choices available to us in those debates. Whether it is debates about the COVID-19 pandemic or debates about social justice, understanding the influence of the think tank industry and their channels of communication and influence becomes crucial to understanding our views of the contemporary world.

References

About State Policy Network. (n.d.). State Policy Network. Retrieved January 6, 2021, from https://spn.org/state-policy-network-about/

Anderson, M., Barthel, M., Perrin, A., & Vogels, E. A. (2020, 10 June). #BlackLivesMatter surges on Twitter after George Floyd's death. *Factank.* https://www.pewresearch.org/fact-tank/2020/06/10/blacklivesmatter-surges-on-twitter-after-george-floyds-death/

Augier, M., & March, J. (2011). *The roots, rituals, and rhetorics of change: North American business schools after the Second World War.* Stanford: Stanford University Press.

Barros, A., & Taylor, S. (2020). Think tanks, business and civil society: The ethics of promoting pro-corporate ideologies. *Journal of Business Ethics, 162.* DOI: https://doi.org/10.1007/s10551-018-4007-y

Bechara, J., Jang, D., & Bottom, W.P. (2021). Social engineers and invisible hands: Rival systems of influence in the interstitial field of public policy think tanks. Working paper.

Bernini, A. (2020). The voice of radio in the battle for equal rights: Evidence from the U.S. South. *SSRN Electronic Journal.* DOI: https://doi.org/10.2139/ssrn.3691947.

Bottom, W.P., Jang, D., & Bechara, J. (2021). Calling the tune: The interlock network of funding sources for public policy think tanks. Working paper.

Bottom, W.P. (2003). Keynes' attack on the Versailles Treaty: An early investigation of the consequences of bounded rationality, framing, and cognitive illusions. *International Negotiation, 8(2)*, 367–402.

Buchanan, L., Bui, Q., & Patel, J. K. (2020, 3 July). *Black Lives Matter may be the largest movement in U.S. history.* The New York Times. https://www.nytimes.com/interactive/2020/07/03/us/george-floyd-protests-crowd-size.html

Burgin, A. (2013). Age of certainty: Galbraith, Friedman, and the public life of economic ideas. *History of Political Economy, 45* (suppl_1),191–219. DOI: https://doi.org/10.1215/00182702-2310998

Burris V. 2008. The interlock structure of the policy-planning network and the right turn in U.S. state policy. *Research in Political Sociology, 17*, 3–42

Butler, S. M. (1990). Assuring affordable health care for all Americans. *Journal of Health Care for the Poor and Underserved, 1*(1), 63–73. DOI: https://doi.org/10.1353/hpu.2010.0057

Chu, J. S., & Davis, G. F. (2016). Who killed the inner circle? The decline of the American corporate interlock network. *American Journal of Sociology, 122*(3), 714–754.

Coronavirus: President Trump defends tweets against US states' lockdowns. (2020, April 18). BBC News. https://www.bbc.com/news/world-us-canada-52330531

Dennison, H. S. (1932). The need for the development of political science engineering. *American Political Science Review, 26*(2), 241–255.

Djelic, M.-L. (1998). *Exporting the American model: The post-war transformation of European business.* Oxford: Oxford University Press.

Ellsworth, P. C., & Smith, C. A. (1988). From appraisal to emotion: Differences among unpleasant feelings. *Motivation and Emotion, 12*(3), 271–302.

Feulner, E. J. Jr. (1986). Waging and winning the war of ideas. *The Heritage Lectures*, 84, the Heritage Foundation pp 1–19.

Feulner, E. J. Jr. (n.d.) Retrieved from: http://www.heritage.org/about/staff/f/edwin-feulner.

Friedman, M. (1970, September 13). The social responsibility of business is to increase its profits. *New York Times Magazine.* https://www.nytimes.com/1970/09/13/archives/a-friedman-doctrine-the-social-responsibility-of-business-is-to.html

Friedman, M. (1962). *Capitalism and freedom.* Chicago: University of Chicago Press.

Furnas, A. C. (2020). Coalitions and coordination in Washington think tanks: board interlock among Washington DC-based policy research and planning organizations. *Applied Network Science*, *5* (1), 1–17.

Groseclose, T., & Milyo, J. (2005). A measure of media bias. *Quarterly Journal of Economics*, *120*(4), 1191–1237.

Hayek, F. A. (1944). *The road to serfdom*. Chicago: University of Chicago Press.

Jacques, P. J., Dunlap, R. E., & Freeman, M. (2008). The organisation of denial: Conservative think tanks and environmental scepticism. *Environmental Politics*, *17*(3), 349–385. DOI: https://doi.org/10.1080/09644010802055576

Jones, D. K., Bradley, K. W. V., & Oberlander, J. (2014). Pascal's wager: Health insurance exchanges, Obamacare, and the Republican dilemma. *Journal of Health Politics, Policy and Law*, *39*(1), 97–137. DOI: https://doi.org/10.1215/03616878-2395190

Kallick, D. D. (2002). *Progressive think tanks: What exists, what's missing?* Open Society Institute.

Keynes, J. M. (1922). *A revision of the treaty*. London: Harcourt, Brace.

Keynes, J. M. (1919). *The economic consequences of the peace*. London: Macmillan.

List of monuments and memorials removed during the George Floyd protests. (2021). In *Wikipedia*. https://en.wikipedia.org/w/index.php?title=List_of_monuments_and_memorials_removed_during_the_George_Floyd_protests&oldid=997671995

List of social platforms with at least 100 million active users. (2020). In *Wikipedia*. https://en.wikipedia.org/w/index.php?title=List_of_social_platforms_with_at_least_100_million_active_users&oldid=993103507

Lyons, G. M. (1969). *The uneasy partnership: Social science and the federal government in the Twentieth Century* (1st edition). Russell Sage Foundation, New York, NY.

Makridis, C., & Rothwell, J. T. (2020). *The real cost of political polarization: Evidence from the COVID-19 pandemic* (SSRN Scholarly Paper ID 3638373). Social Science Research Network. DOI: https://doi.org/10.2139/ssrn.3638373

Medvetz, T. (2012). *Think tanks in America*. Chicago: University of Chicago Press.

Mena, P. (2019). Principles and boundaries of fact-checking: Journalists' perceptions. *Journalism Practice*, *13*(6), 657–672. DOI: https://doi.org/10.1080/17512786.2018.1547655

Meyer, R. (2019, June 12). *The think tank struggling to write the Green New Deal*. The Atlantic. https://www.theatlantic.com/science/archive/2019/06/whats-green-new-deal-nobody-knows/591391/

Mizruchi, M. S. (2013). *The fracturing of the American corporate elite*. Cambridge, MA: Harvard University Press.

Moulton, H. G., & Pasvolsky, L. (1932). *War debts and world prosperity*. Brookings Institution. https://catalog.hathitrust.org/Record/000964926

Ness, E. C., & Gándara, D. (2014). Ideological think tanks in the states: An inventory of their prevalence, networks, and higher education policy activity. *Educational Policy*, *28*(2), 258–280. DOI: https://doi.org/10.1177/0895904813515328

Pennebaker, J. W., Booth, R. J., & Francis, M. E. (2007). *Operator's Manual Linguistic Inquiry and Word Count: LIWC2007*. http://homepage.psy.utexas.edu/homepage/faculty/pennebaker/reprints/LIWC2007_OperatorManual.pdf

Pennebaker, J.W., Boyd, R.L., Jordan, K., & Blackburn, K. (2015). *The development and psychometric properties of LIWC2015*. Austin, TX: University of Texas at Austin.

Petty, R. E., & Cacioppo, J. T. (1986). The elaboration likelihood model of persuasion. In R. E. Petty & J. T. Cacioppo (Eds.), *Communication and Persuasion: Central and Peripheral Routes to Attitude Change* (pp. 1–24). Springer, New York, NY. DOI: https://doi.org/10.1007/978-1-4612-4964-1_1

Petty, R. E., & Wegener, D. T. (1999). The elaboration likelihood model: Current status and controversies. In *Dual-process theories in social psychology* (pp. 37–72). New York, NY: The Guilford Press.

Policy Action Network: About. (2002, June 3). https://web.archive.org/web/20020603235213/http://www.movingideas.org/about/

Restuccia, A., & Bravin, J. (2020, September 9). *Trump releases list of potential Supreme Court nominees.* Wall Street Journal. https://www.wsj.com/articles/trump-releases-list-of-potential-supreme-court-nominees-11599682752

Shoemaker, P. J., & Vos, T. (2009). *Gatekeeping theory.* New York, NY: Routledge.

Singer, J. B. (2007). Contested autonomy. *Journalism Studies, 8*(1), 79–95. DOI: https://doi.org/10.1080/14616700601056866

Skidelsky, R. J. A. (1992). *John Maynard Keynes: The economist as saviour, 1920–1937* (Vol. 2). London: Macmillan.

U.S. Department of State. (2002). The role of think tanks in U.S. foreign policy. *U.S. Foreign Policy Agenda, 7* (3), pp. 1–47.

Weaver, R. K. (1989). The changing world of think tanks. *Political Science and Politics, 22*(3), 563–578.

Wheeler, B. (2012, March 6). *Can Limbaugh survive advertiser boycott?* BBC News Magazine. https://www.bbc.com/news/magazine-17263546

Kathleen M. Vogel & Matthew Schmidt

Chapter 2
AI Platforms and U.S. Intelligence: Opportunities for Collaboration, Dialogue, and Negotiation

Abstract: This chapter discusses a prototype under development, called the Analytic Component System (ACS), which is being designed to provide intelligence analysts with a computational platform that will promote collaboration, dialogue, and workplace efficiency within U.S. intelligence, like Amazon Web Services. This chapter uses this technological object to discuss various socio-technical dimensions to be considered before, during, and after deployment of artificial intelligence and advanced computational tools in the U.S. intelligence workplace, to promote positive aspects of communication and collaboration and decrease potential sources of conflict.

Keywords: artificial intelligence, platforms, socio-technical, organizational culture, intelligence analysis

Introduction

There are a variety of new tools that are being developed to help U.S. intelligence analysts more efficiently harness big data and artificial intelligence (AI) to provide timely intelligence assessments to decision makers (Brantly, 2018; Eldridge et al., 2018; Frank, 2017; Hare & Coghill, 2016; Herhkovitz, 2020; Lim, 2016; Omand et al., 2012; Regens, 2019; Van Puyvelde et al., 2017). The Laboratory for Analytic Sciences, an academia-industry-government collaborative research facility at North Carolina State University, has developed a novel computational architecture called the Analytic Component System (ACS) that aims to improve communication, collaboration, and efficiency in the future of intelligence analysis. This system has three distinct but related development efforts (see Figure 2.1): (1) the Analytic Component Interface (ACI), an interface that would define standard protocols and constructs that enable the interoperability of tools and components; (2) the Analytic Computing Environment (ACE), a service-oriented computing platform that would enable a single analytic workflow to leverage multiple, independently developed analytic technologies in order to execute and solve a given problem; and (3) the Analytic Component Library (ACL), a repository of modular tools, algorithms, and workflows. The ACS system is designed to include a variety of analytic components, such as software programs, automated algorithms, and new AI/machine learning techniques. It is designed

https://doi.org/10.1515/9783110687262-003

to integrate analyst workflows, enable collaboration between various analytic technologies, and help analysts communicate and collaborate with one another. To date, there have been a variety of technical and organizational problems in collaboration and communication among intelligence analysts, and ACS is a new platform system designed to overcome these impediments.

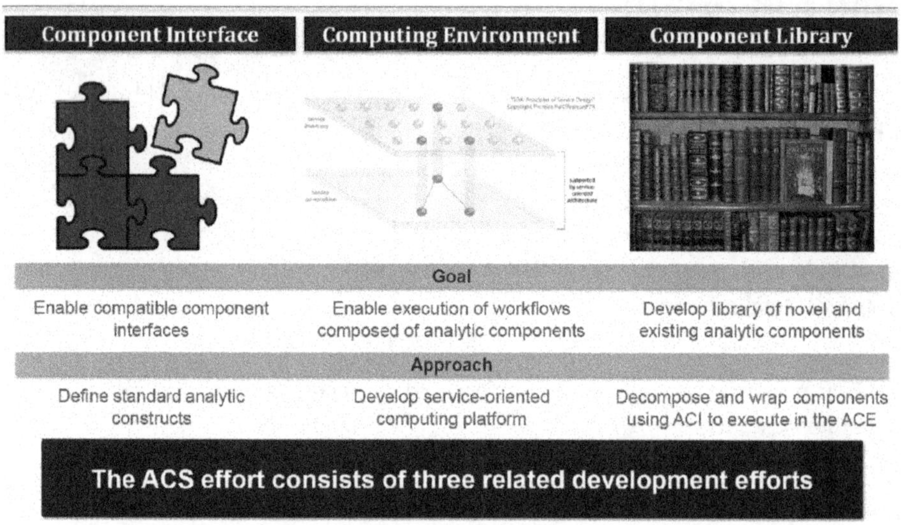

Figure 2.1: Three Elements of the Analytic Component System (ACS): (1) the Analytic Component Interface (ACI); (2) the Analytic Computing Environment (ACE); and (3) the Analytic Component Library (ACL).

ACS has been compared to creating an Amazon Web Services (AWS)–like platform for intelligence analysis – a standardized, service-oriented computing system for enabling the efficient "calling" and integration of different people, IC software and IT tools, data streams, and workflows. It would allow an analyst (or team) to design a robust analytic workflow for a given intelligence problem that would eliminate work friction among systems, tools, and people, and enable the creation of an organized repository of these workflows as a resource available to analysts working on other problems. The aim of this technology is to create a seamless computational architecture for work with new and different algorithms and data that would enable computationally assisted recommendations to analysts about intelligence problems they are working on and rapid assessment outputs, as well as create a reservoir of stored expert knowledge and analytic workflows that an analyst could access at any time.

"Platformization" of Intelligence

Although ACS was a prototype under development and its work was halted in 2018, it provides an opportunity for reflection on the kinds of intelligence platforms being developed by U.S. intelligence and the various considerations that should go into the design, development, and implementation of these systems in the intelligence workplace. The design and early prototyping phase provides a focal point for reflection on the potential socio-technical dimensions of these platforms in intelligence work: the integration of people, algorithms, software, tools, and manual work, and how these dimensions should be incorporated into this phase. Although computational platforms were used previously in intelligence, ACS represents a next-generation system that aims to seamlessly integrate all human, hardware, and software components that are part of intelligence analysis.

Social scientists define a platform as a computational infrastructure of compatible components, upon which other software and applications can be built and run, and upon which developers and users can design additional layers of functionality (Gillespie, 2010; Mansell, 2015). Gillespie (2010), however, discusses how "platform" can embody figurative dimensions (its abstract promises) and architectural dimensions (an open, egalitarian space for expression) (352). Moreover, Gillespie argues that platforms "are 'platforms' not necessarily because they allow code to be written or run, but because they afford an opportunity to communicate, interact, or sell" (351). Martens (2016) adds that platforms can provide mediated exchanges to reduce transaction costs. Other IT scholars discuss how platforms allow participants to (co-)create new forms of knowledge and social networks among users (Helberger et al., 2018; Langlois & Elmer, 2013; Olaison & Revang, 2017; Plantin et al., 2018; Watanabe et al., 2017). Platforms have a variety of beneficial features, including personalization, user participation, flexibility, freedom, and programmability, which can be adapted and altered according to user needs (Hanseth & Lyytinen, 2010; Plantin et al., 2018). In sum, platforms can constitute a powerful infrastructure for knowledge creation and sharing, as well as user participation and expression.

Other social scientists, however, have looked at the more complex and contingent character of how a variety of technical, social, and economic issues can shape platforms' structure, function, and use (Baldwin & Woodward, 2008). Ess (2009) has argued for the need to look closely at platform design and whether/how it suits users, because "Platforms often reinforce the values and preferences of designers, either explicitly or implicitly, while sometimes clashing with the values and preferences of their intended users" (p. 16). This can be further complicated by the fact that platforms are populated by many diverse and sometimes contentious communities, often with competing needs (Gillespie, 2017). Gillespie has raised the concern that platforms can lead to hierarchical information flows because of how they are constructed to organize and channel information in particular ways. Others have raised concerns that platforms lead to "datafication" – the quantification of human life through digital information – and the various biases and errors that can be created through this process (Mejias & Couldry, 2019). Tim Jordan (2015) has aptly asked us to consider the politics of information that encompasses platforms.

What does this all mean for platforms being conceptualized for intelligence analysis? It would be useful to outline three key areas in which we think socio-technical considerations of new platforms for intelligence should be considered before these platforms are implemented: (1) platform governance, (2) cultural work practices, and (3) datafication of intelligence. These issues, however, are merely the starting point for anticipating human factors and their part in any new intelligence platform. We wish to use ACS as a way to illustrate how these issues might play out in a future intelligence workplace, and to open up the conversation among technology developers, intelligence practitioners, and intelligence officials about the various knowledge-management and knowledge-sharing issues these platforms raise – even as they solve current analytic problems. These new issues will have to be anticipated and addressed with new policies, procedures, and training.

Platform Governance

In social science literature on computational platforms, scholars have identified the challenge of "the problem of many hands." This problem, originally coined by Thompson (1980) and taken up more recently by others (Doorn, 2012; van de Poel et al., 2012), refers to a situation in which different people can contribute in different ways to a problem – or its solution – in a manner that makes it difficult to identify who is responsible for which actions and consequences, and on this basis accordingly allocate accountability and responsibility. Platforms provide the ability for many users to create, suggest, and shape knowledge-based system interactions and functions. To minimize chaos, platform designers and developers must structure platform-based user interactions in specific ways (algorithmic sorting, privileging particular data signals, etc.) that then influence content and services that become visible (Bucher, 2018; Pasquale, 2015); through these structuring devices, platforms can moderate what users share and how they interact (Gillespie, 2018a). This, then, leads into the more contentious issue of platform governance (Gillespie, 2018b; Gorwa, 2019).

Considering this issue of platform governance and the ACS prototype has caused us to reflect on the following questions: Who decides what intelligence components and workflows are added to ACS? Would only senior intelligence analysts or senior officials be allowed to add analytic workflows to ACS? What about skilled junior analysts? How can we ensure a diversity of analytic workflows (perhaps even controversial or "devil's advocate" scenarios) are represented in ACS? Who would adjudicate and manage that process? How would these decisions be made? Also, ACS might include a variety of recommender systems, which could give users a choice of different analytic recommendation logics (based on different AI techniques) to solve a given intelligence problem. Some of these recommendation systems could highlight popular choices among analysts (similar to how AWS "recommends" products for a customer to buy). However, a choice's popularity may not make it appropriate for a given analytic problem. One need only consider the groupthink logic – ultimately proved wrong – that pervaded U.S. intelligence analysis regarding Iraq's WMD capabilities before the 2003 war. How should we anticipate groupthink bias within various analytic workflows and AI tools deposited into ACS? What internal policies and procedures should be developed in a particular agency or unit to address these issues? What kinds of training might analysts need to be able to use these systems appropriately? As is evident, although platforms like ACS might be technologically capable of a variety of outputs, humans are going to have to decide how these technological capabilities are translated to the desktop of an intelligence analyst in ways that promote not only efficiency, but also accuracy and confidence of analytic outputs. This would require the development of some formal governance of these analytic platforms before their deployment into the intelligence workplace.

Cultural Work Practices

Organizational culture involves the values, beliefs, and systems that may facilitate or hinder knowledge creation and sharing in an organization (Alavi & Leidner, 2001; Janz & Prasarnphanich, 2003; Michailova & Minbaeva, 2012; Newell et al., 2009). Each organization has a unique culture composed of visible and invisible dimensions (Al-Alawi et al., 2007): the visible part consists of the organization's stated values and mission; the invisible part relates to the norms and values that shape the behavior and actions of employees (and their managers). Scholars also point to how knowledge and knowledge sharing are connected to social structures and local communities of practice within an organization (Razmerita et al., 2016). Organizational culture is recognized to be an important factor for the organization's adoption of new information systems (Hung et al., 2011; Jackson, 2011). Studies show that to successfully implement new technological systems that create new knowledge sharing practices, certain organizational changes may be necessary (Davidson, 2006; Kuettner et al., 2013; Roda et al., 2003). In turning to intelligence organizations, we find certain aspects of culture and knowledge sharing that require consideration for the deployment of new technological systems.

In their study of one intelligence unit, Turnley and McNamara (2007) found that new collaborative information technologies would have the potential to accelerate the flow of information through the analytic chain, but this could change the tempo of operations and decision making. This could create a situation in which the collaborative technology works in practice but may not work organizationally. Further, they found that intelligence analysts often operate in multiple relationships – with their unit, their division, their directorate – in producing intelligence reports. Therefore, introducing a new technology into the intelligence work environment requires that analysts understand how their existing relationships (program, team, individual) may also be altered. Turnley and McNamara also pointed out that intelligence technologies that change information flow or work practices can also impact resource allocation, ownership of information, and their associated power structures. The authors concluded that, because the analytic environment varies across intelligence units and agencies, it is important to consider the social environment in which the tool will be embedded and what existing work processes or practices, at individual or team levels, might promote or hinder use of the technology in its environment – and how these practices could be constructively modified with it.

In considering ACS in this context, questions arise about the future deployment of the ACS system: How might ACS alter the tempo of intelligence work and alter the relationships an analyst has with their unit, division, and directorate in good but problematic ways? How might decisions be made about what tasks and workflows are better left to the AI-enabled ACS versus the human? The ACS system is designed to help analysts (or a group of analysts) determine what role AI and humans should play in a given analytic task. In addition, the ACS system could help with defining once a task is automated with AI, what implications this has for other workflows downstream. This would be particularly helpful in complicated intelligence analyses where there are multiple computational components as well as humans in the loop. For example, in a scenario where an analyst is attempting to identify the malicious activities of a terrorist group, an AI-enabled surveillance drone can be used to rapidly identify and sort through hundreds of trucks in a given area instead of having an analyst do this visually and manually. Such a drone system could allow for the identification of 500 trucks and anomalous activities per hour. This would be much faster than a human could process this information for an assessment. The ACS system could then be used to help the analyst in various ways: (1) it could identify and plug into the assessment other complementary AI-enabled tools that could help analysts sort through the image data; (2) it could provide additional resources (including identifying human expertise) to help the analyst prioritize (or triage) the data of certain trucks in certain areas; (3) it could identify what anomalies in the data need closer human investigation; (4) it could determine what parts of the analytic workflow need to remain under human hands; or (5) it could help the analyst more quickly determine what other downstream tasks would need to be altered to accommodate the new rapid workflow enabled by the AI-enabled surveillance drone. The AI-enabled ACS system could take all of these factors into account and then define a new analytic workflow that would optimally utilize all available resources (human and computational) for the required task.

Moreover, if ACS allows for more rapid automated analysis by AI-enabled tools or linked datasets developed by other units, how would analysts be able to test the veracity of the output before the information is passed on for tactical or strategic decision making? What about the introduction of bias into datasets and algorithms incorporated as a part of the ACS system? It is well known that machine-learning systems can incorrectly categorize data or introduce errors from altered or manipulated data (Nguyen et al., 2015; Su et al., 2019; Martineau, 2019; Open AI, 2017; Matsakis, 2017). Intelligence analysts would need training to understand how AI algorithms may fail or introduce errors. How might managers anticipate these changes and institute policies and procedures to promote beneficial knowledge sharing and knowledge management within ACS? These are all examples of issues that would need to be addressed part and parcel with development of the ACS system.

Gregory Treverton, former Director of the U.S. National Intelligence Council, has also studied how new online tools and platforms in the U.S. intelligence community are adopted (Treverton, 2016). As long noted by Orlikowski (1992b), collaborative technologies do not automatically produce collaboration in organizations unless organizational norms, incentives, and structural factors encourage it. Treverton notes, similarly to Johnston (2005), that collaboration runs against traditional work processes in the intelligence community (IC), which tend to be linear, hierarchical, and focused on individual rewards and recognition (this is a generalization; there are, of course, exceptions). Treverton argues that new IT tools can enable collaboration, but they critically depend on policies and practices that interact with the organizational culture. He notes that development for new technological tools in the IC has been largely from the bottom up, with little push from the top. As a result, problems for adoption arise when there is a lack of appropriate architecture, incentives, and senior support for the technologies. Treverton maintains there is a tension between capabilities that new tools enable and traditional work processes that focus on finished intelligence products; new employees tend to be socialized into the latter. He argues that the new technological capabilities will not be realized if traditional finished intelligence products and processes remain in their dominant current form. Treverton says that new developments in shared IT platforms within and across the U.S. IC, mostly driven by budgetary pressures, could help to change the current way intelligence analysts work – but he argues that senior managerial interventions and policies that support new ways of working should be created and sustained.

For example, if one analyst uses ACS but draws on the datasets and AI-enabled algorithms developed by another intelligence unit (or multiple units) that has been incorporated into ACS, who would get the recognition for the output? Under this arrangement, would another analytic unit have more say about an output if it is their AI-enabled software that is producing the intelligence assessment? Would it be the analyst working with the algorithm of another unit, the other unit that produced the algorithm, or some co-sharing arrangement of recognition? As noted by Treverton and others, currently, the U.S. IC does not have standardized means of sharing recognition among analysts (Vogel, 2013a). This suggests a need for developing memorandums of understanding (MOUs) or other information-sharing protocols within and among intelligence units so that it is clear how recognition is to be allocated as analysts use the ACS system. Ren et al. (2008) also note the importance of having information and training sessions for workers and managers on new technologies and revisiting the organization's incentive systems – before technologies are introduced – to minimize user resistance. In addition, Ren et al. advocate the appointment of a "collaboration engineer" who can work with users of the technologies to modify existing work practices in order to integrate the new technology. All of these practices would be important to address at individual, team, and program levels in a variety of intelligence environments for ACS or any new AI-enabled information technologies that are introduced.

In addition to the problems with new technology use among analysts described above, there can be a rejection of new technological tools by intelligence analysts if they do not trust the algorithms and processes by which the data and analytic output are generated. Beyond the context of intelligence organizations, trust – a major issue being considered with AI-enabled automated intelligence analysis (Yeh, 2015) – has been found to be key to knowledge exchange and uptake within other organizations (Andrews & Delahay, 2000; Chow & Chan, 2008; Hau et al., 2013; Mayer et al., 1995; Tsai & Ghosal, 1998). Factors in increasing trust in knowledge sharing relate to an individual's perception of relevant expertise (Abrams et al., 2003), as well as the belief that others will not take advantage of or misuse that trust (Gefen et al., 2003; Hsu et al., 2007). As a counterpart to trust, fear has been identified as a factor that prevents knowledge sharing in organizations, specifically, fear of criticism, fear of relinquishing power and authority, fear that job security will be reduced, and fear of losing face or misleading community members (Ardichvili et al., 2003; Matschke et al., 2014; Šajeva, 2007).

How would ACS alter information flow and ownership of ideas by intelligence analysts and enhance or challenge existing collaboration practices in intelligence? Will intelligence analysts (and their managers) trust end products from ACS? If so, how should confidence be attained? For automated analyses, would analysts be able to deconstruct the analytic process with ACS (e.g., open the "black box") to ensure the results are reliable? Because the ACS system is imagined to operate similarly to the AWS model, this begs the questions: How much would intelligence analysts need to know about how ACS produces its outputs in order to trust the system? What accountability measures might exist within ACS to check whether the intelligence output is flawed? How much judgment should be devolved to ACS systems? What becomes the analyst's role in a future ACS-enabled analytic unit? Will they trust that they would not be replaced by a machine as some workflows become more automated? How can the IC build trust and decrease fear among analysts in these new platform systems? What additional policies, procedures, and training are needed in the IC to address these organizational culture issues? This is merely a sampling of possible questions to be explored as new platform systems are developed with the capacity to change existing cultural work practices in intelligence.

Datafication of Intelligence Work

As noted earlier, scholars have pointed to the increasing datafication of human life, including in the workplace (Mejias & Couldry, 2019). The question of how big data, AI, and various computational platforms will impact the workforce has been a topic of intense focus by the government, scholars, media, and the public (Davis, 2016; Executive Office of the President, 2016; Kessler, 2018; National Academies of Sciences, Engineering, and Medicine, 2017; Rosenblat, 2018). Key concerns revolve around the shift toward quantification and technological solutions enabled by big data and AI-enabled systems at the expense of other forms of information or understanding and how this will impact various knowledge-worker jobs. Bowker and Star (1999) have discussed how IT infrastructures, as systems for storing, standardizing, and classifying data, tend to structure a particular way of seeing the world that can omit many important factors.

Many aspects of intelligence analysis cannot be easily or fully captured by computational systems – at least in the current and near term. For example, in assessing a state or non-state weapons program, one must understand the tacit knowledge associated with weapons development. Acquisition of such data typically involves using qualitative data and methodologies (e.g., expert interviews, focus groups, laboratory observation, or other forms of ethnography) – and in the case of intelligence, human intelligence (HUMINT). Developing a weapons capability involves not only counting and measuring materials, equipment, documents, and other tangible objects, but also assessing the sociopolitical-cultural factors that shape intent and capability on the ground. It has been shown that a lack of consideration of tacit knowledge and other social factors (e.g., organizational/leadership components and dynamics, and larger micro and macro sociopolitical-economic contexts) has led to erroneous intelligence and policy assessments (Ben Ouagrham-Gormley, 2014; Brugioni, 1995; Duelfer, 2004; Hymans, 2012; Schroeder, 1995; Vogel, 2013a; 2013b; 2019). Explicit forms of knowledge that are readily accessible through big-data/AI approaches do not tell the whole story. Therefore, caution should be taken in relying solely on these approaches to weapons assessments, as these analytics may not capture important details crucial to accurate threat assessment, and more qualitative data and analyses will likely be necessary to inform the big-data picture.

This raises questions for a future ACS system: If quantitative methods and data are easiest to incorporate into an ACS system, how do we ensure that analysts do not rely solely on these approaches for their intelligence assessments? How do we train analysts to be aware of the biases and gaps in various big-data and AI approaches? How do we ensure that hard-to-gather, qualitative data remain prioritized and able to be incorporated in ACS-like systems? How do we ensure that the non-codifiable tacit knowledge of veteran intelligence analysts is accessible and passed on to junior analysts?

Conclusion

From this evaluation of ACS and these socio-technical dimensions, one can see that there are more questions raised than answered. However, we need to have these kinds of dialogues regarding these platform systems now. As individuals involved with the development of the ACS system, we recommend looking more closely at these issues and gathering user data from working-level intelligence analysts and managers to further inform the social and technical ramifications of these technologies. Beyond ACS, the U.S. intelligence community needs to devote more attention and resources to studying how human-machine teaming will occur in a future big-data/AI-enabled intelligence workplace. To date, existing intelligence initiatives have focused largely on the technical problems that need to be addressed with AI intelligence systems. We argue that a similar effort needs to be focused on the socio-technical dimensions of how these systems are to be deployed at the working-level, and how intelligence managers and officials need to think carefully about the variety of impacts these technologies may have on analysts.

References

Abrams, L. C., Cross, R., Lesser, E., & Levin, D. Z. (2003). Nurturing interpersonal trust in knowledge-sharing networks. *Academy of Management Executive, 17*(4): 64–77.

Al-Alawi, A. I., Al-Marzooqi, Y. N., & Mohammed, F. Y. (2007). Organizational culture and knowledge sharing: Critical success factors. *Journal of knowledge management, 11*(2): 22–42.

Alavi, M., & Leidner, D. E. (2001). Review: Knowledge management and knowledge management systems: Conceptual foundations and research issues. *MIS Quarterly, 25*(1): 107–136.

Andrews, K. M., & Delahay, B. L. (2000). Influences on knowledge processes in organizational learning: The psychosocial filter. *Journal of Management Studies, 37*: 797–810.

Ardichvili, A., Page, V., & Wentling, T. (2003). Motivation and barriers to participation in virtual knowledge-sharing communities of practice. *Journal of Knowledge Management, 7*(1): 64–77.

Baldwin, C. Y., & Woodard, J. (2008). *The Architecture of Platforms: A Unified View (31 p.)*. Boston, MA: Harvard Business School. http://www.hbs.edu/faculty/Publication%20Files/09-034_149607b7-2b95-4316-b4b6-1df66dd34e83.pdf https://doi.org/10.2139/ssrn.1265155

Ben Ouagrham-Gormley, S. (2014). *Barriers to Bioweapons*. Ithaca, NY: Cornell University Press.

Bowker G. C., & Star, S. L. (1999). *Sorting things out: Classification and its consequences*. Cambridge, MA: MIT Press.

Brantly, A. F. (2018). When everything becomes intelligence: Machine learning and the connected world. *Intelligence and National Security, 33*(4): 562–573. DOI: 10.1080/02684527.2018.1452555

Brugioni, D. A. (1995). The unidentifieds. In H. Bradford (Ed.), *Inside CIA's Private World: Declassified Articles from the Agency's Internal Journal, 1955–1992* (pp. 8–26). New Haven: Yale University Press.

Bucher, T. (2018). *If . . . then: Algorithmic power and politics*. Oxford, UK: Oxford University Press.

Chow, W.S. and Chan, L.S. (2008). Social network, social trust and shared goals in organizational knowledge sharing. *Information & Management* 45(7): 458-65. DOI: https://doi.org/10.1016/j.im.2008.06.007

Davidson, E. (2006). A technological frames perspective on information technology and organizational change. *Journal of Applied Behavioral Science, 42*(1): 23–39.

Davis, G. F. (2016). *The vanishing American corporation: Navigating the hazards of a new economy.* Oakland, CA: Berrett-Kohler.

Doorn, N. (2012). Responsibility ascriptions in technology development and engineering: Three perspectives. *Science and Engineering Ethics, 18*(1): 69–90.

Duelfer, C. (2004). *Comprehensive report of the Special Advisor to the DCI on Iraq's WMD.* Central Intelligence Agency. https://www.cia.gov/library/reports/general-reports-1/iraq_wmd_2004/

Eldridge, C., Hobbs, C., & Moran, M. (2018). Fusing algorithms and analysts: Open-source intelligence in the age of 'Big Data'. *Intelligence and National Security, 33*(3): 391–406. DOI: https://doi.org/10.1080/02684527.2017.1406677

Ess, C. (2009). Digital Media Ethics. Cambridge, UK: Polity Press. Polity Press.

Executive Office of the President. (2016). *Artificial intelligence, automation, and the economy.* Washington, DC: U.S. Government Printing Office.

Frank, A. (2017). Computational social science and intelligence analysis. *Intelligence and National Security, 32*(5): 579–599, DOI: 10.1080/02684527.2017.1310968

Gefen, D., Karahanna, E., & Straub, D.W. (2003). Trust and TAM in online shopping: An integrated model. *MIS Quarterly, 27*(1): 51–90.

Gillespie, T. (2010). The politics of platforms. *New Media & Society, 12*(3): 347–364.

Gillespie, T. (2017, August 24). The platform metaphor, revisited. *Digital Society Blog.* https://www.hiig.de/en/the-platform-metaphor-revisited/

Gillespie, T. (2018a). *Custodians of the Internet: Platforms, content moderation, and the hidden decisions that shape social media.* New Haven: Yale University Press.

Gillespie, T. (2018b). Platforms are not Intermediaries. *Georgetown Law Technology Review, 2*(2): 198–216.

Gorwa, R. (2019). What is platform governance? *Information, Communication & Society, 22*(6): 1–18. DOI: 10.1080/1369118X.2019.1573914

Hanseth, O., & Lyytinen, K. (2010). Design theory for dynamic complexity in information infrastructures: The case of building Internet. *Journal of Information Technology, 25*: 1–19. DOI: 10.1057/jit.2009.19

Hare, N., & Coghill, P. (2016). The future of the intelligence analysis task. *Intelligence and National Security, 31*(6): 858–870, DOI: 10.1080/02684527.2015.1115238

Hau, Y.S., Kim, B., Lee, H., & Kim, Y.-G. (2013). The effects of individual motivations and social capital on employees' tacit and explicit knowledge sharing intentions. *International Journal of Information Management 33* (2):356-66. DOI: https://doi.org/10.1016/j.ijinfomgt.2012.10.009

Helberger, N., Pierson, J., & Poell, T. (2018). Governing online platforms: From contested to cooperative responsibility. *The Information Society*, 34(1): 1–14. DOI: 10.1080/01972243.2017.1391913

Herhkovitz, S. (2020). Crowdsourced intelligence (Crosint): Using crowds for national security. *International Journal of Intelligence, Security, and Public Affairs, 22*(1): 42–55. DOI: 10.1080/23800992.2020.1744824

Hsu, M.-H., Ju, T. L., Yen, C.-H., & Chang, C.-M. (2007). Knowledge sharing behavior in virtual communities: The relationship between trust, self-efficacy, and outcome expectations. *International Journal of Human-Computer Studies, 65*(2): 153–169.

Hung, S.-Y., Lai, H.-M., & Chang, W.-W. (2011). Knowledge-sharing motivations affecting R&D employees' acceptance of electronic knowledge repository. *Behaviour & Information Technology, 30*(2): 213–230.

Hymans, J. E. C. (2012). *Achieving nuclear ambitions: Scientists, politicians, and proliferation.* Cambridge, UK: Cambridge University Press.

Jackson, S. (2011). Organizational culture and information systems adoption: A three-perspective approach. *Information and Organization*, *21*(2): 57–83.

Janz, B. D., & Prasarnphanich, P. (2003). Understanding the antecedents of effective knowledge management: The importance of a knowledge-centered culture. *Decision Sciences*, *34*(2): 351.

Johnston, R. (2005). *Analytic culture in the U.S. Intelligence Community: An ethnographic study.* Washington, DC: Center for the Study of Intelligence, Central Intelligence Agency.

Jordan, T. (2015). *Information politics: Liberation and exploitation in the digital society.* London: Pluto Press.

Kessler, S. (2018). *Gigged: The gig economy, the end of the job and the future of work.* New York: Random House Business.

Kirchner, K., Razmerita, L., & Sudzina, F. (2008). New forms of interaction and knowledge sharing on Web 2.0. In Miltiadis Lytras & Patricia Ordonez De Pablo (Eds.), *Web2.0: The business model* (pp. 21–37). Berlin: Springer Science and Business Media.

Kuettner, T., Diehl, R., & Schubert, P. (2013). Change factors in Enterprise 2.0 initiatives: Can we learn from ERP? *Electronic Markets*, *23*(40): 329–40.

Langlois, G., & Elmer, G. (2013). The research politics of social media platforms. *Culture Machine*, *14*, 1–17. http://www.culturemachine.net/

Lim, K. (2016). Big data and strategic intelligence. *Intelligence and National Security*, *31*(4): 619–635. DOI: 10.1080/02684527.2015.1062321

Mansell, R. (2015). Platforms of power. *Intermedia*, *43*(1): 20–24. Retrieved from http://eprints.lse.ac.uk/61318/1/__lse.ac.uk_storage_LIBRARY_Secondary_libfile_shared_repository_Content_Mansell,R_Platforms%20power_Mansell_Platform%20power_2015_cover.pdf

Martens, B. (2016, April). *An economic policy perspective on online platforms.* Institute for Prospective Technological Studies Digital Economy JRC101501 [Working paper].

Martineau, K. (2019, July 31). Why did my classifer just mistake a turtle for a rifle? *MIT News*, Cambridge, MA: Massachusetts Institute of Technology.

Matsakis, L. (2017, December 20). Researchers fooled a Google AI into thinking a rifle was a helicopter. *Wired.* https://www.wired.com/story/researcher-fooled-a-google-ai-into-thinking-a-rifle-was-a-helicopter/?mbid=nl_122117_daily_list1_p2

Matschke, C., Moskaliuk, J., Bokhorst, F., Schümmer, T., & Cress, U. (2014). Motivational factors of information exchange in social information spaces. *Computers in Human Behavior, 36*: 549–558.

Mayer, R. C., Davis, J. H., & Schoorman, D. F. (1995). An integrative model of organizational trust. *Academy of Management Review*, *20*(3): 709–734.

Mejias, U. A., & Couldry, N. (2019). Datafication. *Internet Policy Review*, *8* (4). DOI: 10.14763/2019.4.1428. https://policyreview.info/concepts/datafication

Michailova, S., & Minbaeva, D. B. (2012). Organizational values and knowledge sharing in multinational corporations: The Danisco case. *International Business Review*, *21*(1): 59–70.

National Academies of Sciences, Engineering, and Medicine. (2017). *Information technology and the U.S. workforce: Where are we and where do we go from here?* Washington, DC: National Academies Press.

Newell, S., Robertson, M., Scarbrough, H., & Swan, J. (2009). *Managing knowledge work and innovation.* Basingstoke: Palgrave Macmillan.

Nguyen, A., Yosinski, J., & Clune, J. (2015). *Deep neural networks are easily fooled: High confidence predictions for unrecognizable images.* https://arxiv.org/abs/1412.1897

Orlikowski, W.J. (1992a). Learning from notes: Organizational issues in groupware implementation. In M. Mantel & R. Baecker, Eds., *Proceedings of the ACM Conference on Computer-Supported Cooperative Work*, November, Toronto, 362–369.

Olaisen, J., & Revang, O. (2017). Working smarter and greener: Collaborative knowledge sharing in virtual global project teams. *International Journal of Information Management 37*: 1441–1448. DOI: https://doi.org/10.1016/j.ijinfomgt.2016.10.002.

Omand, D., Bartlett, J., & Miller, C. (2012). Introducing social media intelligence (SOCMINT). *Intelligence and National Security, 27*(6): 801–823. DOI: 10.1080/02684527.2012.716965.

Open AI. (2017, July 17). *Robust adversarial inputs.* Robust Adversarial Inputs (openai.com)

Orlikowski, W. J. (1992b). Learning from notes: Organizational issues in groupware implementation. In M. Mantel & R. Baecker (Eds.), *Proceedings of the ACM Conference on Computer-Supported Cooperative Work: An ethnographic study of culture and collaborative technology in the intelligence community* (pp. 362–369). ACM.

Pasquale, F. (2015). *The black box society: The secret algorithms that control money and information.* Cambridge: MA: Harvard University Press.

Phillips, E., Ososky, S., Grove, J., & Jentsch, F. (2011). From tools to teammates: Toward the development of appropriate mental models for intelligent robots. *Proceedings of the Human Factors and Ergonomics Society Annual Meeting, 55*(1): 200–1495. DOI: https://doi.org/10.1177%2F1071181311551310

Plantin, J.-C., Lagose, C., Edwards, P. N., & Sandvig. C. (2018). Infrastructure studies meet platform studies in the age of Google and Facebook. *New Media & Society, 20*: 293–310.

Poell, T., Van Dijck, J., & Nieborg, D. (2019). Platformisation. *Internet Policy Review, 8*(4): 1–13.

Razmerita, L., Kirchner, K., & Nielsen, P. (2016). What factors influence knowledge sharing in organizations? A social dilemma perspective of social media communication. *Journal of Knowledge Management, 20*(6): 1225–1246. DOI: http://dx.doi.org/10.1108/JKM-03-2016-0112.

Regens, J. L. (2019). Augmenting human cognition to enhance strategic, operational, and tactical intelligence. *Intelligence and National Security, 34*(5): 673–687. DOI: 10.1080/02684527.2019.1579410.

Ren, Y., Kiesler, S., & Fussell, S. R. (2008). Multiple group coordination in complex and dynamic task environments: Interruptions, coping mechanisms, and technology.

Roda, C., Angehrn, A., Nabeth, T., & Razmerita, L. (2003). Using conversational agents to support the adoption of knowledge sharing practices. *Interacting with Computers, 15*(1): 57–89.

Rosenblat, A. (2018). *Uberland: How algorithms are rewriting the rules of work.* Oakland, CA: University of California Press.

Šajeva, S. (2007). An Investigation of Critical Barriers to Effective Knowledge Management. *Social Sciences/Socialiniai Mokslai 58*(4): 20–27.

Schroeder, G. (1995). Soviet reality sans Potemkin. In H. Bradford (Ed.), *Inside CIA's private world: Declassified articles from the agency's internal journal, 1955–1992*, (pp. 41–48). New Haven: Yale University Press.

Su, J., Vargas, D. V., & Sakurai, K. (2019). *One pixel attack for fooling deep neural networks.* https://arxiv.org/abs/1710.08864

Thompson, D. F. (1980). Moral responsibility of public officials: The problem of many hands. *American Political Science Review, 74*(4): 905–916.

Treverton, G. F. (2016). *New tools for collaboration: The experience of the U.S. intelligence community.* Lanham: CSIS/Rowman and Littlefield.

Tsai, W., & Ghoshal, S. (1998). Social capital and value creation: The role of intrafirm networks. *Academy of Management Journal, 41*(4): 464–476.

Turnley, J. G., & McNamara, L. A. (2007). An ethnographic study of culture and collaborative technology in the intelligence community. *Sandia Technical Report.* SAND 2007-2593-J.

van de Poel, I., Nihlen Fahlquist, J., Doorn, N., Zwart, S., & Royakkers, L. (2012). The problem of many hands: Climate change as an example. *Science and Engineering Ethics, 18*(1): 49–67.

Van Puyvelde, D., Coutlhart, S., & Shariar Hossain, M. (2017). Beyond the buzzword: Big data and national security decision-making. *International Affairs*, *93*(6): 1397–1416.

Vogel, K. M. (2013a). *Phantom menace or looming danger? A new framework for assessing bioweapons threats*. Baltimore, MD: Johns Hopkins University Press.

Vogel, K. M. (2013b). The need for greater multidisciplinary, sociotechnical analysis: The bioweapons case. *Studies in Intelligence*, *57*(3): 1–10.

Vogel, K. M. (2019). Big data and biodefense: Prospects and pitfalls. In S. K. Singh & J. H. Kuhn (Eds.), *Defense Against Biological Attacks, vol. 1* (pp. 297–316). Cham, Switzerland: Springer Nature.

Watanabe, C., Naveed, K., Neittaanmaki, P., & Fox, B. (2017). Consolidated challenge to social demand for resilient platforms: Lessons from Uber's global expansion. *Technology in Society*, *48*: 33–53.

Yeh, P. F. (2015). The case for using robots in intelligence analysis. *Studies in Intelligence*, *59*(4): 1–8. https://www.cia.gov/library/center-for-the-study-of-intelligence/csi-publications/csi-studies/studies/vol-59-no-4/pdfs/Yeh-Automated-Analysis.pdf

Deborah Goldstein

Chapter 3 Online Deliberative Dialogue with State Leaders: A North Carolina Case Study

Abstract: Established in 2015 in partnership with the Duke Sanford School of Public Policy, the North Carolina Leadership Forum (NCLF) facilitates constructive engagement between North Carolina policy, business, and non-profit leaders across party lines, ideologies, professional experiences, and regional perspectives. NCLF's goal is to develop a cohort of state leaders who have the will, the skills, and the relationships with each other to work constructively with others of different political parties or ideologies. When the program was conducted during the COVID-19 pandemic and a very tense political election, the experience of the online dialogue was unique and unusual. This chapter describes key lessons learned about how an online format can be used to enhance or enable dialogue across differences on highly polarized issues.

Keywords: leadership, democracy, deliberation, relationship-building, state policy

Introduction

Established in 2015 in partnership with the Duke Sanford School of Public Policy, the North Carolina Leadership Forum (NCLF) facilitates constructive engagement between North Carolina policy, business, and non-profit leaders across party lines, ideologies, professional experiences, and regional perspectives. NCLF's goal is to develop a cohort of state leaders who have the will, the skills, and the relationships with each other to work constructively with others of different political parties or ideologies. Over the long-term, NCLF aims to support a healthy and productive policy-making environment for North Carolina and its local governments and provide a model for similar efforts in other states by building a network of such leaders and publicly reinforcing their efforts.

Until 2020, NCLF's program recruited an annual cohort of about 30 statewide leaders for a year-long program in which participants attend four two-day intensive in-person meetings focused on a specific issue and engage in deliberative dialogue and relationship building over that period. When COVID-19 stay-at-home orders took effect, NCLF had just convened its fourth and newest cohort for the group's first two-day in-person introductory session. Realizing we could not hold subsequent meetings in person, NCLF quickly pivoted to convene the new cohort online.

While NCLF leadership initially questioned whether it would be possible to hold meaningful dialogue across differences online, particularly with very busy state

https://doi.org/10.1515/9783110687262-004

leaders during a crisis period, we thought it was critical to continue to build connections and foster conversation during this period. We found that many participants were eager to stay involved and talk to each other and that we were able to foster meaningful relationship-building and respectful dialogue across serious differences of opinion through an online format. We also found that alumni from prior years were eager to participate in online convenings to further connection and brainstorming collectively. At the same time, facilitating constructive dialogue online amid a crisis was not without challenges.

While NCLF facilitators were able to identify resources about successful online group meetings, we found very limited resources to inform leading constructive dialogue across differences in an online context. Ultimately, we adapted the NCLF in-person program to an online format with three main adjustments: increased pace and interactivity, building connection and trust through small groups and optional social time, and using simple, accessible technology with support from separate personnel beyond the facilitators. We learned that participants did not have the same experience as those who have been through in-person cohorts, however, they did report learning a great deal from the program and improving their skills and knowledge. Because the program was conducted during the COVID-19 pandemic and a very tense political election, the experience of the online dialogue was unique and unusual. At the same time, it provided key lessons about how an online format can be used to enhance or enable dialogue across differences on highly polarized issues.

NCLF Practice

Founded in 2015, the NC Leadership Forum has developed a practice for convening a recruited group of multisectoral leaders from across North Carolina to engage in deliberative dialogue across difference. The program includes several techniques that foster relationship building and networking amongst the group alongside a series of carefully facilitated discussions that encourage the leaders to deepen their understanding of a specific issue of importance in the state, both in terms of why others hold different views and what underlies their own values and views on the topic.

The program is planned and led by a diverse steering committee of three Democrats and three Republicans with extensive experience in a range of positions in the public sector. Steering committee members help select the forum topic for the year, support participant recruitment, and take turns facilitating the program and participating in dialogue alongside participants.

Once the topic is selected, the program invites approximately 30 state leaders with expertise or interest in the topic to participate in the forum. Participants are recruited from across the state, with a focus on diversity in many respects: political party, geography (rural and urban, different regions of the state), sector (business leaders, nonprofit advocates from a variety of experiences and political perspectives, and elected officials from the local and state level), race, ethnicity, gender, and age/ experience.

When NCLF is conducted in person, participants are asked to commit to four 2-day sessions, during which the steering committee leads the group through a deliberative dialogue model adapted from frameworks established by the Kettering Foundation/National Issues Forum and other civil dialogue and conflict resolution programs.[1]

Facilitators use the following model to guide discussion of the annual issue:

- Broadly frame a question, such as "How should NC respond to the COVID-19 crisis?";
- Brainstorm a broad list of concerns about the selected issue (participants share their own concerns and collect concerns from their community);
- Categorize and organize the concerns;
- Develop a shared understanding of the underlying values at stake as expressed by participants;
- Where needed, provide basic information about the facts and systems underlying the issue under discussion;
- Brainstorm solutions that address the concerns raised;
- Articulate the benefits and downsides of each proposed solution;
- Determine participants' preferences with regard to whether they favor or oppose solutions and how serious or moderate preferences are for each proposal;
- Deepen understanding of what underlies the different perspectives on the solutions where there is the most polarization; and
- Explore whether modifying any solutions would increase support for proposed solutions.

Alongside these discussions, NCLF incorporates several methods to encourage participants to get to know each other:

- Introduce ground rules for discussions, including a detailed overview of what it means to engage in "active listening";
- Early in the opening session, ask each participant to share with the full group a personal story about a person or event that had a significant impact on who they are;

1 For examples of practice and research around Deliberative Dialogue, see Kettering Foundation. (2019). *Public Deliberation and Divisiveness: An Update on the Research.* https://www.kettering.org/catalog/product/public-deliberation-and-divisiveness-update-research; Rourke, B. (2014). *Developing Materials for Deliberative Forums.* Kettering Foundation. https://www.kettering.org/catalog/product/developing-materials-deliberative-forums; and Essential Partners. (2019). *Fostering Dialogue Across Divides.* https://whatisessential.org/resources/fostering-dialogue-across-divides.

- Assign participants to a diverse "homeroom" group that is led by a steering committee captain. In the in-person version, participants often are grouped by homeroom for meal seating or for small group discussions;
- Pair each participant with a "buddy" that holds a different political perspective, but lives relatively close by (i.e. within an hour). Over the course of the program, buddies are asked to meet between sessions to hold at least one meaningful conversation on a topic of their choosing, with encouragement to meet more;
- Arrange discussions between pairs, in small groups, or the full group depending on the goal and nature of the particular activity. Seating is typically assigned, with deliberate attention given to moving participants around until each person has had an opportunity to interact with every other person at least once;
- When in-person, NCLF hosts the events at a site for two days, with meals provided, typically including an evening reception and dinner, incorporating support for social interaction over meals and in between programmed sessions; and
- Programs typically are scheduled at 2–3 sites around the state so that participants can also have some experience in geographies relevant to the topic or in the "hometown" of some of the participants.

For reports on the proceedings of prior in-person programs, see NCLF's website at https://sites.duke.edu/nclf/.

Adaptation for Online Dialogue

In March 2020, NCLF had just convened its first meeting of its 2020 Cohort to focus on the topic of immigration when North Carolina's first cases of COVID-19 emerged and stay-at-home orders took effect. Three issues quickly became clear: 1) As leaders in the state, many NCLF cohort participants were at the forefront of leading local and statewide efforts to respond to COVID-19; 2) It would be impossible to convene the cohort in person; and 3) NC was experiencing deep polarization around the state and nation's response to COVID-19.

NCLF decided to invite the Cohort to continue its discussions through an online format and to switch topics from immigration to NC's response to COVID-19. Because many state leaders were already familiar with Zoom, we elected to use that format for all of NCLF's conversations. Rather than schedule four two-day sessions, NCLF invited participants to attend two small group discussions, scheduled in April/May and then in June. We then followed up in July, September, and November with 3 full-group sessions – each full-group session was from 2 pm–6 pm or 8 am–12 pm on two sequential days (i.e. 2 pm–6 pm Thursday and 8 am-noon Friday or 8 am–12 pm Wednesday and 8 am–12 pm Thursday).

Between April and November, about 20 NC leaders from around the state convened to talk through their concerns, values, and preferences about a range of responses to how NC was addressing the COVID-19 pandemic. Topics discussed included strongly held views on reopening businesses, reopening schools, the treatment of workers, including farmworkers and those in meat-packing plants, addressing economic needs in the state through the state budget, health care coverage for those impacted by COVID-19, addressing evictions in the state, and the role of the Governor, the legislature, and other elected officials in responding to the crisis. Participants were deeply divided over some of these topics and engaged in spirited conversation in particular around reopening businesses and schools, protecting workers, and the role of government in making decisions during the pandemic on behalf of the community. Values around individual decision making, information sharing and transparency, safety and risk, equity and fairness, creativity and innovation, the role of expertise, and neighborliness/caring for each other were at stake in many of the conversations.

Further, because the dialogue was conducted between April–November 2020, participants were managing their own leadership and home lives during a pandemic, confronting issues of racial justice and protests in their hometowns and on TV, and a very tense election cycle. Participants engaged in some discussion of these challenges and reflected on what they could learn to inform their own approach to leadership, active listening, and engagement in their communities. Feedback from the group suggested that they found the conversations helpful in informing how they approach leadership, added nuance and information to their understanding of issues, and provided a new network of colleagues during a period in which they were more isolated than is typical.

After each NCLF cohort finishes their series of meetings, we conduct an immediate post-program survey to assess whether the program had an impact on participants and which parts were most effective. A comparison of the post-program surveys from our most recent in-person cohort in 2019 and the online cohort in 2020 shows that participants in the online cohort did experience similar outcomes as the in-person cohort but to a weaker degree. For example, 88% of online participants said they built relationships with people of differing views, compared to 95% of in-person participants, but respondents from the online group on the survey were split between "strongly agree" and "somewhat agree", while 86% of the in-person group selected "strongly agree." A similar pattern holds for improved understanding about the issue, the views of others, and developing strong skills at constructive engagement – responses of the online group are about 10–15% lower than the in-person group overall but still very positive (See Table 3.1).

Table 3.1: Post-Program Survey of Participants (2019–2020).

	Online Cohort March-Nov 2020	In-Person Cohort Jan-Aug 2019
Building Relationships *I formed relationships with one or more people of differing views that I would not have otherwise formed*	Strongly agree: 52.94% Somewhat agree: 35.29% Neither agree/disagree: 11.76% Somewhat disagree: 0 Strongly disagree: 0	Strongly agree: 86.36% Somewhat agree: 9.09% Neither agree/disagree: 0 Somewhat disagree: 0 Strongly disagree: 4.55%
Understanding the issues *I learned more about [topic]*	Strongly agree: 29.41% Somewhat agree: 52.94% Neither agree/disagree: 17.65% Somewhat disagree: 0 Strongly disagree: 0	Strongly agree: 65.22% Somewhat agree: 30.43% Neither agree/disagree: 4.35% Somewhat disagree: 0 Strongly disagree: 0
Understanding the Views of Others *I better understand the values, opinions, or priorities about [topic] held by people with different perspectives than mine.*	Strongly agree: 47.06% Somewhat agree: 47.06% Neither agree/disagree: 5.88% Somewhat disagree: 0 Strongly disagree: 0	Strongly agree: 65.22% Somewhat agree: 34.78% Neither agree/disagree: 0 Somewhat disagree: 0 Strongly disagree: 0
The Skill of Seeking to Understand *I gained skills that will help me engage constructively with people of different views*	Strongly agree: 41.18% Somewhat agree: 35.29% Neither agree/disagree: 17.65% Somewhat disagree: 5.88% Strongly disagree: 0	Strongly agree: 72.73% Somewhat agree: 13.64% Neither agree/disagree: 9.09% Somewhat disagree: 4.55% Strongly disagree: 0

Approaches for Enhancing Online Dialogue

While NCLF leaders were able to find some resources on how to run an effective group meeting online via Zoom, we found little guidance about facilitating online dialogue among people with deeply different views. However, with detailed planning, debriefs after each program, and a willingness to be flexible, we were able to facilitate a program that engaged participants, introduced meaningful discussion on a challenging and important topic, and increased the attendees' reported will, skills, and relationships.

In conducting the NCLF program online, we focused on three key areas as priorities:

- In order to keep the attention and focus of participants, we adapted and accelerated the pace of each conversation within the full program. We also focused on encouraging high levels of interaction through activities and increased use of small group discussions;

- Recognizing the loss of in-person interaction, we prioritized building connection and trust, such as through increased use of carefully assigned small groups and optional social time before the meeting. We learned that being online also offered new opportunities for participants to share parts of their personality; and
- To make the program accessible and support the flow and pace, we had separate people manage facilitating the conversation and manage technology and logistics, and we also kept technological tools simple.

We learned that online programs had some unanticipated advantages. For example, some participants remarked that the focus and close-up facial views during small group discussion encouraged authenticity and honesty in a way that in-person large groups may not. Second, the reduced time commitment and lack of travel made it easier for some members of the cohort to participate.

On the other hand, we also experienced some challenges. New constraints on resolving tension after difficult conversations emerged. Participants also expressed frustration about the reduced opportunities to network with each other informally. Finally, we were less successful at fostering the "buddy" relationships that have been a hallmark of past annual programs.

Accelerated pace and increased interactivity. While NCLF usually convenes each session for one and a half days, we recognized that online discussion requires a significantly quicker pace for discussion and that participants would not be willing or able to focus in an online format for more than 3–4 hours at a time. We also assumed that in order to retain attention and focus, every session had to be highly interactive – one resource we consulted suggested asking people to participate every 5–7 minutes.

NCLF first adapted its format to incorporate two 90-minute small group discussions about a month apart. The first focused on a basic check-in to connect with others about how they were responding to the COVID-19 pandemic, and the second asked participants to think about how the COVID-19 pandemic was impacting immigrants and what solutions might address immigrant needs during this crisis period. Those sessions helped facilitate relationship-building within the cohort early on and bridged the change in topic from immigration to the COVID-19 pandemic. Given the stress of managing work, family, and other needs during the early months of the pandemic, it was particularly important to pay attention to the personal needs of participants.

By prioritizing the people first, rather than our program or topic, and fostering a personal connection with others who were confronting the pandemic both as leaders and family members in other parts of the state, participants found a value and purpose to continuing with the program. It was also important to acknowledge the change in topic – while some participants were clear that the pandemic was the only topic that they could consider in the moment, others had joined the group specifically to talk about immigration, and building a transition to connect the two topics fostered continued engagement for many, though not all, members of the group.

Once it was clear that a large proportion of participants were engaged and interested in continuing, NCLF planned sessions that were held on two adjacent half-days. Within each half-day session, we limited each discussion topic to an hour or less, and we typically divided the group into smaller breakout discussions of no more than 10 people, led by 1–2 facilitators. Report-outs and closure exercises were kept very brief. Even within the half-day format, we provided a 15-minute break at a midway point to allow participants to step away from their computer, handle other business, or address personal needs. We shared agendas in advance and made it clear that we wanted full attention during sessions, acknowledging that some may need to step out and that breaks would make that easier.

NCLF followed the same structure for the half-day sessions that it would have used in a full-day dialogue (i.e. discussion 1, identify concerns; discussion 2, explore values in tension; discussion 3, vote on preferences and discuss differing perspectives, etc.). However, in the online format, we shortened the time for each discussion and relied more heavily on small groups over full-group discussions.

During in-person sessions, we frequently ask participants to create visual representations of their preferences by placing stickers on statements posted on the wall – typically at the end of a session, as we transitioned to the next discussion. We replaced this technique in two ways: we used the Zoom polling feature to ask participants to vote on three statements, and we asked participants to complete a short survey in the evening between day 1 and day 2. In both cases, we used PowerPoint slides to reflect the results back to the participants at the start of the second day and solicited reactions and clarification of why people voted as they had.

In the past, NCLF's in-person sessions have incorporated some presentations of data or case studies, typically either by NCLF staff, experts in the field, or local practitioners with relevant perspectives. We did not think such presentations would hold the attention of participants in an online format, and generally replaced them with short, recommended reading lists of articles prior to the online session. Participants also frequently shared articles of interest via the chat function in Zoom as an organic part of the conversation, with NCLF reinforcing this effort by compiling the links and resending them post-program.

Cultivating connection and trust online. NCLF facilitators were very concerned that it would be difficult to replicate the relationship-building components of our in-person program online but found several techniques that supported connection and trust through Zoom.

First, we relied heavily on small groups of no more than 10, and often closer to 5 people, to encourage participation and connection. We typically assign cohort participants to homerooms that are intentionally designed to represent a cross-section of the diversity of the full group. In the live in-person version, we also assign seating during full group sessions such that people rotate until they have sat next to almost every other person who has a different ideological perspective than their own. We adapted this approach for online breakout assignments, making sure the homeroom configuration repeated several times, but also rotating people through small breakouts until they had been in one with almost everyone else. Because of the nature of the dialogue, we paid close attention to creating diverse groups and often made last-minute adjustments to groups to accommodate changes in attendance and still maintain diversity.

Second, we started morning sessions with an invitation to join up to 30 minutes early for an optional "breakfast" with the group that was intentionally set as social time without an agenda. We were surprised at how many participants elected to join these breakfasts and found them to be successful at encouraging relationship building. As an example, at one breakfast, participants began sharing stories of their childhood experiences getting to school in the morning or even driving the bus as teenagers to take other kids to school. This shared camaraderie fostered getting to know each other and shared storytelling that reached across different parts of North Carolina.

Third, we also learned that for some people, the format of online zoom calls fostered intimacy and authenticity that was not available in a formal in-person setting. People seemed particularly focused on the conversation because they did not have other distractions that might have been present at a live setting. Via Zoom, people had a close-up view of each other's faces during the conversation, this appeared to encourage sharing when in small groups. We also had the added advantage of seeing into people's personal lives as they participated – participants got to know one facilitator's cat, we saw musical instruments hanging on the wall behind several attendees, and we met a few people's children when they came in to say hello or walked through the room. A few participants also changed their background to reflect some aspect of their personality – a favorite dish they liked to cook or a place they had visited and loved.

While we can't know for certain how these details compare to in-person interaction, they are good examples of how online interaction can still feel personal and foster relationship-building with new people. In future cohorts, we could imagine incorporating more of these personal details into a gathering, such as by asking people to share an object from their home or by using some online small group or paired discussions to encourage conversation in between policy discussions.

Finally, one obvious advantage of the online dialogues was that people who lived several hours apart had an easy and accessible way to engage in conversation, particularly during a period of isolation. Our regular in-person dialogues require people to travel up to 4 hours to attend and to stay overnight. By meeting online, we were able to accommodate scheduling needs like childcare or preparing dinner, and still allow participants to engage in leadership conversations with others from around the state. Given that differences are often rooted in dramatically different experiences at the local level, online dialogue enabled meaningful discussions between someone in rural Eastern North Carolina and an entrepreneur in Charlotte, learning about how each experienced the pandemic's impact differently. Further, because we started conducting our program during the early months of stay-at-home orders, participants were particularly appreciative of the opportunity to connect with new people and exchange ideas – this experience exposed them to connection and dialogue during a period where their day-to-day experience was more isolated and polarized than normal.

Assign different personnel to facilitation and technology and keep technology tools simple. In planning NCLF dialogues, we made a choice to keep technological tools simple and consolidated as much as possible to minimize technological demands on participants. We also found it extremely helpful to devote specific personnel support to technology and logistics so that facilitators and participants could focus on the conversation rather than worry about managing technology.

For each dialogue, we shared a copy of the agenda with participants using Google Docs and used the Google Doc during the meeting as a guide. When we sent groups into breakouts, we asked the group to take notes at the bottom of the same google doc in an assigned section. In some sessions, we were able to enlist students or administrative support in notetaking, which led to much more detailed records of conversations. Participants were willing to take notes, but some were unable to juggle the online discussion and a shared document (especially if they were working with an iPad or one screen). Given the reliance on small groups, it was often helpful to use the notes to summarize discussions and redistribute a summary in advance of the next session. NCLF made a choice not to record sessions because of a concern that recordings would lead people to be more guarded in conversation. However, where it is feasible to record and use the recordings internally for reference in future sessions, that could be helpful.

Due to the increased use of Zoom generally during the COVID-19 pandemic, we did find that most participants learned to use Zoom as a web-based video tool quickly or were able to secure assistance on their own. To keep the program accessible, we stayed with the Zoom tool and did not integrate other conversation applications or interactive tools. We strongly encouraged participants to use a laptop/iPad rather than a phone and to keep their video on; they were generally willing. With Zoom, it was extremely helpful to have two people from the planning team work together to manage people coming in and out of the meeting, handle any technical issues that arose, and facilitate moving people in and out of breakout sessions. These assigned technology/logistics managers also aided facilitators by pointing out if someone was trying to speak and keeping track of the order of speakers in large group settings. This technology support made a significant difference in ensuring the program ran smoothly – facilitators were able to focus on the content of discussions and working with participants, while the two staff assigned to technology and logistics attended to various technological challenges that arose.

During dialogue sessions, participants chose to use the chat function to add to the conversation. In large part, they wanted to share additional resources such as an article they had written or read on the relevant topic. Sometimes they used the chat to clarify a point. We supported use of the chat and compiled the notes from the chat for the record of proceedings, and re-shared any articles posted in the chat with participants after each session.

As noted above, we occasionally asked the group to vote, adapting methodologies we would have used to gauge preferences during an in-person session. For example, we posed three questions asking participants to take a position on reopening businesses, reopening schools, and putting a moratorium on deportations during the COVID pandemic. Because the results were highly polarized for the first two questions, we used the data to solicit discussion on why people held their views, what values were at stake, and what tradeoffs they heard from others with opposing views. We also conducted a survey in which we asked people to rate how important an issue was from low to high and whether they could tolerate the issues' downsides from low to high. Sharing these polarity charts helped us to focus the conversation on areas where people were most at extremes and also visually show the group that on some issues, they disagreed, but viewed the differences as less important. Again, these votes and polarity charts were used to encourage conversation in more depth and clarify why different people viewed the issue very differently.

Challenges and Possible Improvements

The transition to online did result in two changes in participation – a drop-off from the original group and unpredictable and inconsistent participation. For various reasons, including a change in topic and the COVID-19 pandemic, about one-third of our group did not continue with the online dialogues. We did find that participants who attended an early session tended to stick with the full program, while others opted out completely. Our approach of keeping the initial online sessions to one hour, focusing on social and personal interaction during those sessions, and choosing topics that bridged the group to a more intense dialogue, did help increase buy-in for future participation in longer sessions. Presumably however, some participants simply did not want to participate via an online format and planners should assume that will be the case for any group.

Second, while online dialogues can make the events more accessible for participants who live in geographically disparate locations, it is also easier for participants to elect to attend only part of a program. Participants also tended to decide to participate or opt out at the last minute. Having inconsistent participation likely hampered the goals of deepening dialogue and relationship building.

It is critical to plan flexibility into online discussions and be ready to adapt as the group grows or changes. We found that we needed to plan for a full group and think through breakouts and discussions in advance, but always be prepared for some attendees to join or drop-out at the last minute and allow time to rearrange accordingly. As noted above, having specific planning staff on standby to focus on technology and logistics enabled the facilitators to focus on the content of dialogues, while the other personnel can adjust mid-program to group assignments, help a participant who had left and re-entered to get oriented, or manage other scheduling adjustments.

While we had a great deal of success at encouraging social interaction and relationship-building online, we found that it could not replace many of the benefits of in-person programs. Many participants in the program noted that they had agreed to join the cohort because they saw the networking as a primary benefit, and while they met people, they were unable to network with the same depth. Without meals together during a full-day in-person program, conversation over coffee between sessions, or at the bar after dinner, participants simply had less time to talk with others in the group. While we compensated as much as we could with small groups and the breakfast social time, it was much less time, less opportunity for one-on-one discussion, and less serendipitous conversation than one would experience in person.

In addition, we also found that during some of our dialogues, managing a formal agenda with time limits posed new challenges in an online format. First, in our efforts to keep the online time to a half-day, we sometimes tackled difficult topics in 45–60 minutes, where we would have allowed 2 hours in person. As a result, we sometimes truncated conversation just as people were warming up or as tension peaked, without addressing key conflicts in depth. While we resolved this by returning to the question later, it was not ideal. At the end of the program, participants suggested that we build more flexibility into the agenda to allow an extension of some discussions as needed.

Second, based on prior experience, we believe that in some cases, when tensions run high during a disagreement during a dialogue session, participants are often able to then follow up in person with supportive, congenial interaction "at the water cooler" during the break. By holding dialogues and then concluding the session turning off computers, people walked away from each other without the opportunity to resolve personal reactions.

Finally, we continually learned as we held sessions that we needed to give extra attention to online group dynamics in ways that came more naturally to facilitators experienced with in-person conversation. While in person, facilitators use eye contact and visual cues to manage and deepen the conversation, it is difficult to adapt these approaches on the Zoom interface. When we were in a full group in particular, some participants spoke frequently while others held back, especially on more controversial topics, and it is harder to manage that participation on Zoom. One technique used to facilitate wider participation was a Round Robin approach – we would go around the screen and invite each person to comment in order. Another was to use some personnel to pay attention to people trying to add to the conversation and flag that for the facilitator. We also learned that it is important to allow longer pauses of silence, to give people time to react and process and encourage them to speak up.

Typically, the best approach to encourage participation was facilitated small group discussions that then came together in a full group. In general, we put special effort into planning groups that were diverse in terms of opinion and perspective. For one session, we also allowed participants to self-select into one of two "affinity groups", invited each affinity group to talk about how they were feeling, and then came together as a full group to invite each affinity group to share with each other and then engage in a full group discussion, and this enabled participants to put thoughts into the room they may not have felt comfortable sharing in a more diverse group.

Conclusion

At the conclusion of the program, we asked participants to name one way that their views were modified as a result of their participation in the program. Comments included,

> I have listened to other members of NCLF, making passionate, factual, intelligent comments that I had never considered. These comments were not emotional, which is what I generally hear. As a result, my views on some issues were modified.
>
> My understanding of [XX] Party and its base has significantly improved. I am more familiar with the nuances and the diversity of this political and ideological camp that I am not a part of.
>
> Issues are not black and white. Discussions with people of varying views has helped to moderate my opinions on COVID responses and immigration.

While the online format was challenging, we learned that with careful planning, attention to social interaction (not just the topic), and flexibility, it was possible to facilitate a meaningful dialogue online that kept participants engaged. Increasing the pace, using small groups, and providing technology and logistics support separately from facilitation, were all very helpful to making the dialogues run smoothly.

NCLF will continue to host in-person programming for future cohorts once it is possible to do so. However, we have learned that we can integrate online dialogue sessions for our groups to make conversations more accessible and potentially more intimate. We also hope to incorporate online programming for alumni as a way of continuing their engagement and enhancing their leadership skills and network connections. Any future online dialogues hosted by NCLF will continue to incorporate lessons learned by shortening time spent in discussion and increasing interactivity, focusing on small group discussions, keeping technology simple, and incorporating technology support alongside facilitation. We would also build in more flexibility for extending discussion as needed when the time is insufficient and look for more ways to incorporate increased social interaction. We hope the lessons we learned about how to effectively manage online dialogue will be a resource to other groups considering this approach.

Jeanne Felicity Zimmer, D.G. Mawn, Lori Dieckman, & Melinda Burrell

Chapter 4 Connecting Communities Virtually Through Community Mediation

Abstract: The National Association for Community Mediation (NAFCM) connects and supports hundreds of community mediation centers and community mediators around the country. These centers and individuals help communities undertake the hard conversations necessary to explore and resolve disputes as well as to promote justice. Because of this nation-wide reach, NAFCM has been using a combination of virtual and in-person meetings for years and therefore was well-positioned for the COVID-necessitated switch to virtual. This chapter outlines how NAFCM built on that experience: immediately holding Zoom trainings and town halls for mediators seeking to address the initial panic and fear around the pandemic; then utilizing the JAMS Foundation gift of a Zoom license for qualified member centers which enabled centers to expand and deepen their outreach. NAFCM, joined with Mediators Beyond Borders International and PIRUSA, combining their shared technical sophistication, co-created the Trust Network. This network uses technological platforms to track and aid responses to incidents of partisan violence and to build social cohesion. During this time, NAFCM also continued to provide virtual learning circles for centers and peacebuilders, including through JAMS Foundation capacity building grants and an online certificate course with the Carter Center at George Mason University. The chapter concludes with recommendations for ever better use of technology for mediation and peacebuilding.

Keywords: community mediation, community mediation centers, conflict resolution, National Association for Community Mediation (NAFCM), virtual mediation

---

Acknowledgments: This chapter was adapted from the "Virtual Interpersonal Community Mediation: NAFCM Think Tank Report" to Mediate.com in their work to develop best-practice recommendations regarding online services with the goal of supporting the field of community mediation to embrace and offer online mediation services and utilize and benefit from basic and ongoing online mediation training. The authors would like to thank the members of the NAFCM workgroups, including: Aaron Addison, Piedmont Dispute Resolution Center (Virginia); Kabrina Bass, Midlands Mediation (South Carolina); Brandon Brown, George Mason University's Carter School for Peace and Conflict Resolution (Maine); Sara Campos, Loyola Marymount Law School's Center for Conflict Resolution (California); Philip Hong, Pepperdine School of Law (California); Corinne "Cookie" Levitz, Center for Conflict Resolution in Chicago (Illinois): Charles A. Lieske, Mediation West (Nebraska), Norma López, Orange County Human Relations (California); and, Felicia Washington, NAFCM (Virginia).

https://doi.org/10.1515/9783110687262-005

Introduction

The National Association for Community Mediation (NAFCM), established in 1994, is a member association that supports and promotes a national network of local Community Mediation Centers (CMCs), which offer a variety of services to empower individuals and communities to resolve conflict. Guided by the nine NAFCM hallmarks, CMCs provide a holistic approach to addressing conflict and harm that values all voices, encourages collaborative community relations, and focuses on effecting systemic change. CMCs work directly with individuals and organizations seeking to reduce social inequities and have participated in NAFCM-facilitated, virtual national learning communities pursuing projects focused on community policing, homelessness, formerly incarcerated adults, and navigating cultural differences. CMCs can respond quickly to identified needs or instances of structural inequality. Given the versatility of community mediation, a wide variety of organizations partner with CMCs including, but not limited to, government agencies, police departments, schools, courts, housing organizations, community advocates, and faith communities. As community anchors, the CMCs, with NAFCM as the hub, are well positioned to collaborate with data collection and analysis, to convene stakeholders for listening sessions, workshops, and trainings, to disseminate information and findings, and generally to promote and inform the development of restorative justice knowledge and practices.

NAFCM is able to help CMCs have an impact on the overarching structural inequalities of our society, because NAFCM believes community mediation is community mobilization. NAFCM draws on the experiences of the CMCs to educate policymakers and decision makers about the benefits and effectiveness of community mediation and restorative justice. The association's strong communication network includes a dedicated website with a Virtual Library of research and evaluation on community mediation.

NAFCM exists in a virtual space with no fixed office and a geographically diverse leadership team. NAFCM's Board of Directors has met virtually for decades. Even though NAFCM exists virtually, it still values face-to-face interactions and consciously builds those into its work. The Board meets in person at the start of each fiscal year with a retreat which builds and grounds relationships. NAFCM walks its talk by using consensus decision making in its virtual Board and committee meetings, and online technology helps ensure that all voices are heard.

When the pandemic hit the United States, NAFCM responded immediately, as it has done for decades, using cutting-edge virtual technology to promote collaboration. This chapter will highlight how NAFCM used technology to foster connection and collaboration between CMCs, community members, and like-minded organizations and individuals to address current issues in the moment. Some examples that will be discussed further in this chapter include:

- In partnership with Mediators Beyond Borders International (MBBI), NAFCM co-hosted the first of several international town hall forums beginning on March 21, 2020, within days of the closure of in-person activities across North

America. These forums served as both a mechanism of support for members as well as a way to prompt creative activities. One such realization was to ask people to keep a "physical distance" not a "social distance." Recognizing that words have meaning, and during a time when people were hunkering at home with community and social bonds frayed, NAFCM acknowledged that people need not tell themselves multiple times a day that they are distant from others. Rather, everyone needed to be reminded that they are still connected in those very important ways. This realization led to creating methods for members and those they serve to remain socially close while physically apart with an expanded array of online options for connecting.

- The NAFCM Board developed and facilitated training in how to use Zoom to increase the ease and efficacy of offering services through this virtual interpersonal method. Through the partnership with the JAMS Foundation, this was followed by the ability for NAFCM to obtain premium Zoom licenses to be distributed to member centers.
- NAFCM hosted multiple domestic town hall meetings on urgent, emergent issues such as eviction mediation, structural marginalization, and reimagining safety.

These are all examples not only of how NAFCM serves its members but also how NAFCM is a leader in creative contemporary conflict resolution.

About NAFCM

NAFCM's work is grounded in the Nine Hallmarks of Community Mediation which were outlined by CMC leaders in Portland, Oregon, in 1993 and finalized during a larger gathering of CMC leaders in Las Vegas, Nevada, in 1994.

The Hallmarks are intended to identify a set of guiding principles which could be applied in a variety of contexts but, at their heart, define the practice of community mediation. In keeping with the importance the Hallmarks place on inclusivity, CMCs will apply them as best fits the needs of the local community they serve along with the skill set present within the center. This is done with the recognition that many approaches to dispute management and conflict resolution can be used, provided the intent behind them is focused on Hallmark-articulated principles of access, diversity, education, quality of service, and attention to local community norms and values. These other approaches include conflict coaching, community dialogues, facilitation, listening sessions, and restorative practices.

Although each community mediation center is unique, all CMCs are characterized by, and committed to these Hallmarks:

Community-Based (1) A private non-profit or public agency or program thereof, with mediators, staff, and a governing/advisory board representative of the diversity of the community served.

Open (2) The use of trained community volunteers as providers of mediation services; the practice of mediation is open to all persons.

Accessible (3) Providing direct access to the public through self-referral and striving to reduce barriers to service including physical, linguistic, cultural, programmatic, and economic.

Low Cost (4) Providing service to clients regardless of their ability to pay.

Inclusive (5) Providing service and hiring without discrimination on the basis of race, color, religion, gender, age, disabilities, national origin, marital status, personal appearance, gender identity, sexual orientation, family responsibilities, matriculation, political affiliation, source of income.

Timely (6) Providing a forum for dispute resolution at the earliest stage of conflict.

Innovative (7) Providing an alternative to the judicial system at any stage of a conflict

Outcome Oriented (8) Initiating, facilitating, and educating for collaborative community relationships to effect positive systemic change.

Newsworthy (9) Engaging in public awareness and educational activities about the values and practices of mediation.

From these guiding principles, the National Association for Community Mediation was born in 1994. The NAFCM leadership team represents communities across the United States and Canada. Its members are also geographically diverse, so NAFCM has historically communicated and supported its members through virtually hosted webinars, town hall meetings, and through its online resource library.

Virtual Learning Communities

With funding and administrative guidance from the JAMS Foundation, NAFCM has facilitated virtual Learning Communities for over seven years on a wide range of topics involving CMCs across the United States of America and Canada. NAFCM's Learning Communities have created replicable projects around elder issues, prisoner reentry, and the reintegration of military families. The Learning Community is an online, structured, and collaborative peer working group facilitated by NAFCM. This structure serves as an incubator for innovation by aiding in the development of "good practices." Written materials developed through these grants are shared with CMCs and mediators across the continent. By distributing these materials, sharing programmatic resources, providing training, and developing national partnerships, NAFCM supports the replication of these service models and ensures the Program's impact on an international level.

Each Learning Community meets virtually twice a month for the first six months, and monthly thereafter, using a specified online meeting platform. The Learning Communities follow the "Listening for Action" structured guidance offered by NAFCM that strengthens the unique work of each project and creates an online executive learning environment that allows the members to grow both individually and professionally.

These are the focus areas and states, provinces, and districts with CMCs involved in the virtual Learning Communities:

2014–2016	Veterans and Returning Combatants States: Arkansas, California, Maine, Massachusetts
2015–2017	Implementing Community Policing in the 21st Century States: Louisiana, Maryland, Ohio, Virginia
2016–2018	Transitioning Communities: Immigrants and Foster Care States: California, Massachusetts
2017–2019	Older Adults States and Provinces: California, Michigan, Minnesota, Ontario, Tennessee, Vermont
2018–2020	Houselessness States and Districts: California, District of Columbia, Illinois
2019–2021	Formerly Incarcerated Adults States: Indiana, Ohio, Oregon, Pennsylvania, Washington
2020–2022	Young Adults: Community and Social Bonding States: California, Georgia, Louisiana, Oregon
2021–2023	Community Cohesion: Facing Historical Barriers States: California, Maryland, Massachusetts

Use of Virtual Platforms Pre-COVID-19, During 2020, and in 2021

Community mediation is focused locally, fostering face-to-face connection among the community mediation center staff, volunteers, and the community members served. The abrupt onset of physical distancing forced the previous hybrid model that mixed virtual services with in-person services to be online only.

This raised concerns about how to continue to provide the full array of services, especially considering how the pandemic heightened, not lessened, conflict. CMCs are participant-focused and have been providing both face-to-face and virtual mediation sessions for decades, as well as virtual training and continuing-education sessions. According to the 2019 State of Community Mediation Report, 47% of the CMCs used teleconferencing as part of their community services and programs and 36.6% used video/web. 8.4% used disability assistance technologies, 4.9% used other unspecified technologies, and 2.8% used online chat rooms as part of their services and programs.

As the pandemic moved everyone and everything online, many CMCs found themselves "forced" to adopt virtual practices. Even though many centers found the move to serve totally online antithetical to the values of community mediation, they adapted. This was borne out when, in mid-2020, the members of NAFCM's Board of Directors made check-in phone calls to all member CMCs and found that CMCs were flexible, adaptable, and able to pivot quickly to both train volunteer community mediators and provide services online, helping those experiencing conflict to manage their conflicts in online spaces.

Some CMCs that had been resistant to providing online services found themselves pleasantly surprised by the benefits of virtual services, as they learned the capacity of technology to transform conflict communication in homes, workplaces, faith communities, and neighborhoods. Often this was because the virtual platform made mediation accessible to people who had not had access before, such as family mediations involving people in different states or countries. Other CMCs had been offering virtual services – going back to phone mediations prior to the internet – to benefit prospective participants separated geographically.

In general, CMCs have reported the additional benefits of Zoom as providing increased access to services through flexible scheduling options and reduction of costs to participants since they did not have to travel to in-person mediation sessions and incur costs such as parking and childcare. Follow-up calls to CMCs by NAFCM board members in 2021 found that many participants not only benefited from virtual mediation services, but many preferred the opportunity to mediate via Zoom. For example, some centers found people were more comfortable in their home environments and therefore more ready to engage in the mediation process. CMCs were creative when participants faced barriers such as shared or limited technology; for example, some CMCs provided space in their offices for participants to mediate via Zoom.

As participant-centered providers, both in-person and virtual services will likely be part of the service delivery mix for CMCs going forward. Similarly, online training for prospective volunteer community mediators may be part of the future of community mediation, but again, not exclusively. Unlike mediators in private practice, CMCs create cohorts of volunteers and utilize experienced volunteer mediators to both coach and provide apprenticeship and mentorship opportunities. This is part of the relational foundation of community mediation. Today, most CMCs have volunteers trained in virtual mediation, so they are able to complement their existing capacity for in-person mediation, as well as the provision of other services.

CMCs are hands-on in their training of prospective volunteer mediators and restorative-justice facilitators because CMCs will have an ongoing relationship with these volunteers and the quality of services they provide through the CMCs (unlike other providers of training who have no ongoing commitment or oversight of their trainees). Quality assurance is key to CMCs and the ongoing oversight and engagement as part of the development of reflective practitioners is essential to CMCs' service provision. Training and supporting volunteer community mediators virtually includes the elements of relationship building and reflective practice. The shift to all virtual services among our members in both the United States of America and Canada facilitated collaborations that might not have happened otherwise, such as a basic mediation skills training conducted jointly by CMCs in Maryland and Minnesota, facilitating the inclusion of a wider diversity of both presenters and content.

JAMS Foundation Donation of Zoom Licenses

When the pandemic shuttered in-person gatherings in early 2020, NAFCM acted quickly to garner resources to support local CMCs. In July 2020, the JAMS Foundation purchased 200 Zoom Pro licenses to be distributed to NAFCM member centers and these licenses are active through July 2022. The Pro licenses have features which are critical to conducting virtual mediations including the ability to create break out rooms and to schedule meetings for longer than 40 minutes with multiple participants.

To date, 110 CMCs have qualified for these licenses, with these CMCs receiving one, two, or three licenses based on their demonstrated need. As of August 31, 2021, these centers have hosted 17,653 meetings totaling 10,567,852 minutes and including 120,970 participants. These numbers are significant and illustrate the importance of this JAMS Foundation gift to the CMCs' staff, volunteers, and customers.

The abrupt shift to virtual gatherings created challenges for CMCs who relied on physical space rather than technology to conduct mediations, meetings, and training. Budgets were strained as the demand for mediation services continued. CMCs reported that additional Zoom Pro licenses made a meaningful difference in meeting the needs of their clients. The Zoom accounts are also used for staff and volunteer meetings and training events while eliminating geographic barriers to attendance.

- One CMC reported that the largest scale event the account made possible was their Restorative Justice Summit. This involved inviting a well-known outside keynote speaker from a different part of the country, many guest speakers who have experienced their programs directly, and, of course, lots of interested community members. Part of the great success was because of the technological freedoms a Pro Zoom account allowed.

- Another CMC reported that the Pro Zoom account enabled them to increase access to their services in numerous ways including providing simultaneous language translation for parenting seminars, hosting community classes, monthly workshops for court-involved youth to teach conflict resolution skills, and 40-hour mediation training for a new cadre of mediators.

The graph in Figure 4.1 shows the increase in Zoom use by the CMCs over a 12-month period from September 2020 through August 2021.

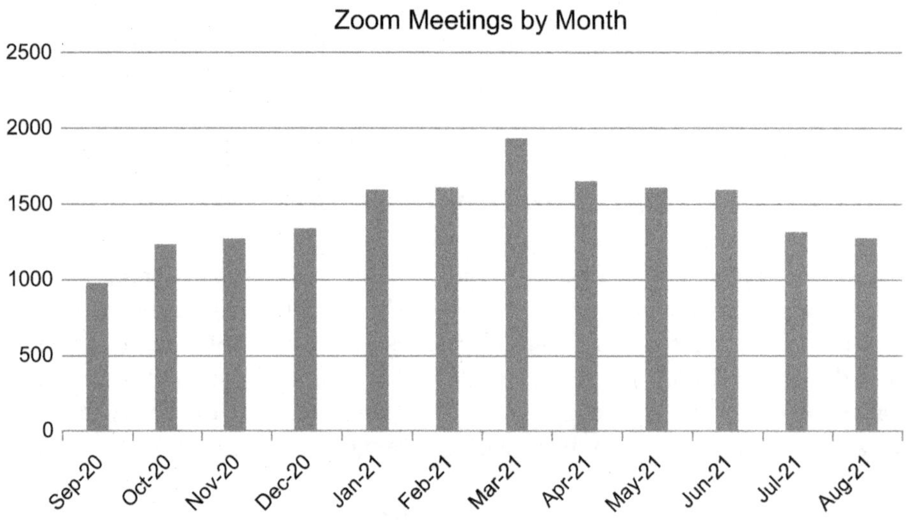

Figure 4.1: Zoom Use by CMCs Over a 12-month Period from September 2020 through August 2021.

The TRUST Network

Another example of how NAFCM has used technology to promote dialogue is found in the formation of the TRUST Network. In the Autumn of 2020 NAFCM joined with Mediators Beyond Borders International (MBBI) and Political Incident Reporting USA (PIRUSA, formerly EIRUSA) to create a space titled the TRUST Network. The TRUST Network was developed to braid the work and energy of national organizations working in the democracy, social justice, and peace space and to support community responses through established community organizations.

With the leadership of PIRUSA, online platforms, and in particular social media accounts, were used as a basis to begin to triangulate the data and reveal hot spots of current or emerging violence. PIRUSA brought their years of experience collecting and disseminating information about on-the-ground dynamics during crises around the world.

Together with NAFCM and all the partners that came together under the TRUST Network umbrella, virtual technology was employed that both alerted local communities of the possibility of violence as well as worked with these communities to support prevention action. Through technology including Zoom, Slack, and Ushahidi, the TRUST Network national and local partnerships helped to deflate potential hot spots as well as to prevent a hot spot from emerging.

NAFCM is already implementing both short- and long-term democracy-strengthening work, much of the effort being expended through online platforms. With TRUST Network funding from the Packard Foundation and Humanity United, nine communities in six states have been able to grow and strengthen their community resolve to address the divides that are fracturing their communities, with most of this effort infused through virtual learning and listening. CMCs and other local pro-democracy initiatives are the heart of the network. During Stop the Steal rallies, Resolution Virginia encouraged state legislators to remind their constituents to protest peacefully. DC Peace Team and local teams from Nonviolent Peaceforce de-escalate violence directly so that the voices obscured by violence could be heard. Much of the coordination and implementation of these and similar efforts occurred through online platforms.

Collaboration with George Mason University/Jimmy and Rosalynn Carter (SPCR)

In another example of how NAFCM is using technology for ever better conflict resolution work, the President of NAFCM and the Associate Dean of The Jimmy and Rosalynn Carter School for Peace and Conflict Resolution, George Mason University, worked together to develop a certificate program for working professionals across the world that will have online elements. The "Contemporary Dispute Resolution Certificate," developed with input from a diverse group of conflict resolution professionals through virtual group interviews, will sharpen students' skills to cultivate socially just dispute resolution practices in complex organizations.

The Carter School and NAFCM have collaborated in several ways. The most notable was an 18-month project to conduct a nationwide State of Community Mediation report. This report included a nationwide survey of the more than 300 members of NAFCM and was followed by focus groups and Listening Sessions to gather larger community feedback on the efficacy, ethics, and priorities of CMCs in their local communities. All of this research had virtual as well as online components. The resulting report is informing the work and priorities of CMCs as well as providing input for local, state, and national policymakers about the purpose and results of local-level expertise in restorative justice and collaborative decision-making processes. The Carter School and NAFCM model an effective collaboration between a research university and a national association with hundreds of local partners across the United States of America and Canada.

Launched virtually in 2021, the certificate includes courses in negotiation, facilitation, coaching, and mediation, as well as hands-on experience through a practicum. The inaugural cohort of participants is now in the first semester of coursework. The certificate offers opportunities for students to analyze and appreciate disputes in the context of larger social structures such as economic and racial inequality, unequal access to justice, and the education system. These opportunities include identifying and implementing appropriate dispute resolution strategies, analyzing the factors underlying disputes, recognizing power differentials among disputants, and choosing appropriate strategies to address those factors. Upon completing the certificate individuals will be prepared with the analytical and practical skills to implement processes such as mediation, negotiation, coaching, or facilitation – in virtual and physical spaces – in a manner that meets the participants' needs. They therefore will be better able to deal effectively with disputes in work settings including schools, businesses, and local and state government. From a perspective grounded in empathy, with a focus on how the impact of social injustice, negative peace, and intentional community dis-engagement, may have had on the conflict and those in conflict, these practitioners will be better equipped to assist those in conflict to create choices that are sustainable. They also will be able to revolutionize the conflict by raising for discussion the underlying facilitators of that conflict.

Visions for the Virtual Future

As part of the Mediate.com Online Mediation Training Task Force that met during the Winter and Spring of 2021, NAFCM convened a diverse group to respond to the question, "How can we best assist and support community mediation centers and other non-profit mediation organizations to embrace and offer online mediation services and to utilize and benefit from basic and ongoing online mediation training that will help the underserved?"

Technology has helped strengthen CMCs and can bolster the ability of community mediation to be infused into formal and informal dispute resolution practices. However, for technology to be even more effective in helping resolve disputes, the following recommendations are made for the following audiences: policy makers, foundations, CMCs, and all those who support the work of CMCs to continue to respond to the call of the 1964 Civil Rights Act, Section 10.

The virtual space will continue to strengthen CMCs' ability and capacity through online training in the wide range of services that CMCs provide. A short list includes family mediation; small claims; workplace conflict mediation; teenager/parent mediation; juvenile/court-connected cases; city ordinance violations; restorative justice; and domestic violence. Possibilities include creating basic modules in the NAFCM's Virtual Library that could be accessed by all. While this may result in cost-savings for CMCs, NAFCM also honors local control of trainings by CMCs. In particular, NAFCM developed standards of quality and integrity based on the nine Hallmarks and invited member CMCs to have their online basic community mediation training evaluated. From these evaluations, the NAFCM Online Community Mediation Training Booklet was created and has been published and distributed for broader use of these services.

Accessibility Is an Ongoing Need for the Users of CMCs

Because CMCs offer services at low or no cost to participants, we need to note that access to online services can be a barrier to participants – particularly those in rural communities. The ability to use broadband provided by libraries or to provide services over the phone or using cellphones can bridge the access gap. This has been mitigated through partnerships with libraries, offering Zoom spaces in centers, and through the JAMS Foundation gift of Pro Zoom licenses to NAFCM member CMCs. Further, some communities, especially in rural areas, do not have the same technology capacity or accessibility and prefer in-person trainings. Mobile-friendly services are needed.

CMCs conduct training, mediations, and other conflict resolution services in the language of the participants or using interpreters in virtual sessions, as well as recruiting and training mediators and facilitators from targeted communities. Additional needs include the development of shared materials in multiple languages.

Strengthening CMCs' Footprint in Conflict Resolution Activities

CMCs need to be part of the justice infrastructure of the country. Two overarching ways are through funding and partnerships, further exploring ways to facilitate connectivity between systems and CMCs in the virtual space. To increase the use of community mediation instead of the judicial institution, there is a need to advertise alternatives boldly for visitors to the site. Something needs to catch people's eyes on the site that directs them to mediation as an alternative to judicial processes and do so at the beginning of a conflict. CMCs' work extends beyond interpersonal conflicts. They also facilitate group work that is specific to their communities. NAFCM and CMCs create virtual trainings that equip mediators with specific skills that are more group- and community-based. A current example of this would be a training about facilitating conversations between communities and police, communities, and political figures, and/or communities and the courts.

NAFCM supports the development of ongoing online trainings that are specific to addressing the needs of systemically underserved/marginalized people and communities.

Strengthening the Awareness of Community Mediation Centers

Technology has expanded the knowledge and openness of the broader community to the value and use of community mediation. CMCs need to create virtual learning opportunities to support local grassroots organizations that are working with underserved communities to increase their knowledge of community mediation, facilitate planning processes on how community mediation can enhance the capacity of those they serve, and create avenues for funding new community mediation ventures. Through such efforts CMCs will no longer remain their community's "best kept secret."

Members of the public who could benefit from community mediation may not be aware of what mediation involves. One way to increase systems capacity and access to justice would be to provide free collateral materials for the public, online and physically, such as general Frequently Asked Questions (FAQs) sheets and short videos and podcasts aimed at educating the public about mediation.

There is much work yet to be done, especially considering the ever-growing polarization in our communities and institutions. CMCs are anchored in their communities and therefore are well suited to serve and work with their individual communities. No two centers are alike. While most offer an array of services to the expansive diversity of their communities, others focus on non-geographic communities such as faith-based, veterans, housing-insecure, and LGBTQ+ communities.

The possibilities for utilizing technology inspire imagination and creativity. As NAFCM continues to serve as a hub for connecting local CMCs and supporters to resources, one could envision a future where services could be provided across communities nationally or even internationally using a common virtual platform. A virtual community mediation center has the potential to decrease polarization, which has negatively impacted the willingness and ability of people to engage in productive dialogue. A virtual CMC could also build bridges and foster the acknowledgement and appreciation needed to increase the communities' cohesion and security.

Conclusion

Even the most tentative CMCs have successfully adapted to online technologies – some administratively, some for training, some for-service delivery (mediation, restorative justice, facilitation), and some for all of the above. Some centers may remain entirely virtual, but most will likely be hybrid. While the myriad benefits of virtual interpersonal mediation are detailed here, there is no substitute for breaking bread, engaging in appropriate physical touch, and communing in person. Knowing this, and as a relational organization, NAFCM is able to create community in physical and virtual spaces. NAFCM and CMCs continue to utilize cutting-edge technologies to better serve their communities.

Reference

Washington, Felicia, M.S., Mawn, D.G., M.A., J.D., Shedd, Julie, Ph.D. (2019) State of Community Mediation 2019.

Arik Segal & Yotam Keduri

Chapter 5
Going Hybrid: Using Facebook Groups for People-to-People Dialogue

Abstract: International conflicts in the 21st century pose a dire challenge for peace and conflict professionals due to the influx of non-state actors, globalization and development of communication technology. Within this context, 'Track III' diplomacy efforts engaging non-state actors through 'people-to-people' dialogue have been the tool of choice for many grassroots organizations seeking to build peace using 'bottom-up' approaches to conflict resolution. This chapter aims to give an overview of the opportunities online dialogue platforms hold in improving existing dialogue methodologies. It is based on observation and research of an online, Israeli-Palestinian people-to-people dialogue project, the "Yala Young Leaders' MENA Leaders for Change Program", that took place during the 2014 Gaza Engagement, mostly on Facebook. The present study represents an early attempt to overcome this lacuna by integrating established analytical tools from parallel fields – notably Gottman etal.'s Rapid Couples Interaction Scoring System, designed to analyze the intractability of conflictual statements in discourse between married couples. The resulting adaptation of this scale, the Online Conflict Dynamics Matrix ('ODCM') is designed to codify utterances by type and analyze the resulting sequences in order to assess the dynamics that lead up to confrontation, resolution, or stalemate. A first of its kind, this matrix represents an important step in the development of discourse analysis to in the field of conflict research – a critical tool for assessing how technological innovations can contribute to the conduct of peacebuilding projects and to the field of peace and conflict.

Keywords: dialogue, peacebuilding, facebook groups, people-to-people, intergroup conflict

Introduction

Following the World Health Organization's March 11, 2020 declaration that COVID-19 can be characterized as a global pandemic, many countries responded with emergency measures restricting mobility and enforcing what is now known as "social

Acknowledgements: The US Embassy in Jerusalem and Yala Palestine, The Peres Center for Peace and Search for Common Ground for their support and management of the MENA Leaders for Change project. The Lauder School of Governance at Reichman University for granting this study the "Academic Advancement Award". Special thanks to Danni Reches for her input and research assistance.

https://doi.org/10.1515/9783110687262-006

distancing" to curb the spread of the virus. The unprecedented situation forced organizations to think of creative ways to continue activities such as teaching, officework, and conferencing without people meeting face-to-face. Among those affected are peacebuilding and conflict resolution organizations that had to find immediate solutions for "people-to-people dialogue" meetings, which were traditionally conducted in physical locations.

This chapter discusses a study that was conducted prior to the pandemic; however, it holds important insights that can assist conflict resolution and peacebuilding organizations struggling to find digital solutions in times of social distancing. The study in question is a case study of an Israeli-Palestinian digital-physical peacebuilding project utilizing Facebook as a main communication platform to facilitate continuous dialogue. For this reason, this chapter will be relevant to both scholars and practitioners in laying out a new methodology for digital peacebuilding and its evaluation. The first section discusses people-to-people dialogue and the contribution of digital technologies to peacebuilding. The next section gives an overview of the 'MENA Leaders for Change Facebook Community Project' established through the Yala Young Leaders' movement. The third section examines the opportunities and prospects for digital engagement and the final section includes our concluding remarks. Introducing this unique case study from the field will offer important tips for future directions of digitized peacebuilding.

Part I: People-to-People Dialogue and the Contribution of Digital Technologies

Signing a peace treaty or making peace between political elites is hardly sufficient to put an end to conflicts, not to mention the social and psychological damage the conflicts have caused (Handelman & Chowdhury, 2017). It is crucial to include civil society and community level relationship building in managing conflicts given the importance of grassroots activism in events, such as the Arab Spring uprisings. Therefore, while official diplomacy is necessary in maintaining diplomatic channels, integrating citizens is a vital component of resolving ethno-political conflicts in the long-run (Cochrane & Dunn, 2002).

People-to-People (P2P) dialogue has been the main tool used by grassroots organizations that aim to build peace using a "bottom-up" approach to conflict resolution. Unlike theoretical models of negotiation for example, there has yet to be found a theory that sufficiently deals with the complexities of a bottom-up approach. Many practitioners of conflict resolution base their approaches on Allport's 'contact theory,' which posits that "the best way to reduce tensions between groups in conflict is to bring them together since the basis of evil is the unknown" (Allport, 1954). Despite its wide use, contact theory suffers from shortcomings and has received substantial criticism. Primarily, it tends to avoid discussing conflictual or incendiary topics, since it intends to encourage positive interaction (Checkoway, 2003). As a result, dialogue programs continue to be common practice in many ethno-political conflict zones since no alternative has been found.

The ascendance of technology and social media platforms have created new opportunities for improving the effectiveness, monitoring, and evaluation of people-to -people dialogue programs. The use of digital technologies in peacebuilding is a relatively new venue, which has its roots in online mediation. The origins of Online Dispute Resolution (ODR) date back to the 1990s when the World Wide Web started to gain popular use and online disputes increased. Whereas many viewed computer mediated communication (CMC) as something that would sustain positive social and professional international relations, anti-social outcomes including impersonalization and verbal hostility were widely reported (Walther, 1997). The first article about ODR was published in 1996 when the first conference on ODR was organized, marking the field's infrastructure establishment (Wahab, Katsh, & Rainey, 2012). Since then, ODR has developed mainly in the context of business disputes between providers and consumers. While there is research on the ways online platforms help resolve family disputes (Augar & Zeleznikow, 2014, see also Zeleznikow, this volume) and its application to law and litigation (Katsh, 2007), there has been limited research on international political conflict resolution and online technologies.

ODR practitioners have relied on conflict resolution theory designed for face-to-face meetings. Because its base comes from the offline world, most critique of ODR focuses on the loss of traditional nonverbal cues. Other perceived issues include the different communication strategies and ODR's less formal setting. Here, rules play an increased role in controlling communication, social interaction, and the information flow between disputing parties. One could think of rules of evidence, the role of third parties, and the increased use of text in the proceedings (Wahab, Katsh, & Rainey, 2012). In ODR, where the written word and visual dimensions of the screen are central to the interaction, the type of technology (also known as the "fourth party," Rifkin 2001), chosen by an organization carries weight and has to be carefully selected. In face-to-face meetings, the spoken word and body language constitute the primary elements in the communication process.

ODR is also used for people-to-people dialogue programs. Previous research that touches upon principles and advantages of online platforms for dialogue are for example Figallo and Pyser's (2004) examination of the use of massive online dialogue among citizens of New York. They argue that online dialogue can be used to promote trust and collaboration. In addition, the use of ICT (Information Communication Technologies) in peacebuilding platforms promotes a wide range of grassroots actors and groups in post-conflict zones (Telidis & Kappler, 2016). A good example is an online dialogue program with Bosnians and Serbs that was analyzed by Selvanathan et al. (2019). The study concluded that participants showed greater group identification and demands for justice after the dialogue. Expressions of anger and anxiety decreased, whereas time orientations toward the present increased.

The ways in which social media, specifically Facebook, is used to promote intergroup dialogue and reconciliation in the context of the conflict between Israeli-Jews and Palestinians have been examined as well (Mor, Ron, & Maoz, 2016; Ron, Suleiman, & Maoz, 2020). These studies concluded that on the one hand, exposure to pain and suffering led to a predominantly negative intergroup exchange, and that social media can be used as a mechanism for expressing and mobilizing intergroup disengagement and animosity. On the other hand, the exposure to such moderate and peace seeking voices facilitated a positive dialogue between Israeli-Jews and Palestinians, expressing hope, sympathy, and acceptance. Through Facebook groups and pages people were mobilized to call for solidarity, maintain engagement, and directly call for and organize action.

Surprisingly however, even during the COVID-19 pandemic, trained facilitators have not flocked to social media and the tools it has to offer. This might have to do firstly with the shortcomings and criticism that people-to-people dialogue programs face based on Allport's contact theory, and secondly with findings that the use of only online tools for dialogue projects could have negative effects. Contact theory contains a long list of conditions for a successful face-to-face contact that result in reducing intergroup conflict. There are significant barriers to meeting those conditions, thus limiting the amount of contact actually taking place. These challenges include the complexity and costs of arranging a meeting between rival groups (including political barriers such as entry permits in the case of Israel; Albeck, Adwan, & Bar-on, 2002), high anxiety among participants, and the difficulties in generalizing out from a specific contact with specific outgroup individuals to inform interactions with the outgroup as a whole. Nevertheless, Amichai-Hamburger et al. (2006; 2015) argue that these challenges can be overcome with the use of the internet. Our study provides empirical evidence that supports many of their points, as will be elaborated upon later.

Despite the advantages of the use of the internet for dialogue programs, Reilly (2012) argues that online interaction alone does not suffice to promote understanding and trust, based on the findings of the use of social media in facilitating inter-group conflict in Northern Ireland. A study by Cao and Lin (2017) focused on different types of CMC and argues that video communication yields better results on attitudes of the outgroup than text-based communication. Another relevant study by Ellis and Maoz (2007) examined the differences in online and face-to-face communication between groups of Israelis and Palestinians. They emphasize the lack of constructive arguments in the online dialogue process. The important contributions of our study therefore are that it focuses on the delivery of a conflict transformation process through Facebook groups, which demonstrates how online and physical dialogue can overcome many of the difficulties posed by contact theory. This is supported by the people-to-people dialogue project and a case study of the MENA Young Leaders Facebook Community.

Part II: MENA Young Leaders Facebook Community Project

The events of the Arab Spring have served as an example of the power of civic activism in the age of social media. The speed and manner in which activists were able to mobilize and spread aspirations for democracy across borders gave hope that social media could play a critical role in reinvigorating civil society, democracy, and peace across the region (Howard et al., 2011; Anderson, 2011).

The project which forms the subject of this chapter represents a unique offshoot of this persuasion, with its belief that these same principles might be applied successfully to the Israeli-Palestinian conflict. It is predicated, in part, on the belief that linking Israeli and Palestinian young leaders with a wider network of activists from across the MENA region might serve to liberate them from the various blind-spots imposed by the conflict's strict borders. An enduring and shared social media platform could lend their work geographic breadth and a sustainability rare in most peacebuilding efforts. As such, the project has the potential to provide the spark for an upsurge in regional social change and democratization.

The *Yala Young Leaders' MENA Leaders for Change Program* (MLC) was an Israeli-Arab people-to-people online and onsite dialogue project that took place from June to November 2014. The project was funded by the US Department of State and managed by the Peres Center for Peace, Search for Common Ground, and Yala Palestine. It was designed as a multi-stage intervention, structured around a preliminary skills training workshop, ongoing guided interaction and discussion in the Facebook closed and secret group, and, for a select group of participants, participation in a three-day summative conference in Jordan. The project's participants came from Israel, the Palestinian Authority, Jordan, Egypt, Iraq, Morocco, Tunisia, Algeria, Yemen, Saudi Arabia, and Syria. The project's methodology included five dimensions: facilitated online discussions about the grievances and difficult emotions each side holds for the other, online and onsite learning of negotiation skills, several in-person team building meetings, facilitated online dialogue that aimed to reveal shared interests and values, and lastly joint creation of peacebuilding projects.

Reports on participation in the Facebook group indicate that actual use was well in excess of program minima: while 22.8% of participants visited the MLC Facebook group on a weekly basis (per program requirements), the majority of participants (74.2%) visited the platform more frequently; 49.5% visiting daily, and 16.8% more than twice a day. Only 3.0% said they did not visit the group regularly. In terms of self-assessed future use, 52.5% said they foresaw visiting the group on a weekly basis, 34.7% daily, and 8.9% more than this. 4.0% did not see themselves visiting in the future.

The vast majority (80%) saw themselves using the Facebook platform to keep in touch with other respondents. A large number of participants, 67%, thought they would use it to share their thoughts with others, 62% foresaw using it as a forum to discuss ideas, and 59% envisioned using the group as a platform for actually working together. Few (18%) thought they would use the platform to request emergency assistance. A small minority felt they would not use it at all (5%).

Overall, participants felt the Facebook group was a somewhat effective way (4.92 out of 7) to engage participants around peacebuilding, and a somewhat effective way (4.87 out of 7) to mobilize people across the MENA region in peacebuilding. Controlled for demography, Israeli Jews were most skeptical with regards to the former (mean of 3.9), while MENA participants were most optimistic (5.84). For the latter, MENA citizens were most enthusiastic (5.6) about the platform's potential regionally. Gender differences also mattered, with women more skeptical (4.6) than men (5.2) regarding the platform's effectiveness.

Applying the Online Discourse Analysis Matrix (ODM) to P2P dialogue on Facebook

The availability of reams of written exchanges undertaken in real time on potentially incendiary (and certainly controversial) topics afforded the evaluators of the MENA Young Leaders Facebook Community Project a unique opportunity that is rarely afforded in conflict research: the opportunity to undertake close narrative analysis of conflict dynamics in online speech.

The abundant research on conflict theory has been mostly concerned with issues of identity, attitudes, and the dynamics of conflict escalation. As a result, they have been well-served by a wide variety of survey and case-study designs. Analysis of conflicts in conversation (as would befit an analysis of postings on Facebook) has been less frequent. With that, the growth in online communication as an emerging platform in conflicts (for example, among terrorist groups; Chiluwa, 2017, 2019) as well as the rise of conflicts online as an issue of concern for virtual communities (cf. de Souza & Preece, 2004, Schneider & von der Emde, 2006) have pointed to the need for an analytical framework to understand verbal escalation. While the critical discourse analysis (CDA) or semiotic analysis strategies these studies have endorsed do very well to place a given utterance within a wider cultural or power context, research over the past decade has highlighted the need for reliable frameworks with predictive validity that can track and describe verbal escalation online, specifically using coding analysis techniques (Bui-Wrzosinska et al, 2013). Fortunately, such frameworks are a staple of gender studies and couples research (e.g. Tannen, 1990, 1994, 1996). One well- known example is Gottman et al.'s *Rapid Couples Interaction Scoring System* (RCISS). Designed to predict the likelihood for divorce among married couples by codifying statements made over the course of discussions on issues of contention between the couple, the scale lends itself readily to conflict analysis for its focus on conflicts and the dynamics that lead up to confrontation, resolution, or stalemate.

For the purposes of evaluating our program, Gottman's scale was adapted into a code whose categories would account for the full variety of responses that could be seen in a Facebook feed spanning several months. Since the context for which the RCISS was developed was quite different from the context of the interactions in the project, the RCISS was not used in its original form but instead adapted to the present study.

The code was developed over several iterations using a 'grounded method' (Glaser & Strauss, 1967), in which the print-outs ("feeds") of several days worth of Facebook exchanges were reviewed and assigned categories, which were then honed and re-honed until they fully and accurately accounted for every statement-type identified in the feeds.

The code features a general matrix of responses by type, including "neutral", "positive", "reinforcement", "repair/mitigation", and "contentious" statements, according to which the full range of statements made by participants could be classified. Five main types of "positive" statements were identified: "best wishes" made to participants by other participants (including expressions of thankfulness and appreciation), "personal expressions" (including the sharing of personal experiences, positive views, opinions and attitudes towards other participants and the shared format of the program), "exhortations to peace," "expressions of personal concern and commiseration" for and with other participants (especially during the height of the 2014 Gaza War), and "expressions of solidarity" with the group. "Reinforcement" statements included facebook likes, compliments, and "agreement/concession" with a statement made by another participant. Seven "repair/mitigation" statements were identified, including "divertive" (often joking or amusing) comments meant to deflect an impending conflict, "clarifications" of a potential conflictual point or statement (including defenses of a position made that were nonetheless designed to deflect the conversation away from conflict), "requests for clarifications" of a point, "appeals to neutrality and objectivity" in situations where conversations became heated, "appeals to solidarity", "exhortations to peace" (in the service of defusing a heated exchange) and "apologies." Finally, three types of "contentious" statements were identified, each representing a further step towards intractability: "potentially controversial statements" (including the posting of partisan content, commentary or coverage of an incident in the Gaza escalation), "direct challenges" to a statement or comment made by another participant, and "intractable statements" including condemnations of a participant, their community/nationality or their side in the Gaza conflict, insults, sarcasm, and rhetorical statements. To simplify the coding, each of the above statements was assigned a random letter. (The choice of the letters was random, and used solely as an identifier. "Exhortations to peace" in their positive context, for example, were accorded a "g" while those in a reparative context were given an "s." For their part, "potentially controversial statements" were accorded an "x," "direct challenges" a "y", and "intractable statements" a "z").

In analyzing the exchanges, statements made by individual participants in a given exchange (or "string") were coded using a letter (or sequential series of letters, in cases where a participant's comments might move, for instance, from a repair to a positive statement). Analysis of the sequences was then used to see how conflictual statements escalated, how and when they were negotiated and repaired, and which repairs were the most recurring or successful. (As part of this approach, cases where the program moderator would intervene to defuse a heated exchange were accorded a separate letter, "w"). This approach marks a second departure from the RCISS whose matrix is used to separately code the speaker and the listener in the interaction; the ODM matrix, by contrast, was not focused on differentiating each of the different speakers in an exchange, but instead on the dynamics of the interaction (the sequence of individual statements) in the group setting. (The only exception to this rule was in instances where the moderator would make a statement, which were always coded as "w.")

A feed representing four months of discussion was selected, and scoured for any and all potential conflicts (i.e. strings of conversation in which an x, y, or z formed the basis for a subsequent comment or series of comments). The full string was then analyzed to its conclusion (marked by a "v"). The final analyzed string would thus be able to provide a schema delineating the length of the conflict, the way it was resolved, and the types of responses offered by participants to mitigate or exacerbate conflictual situations. (This focus in processing marks the third major departure from the RCISS, in which the overall negative scores accorded to speaker and listener are subtracted from their positive scores to yield a slope that is then the basis for further analysis. In the ODM, by contrast, the focus was on identifying recurring sequences and, particularly, sequences where potentially controversial statements, "x"s, escalated into intractable ones, "z"s, and those strategies or statement types that prevented these escalations from occurring.)

Over three months' worth of posts (June 15–September 15) were reviewed employing the coding system developed for the evaluation. Within that time frame, 22 "contentious" exchanges (i.e. those featuring a post or response coded either as an "x," a "y," or a "z") comprising a total of 481 distinct "posts" were identified. (A small number by any standard, these isolated controversies represented a fraction of the discussion even during the height of the escalation in Gaza.) It is important to note that much of these discussions were undertaken between a relatively small group of participants (in some strings as few as three, the longest having no more than 11).

Of the controversies, three were left unresolved (ending in an unanswered string, often an "x") and four were put to rest by the moderator. The remaining 15 conflicts (roughly two-thirds of all controversies) were resolved by the participants themselves. (All controversies revolved around the Gaza war, in virtually every case as the result of a statement made in justification of one side of the conflict.) In all, the moderator intervened 29 times within a total 481 posts, or an average of once for every 16 posts. In reality, however, discussions did not require even this amount of intervention: of the 29 occasions, 10 occurred over the course of one string from late July. The average number of interventions was closer to less than once per string (0.904).[1]

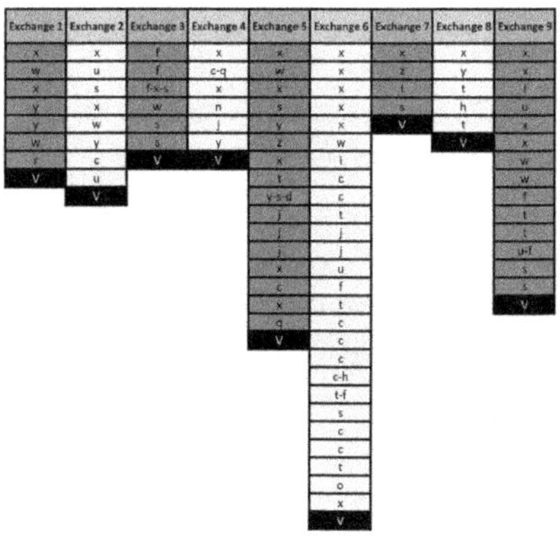

Figure 5.1: The Strings of "Contentious" Exchanges.

Over the course of these strings, there were 82 x's, 77 y's and 29 z's (Figure 5.1 provides a sample view). That is to say: 30% of all interaction was made up of potentially controversial or polarizing content, the remainder dedicated to mitigation, clarification, and repair. (It is important to note that these strings were exceptions in virtually *all* contact through the Facebook platform. On the whole, interactions were highly amicable, generous, and optimistic. In fact, an overall review of the entirety of the Facebook content would see a predominance of "neutral" and "positive" comments.)

If x's comprised *potentially* controversial posts (not necessarily comprising an agenda or argument), and y's a direct challenge to the views of another participant which could still be positively addressed, it is heartening to note that roughly 1/5 of all these statements (22% in the case of x's, 20% in the case of y's) were mitigated – that is, defused using language or conventions designed to soften the impact of the statement. For example: "i trully [sic] emphesize with your cry and pain it is trully [sic] unfair the situation you are stuck in. What upsets me is . . . ". "Z" statements were rarely mitigated for obvious reasons (z's representing intractable views, characterized by denigration or refusal to communicate). At the same time it is encouraging that, in a period of time marred by violent conflict in which the governments of some 1/3 of all participants were directly involved, only 27 such statements were

1 This number cannot take into account the facilitation staff conducted with participants outside of the context of the platform, such as ongoing direct 1:1 correspondences – especially in cases where a participant began showing signs of increased antagonism.

recorded. In all but two occasions, each z was preceded either by a "y" or another "z" occurring 1–3 statements earlier. That is to say: practically all z's were reactive.

The strategies that were employed by participants in controversial exchanges can be viewed by frequency in table 5.1. It shows that the most common strategy for defusing conflicts which participants employed in their conversations was the clarification of their views on a previous ideological position or statement. This reparative strategy was used in 116 of all 481 posts (24.1% of all postings), in 55 cases (47.4% of the time) in conjunction with other strategies. The next most-used defusing device was a more positive strategy: reverting the conversation back to a personal or general philosophical stance. For example, in response to a heated and polarized debate in which both Jewish and Palestinian historical claims to the land were challenged (string 14), one participant writes: "Hi everyone, after reading your dialogue it made me think alot. It is important for both sides to reflect and share their narrative and it is important for us to understand each other history, but focusing only in the past won't bring us anywhere."

While there is some use of this strategy in the early strings, on average this was rarely done until a series of interventions by the moderator in string 16, culminating in the following suggestion to the correspondents: "would like to make an experiment: let's try to discuss things without using the tool of comparison. State your opinion, views, questions and wills but don't say 'but X did that!' or 'We can do this cause Y does that'. Comparisons usually provide us with an easy way out of deep thinking." After this, use of the strategy more than doubled, from 1.3 times per string to 3. By the final string, one month later, it is used more than 12 times. In fact, the final conflict is dedicated more to an exchange of views than actual confrontational or intractable content.

Table 5.1: Strategies Employed by Participants in Controversial Exchanges, by Frequency.

Matrix Category	Strategy	CODE LETTER	Total	Used on its own
Repair	Clarifications	C	116	61
Positive	"Personal Expressions" Presentation of personal philosophy	F	52	30
Repair	Requests for clarification	J	38	23
Repair	Exhortations to the importance of peace	S	31	19
Repair	Miscellaneous	U	29	26
Repair	"Exhortations to solidarity," or appeals to the common cause of the group	T	22	12
Neutral	Opening the floor	D	21	10
Reinforcement	Agreement/Concession	Q	21	10

Table 5.1 (continued)

Matrix Category	Strategy	CODE LETTER	Total	Used on its own
Repair	"Appeals to neutrality/objectivity"/Calls to view "both sides" of an issue	H	17	4
Reinforcement	Like	O	12	11
Positive	Commiseration	K	9	3
Repair	Apologies	I	6	2
Positive	Best wishes	E	4	3
Repair	Deflection	R	3	3

Summary

Employment of the ODM thus finds that:

- In the analyzed strings (which were chosen for their containing "conflictual" episodes), virtually all intractable statements ("z"s) were preceded by potentially conflictual statements ("x"s) and challenges ("y"s) which were not defused or mitigated;
- Of the 22 conflictual episodes, all but three were resolved successfully. Of these 19, the majority (*n*=15) were resolved by the participants themselves, without the need for intervention by the moderator.
- Of the potentially conflictual statements ("x"s) and challenges ("y"s) that were mitigated, *clarifications of the stater's position* and *requests for clarification* by other participants were the most common "repair" strategies, which often resulted in the softening of conflictual content on the part of the speaker. *Personal expressions* and *exhortations to peace* (the latter in its repair function) also featured highly in successful efforts to defuse conflictual positions.

It is important to remember that both the prevalence of these conflictual episodes and of these repair strategies are a reflection of a specific conflict context: discussions between a highly diverse group of participants who, on the one hand, have assembled out of a commitment to peace and on the other, are doing so during a time of intense polarization and conflict escalation (the 2014 Gaza War).

Though a highly innovative approach to the problem of analyzing conversational data, the Online Discourse Analysis Matrix (ODM) we applied to this study is limited precisely because of its novelty. Unlike the scale on which it is based, which has had several decades of iterations to hone its categories, decades in which findings could be compared to actual outcomes (i.e., divorces), the ODM can only give a window onto conversation dynamics in real time. Until it has undergone numerous iterations it can offer little predictive value. Further, dominated as many of these online exchanges are by a relatively small group of more vocal participants, the matrix cannot give a precise window onto how all participants learned to negotiate differences in and outside of the auspices of the project. All it can do is show how a certain number of select conflicts evolved and the dynamics by which they were mediated by those involved (including the degree to which program moderators were needed). The design is thus still at an exploratory stage. If continued to be developed and tested on further groups, however, it poses a great deal of potential to serve as a predictive tool in contending with online and discursive conflicts in real time.

An Impact Assessment of the Project

High levels of use of the ODM aside, the real question we want to answer is "what is the value of using a Facebook group for peacebuilding". A preliminary answer can be found in the responses to a question about future plans to engage with programs or members of this project, which was solicited in the conference questionnaire. This questionnaire was distributed to participants at the project's final conference in Jordan, on October 28, 2014 (of which 57 fully-completed questionnaires were processed) and comprised 16 questions representing a mix of closed (Likert-scaled and categorical) questions on various aspects of the program, participant behavior or attitudes, satisfaction with course and program components, the number and durability of friendships made by participants, and use of the group's *Facebook* page and activism (specifically peace activism) outside of the project. One of the questions read "Do you think you will collaborate with any of these people on future peacebuilding work?" A follow-up question asked: "If *Yes*, please write the name of the project or a brief description of it below." Of the 28 programs cited in response to this open-ended question, the top three are all online-based platforms. This suggests that a number of participants expect that their participation in peace programs will include affiliation with additional online networks. There are a number of possible reasons for this.

Firstly, many of the participants were newcomers to the world of peacebuilding and online communities may have been the best and easiest way to proceed; a way of being networked (even if as passive participants) in wider platforms based primarily on more networking and contact. A second reason can be distilled from the difference in views vis-à-vis the online nature of the program among different demographic groups. Results from the post-conference questionnaire indicated that participants from Gaza and other MENA countries indicated that the online nature of the program was very important in their decision to enroll (5.86 and 4.90 out of 7 respectively). Closed borders and geographic distances represent significant hindrances to face-to-face encounters with their counterparts. In the absence of a real space in which to work together, it is no surprise that many participants embraced the online platform as a productive way to mobilize and promote peace. Israelis, by contrast, tended to be less enthused about the online platform.

Nonetheless, participants did not seem divided on the utility of the Facebook platform in certain areas. The post conference questionnaire results suggest that the platform was seen, overall, as a viable medium through which much of the preliminary work of peacebuilding could be accomplished, from networking (80% of respondents saying they would use it to stay in touch, 67% to share thoughts and 62% to discuss events) to planning collaborative projects (59%). While the long-term value of online participation (or, as certain civil society researchers would say, passive involvement) in promoting a peaceful resolution to the Israeli-Palestinian conflict remains to be seen, as far as consensus-building was concerned, the proceedings on the Facebook group (30%) proved to be just as decisive as face-to-face contact between participants (30%).

The second and more notable difference between this program and counterparts in the traditional approach to bridging Israelis and Palestinians is its emphasis on dealing directly with conflict related issues. The central criticism of the majority of Israeli-Palestinian encounter programs has been their emphasis on the finding of common ground, to the point that they have shied away from contentious issues (Maoz, 2011). Our project encouraged the opposite, making the negotiation of highly politicized and contentious differences between participants a central focus.

Further, the project staff seem to have taken the proper steps to ensure that the ensuing interactions did not thoroughly undermine the program. Participants were screened carefully before being accepted, underwent online training segments from which they claim to have developed their negotiation skills and motivation to understand, and finally, were given an online forum in which to interact while carefully monitored and guided. Without these, even the most well-intentioned interactions could easily have devolved into factionalism, as is illustrated by a close analysis of the Facebook feeds. Given the proportionally very small number of criticisms and dropouts from the program as a result, this approach should be seen as a resounding success.

In terms of changes in attitudes, participants strongly agreed (5.38 out of 7) that as a result of the program they developed a better understanding of "the other side" and that they felt that their views about participants from other countries changed over the course of the program (5.18). On the whole, views changed for the better, with respondents citing an average of 3.55 different communities for whom they had developed a newfound respect. While it is unrealistic to assume that several months of mediated online correspondence can compete with the views and attitudes participants hear continuously around them, both socially and through their respective national media, the ability of program participants to continue their interaction despite a highly divisive war in Gaza seems in itself a strong endorsement of both the program's curriculum and the work of its staff. Though participants still have a way to go before they truly see eye to eye on these issues, it seems that the program has done its part in setting the stage for truly resilient "bridging". The optimism expressed by the majority of participants, the numbers and extent of participants' friendships, and the degree to which participants seemed invested in continuing to work together all attest to the program's accomplishments in negotiating a very complex terrain.

Part III: The Advantages of Online Dialogue Programs – Reflections from the Field

The results of the project demonstrate how using social media platforms, particularly Facebook, assist in managing challenges of people-to-people dialogue. In this final section we elaborate on those challenges and offer five advantages of online platforms: (1) effective participation; (2) confronting "re-entry"; (3) cost effectiveness; (4) balance of power; and (5) measurability and evaluation.

1 Effective Participation

With P2P, participants are selected by conflict resolution and peacebuilding organizations according to the project's goal. Dialogue projects target the wide public or segments of it. The goals are defined as changing attitudes and negative perceptions and have a wide impact among the masses (Knight, 2014). Nevertheless, such projects have encountered difficulties in achieving their goals due to challenges of effective participation.

Dialogue projects involving intergroup conflict usually suffer from selection bias; they attract those who are willing and motivated to meet with the other side. Their attitudes and perceptions do not need to be changed, therefore the entire project loses its relevance (Svensson & Brounéus, 2013). It is difficult to find a positive target group for intergroup dialogue projects such as hardliners, minorities, or influential people in communities who are the actual agents of change. Those individuals usually lack the interest to meet the so-called enemy, and therefore do not make the time and effort to attend. In today's mega busy world, there must be an incentive for the participants to make the effort and time commitment to a peacebuilding project. Finally, in areas of harsh intractable conflicts, it is unpleasant and even dangerous to be seen talking to and being in the same room with members of a conflicting community. The costs of criticism and threats to safety often outweigh the perceived benefits of intergroup dialogue.

Social media platforms offer a partial solution for the challenge of participation. The platforms are characterized as popular, attractive, and user friendly, which facilitates effective recruitment. Hardliners have fewer objections to engaging in a dialogue that is based on a virtual platform, where they can first simply be bystanders and then decide if they wish to actively participate. The online platform serves as an easy entry point from which one can then dive into more difficult discussions. Those who fear hearing accusations and difficult stories are able to easily log off.

Moreover, time difference and physical distance are removed as obstacles to participation. Busy participants are able to spend a few minutes every day to check the latest updates in the online group. Participation in an online P2P also requires less physical and emotional effort. For those who fear to be seen in a physical gathering, the online platform holds a unique advantage in the form of creating a fake and/or secret profile. By remaining anonymous, participants can overcome identity challenges. In addition, participants engaging in the contact from the comfort of their homes are more likely to feel less anxious. Scholars have found that a private setting contributes to the decreasing use of stereotypes and helps participants to be more open and receptive to altering one's own response (Amichai-Hamburger & McKenna, 2006).

2 Confronting "Re-entry"

Another limitation for the effectiveness of P2P projects is the re-entry problem (when participants leave the dialogue setting and return to their own communities) between each meeting session or at the end of the program (Dessel & Ali, 2012). The attitude-perception changing process which the participants are going through (Knight, 2014), is only effective when the process continues for a long period of time. Generally, dialogue projects are limited in time due to the budget and other technical or political obstacles. The resources included in a project such as funds, availability of staff, and political stability allow the interaction to be held for a relatively short time and in little recurrence.

Social media can contribute to coping with the problem of re-entry by offering limitless and continuous interaction. As Amichai-Hamburger and McKenna (2006) have pointed out, instead of one intensive meeting taking place over a few hours, the internet offers contacts to be arranged over days or weeks. Furthermore, participants who become Facebook friends, or communicate via Twitter, Linkedin, WhatsApp, or similar platforms are exposed to the opinions, thoughts, and daily happenings of each other. The continuous interaction contributes to the effectiveness of the conflict transformation process because it promotes a smoother flow and progress, without the need to frequently restart building trust and relationships from the beginning.

3 Cost Effective

Peacebuilding dialogue encounters require infrastructure and resources including funds and therefore organizations spend considerable time on proposal writing (Kosic & Byrne, 2009). Most of the funding goes towards meeting facilities, such as conference rooms, and transportation. The problem is exacerbated when there is a need to find a neutral ground to hold the meetings which often narrows down possibilities to distant and pricy locations, especially in violent conflict zones. A major advantage of holding the dialogue on a social media platform is that it saves costs and it represents a virtual, safe, easy to access, and free of charge venue. Additionally, it saves energy and contributes to a clean and sustainable environment.

4 Balance of Power

In most conflicts there is an imbalance of power between parties due to differences in military, economic, and diplomatic power. When trying to facilitate a dialogue between conflicting parties, it is crucial to ensure that the environment balances the power asymmetry (Pfeil, 2015), allowing the groups a safe place where they can feel comfortable to express and discuss their points of view. A balanced dialogue environment also helps create trust between parties and organizing institutions, therefore supporting the effectiveness of the process (Maoz, 2004).

The virtual world could serve as a neutral meeting place where power asymmetry is not as visible. Under such conditions, the facilitation of the process is under full control of the organizing institution which can use the technological software to ensure power balance throughout the process. Other advantages are that subtle cues that indicate status are not immediately obvious online. Equal status increases the likelihood for perceived similarities between groups. Additionally, research has shown that existing internal status (e.g., the internal pecking order within one's own and the hierarchy within the other group) does not carry as much weight online as it does in face-to-face meetings, and thus does not affect the behavior of the group members as much. Therefore, electronic interaction makes power less of an issue during discussion, leading group members to contribute more. Since participants have more control over how they present themselves and their views online, they should tend to feel more comfortable and in control of the situation (Amichai-Hamburger & McKenna, 2006).

5 Measurability and Evaluation

One of the criticisms of P2P is their ineffectiveness and limited impact on the conflict. When there is no agreement to sign, the question is "what has been achieved through the joint dialogue and meeting?" Furthermore, goals such as "changing attitudes", "bridge building" and "creating understanding" are difficult to quantify and measure. The most common tools used to evaluate dialogue programs are surveys that are handed out in different time spans throughout the program (Svensson & Brounéus, 2013). The validity of surveys is questionable since they represent an opinion in a certain moment and depend on the understanding of a certain question.

For a dialogue to be successful, both sides should participate jointly in a task of which the completion is important to both groups. Evidence from previous studies (Amichai-Hamburger & McKenna, 2006) indicates that tasks performed by virtual teams are done equally well (and not well) as those conducted by teams who met face-to-face. Internet interactions have even shown a tendency for participants to engage in greater self-disclosure and more intimate exchanges.

Projects similar to ours can conduct a comparable analysis of the data to enable the development of a new evaluation system. As the entire communication between the parties is transcribed in real-time, it is possible to follow the dynamics of the dialogue, analyze it, and draw conclusions regarding the program's goals. Using tools like the Online Discourse Matrix (ODM), rigorous analyses of conflict dynamics can be further developed, to the point of predictive validity.

Conclusion

The COVID-19 pandemic drove peacebuilding organizations to adapt and adjust to working via digital platforms. Despite common fears about losing the human connection when using social media, Facebook and other digital platforms can serve as effective complementary tools to physical encounters. This insight will remain relevant also in the post-pandemic world, thus strengthening these conflict resolution practices. The case study presented in this chapter demonstrates how conducting people-to-people dialogue programs online through social media along with physical meetings can yield successful peacebuilding projects. The application of online social media platforms such as Facebook in conflict resolution processes is not only helpful, but imperative since human communication nowadays takes place in the virtual space at least as much as it does on the physical one. Our project offers conflict resolution researchers and practitioners not just a new methodology, but a new path to think about, analyze, and address international conflicts through technology.

The use of Facebook communities does hold several challenges. First, the project must take place where potential participants have free and easy access to the internet and where social media platforms are popular. Secondly, the ongoing, almost non-stop online facilitation requires special preparation for facilitators and funds allocated for training. The tool described here for assessing the efficacy of this programming (the ODM) also needs to be developed into a rigorous, predictive tool – a process that requires ongoing iterations and testing. Finally, the long-term, scalable impact of online peacebuilding on the conflict remains ambiguous. When violent, intractable conflicts take place alongside the initiatives, it is very difficult to change perceptions and reach understanding among people who fight each other outside the Facebook group. The ongoing violence in the Israeli-Palestinian conflict and lack of a peace process limit the hope for peace and the effectiveness of peacebuilding programs to create change. It is therefore the obligation of researchers and practitioners to keep finding new, innovative ways to address conflicts through peacebuilding.

References

Albeck, J., Adwan, S., & Bar-On, D. (2002). Dialogue Groups: TRT's Guidelines for Working Through Intractable Conflicts by Personal Storytelling. *Peace & Conflict*, 8(4),301–322.

Allport, G.W. (1954). *The nature of prejudice*. Cambridge, Mass.: Addison-Wesley Pub. Co.

Amichai-Hamburger, Y., & McKenna, K.Y. (2006). The contact hypothesis reconsidered: Interacting via the Internet. *Journal of Computer-Mediated Communication*, 11(3), 825–843.

Amichai-Hamburger, Y., Hasler, B. & Shani-Sherman, T. (2015). Structured and unstructured intergroup contact in the digital age. *Computers In Human Behavior*, 52, 515–522.

Anderson, L. (2011). Demystifying the Arab Spring: Parsing the differences between Tunisia, Egypt, and Libya. *Foreign Affairs*, 90(3),2–7.

Augar, N. & Zeleznikow, J. (2014). Developing Online Support and Counseling to Enhance Family Dispute Resolution in Australia. *Group Decision & Negotiation*, 23(3),515–532.

Bui-Wrzosinska, L., Gelfand, M., Nowak, A., & Severance, L. (2013). Studying trajectories of conflict escalation. In M. Sycara, M. Gelfand and A. Abbe (Eds.) *Models for intercultural collaboration and negotiation* (145–156). Springer, Dordrecht.

Cao, B. & Lin, W.Y. (2017). Revisiting the contact hypothesis: Effects of different modes of computer-mediated communication on intergroup relationships. *International Journal of Intercultural Relations*, 58, 23–30.

Checkoway, B. (2003). Multicultural community participation for diverse democracy: Building common ground in an Israeli neighborhood. *International Institute Journal*, 11(3).

Chiluwa, I. (2017). The discourse of terror threats: Assessing online written threats by Nigerian terrorist groups. *Studies in Conflict & Terrorism*, 40(4), 318–338.

Chiluwa, I. (2019). Discourse analysis and conflict studies. In *SAGE Research Methods Cases*. https://dx.doi.org/10.4135/9781526468208

Cochrane, F. & Dunn, S. (2002). People power? The role of the voluntary and community sector in the Northern Ireland Conflict. Cork: Cork University Press.

De Souza, C.S. & Preece, J. (2004). A framework for analyzing and understanding online communities. *Interacting with Computers*, 16, 579–610.

Dessel, A.B. & Ali, N. (2012). The Minds of Peace and intergroup dialogue: two complementary approaches to peace. *Israel Affairs*, 18(1),123–139.

Ellis, D. & Maoz, I. (2007). Online Argument Between Israeli Jews and Palestinians. *Human Communication Research*, 33(3),291–309.

Figallo, C. & Pyser, S. (2004). The "Listening to the City" Online Dialogues Experience: The Impact of a Full Value Contract. *Conflict Resolution Quarterly*, 21(3),381–39.

Glaser, B.G. & Strauss, A.L. (1967). *The discovery of grounded theory: strategies for qualitative research*. Aldine Publishing, Chicago.

Gottman, J.M. (1993). The roles of conflict engagement, escalation, and avoidance in marital interaction: A longitudinal view of five types of couples. *Journal of Consulting and Clinical Psychology*, 61(1),6–15.
Handelman, S. & Chowdhury, J. (2017). The limits of political-elite diplomacy: leaders, people and social conflicts. *Israel Affairs*, 23(3),468–495.
Howard, P.N., Duffy, A., Freelon, D., Hussain, M.M., Mari, W., & Maziad, M. (2011). Opening closed regimes: What was the role of social media during the Arab Spring? Project on Information Technology and Political Islam (1–30). *Seattle: Department of Communication, University of Washington*. Available at SSRN 2595096.
Katsh, E. (2007). Online Dispute Resolution: Some Implications for the Emergence of Law in Cyberspace. *International Review Of Law, Computers & Technology*, 21(2),97–107.
Knight, H. (2014). Articulating injustice: an exploration of young people's experiences of participation in a conflict transformation programme that utilises the arts as a form of dialogue. *Compare: A Journal of Comparative and International Education*, 44(1),77–96.
Kosic, A. & Byrne, S. (2009). Community Relations Work with Young People in Vukovas, Croatia: An Exploratory Study in Coexistence Building. Peace and Conflict Studies 15(2),61–79.
Maoz, I. (2004). Peace Building in Violent Conflict: Israeli-Palestinian Post-Oslo People-to-People Activities. *International Journal of Politics, Culture and Society* 17(3),563–574.
Maoz, I. (2011). Does contact work in protracted asymmetrical conflict? Appraising 20 years of reconciliation-aimed encounters between Israeli Jews and Palestinians. *Journal of Peace Research*, 48(1),115–125.
Mor, Y., Ron, Y., & Maoz, I. (2016). "Likes" for peace: Can Facebook promote dialogue in the Israeli–Palestinian conflict?. *Media and Communication*, 4(1), 15–26.
Pfeil, H. (2015). Understanding the Dynamics of Israeli-Palestinian Grassroots Dialogue Workshops: the Contribution of a Habermasian Approach. *International Journal of Politics, Culture, and Society*, 28(2),119–141.
Reilly, P. (2012). Community Worker Perspectives on the Use of New Media to Reconfigure Socio-spatial Relations in Belfast. *Urban Studies*, 49(15),3385–3401.
Rifkin, J. (2001). Online Dispute Resolution: Theory and Practice of the Fourth Party. *Conflict Resolution Quarterly*, 19(1),117–124.
Ron, Y., Suleiman, C., & Maoz, I. (2020). Women for Peace: Promoting Dialogue and Peace through Facebook?. *Social Media+ Society*, 6(4), 1–11.
Schneider, J. & von der Emde, S. (2006). Conflicts in cyberspace: From communication breakdown to intercultural dialogue in online collaborations. In J.A. Belz and S.L. Thorne (Eds.) *Program Direction Internet-mediated Intercultural Foreign Language Education/AAUCS Issues in Language* (178–206). Boston, Heinle.
Selvanathan, H.P., Leidner, B., Petrovic, N., Prelic, N., Ivanek, I., Krugel J., & Bjekic, J. (2019). Wedialog.net: A Quantitative Field Test of the Effects of Online Intergroup Dialogue in Promoting Justice – Versus Harmony-Oriented Outcomes in Bosnia and Serbia. *Peace and Conflict: Journal of Peace Psychology*, 25(4),287–299.
Svensson, I. & Brounéus, K. (2013). Dialogue and interethnic trust: A randomized field trial of 'sustained dialogue'in Ethiopia. *Journal of Peace Research*, *50*(5), 563–575.
Tannen, D. (1990). *You just don't understand: Women and men in conversation*. Morrow.
Tannen, D. (1994). *Gender and discourse*. New York, Oxford University Press.
Tannen, D. (1996). Researching gender-related patterns in classroom discourse. *Tesol Quarterly*, 30(2),341–344.
Tellidis, I. & Kappler, S. (2016). Information and communication technologies in peacebuilding: Implications, opportunities and challenges. *Cooperation and Conflict*, 51(1),75–93.

Wahab, M.S.A, Katsh, M.E. & Rainey D. (2012). *Online Dispute Resolution: Theory and Practice: A Treatise on Technology and Dispute Resolution*. The Hague, Eleven International Publishing.
Walther, J.B., (1997). Group and Interpersonal Effects in International Computer-Mediated. Collaboration. *Human Communication Research*, 23(3),342–369.
Yala "Mena Leaders for Change 2013–14" Program: Empowering Emerging Leaders to Advance Peace and Positive Change in the Mena Region. Submitted by The Peres Center For Peace.

Candice Edrington

Chapter 6
Can You Hear Me Now? How #ShareTheMicNow used Dialogue and Collaboration to Amplify the Voices of Black Women

Abstract: The first half of 2020 proved to be very busy as Americans were forced to tackle two pandemics: COVID-19 and racism. While COVID-19 began in other countries before making its way to the U.S., the racial injustices that were taking place in the United States sparked unprecedented protests around the globe. The stay-at-home orders established due to the COVID-19 pandemic forced citizens to not only take a break, but to take inventory of the harsh realizations lived by African Americans every day. Three deaths of unarmed Black people (Ahmaud Arbery, Breonna Taylor, and George Floyd) over the span of a few months prompted a resurgence of the Black Lives Matter movement both online and offline. Although the deaths of Arbery and Floyd received much attention from the media, Taylor's death was not publicized nearly as much. The lack of media attention surrounding Taylor's death, in comparison to both Arbery and Floyd, illuminated the intersectional invisibility of Black women and their voices. Created for the purpose of amplifying the voices of Black women, Bozoma Saint John initiated the #SharetheMicNow campaign. This campaign suggested that relationships between White women of power and Black women are a step in the right direction in the fight for social justice. The goal of this chapter is to highlight how White women of celebrity stature allowed Black women activists and celebrities to take over their Instagram accounts for a day to discuss their social justice efforts and to share how others could get involved. Using a case study approach, this chapter will seek to reveal how the #SharetheMicNow campaign used technology to promote dialogue and collaboration during a time of heightened awareness of racial injustice.

Keywords: #SharetheMicNow, collaboration, hashtag activism, amplification, Instagram

Introduction

The first half of 2020 proved to be very busy as Americans were forced to tackle two pandemics: COVID-19 and racism. While COVID-19 began in other countries before making its way to the U.S., the racial injustices that were taking place in the United States sparked unprecedented protests around the globe. The stay-at-home orders established due to the COVID-19 pandemic demanded citizens to not only take a break

https://doi.org/10.1515/9783110687262-007

from their normal lives and routines, but to take inventory of the harsh realizations lived by African Americans every day. Three deaths of unarmed Black people (Ahmaud Arbery, Breonna Taylor, and George Floyd) over the span of a few months prompted a climactic point in the Black Lives Matter movement (BLM) both online and offline.

Although the deaths of Arbery and Floyd received much attention from the media, Taylor's death was not publicized nearly as much. Glamour writes, "between the coronavirus pandemic and the justified outrage over the killings of Ahmaud Arbery and George Floyd, the name Breonna Taylor didn't rise to the top of most people's full newsfeeds" (para. 11). The lack of media attention surrounding Taylor's death, in comparison to both Arbery and Floyd, illuminated the intersectional invisibility (Purdie-Vaughns & Eibach, 2008; Sesko & Biernat, 2010) of Black women, their lives, and their voices. News media attention and social media chatter of Taylor's death was misplaced and somewhat lost as the world proceeded to mourn the death of Floyd. It wasn't until her birthday, June 5, that the hashtag #birthdayforBreonna began to remind us that she too was to be remembered as part of the Black Lives Matter movement.

Noticeably different from the other prominently publicized protests of BLM in previous years was the stark increase of people from different races, ethnicities, and countries participating in the movement. Also different were the sentiments surrounding the BLM movement. Conversations of equality and justice for African Americans beyond the scope of police brutality emerged. Black activists and scholars urged others to not only think of racial injustices from the periphery of state-sanctioned violence, but through a lens of institutionalized systems such as education, healthcare, and employment. This prompted the dialogue about antiracism, a concept that surpasses allyship. Talks of antiracism transformed the rhetorical landscape of social media, as it related to BLM, with people from other races asking how to help the movement and become an antiracist. Conversations such as these generated a space for digital dialogue and collaboration. As a result, the social media campaign #SharetheMicNow was created.

Organized for the purpose of amplifying the voices of Black women, who otherwise are rendered silent in their efforts toward social justice (Barnett, 1993), organizers Bozoma Saint John, Glennon Doyle, Luvvie Ajayi Jones, and Stacey Bendet initiated the #SharetheMicNow campaign. This campaign was constructed on the hopes that relationships between White women and Black women are a step in the right direction in the fight for social justice. Using Instagram, White women of celebrity stature and influence allowed Black women activists and celebrities to take over their accounts for a day to discuss their social justice efforts and to share how others could get involved.

The goal of this chapter is to highlight how the #SharetheMicNow campaign used technology to promote dialogue and collaboration during a time of heightened awareness of racial injustice. By analyzing the Instagram Live videos highlighted on the official Instagram page, this chapter seeks to reveal some of the key themes that emerged from the conversations between the women involved in this campaign as well as to discuss the implications this campaign has for dialogue and collaboration in a digital landscape as it relates to conflict and communication.

The Reckoning

Ahmaud Arbery, a 25-year-old Black man, was murdered in February of 2020 after being pursued by two White men in a South Georgia neighborhood. The crime: jogging while Black. Video of the murder was captured and began to circulate the Internet. The hashtag #blacklivesmatter was used to reference his death but on his birthday, a new hashtag campaign (#irunwithmaud) was created. The idea of the campaign was to honor Arbery on his birthday (May 8) by running 2.23 miles, symbolic of the day his life was senselessly taken.

Breonna Taylor, a 26-year-old EMT worker, was killed in March of 2020 after being struck eight times by bullets fired by police officers into her apartment. Her death was a result of a no-knock warrant in which her apartment was raided under the premise that it was being used to store drugs. There was not any video footage of this incident as the police officers involved were in plain clothing and were not equipped with body cameras. Following the news of her death, her name was associated with the #blacklivesmatter and #sayhername hashtags. This was the second publicized death of an unarmed Black person that occurred within a few weeks of each other.

While national protests and social media campaigns ensued after the deaths of both Arbery and Taylor, the death of George Floyd in May of 2020 ignited global unrest. Floyd was arrested under the pretense of a counterfeit $20 bill. His arrest and murder were both recorded and widely circulated on all social media platforms. Lasting longer than nine minutes, the video of a White police officer kneeling on the neck of a handcuffed Floyd perpetuated the state-sanctioned violence and racial injustices that the Black Lives Matter movement has condemned since its inception. The wide circulation of the video fomented national and international demonstrative acts such as protests and other forms of solidarity. According to the Pew Research Center (2020), the #blacklivesmatter hashtag was used a record-breaking 8.8 million times on Twitter just three days after Floyd's death (para. 3).

#ShareTheMicNow

With a long history of involvement in movements and initiatives surrounding social justice, Black women are often the ones less notably publicized in the media for their efforts. Purdie-Vaughns and Eibach (2008) suggest that "the intersection of race and gender marginalizes Black women's historical contribution" (p. 384). Additionally, Barnett (1993) notes "the invisibility of modern Black women leaders and activists is in part a result of gender, race, and class biases prevalent in both the social movement literature and feminist scholarship" (p. 163). Thus, the need for the #ShareTheMicNow campaign. Created with the sole purpose of amplifying the voices of Black women, the #ShareTheMicNow campaign utilized the social media platform of Instagram to illuminate the Black women and White women who would participate in the campaign on June 10, 2020. The official Instagram account for the #ShareTheMicNow campaign was created on June 9, 2020, just one day before the social media takeover began. In the bio section of the Instagram page for the campaign, the organizers write, "magnifying Black women and the important work that they're doing in order to catalyze change. White women, #Sharethemicnow" (ShareTheMicNow, 2020).

The idea of this social media campaign was that influential White women would hand over their Instagram account to a Black woman. In turn, the Black woman would share her story, provide resources as they relate to the Black Lives Matter movement, and/or challenge viewers to become anti-racists and help with the fight to end racial injustices faced by the Black community. According to the second post,

> When the world listens to women, it listens to white women. For far too long, Black women's voices have gone unheard, even though they've been using their voices loudly for centuries to enact change, Today, more than ever, it is NECESSARY that we create a unifying action to center Black women's lives, stories, and calls to action. We need to listen to Black women. This is why we created #ShareTheMicNow. Tomorrow, Black women will speak from the Instagram accounts of White women. The intention of this campaign is to magnify Black women and the important work that they're doing in order to catalyze the change that will only come when we truly hear each other's voices. (ShareTheMicNow, 2020)

With over 45k followers, the page only features a total of seven posts. The seven posts highlight the creators of the campaign, the mission of the campaign, the participants of the campaign, the Instagram handles of all the contributors, a video speaking Breonna Taylor's name, and a message to 'continue sharing the mic'. In the highlights section of the #Sharethemicnow page, there are recaps and links to the Instagram Live recordings that happened on June 10, 2020. A list of the pairings participating in the campaign can be found in Table 6.1. The pairings bolded are those with live videos that were saved to the highlights section of the #ShareTheMicNow Instagram account.

Presentation of Findings

There were a total of 52 pairs of women participating in the #ShareTheMicNow campaign. Throughout the entire day of June 10, 2020, prominent White women handed over their Instagram accounts to Black women to share their experiences, provide resources as they pertained to the Black Lives Matter movement and anti-racism, and to highlight the work they were involved in regarding social justice and activism efforts. Collectively, the campaign had the opportunity to make over 280 million media impressions with 280 million followers belonging to the White women participants as compared to only 6 million followers belonging to the Black women participants (at the time of the campaign).

Handing over the Instagram accounts included allowing the Black women to post on their regular feed, post to their Instagram stories, and also broadcast to their followers live using the Instagram Live feature on the platform. Because this

Table 6.1: Pairs Participating in the #ShareTheMicNow Campaign.

Black Woman	White Woman	Black Woman	White Woman
Tiffany Aliche 440k followers	**Ashlyn Harris** 765k followers	Elaine Welteroth 656k followers	Michelle Monaghan 1.4m followers
Yaba Blay 75.4k followers	**Abby Wambach** 910k followers	**Eunique Jones Gibson** 51.9k followers	**Katie Couric** 1.1m followers
Elle Hearns 13.6k followers	**Cameron Esposito** 112k followers	Fresco Steez 5,884 followers	Megan Rapinoe 2.2m followers
Yvette Noel Schure 131k followers	**Esther Perel** 603k followers	**Gia Peppers** 54.1k followers	**Jenny Mollen** 417k followers
Stephanie Thomas 23.1k followers	**Selma Blair** 2.4m followers	**Jamia Wilson** 22.6k followers	**Sarah Sophie Flicker** 88.1k followers
Stephanie Young 7,978 followers	**Chrissy Metz** 1.6m followers	**Jessica O. Matthews** 15.7k followers	**Ashley Judd** 442k followers
Tai Beauchamp 68.5k followers	**Kimberly Williams-Paisley** 621k followers	**Candace Marie** 40.8k followers	**Ali Krieger** 888k followers
Thasunda Brown Duckett 23.2k followers	Jessica Seinfeld 505k followers	**Cari Champion** 419k followers	**Busy Phillips** 2.1m followers
Nicole Waters 193k followers	**Hilarie Burton Morgan** 1.3m followers	**Christina Rice** 24.3k followers	**Melissa Urban** 316k followers
Nikki Ogunnaike 57.5k followers	**Arianna Huffington** 716k followers	**Danielle Young** 45.3k followers	**Catt Sadler** 471k followers
Nimotalai Ganiyu **4,610** followers	**Sarah McBride** 113k followers	**Deesha Dyer** 21.8k followers	**Kathryn Budig** 215k followers
Opal Tometi 180k followers	**Ashley Graham** 12m followers	**Devi Brown** 96.1k followers	**Barb Schmidt** 248k followers
Rachel Cargle **1.8m** followers	**Sarah Paulson** 3.5m followers	**Alencia Johnson** 21.2k followers	**Jen Hatmaker** 523k followers
Seun Adigun 75.1k followers	**Sue Bird** 512k followers	**Alexa Idama** 20.8k followers	**Seane Corn** 110k followers
Lindsay Peoples Wagner 144k followers	**Diane Von Furstenberg** 261k followers	**Alexis Mcgill Johnson** 9,183 followers	**Sen. Elizabeth Warren** 3.6m followers
Melina Abdullah 64.6k followers	**Chelsea Handler** 4m followers	**Angelica Ross** 395k followers	**Hilary Swank** 1.1m followers

Table 6.1 (continued)

Black Woman	White Woman	Black Woman	White Woman
Miatta Johnson 12.3k followers	**Brandi Carlile** 518k followers	Austin Channing Brown 405k followers	Brene Brown 3.3m followers
Monique Melton 304k followers	**Debra Messing** 1.4m followers	**Brittney Cooper** 45.5k followers	**Elizabeth Gilbert** 1m followers
Myleik Teele 197k followers	**Cheryl Strayed** 316k followers	**Bozoma Saint John** 347k followers	**Kourtney Kardashian** **109m** followers
Naima Cochrane 8,029 followers	**Liz Plank** 240k followers	**Luvvie Ajayi Jones** 343k followers	**Sophia Bush** 3.7m followers
Jovian Zayne 18.9k followers	**Mandy Moore** 4.4m followers	**Tarana Burke** 306k followers	**Glennon Doyle** 1.5m followers
Justina Omokhua 11.3k followers	**Brie Larson** 6.6m followers	**Julee Wilson** 63.2k followers	**Stacey Bendet** 1.1m followers
Keah Brown 14.6k followers	**Nina Tame** **35.2k** followers	Ibtihaj Muhammad 373k followers	Alex Morgan 9.2m followers
Kimberly Blackwell 40.3k followers	**Julianne Hough** 4.9m followers	Blessing Omakwu 7,315 followers	Melinda Gates 793k followers
Latham Thomas 129k followers	**Gwyneth Paltrow** 7.4m followers	Zerlina Maxwell 48.2k followers	Hillary Clinton 5.4m followers
Lauren Wesley Wilson 12.6k followers	**Sara Bareilles** 724k followers	Kahlana Barfield Brown 266k followers	Julia Roberts 9.2m followers

analysis occurred after the campaign, some information was not available for analysis due to the nature of some Instagram features (stories are only housed on the platform for 24 hours after the original posting). Additionally, all live broadcastings were not saved and were no longer available for analysis. Fortunately, 43 Instagram Live videos were saved in the "highlights" section of the #ShareTheMicNow campaign. The following findings are from those 43 videos.

Themes

In watching and analyzing the 43 videos still retrievable from the highlights section of the #ShareTheMicNow Instagram page, seven key themes became prominent. These themes included: allyship, the Black experience, racism, anti-racism, Whiteness, activism, and moving forward. Subthemes were also present in some instances. These included White womanhood, White privilege, colorblindness, Black womanhood, institutionalized racism, inherent bias, communication, education, and digital storytelling.

Allyship

Before the start of the live broadcasts using the Instagram Live feature, Black women participants of the campaign solicited questions from the followers of the White women participants to be answered when they shared the mic. A resounding number of participants received the question of "what can I do as a White person to help". This prompted the conversation on allyship. Not only what it meant to be an ally, but what it meant to move *beyond* an ally. The majority of the women addressing the questions stated that allyship was the bare minimum. Instead, what the movement needs are disruptors, accomplices, and coconspirators.

> Black people need you as allies right now, even more than an ally we need you as a disruptor; a disruptor is somebody who is going to stand on the front lines with me and acknowledge that there is a serious problem in this country; now that people are hungry and willing to pay attention and we have their ears and eyes, this movement is for you to see us; I want you to see me, all of me; when you see that black woman in your space, know that she is very much the same as you are. We need you to be disruptors and call out those people when they are not being fair. Being the first is a difficult thing. You don't realize you are biased until someone points it out to you. An ally is someone who will say no that's wrong, but a disruptor is somebody who puts it all out there and makes you uncomfortable when you make a racist statement. – Cari Champion @carichampion

> We need advocates, accomplices, and coconspirators. I don't need you to stand with me, I need you to fight with me. You have to admit your bias, fix your bias. We are dismantling and rebuilding a broken system. If you are ready that means that you have to be uncomfortable and unpopular. When you do nothing, we (Black women) have to step in and do it all.
> – Deesha Dyer @deedyer267

> You don't have to be Black to be outraged by someone being killed in the street. Even if you don't have a proximity to Black people, you still have a proximity to people as a human with a heart. – Julee Wilson @missjulee

> The difference between and ally and an accomplice are that an accomplice understands that they need to bring you to the center but then move out of the way. We won't be heard or accepted until we have a conduit, it's unfortunate but a reality. – Dr. Yaba Blay @yababla y

> Everyone has an opportunity to be a part of the solution. Allyship starts with listening.
> – Tai Beauchamp @taibeau

> There is a need for accomplices; people who are willing to show up and not just say I see you but to show up and say I am an accomplice to upending the systems. – Rachel Cargle @rachel.cargle

> This is a moment in time when we are looking for yes people. We need yes people who do know that now is absolutely the time. What does your purposeful protest look like? How will you stay in this for the long haul? – Jovian Zayne @jovianzayne

I don't need you to curate the movement and tell me what to say, all I need you to do is show up and put your body and money on the line . . . that's an accomplice and not allyship
– Tamika Mallory with Kim Blackwell @kimblackwellpmm

Allyship is being the leader in making equality cool. – Lauren Wesley Wilson @laurenwesleywilson

Black people can't dismantle racism. It's like telling people who don't have the key to the house to open the door. Speaking truth to power is actually putting in the work and pointing it out. As women our voice and our ability to create something good is our power. You can't run out of privilege. You don't lose power by pulling other people up. – Luvvie Ajayi Jones @luvvie

Speak up and be an ally. Teach your children early enough to be allies and to speak up. Teach your children that there is no color. – Christina Rice @christinamrice

The Black Experience

The second theme to become prominent during the analysis of the live videos was the Black experience. When starting the live broadcasting to the White women's audiences, many of the Black women participants found it necessary to not only introduce themselves, but to also share their personal experiences with being Black in America. This was done through digital storytelling and personal narrative sharing. It became apparent to viewers that Black women feel as though they are rendered invisible and rarely listened to, and that not all Black people are the same.

I've felt at times I've had to minimize my own experience or think twice before we say something or else, we'll be called aggressive. – Alencia Johnson @alenciajohnson

Being Black is a very hard job. Now that we are in this reckoning, part of me doesn't want to do anything because I am tired. Being Black in America is beautiful but exhausting; we do not have privilege. – Deesha Dyer @deedyer267

What you are seeing is the empowerment of Black people, Black people who are unafraid to declare that we have had enough but that we are also equipped and prepared to defend ourselves. Black women are always taking care of the entire world and selfcare for us is an afterthought. – Elle Hearns @soulfreedreams – Jovian Zayne @jovianzayne

All of us are just trying to live our best lives, thrive, and live our goals. These stories, our stories, need to be told to show the world that we are just trying to be. We not only have ancestorial trauma that we are carrying but what we may see when we turn on the tv. – Julee Wilson @missjulee

Black people are not a monolith. – Tarana Burke @taranajaneen

As a Black woman, I am ready to interrogate the way that I am taking in too much of the internalized oppression that has been offered to my people. – Jovian Zayne @jovianzayne

The stuff that I say as a Black woman to everyone needs a conduit because that's racism and white supremacy; constantly being in a space of vulnerability or a place of I don't know to have me teach you everything. I cannot be oppressed from a system and then asked to teach you about how you benefitted from it. This movement was centered around the invisibility of Black women. People have to look at intersectional and how racism and sexism embeds itself in social justice. If you don't see the faces and hear the names, then you won't recognize yourself in them. Say her name! – Dr. Yaba Blay @yabablay

You think that if you are good and do the right things that these instances won't happen to you. When I get pulled over, I narrate my actions because I want the police officer to be comfortable and not view me as a threat and because I want to go home, I have kids. – Nicole Walters @nicolewalters

As a black person, it is very difficult to navigate the world and be seen as other. – Justina Omokhua @justeenahoh

We can't just be good; we have to be better than. – Miatta johnson @miattajohnson

I am successful but every single day its some bs . . . it's like being in an abusive relationship with America and you have normalized the abuse. – Tiffany Aliche @thebudgetnista

Whiteness

Another theme present in the 43 saved live videos was Whiteness. The majority of the Black women also addressed this topic but approached it in different ways thus leading to subthemes for Whiteness. White womanhood, colorblindness, and White privilege could be identified as subcategories for this theme.

White Women

When women speak up, most of the times they listen to White women's voices. White women violence is the history of the United States. Malcolm X said that most disrespected person in America is the Black woman. I say the most protected person in the United States is the White woman. White women benefitting from a Black woman sharing her experiences is what is unjust. We need white women to think about the ways in which they engage with Black women such as microaggressions. – Alencia Johnson @alneciajohnson

Feminism is a multiracial project and doesn't belong to White women. White women get to weaponize femininity. Think about what the relationships are between Black women and White women and what that means for politics . . . it models what we mean when we begin to talk about White privilege. Racism is a system that we are all born into; we don't get past these murders unless we can really get real about how we got here . . . . thinking together as women and thinking about what our responsibilities to each other are and what White women's responsibility is. Begin to have some accountability about how you are complicit in White supremacy. If we have some real dialogue, then maybe folks will change. White women have to reckon with whiteness. This campaign represents a seeding of power. White people have to actually give something up (privilege). If there are folks who are underprivileged then there are also folks who are overprivileged. Justice is a gain; freedom is a gain. – Brittany Cooper @professor_crunk

ColorBlindness

So many times, we hear from our White friends that I don't see color and that statement alone is dismissive and ignorant to the fact of what we have endured. Seeing it makes us human and makes you aware and compassionate. – Christina Rice @christinamrice

Saying that I don't see color is not the reality for Black Americans. It's important that we honor other people's process. – Devi Brown @devibrown

The first thing you can do is to not raise your kids to be colorblind . . . you can't treat Black people the same, we need a little bit more. White people have a magic power that when they say something people listen. – Nicole Walters @nicolewalters

It's very important that you see color and you accept and acknowledge it. If we don't talk about it then we run the risk of forgetting or being forgotten. – Keah Brown @keah_maria

White Privilege

People need to realize that White privilege is what contributes to all of this. If you are ready to do the work, then you are ready to recognize your role in racism. – Deesha Dyer @deedyer267

It's about having access and being born with power. – Justina Omokhua @justeenahoh

What a privilege to tune out when we start talking about race. – Angelica Ross @angelicaross

Racism

Without being prompted, many of the Black women participants of the #ShareTheMicNow campaign felt it vital to discuss the topic of racism. This conversation seemed to naturally flow as many of them were discussing their personal and professional experiences, particularly in corporate America and the health and wellness industry. Inherent biases, microaggressions, and institutionalized racism were all subtopics of the overall conversation surrounding racism. In particular, institutionalized racism appeared to be a topic that many Black women participants experienced. These conversations addressed how systems in America were intentionally created for non-Black people. Knowing this, many of these women elaborated on how they created spaces for Black women in an effort to no longer be silenced.

Inherent Biases

Do your own research and find out how you can work through your own biases
– Alencia Johnson @alneciajohnson

Sometimes your inherent bias is not even intentional. Ignorance is not a negative word; it literally just means that you don't know and you have not taken the time to think about another's perspective in a considerate way. – Naima Cochrane @naimagram

Only following Black famous people is still problematic because they are the safe diversity. Following others pinpoints where your bias comes from. – Luvvie Ajayi Jones @luvvie

People are going to have to step back and take a look at where these biases come from. We are all a part of the human race. – Stephanie Young @slynnyoung

Institutionalized Racism

Feel free to create your own space if there isn't one for you. A number of outlets realize the power in Black eyeballs and that diversity is good business. – Nikki Ogunnaike @nikkiogun

Challenge your education systems to show the comprehensive history of this nation. I believe that healthcare is a fundamental human right. – Alencia Johnson @alenciajohnson

Silencing comes in many forms. Very often the voice of people of color are silenced in the health industry . . . .it's very apparent that we are silenced in images. When you don't see a certain group of people and you don't hear their voices, they are effectively silenced. Why is silencing an issue? Why do we need to hear everybody's voice? If the narrative is only ever told from one perspective and if that is the only perspective to ever count then that is taken to be the truth. – Alexa Idama @lowimpactfit

Corporate is a system that was not designed thinking about Black people, period. I was going to have to work that much harder to level out the playing field. If the system was built for us, it would take into account that we are already 400 years behind. – Candace Marie @marie_mag_

When Black women create these spaces, it is because we are run out of the other spaces and forced to create our own. We have to find safe spaces and so we create our own.
– Christina Rice @christinamrice

Being Black was not something that was seen as positive in this country.
– Deesha Dyer @deedyer267

Racism is not just being called the n-word or being beaten; it is a series of systems in place that disempower. This is a system that has been in place to protect the status quo. Children are overpoliced in the school system. Illegal traffic stops. We are overpoliced at rates that are egregious; Black on Black crime is a term that was made up to devalue Black people and it works. There have been laws made to put Black people in jail longer. – Tiffany Aliche @thebudgetnista

Understand that we're not valuable because of degrees or work, I'm intrinsically valuable because I am here. – Stephanie Thomas @disabilityfashionstylist

Generations before us have set up systems that we now are trying to clean up but it takes all of us and Black people are tired. Systematically we have been taught that the darker our skin, the more we are a problem and a threat, even as a young kid. These protests that we are in are a protest against the constitution. Black people were not brought to this country to be considered as equal or counterparts. – Seun Adigun @seun_msamazing

The issues of racism and discrimination and the substandard treatment is not just an issue around police brutality. – Opal Tometi @opalayo

We have to make room for Black women in the workplace because the world is changing demographically, and we need more voices in leadership in the workplace. We have to make room by recognizing our bias; you have to make room by holding your leaders accountable. You can't be diverse just by checking a box and it's not a one-time thing. You have to make room by recruiting Black people and sponsoring Black people. – Myleik Teele @myleik

If you don't fit in it probably means that the structures need to change so that more people can be brought in. – Jamia Wilson @jamiaawilson

For more than 400 years, the systems that built and have upheld American society have shown a disregard for Black people. – Alexis Mcgill Johnson @alexismcgilljohnson

Is my hair style going to immediately cut me off from being a candidate? Natural hair is illegal in many states. – Julee Wilson @missjulee

I would never be able to wear my hair in braids. You speak well for a Black girl; you're smart for a Black girl. Microaggressions and comments like that hold us back and don't push us forward. – Lauren Wesley Wilson @laurenwesleywilson

Every day that I walk into corporate spaces, I represent beauty in blackness . . . not just the outward beauty but all parts that are beautiful (culture, music, fashion, food, wisdom, religion, learning and knowledge). – Bozoma Saint John @badassboz

Anti-racism

Anti-racism was also a prominent theme throughout the live videos highlighted on the #ShareTheMicNow Instagram page. Women who shared information on what anti-racism is were not prompted with the question but instead decided to teach the audience members of the White women what it meant. Women speaking on this topic included anti-racism educators.

I have a theoretical framework for antiracism: knowledge + empathy + action. Knowledge is looking at the ways in which we are showing up to listen to the voices (let people tell their own stories), deciding who you listen to. Empathy (I see what you are experiencing and I'm critical in how I play a part in that). Action! Anti-racism work is not self-improvement work for White people; it doesn't end with a donation, post, or letter you write. It ends when this country as a whole recognizes that Black lives actually matter. I encourage you to figure out ways to incorporate antiracism work in your everyday lives. – Rachel Cargle @rachel.cargle

Change the framing of how you watch something, not for entertainment but for understanding. – Naima Cochrane @naimagram

> It's an ongoing learning process that takes a long time. It is a process of identifying and eliminating racism (you have to see it and get rid of it). The purpose is to redistribute power and resources so that everyone can live freely. You use the inside out approach . . . you do the work within yourself first. Antiracism is the responsibility of White people and those that hold White privilege. This is not about being enlightened, but about taking on the responsibility. Antiracism is not anti-White people . . . it is not something that you're naturally and equipped to do. The White collective have never made the commitment to end the violence on Black people. Losing things will make you feel uncomfortable, but it won't put you in danger. – Monique Melton @moemotivate

Activism

Activism proved to be another prominent theme throughout the live videos. The Black women participants thought it vital to provide the audience members of the videos action points on how to move forward. Notably, some of these conversations included thoughts on institutionalized racism as well. However, these particular quotes were chosen as activism because they provided tangible tactics to break the unjust systems. These "action points" included voting, supporting Black-owned businesses, and recruiting at HBCUs and lower-income communities.

> A lot of the policies that really impact our lives are actually dealt with on a local level. I challenge you to have these conversations with your elected officials to see if they look like the community. – Alencia Johnson @alenciajohnson

> It goes beyond just an IG post; it goes into action. Action that makes you uncomfortable. – Deesha Dyer @deedyer267

> Everyone has a role and can take action in different ways. Honoring and serving and protecting Black lives is costly. Invest in Blackness, not just Black culture. – Tarana Burke @taranajaneen

> Really understand how we can move forward in order to heal together. Support Black owned businesses so that we are helping to close the wealth gap. Support the next generation of leaders. Support any HBCU. Vote! – Tai Beauchamp @taibeau

> We have a lot of work to do and the only way we can do that is through a collective voice of people who are interested in making an impact on the country. Voting not only in the big election but on the local levels. Another way that systematic change happens is at the ballot box. Everyone has different responsibilities, but we can all make sure that we are registered to vote. Vote, and make sure that we are voting for people that represent our values and our best selves as a country. – Stephanie Young @slynnyoung

> What can kids do in activism? Circulate petitions. Make sure your friends and parents are donating. Make sure that you are getting in contact with organizations who have been doing the groundwork. – Melina Abdullah's daughter @docmellymel

> Recruiting in low-income communities and from HBCUs. – Candace Marie @marie_mag_

> Be a part of organizations that are doing the work. – Christina Rice @christinamrice

It's very easy to go on social media and say one thing but it's another to actually do it in real life. – Lindsay Peoples Wagner @lpeopleswagner

Communication

The last theme that was deemed prominent throughout the live videos was communication. The notion of communication came in many forms. This included having uncomfortable conversations, communicating with others from the Black community, educating oneself through various sources of literature, and listening to others from a different background. All of these forms of communication were presented as starting points towards positive transformation in America.

I hope White women will listen to our experiences even if you feel differently and will elevate us even if you don't understand it; it's ok to be a little bit uncomfortable.
– Alencia Johnson @alenciajohnson

Be comfortable with being uncomfortable because that is what it is like being a Black woman in this world . . . we live in an uncomfortable space; read a series of books by Black authors to learn the Black experience; all we ask for is equality and not revenge.
– Cari Champion @carichampion

Educate yourself because Black people cannot do the emotional labor; listen when you speak to your Black friends, let them have the floor without judging, trying to change or being defensive. – Christina Rice @christinamrice

It is an opportunity for all of us to deepen our knowledge of everyone; We are meant to learn and grow through our human experience. – Devi Brown @devibrown

The hope is to move from this moment with positivity but ready to do the work; the hope is to move forward and be able to have easier conversations about race; It's one thing to be in your own circles and have these conversations but it's another thing to infiltrate these spaces that you wouldn't normally be in. – Gia Peppers @giapeppers

Have the conversations even though they are going to be uncomfortable.
– Tai Beauchamp @taibeau

The only way that we can change racism is to create spaces like this and have dialogue.
– Stephanie Young @slynnyoung

Get a little uncomfortable from your protected home; read some uncomfortable literature and talk to your kids. – Nicole Walters @nicolewalters

We as a people need to get comfortable with being uncomfortable; the reality is that we need to have the conversation. – Justina Omokhua @justeenahoh

Diversify your feed on social media but also give people opportunities.
– Lindsay Peoples Wagner @lpeopleswagner

> Reach each other and listen to each other in a way that we never have before; if I'm able to bring parts of my culture to the conversations I have then I'm better able to identify the connections that I have with other people. We are not all really that different; bring your whole self to the spaces you are in. Bringing your whole self is how we will actually get empathy in the world. If you recognize and get to see all of me, then maybe you'll view me as less of a stranger; it starts with diversifying the content we see, the feeds we are a part of. – Bozoma Saint John @badassboz

Discussion

Using the Internet to foster dialogic communication is one way that activist organizations can build relationships (Taylor, Kent, & White, 2001). The goal of the #ShareTheMicNow campaign was to not only amplify the voices and stories of Black women but to also use the influence of White women as a means of collaboration to foster relationships. There were thousands of viewers tuned in to each of the 43 live videos analyzed. When reviewing the comments under the posts on the official Instagram page of the campaign, in addition to the comments posted under the live videos, viewers were receptive to the initiative and oftentimes requested more content. Some viewers even wrote that they left the video more informed and aware of their privilege and biases. Furthermore, viewers of the live videos and other material posted during the #ShareTheMicNow campaign asked for this initiative to be continued beyond this intended one-time event.

Although #ShareTheMicNow received much positivity, negative comments and sentiments surrounding the campaign were also present. In particular, there were some comments under the posts on the main Instagram page for #ShareTheMicNow that questioned Julianne Hough's participation in the campaign as she had previously been involved in a scandal in which she wore blackface as a Halloween costume in 2013. Other negative comments were found on some of the White women's pages under the live videos. These comments were of followers who were outraged by the White women celebrities taking part in the campaign and supporting the Black Lives Matter movement as a whole. To these comments, the White women participating in the campaign responded with unwavering support and solidarity of both the campaign and movement. While real-time comments were not visible on the screen of the saved live videos, it was apparent from some of the Black women's commentary and reactions during these videos that the comments and questions they were receiving were also negative.

Notwithstanding, by allowing viewers to comment under posts and interact with the Black women participants during the live videos, whether negative or positive, this shows that the #ShareTheMicNow campaign was created to foster both dialogue and collaboration in a digital space. When defining dialogue, Broome (2009) writes, "dialogue represents a form of discourse that emphasizes listening and inquiry, with the aims of fostering mutual respect and understanding. Dialogue allows communicators to become aware of the different ways that individuals interpret and give meaning to similar experiences" (p. 302). As the analysis of these live videos suggest, both Black and White women participants understand the power in using dialogic communication to build relationships.

While dialogue is important to build relationships, identification is also vital in order to generate participation and build community in social justice efforts and to actually *move* movements forward. There is a relationship between identification and activism (McAdam & Paulsen, 1993). Sommerfeldt suggested that "identification is an important part of relationship building and essential to an individual's participation in collective action" (2008, p. 15). The sharing of personal narratives and experiences by the Black women participants during the live videos resembled digital storytelling. The collaboration between influential White women and Black women was significant in that these personal narratives could reach otherwise unreachable audiences. The personal narratives and experiences shared by the Black women participating in the #ShareTheMicNow campaign functioned rhetorically to disregard established caricatures by evoking shared humanity, to create recognition of others through particularity, and to make abstract concepts knowable (Gallagher & Zagacki, 2005). This is evident through the comments from White audience members under the posts and videos who stated that they felt more informed, understood the issue, and wanted to learn more ways in which they could help the issue.

The use of social media as a digital vehicle to facilitate these conversations and build community as opposed to other platforms is apparently strategic on behalf of the campaign organizers. Sobre-Denton (2016) posits that "social media facilitates a global-local orientation to the world that allows individuals to engage in virtual community-building and participate in communication to build global citizenship" (p. 1715). Unlike other social media platforms, Instagram combines many existing technological features, such as the hashtag, to make it the best choice for this particular initiative. Similar to Twitter, Instagram users utilize hashtags to chronicle and archive conversations albeit different than Twitter in that live videos, highlights, stories, and posts to a user's page can be stored for future review. In the posts to the Instagram page of the campaign, #ShareTheMicNow was used to create a conversation thread. Kuo (2018) declares,

> the significant impact of hashtags isn't just message content, hashtags form networks that move discourse beyond insular discussion to speak across borders and boundaries; any participation in the discussion aids the messages' ability to spread quicker and wider across multiple clusters and generate a larger network (p. 511).

Moving beyond insular discussion to speak across borders and boundaries speaks to the purpose of the campaign overall. Other hashtags such as #DropTheMic and #KeepSharingTheMic were also used on the page to encourage others to 'drop the mic' and take action, and to keep sharing the mic beyond the campaign.

The collaboration between White women of influence and Black women was a great way to not only create dialogue, but to build community with unlikely participants in hopes of getting them to join the movement. In order for participants to join a social movement, McAdam and Paulsen posited

> the decision to join or not join a movement will be mediated by the salience of the identity invoked by the movement and by the support or lack thereof that the recruit receives from those persons who normally serve to sustain or reinforce the identity in question (1993, p. 647).

In other words, the decision to join or not join a social movement is oftentimes determined by the potential participants seeing themselves (their identity) currently involved in the movement. Understanding this, the organizers of the #ShareTheMicNow campaign used collaboration as a means to amplify the voices of Black women, but to also get unlikely participants involved. With an overwhelming outpour of positivity found in the comments of the posts to the campaign's Instagram account and the live videos highlighted, it could be assumed that this was a successful endeavor. Of course, this cannot be determined solely based on social media comments.

Conclusion

Americans were forced to tackle two pandemics: COVID-19 and racism during the first half of 2020. Three deaths of unarmed Black people (Ahmaud Arbery, Breonna Taylor, and George Floyd) over the span of a few months prompted a resurgence of the Black Lives Matter movement both online and offline. Although the deaths of Arbery and Floyd received much attention from the media, Taylor's death was not publicized nearly as much. Sesko and Biernat (2010) write, "invisibility is a unique form of discrimination" (p. 360). The lack of media attention surrounding Taylor's death, in comparison to both Arbery and Floyd, illuminated the intersectional invisibility of Black women and their voices. Created for the purpose of amplifying the voices of Black women, four organizers (two White women and two Black women) initiated the #SharetheMicNow campaign. This campaign suggested that relationships between White women of power and Black women are a step in the right direction in the fight for social justice.

The #ShareTheMicNow campaign used "discursive protest on social media united through a hashtagged word, phrase or sentence" (Yang, 2016, p.13) to promote dialogue and collaboration during a time of heightened awareness of racial injustice. Through mass self-communication (Castells, 2015), Black women discussed allyship, the Black experience, racism, anti-racism, Whiteness, activism, and ways to move forward. In a recent study, Edrington and Lee (2018) found that although it is important to share information and calls to action, using social media as a community-building function is more likely to actually grow a community through amplification. The amplification of Black women and their voices through the collaboration of White and Black women proved to be successful in that it helped to create dialogue, cultivate identity, and build a community of people willing to get uncomfortable, learn, and do the work needed to end racism and racial injustices that affect the Black community. The use of social media and the hashtag function helped to move these conversations in spaces they otherwise would not be invited in. This is not only evident by the comments found under the posts and highlighted live videos, but by the creation of other #ShareTheMicNow Instagram pages both nationally and internationally. Beyond June 10, 2020, activists in Minnesota, Birmingham, the UK, Texas, Australia, Detroit, the Netherlands, Italy, Washington D.C., Charlotte, and Kentucky took up this initiative and decided to #KeepSharingTheMic.

References

Anderson, M., Barthel, M., Perrin, A., & Vogels, E. A. (2020, June 10). #BlackLivesMatter surges on Twitter after George Floyd's death. *Pew Research Center*. Retrieved from https://www.pewresearch.org/fact-tank/2020/06/10/blacklivesmatter-surges-on-twitter-after-george-floyds-death/

Barnett, B. M. (1993). Invisible southern black women leaders in the civil rights movement: The triple constraints of gender, race, and class. *Gender and Society*, *7*(2), 162–182.

Broome, B. (2009). Dialogue theories. In S. W. Littlejohn, & K. A. Foss (Eds.), *Encyclopedia of communication theory* (Vol. 1, pp. 302–306). Thousand Oaks, CA. SAGE Publications, Inc., https://www.doi.org/10.4135/9781412959384.n111

Castells, M. (2015). *Networks of outrage and hope: Social movements in the internet age, 2nd Ed.* Cambridge, UK: Polity Press.

Edrington, C. L., & Lee, N. M. (2018). Tweeting a social movement: Black Lives Matter and its use of Twitter to share information, promote action, and build community. *Journal of Public Interest Communications*, *2*(2), 289–306.

Gallagher, V. J., & Zagacki, K. S. (2005). Visibility and rhetoric: The power of visual images in Norman Rockwell's depictions of civil rights. *Quarterly Journal of Speech*, *91*(2), 175–200.

Kuo, R. (2018). Racial justice activist hashtags: Counterpublics and discourse circulation. *New Media & Society*, *20*(2), 495–514. doi:10.1177/1461444816663485

McAdam, D., & Paulsen, R. (1993). Specifying the relationship between social ties and activism. *American Journal of Sociology*, *99*, 640–667.

Purdie-Vaughns, V., & Eibach, R. P. (2008). Intersectional Invisibility: The distinctive advantages and disadvantages of multiple subordinate-group identities. *Sex Roles*, *59*(5–6), 377–391. doi:10.1007/s11199-008-9424-4

Sesko, A. K., & Biernat, M. (2010). Prototypes of race and gender: The invisibility of Black women. *Journal of Experimental Social Psychology*, *46*, 356–360.

ShareTheMicNow (@sharethemicnow). (2020). Posts [Instagram profile]. Instagram. Retrieved January 18, 2021, from https://www.instagram.com/sharethemicnow/

ShareTheMicNow (@sharethemicnow). (2020). Highlights [Instagram profile]. Instagram. Retrieved January 18, 2021, from https://www.instagram.com/stories/highlights/17875773961704970/

Singer, J. (2020, June 5). Breonna Taylor should be celebrating her 27th birthday. Here's how to help bring her killers to justice. *Glamour*. Retrieved from https://www.glamour.com/story/breonna-taylor-birthday-campaign

Sobre-Denton, M. (2016). Virtual intercultural bridgework: Social media, virtual cosmopolitanism, and activist community-building. *New Media and Society*, 1715–1731.

Sommerfeldt, E. (2008). Activism, relationship building, and the internet: The case of MoveOn.org. *Presented at the National Communication Association*, San Diego, CA.

Taylor, M., Kent, M., & White, W. (2001). How activist organizations are using the internet to build relationships. *Public Relations Review*, *27*(3), 263–263.

Yang, G. (2016). Narrative agency in hashtag activism: The case of #BlackLivesMatter. *Media and Communication*, *4*(4), 13–17.

Part II: **Conflict Communication on Social Media**

Malaka Friedman

Chapter 7
The Right to Tweet Freely: Citizen-Government Social Media Conflict

Abstract: This chapter explores the publicness of conflict by exploring the question of whether conflict online is a public or private matter. Using *Knight First Amendment Institute at Columbia University vs. Trump* as a case study, this chapter explores how Twitter was used by President Trump when engaging with individuals during his presidential campaign and in his presidency. President Trump blocked several individuals from his public Twitter account, effectively treating the space as a private rather than a public forum. The resulting court case and the continuing challenges to its ruling provides insights into how public citizens and political figures in power navigate conflict in online spaces, while also providing implications for future expectations of conflict communication in those spaces.

Keywords: Twitter, public vs. private, hierarchy, imagined audiences, socio-political conflict

Introduction

On January 8, 2021, Twitter officially suspended the @realDonaldTrump account permanently due to "the risk of further incitement of violence." The violence Twitter was referencing was the Capitol insurrection that had taken place two days earlier, which many individuals felt was due in part to Donald Trump using his platform to urge his followers to challenge the recent United States election results. In the aftermath of violence and the deaths of five individuals, many social media platforms concluded that Donald Trump's misuse of his platform contributed to his supporters storming the United States Capitol. In a presidency notable for unprecedented use of social media from the beginning of his campaign, Donald Trump spent the last two weeks of his presidency barred from his preferred method of communication.

In 2016 Donald Trump was elected the 45th president of the United States. While well known as a public figure, Trump was able to interact with social media in a way that was afforded to private citizens and with that the rights often associated with social media communication. Trump's method of conflict resolution was primarily through the blocking function used on Twitter, a common practice amongst social media users, in response to those who disagreed with him or whom he decided not to address. This practice was kept through the transition to his presidency, with Trump blocking social media users online with a click of a button at least until the legal case

https://doi.org/10.1515/9783110687262-008

of *Knight First Amendment Institute at Columbia University vs. Trump* (2018). Several Twitter users who were blocked by Trump challenged the former President's right to restrict their ability to engage with him in the public space of social media, predicated on the idea that his social media account constituted a "public forum." This case exemplifies the shift in the perception of social media as a public versus a private forum, with implications for how individuals manage conflict on social media. Considering the role of participation in a public space with regards to government, and the subsequent censoring of a political figure in the face of conflict, there could be future implications for how users interact with government officials or others in positions of power and whether these social media spaces are indeed public or private. Understanding this case study, and the subsequent events that occurred during this presidency over social media, will undoubtedly be explored in years to come. This chapter serves as a start to this conversation by demonstrating how this case study illustrates the way social media can influence and facilitate participation in socio-political conflict.

Social Media as Public versus Private

Public methods of communication are not a new concept to humans. One merely needs to look towards the use of forums themselves from ancient Rome to the political debates in town halls today. Public spaces allow "strangers [to] co-exist, a setting over which individuals have little control" which can often lead to issues. (de Souza e Silva & Frith, 2012, 54). Social media as a space seems to fit this definition of a public space at first glance, though there are some caveats to defining social media spaces as fully public. Take for example the embedding of Facebook comments underneath a news article, thus allowing individuals to engage with each other in a public manner over the topic at hand. While this instance is a common enough practice, it is also equally as common for a news site to not allow any public posts as well. This move can be seen in NPR's 2016 decision to shift public discussions off its website itself and to allow "social media to pick up the slack" (Jensen, 2016). This move makes a news website a private, or in other words, "a controlled space . . . where interactions with others tend to happen on terms that are more comfortable to the individual" (de Souza e Silva & Frith, 2012, 54). In this NPR example social media is seen as a way for public discourse to still occur, but to be controlled in some manner. As Baym and boyd (2011) note, social media is a quasi-public space where the "publicness" can be difficult to determine and therefore the level of conflict that may result is hard to predict.

Part of the challenge of these social dynamics is due to the ambiguity around who is participating in social media platforms; or, as Marwick and boyd (2011) refer to it, the "imagined audiences" at play online. Imagined audiences have always played a part in social networks that emerge in online spaces. A popular place for communication building prior to Web2.0 (social media) was the introduction of MUDs or multi-user dungeons/dimensions. Within these online communities, there was a social control in place in order to establish how social dynamics were allowed to play out. Reid (1999) analyzed how in these spaces the individual with the most power usually controlled the platform, emphasizing again the role of control when it comes to power in seemingly public spaces. Similar to how social media operates now, the level of pseudonymity online allowed users to be more open in these public spaces but also allowed more opportunities for negative emotional responses to influence these spaces. Reid quotes Hiltz and Turoff (1978) by noting how users within these spaces come to feel that their very best and closest friends are members of their electronic group, whom they seldom or never see" (p.11). In essence, MUDs allowed participants to create imagined audiences that gave individuals a semblance of social control in these public platforms. Understanding the imagined audiences similarly in social media could help to provide insights into the tweets noted in *Knight First Amendment Institute at Columbia University vs. Trump* (2018) through the eyes of the plaintiffs and defendants. This has implications for examining how each side views Twitter as a potential public/private space in the context of citizen-government communication and conflict.

Social Media in Politics

Social media has allowed politicians in the United States to more easily engage with individuals. In some ways, this level of engagement can be attributed to the rise of the internet itself, especially given the ubiquity and accessibility of social media. A well-known example of the media's effect on elections would be the first televised United States presidential debate between John F. Kennedy and Richard Nixon in 1960, which is widely believed to have influenced Kennedy's win over Nixon. The introduction of visual media in this manner has since influenced the manner in which television is used, with ads for politicians being common practice, for example. It was only a matter of time for future media to also have such an effect. For social media use in the United States the most prominent example was Barack Obama's 2008 presidential bid, during which his campaign used a variety of social media platforms to engage voters from different audiences. Social media allows for a context collapse of the personal and professional aspects of a politician's identities, in some cases a balancing act that allows two identities to combine together in an online space (Marwick & boyd, 2011). Obama further challenged notions of space, specifically political space, by creating the first virtual town hall meeting via Twitter in July 2011, which challenged the idea of a physical town hall taking place for only those physically nearby or able to watch through digital devices. This virtual meeting allowed users to tweet at Obama and gain answers to questions about his potential presidency. While this new use of media did challenge spaces, it was still "self-selective" technology (Hong, 2013) as it was used strictly in a specific context with ties to the idea of a physical space. As such the way this space operated in this context was reflective of the norms of a typical town hall meeting while creating a hybrid experience that opened up the imagined audience. By situating this space as a town hall, this social media space was connected to a local forum and Obama was able to construct the power dynamics of this space as it tied to governmental hierarchies in an abstract way. The manner in which users engaged with him as a consequence was informed by norms established in a town hall, such as asking open-ended questions rather than making blanket statements of opinion that were made consciously with regard to Obama's hierarchy as a political user online.

Since Obama's presidency, the effect of social media has now led to what is called a Twitter Influence Index, which notes how the Twitter habits of election candidates may affect the outcome of a general election. Compared to the days of television being the biggest indicator of potential election success, Lee (2013) notes how the immediate feedback of Twitter allows it to be more effective as a tool for politicians to engage with potential voters and to allow voters to feel more connected to a candidate. Additionally, the more "high-interactivity" of a Twitter page, the stronger the social presence and positive evaluations of a candidate are likely to happen. Kruikemeier (2014) supports this notion as their research has found that the number of Twitter followers often predicts more votes for a candidate rather than the number of Twitter posts. Interestingly, Kruikemeier notes additional questions of space and identity by stating that Twitter was used by candidates as a way to explore their "private persona," which they elaborate could refer to a candidate's emotions, private life, or professional activities they conduct on Twitter. Again, this idea of what is private or public when it comes to digital spaces is broadly defined, supporting the notion that spaces such as Twitter are more of a hybrid space. While the identity Kruikemeier notes is private, it is still available to users for public consumption, which implies that once a user has status within a hierarchy, physical or digital, their information is considered public.

Twitter as a social media platform however currently resides as a hybrid space between private and public and therefore can be influenced by physical markers of power, such as governments. One way this influence can be seen is how laws can be adapted to the nature of temporal social media posts. Take the Presidential Records Act of 1978, an act that is meant to preserve official records of documents that occur over a presidency and vice presidency, and how it was meant to primarily address physical documents and has had to be amended in the realm of digital documents. In the realm of social media, this was done during Obama's presidency through social media content being transferred to the National Archives and Records Administration (NARA) where information regarding his and Michelle Obama's (in her role as First Lady of the United States) information was collected. Acker and Kreisberg (2017) note that this type of data collection is difficult to do as social media data is in some ways not considered "open." The authors refer to this type of data collection as a "kind of sandbox" that required Twitter handles associated with the Obamas (@POTUS44 and

@FLOTUS44) to be turned off to prevent data from falling through. This falling through of data occurs as individuals who tag these accounts in posts may have private accounts that may not be seen, meaning that posts cannot be archived as a result and thus cannot be saved as public information. Information will inherently never show a complete picture as a result, especially when considering how deleted accounts or posts lends itself to a loss of potential public data. As a result, only a snapshot of data collection of a presidency online in these formats can be presented with the understanding it will shift over time. The consideration of social media in governments and this shifting is still rather new, with the @WhiteHouse Twitter handle only coming into existence in 2007 and the @POTUS handle being officially verified in 2015. Considering this shift and what it means to be a president in the age of social media led to Obama being considered the first social media president, emphasizing his public role and power within the space of Twitter and other social media platforms.

In contrast, this context collapse of personal and private identities was not as effectively seen within the Trump presidency as it was in the Obama presidency. Part of this reasoning could be because Obama's posts were primarily done by his campaign staff, emphasizing his professional identity in both accounts, and the relative newness of using social media accounts to represent government accounts online. In contrast, Trump's posts were seemingly done primarily by himself and he often used his personal account over the White House official account, which could have been due to his presence on Twitter starting in 2009. His original Twitter account was created well before the @POTUS Twitter handle was even verified and only two years after the @WhiteHouse Twitter handle existed. As a result, Trump's Twitter presence was being established at the same time as the accounts that he would then be able to access in 2016. Because Trump had an existing social media presence and his official presidential account and personal accounts were linked together, in February 2017 the National Archives and Records Administration declared that Trump's use of social media would be covered under the Presidential Records Act of 1978. Trump's tendency to additionally use his personal account to announce content that would normally be under his official presidential account could also have played a part in this determination. The dramatic shift in this presidency in comparison to the first social media presence of a United States President – that of President Obama – needs to be closely analyzed, especially as it may set the standard for the way future presidencies are managed in digital spaces.

Case Study of Knight First Amendment Institute at Columbia University vs. Trump

Prominent figures like politicians already have a hierarchy in in-person public spaces, which carries forward into digital spaces in the classifications of verification processes for some platforms, such as Twitter's use of blue check marked accounts to identify a user as a person of public interest. The figure's hierarchy is mimicked in these online spaces, granting them the ability to have a larger platform (though given their verified status they may already have had a larger platform), with all the benefits granted to individual users. With the 2018 case of *Knight First Amendment Institute at Columbia University vs. Trump,* however, Donald Trump's blocking of certain Twitter users through his personal account of @realDonaldTrump was proven to be a violation of the First Amendment rights of the American public. This decision made by the U.S. Court of Appeals for the Second Circuit not only confirmed that social media users' abilities have shifted but also cemented Twitter's platform as a public one with regards to political discourse. Based on statements and documents provided by the Knight Institute, users were still blocked from interacting with @realDonaldTrump when it was active, suggesting that whether Twitter is a publicly or privately controlled space will be a continuing discussion in US politics. Current research on social media focuses on the role of audiences in public interaction. For example, Baym and boyd (2012) discuss how audiences guide the types of posts users made, while Marwick and boyd (2011) take this analysis a step further by discussing how the perceived imagined audiences affect these public interactions. I use Marwick and boyd (2011), as well as Lee (2013) to guide my analysis, as there is now a shift in the way that public spaces are defined in the digital age when it comes to online interaction with politicians, and in this specific case, those who are also celebrities.

While the case *Knight First Amendment Institute at Columbia University vs. Trump* (2018) is tenuous given the blocking of the @realDonaldTrump account, I intend to use the data available based on the original court documents for this chapter. Through data analysis of the seven users noted in the original complaint filed, I intend to analyze how ideas of audience and "publicness" have played a part in the shift towards free speech online. I use the Knight Institute's websites to provide context to this case, as they include the original law documents filed in addition to testimonials provided by the seven plaintiffs. The additional context provided here will allow me to provide a more comprehensive view of the individuals involved in the case, especially in regard to hierarchies on Twitter's platform and the sense of control that users feel they have in these spaces.

The limitations of this case study are that while this is a landmark case for social media with regard to what is considered public or private, it does ignore potential other users who may have been blocked online by Trump. Currently, there are almost 50 Twitter users who have reported being blocked by Trump online, but this number does not reflect users who may not have reported to the Knight Institute or are perhaps seeking legal advice through a different entity. This study also is very centric on the political system of the United States, which does note freedom of speech as a right to its citizens. Social media censorship is a widely debated topic in several countries, especially given the role of social media in uprisings such as Arab Spring. There is the possibility that in other countries where social media access is controlled by governments, this research may allow individuals to consider ways to challenge their access to the publicness of social media, especially given how hierarchies appear to be transferring from the physical to the digital realm.

The Public versus the Public?

All seven users in the original complaint filed by the Knight Institute were verified Twitter users with follower counts ranging from 5,000 followers to almost 88,000 followers. The majority of the users tended to have around 10,000 followers, which creates a significant public audience for the individual users. Given the number of followers and wide scope of their potential audience, it stands to reason that the number of followers could have influenced Trump to block these individuals versus those with fewer followers. Regardless of the exact number, each of the seven users were well below Trump's follower count of 56.2 million (as of December 2018). The seven plaintiffs/users include Philip Cohen, Eugene Gu, Holly Figueroa, Nicholas Pappas, Joseph Papp, Rebecca Buckwalter, and Brandon Neely. These individuals have a range of professions and all noted their experiences of being blocked through the Knight Institute. Table 7.1 presents the individuals, their profession, follower count, and the specific tweet that led to their blocking as reported to the Knight Institute.

Table 7.1: Plaintiffs in the Knight Institute Lawsuit.

Name	Twitter Handle	Profession	Follower Count (At time of complaint letter)	Blocked Text Tweet (Date of tweet)
Rebecca Buckwalter-Poza	@rpbp	Writer and Legal Analyst	5,247	"To be fair you didn't win the WH: Russia won it for you." (6/6/17)
Philip Cohen	@familyunequal	University Professor	9,900	"Corrupt Incompetent Authoritarian. And then there are the policies. Resist." (6/6/17)
Holly Figueroa	@AynRandPaulRyan	Songwriter and Political Organizer	87,600	"This is pretty much how the whole world sees you. #AMJoy #SundayMorning." (5/28/17)
Eugene Gu	@eugenegu	Surgeon	9,300	"Covfefe: The same guy who doesn't proofread his Twitter handles the nuclear button." (6/18/17)

Table 7.1 (continued)

Name	Twitter Handle	Profession	Follower Count (At time of complaint letter)	Blocked Text Tweet (Date of tweet)
Neely	@BrandonTXNeely	Police Officer	6,700	"Congrats and now black lung won't be covered under #TrumpCare." (6/12/17)
Joseph Papp	@joepabike	Author and Former Cyclist	11,600	"Why didn't you attend your #PittsburghNotParis rally in DC, Sir? #fakeleader." (6/3/17)
Nicholas Pappas	@Pappiness	Comedy Writer	37,400	"Trump is right. The government should protect the people. That's why the courts are protecting us from him." (6/5/17)

Within the lawsuit itself, Twitter was defined as a "public forum" or "interactive space" that allowed the plaintiffs to explore their First Amendment rights when they engaged in conversation with Trump's personal Twitter handle. All users previously had commented on Trump's posts either through replying directly to some of his posts or by retweeting direct messages at his personal Twitter handle. All users were noted in the complaint as being "active" participants when it came to interacting with the @realDonaldTrump handle, with the exception of Gu who was noted to be more of an occasional user. The responses these users posted were often picked up by other Twitter handles through likes or retweets, which increased the audience for the original post. As such, the imagined audience for these tweets can be perceived to be limitless, specifically as responses are not just tied to the follower count of the individuals but also to the follower accounts of those who engaged with the plaintiff's original posts through a matter or liking, retweeting, and commenting. Adding another layer to the possible imagined audiences for this post is the tendency for social media platforms to filter posts based on popularity or status themselves. According to the Knight Institute, Neely even noted that due to his position as a "verified" Twitter user, his tweets were often mentioned early on in @realDonaldTrump's postings or threads (a link of conversations to the original post). Of the seven users, Neely was the only one to acknowledge his own digital hierarchy and subsequent influence on his potential imagined audience. Neely indicated that as such his post may have brought additional attention to his account and led to his blocking. He was not the only plaintiff to be aware of their digital persona and influencing power on Twitter. Other plaintiffs, like Figueroa, acknowledged that they opted out of seeking a different account or handle to communicate with the @realDonaldTrump handle after their blocking as they felt that they had built up a certain audience and did not want to risk losing their status in this space. This status further reinforces the power of digital hierarchies of communication on social media, with these verified users being more prominent within a public space.

Through the Knight Institute, all seven plaintiffs noted their frustration with being blocked, as well as their reasoning behind participating in the lawsuit. Several noted that Twitter is a place for them to speak out and connect with other people within their networks. This point was especially noted by Pappas, Buckwalter, Gu, and Cohen as all noted that Twitter allows them to explore their personal and professional identities at the same time. Cohen for instance noted that within the scope of his academic circles his potential audience is limited to those who are geographically present within the area, whereas this audience is expanded on social media. He further elaborated that "Twitter gives me the broadest audience most immediately," which allows him to engage with others in a larger public sense rather than just those within the scope of academia. In comparison, Buckwalter and Pappas note that as writers and journalists their professional identities should guarantee access as they view seeing public posts as a professional and personal responsibility. Pappas took this one step further by stating that "my Twitter account stands for my identity, demonstrating my views and reputation." Hierarchy, especially in a digital space, mattered to all the individuals who perceived themselves to have more weight in this space than a more physical one. Unlike a physical space, all users felt comfortable engaging with the handle in ways that are reminiscent of Reid's (1999) analysis of MUDs when it comes to posting conversations at certain individuals. In the case of this lawsuit, a few users continually challenged the @realDonaldTrump handle with Pappas and Figueroa noting in the Knight Institute's documents that they monitor posts by Trump in order to create responses. Since the decision of the case, Figueroa even uses this win as part of her bio information.

While it is important to consider the identities of the plaintiffs discussed here, equal attention must be placed on examining Trump's identity within Twitter as a space. In terms of physical hierarchies, Trump is ranked highly when it comes to the government, but he is also in the unique position of having a presence online due to his position as a public figure prior to his presidency. Trump is not the first president to move from celebrity status to one within the realm of politics. Ribke (2015) analyzed similar case studies of Brazilian politicians who moved from their status as celebrities to politicians. Ribke refers to the status of celebrity as a system, one that contains its own hierarchies separate from political ones. The merging of Trump's celebrity and political identities can be referred to as a sort of "multiplicity," (Turkle, 1995) meaning that Trump has rapidly cycled with his various identities online, leading to a possible blurring of his affordances of being a private citizen versus a public citizen prior to the 2016 election. Adding another layer to the sense of identity in this public space is how Trump attempts to create a private space through his personal Twitter handle, through exhibiting the same behavior online as he did before his election. This online communication is similar to Turkle's case study of MUDs and a user referred to as Stewart who would "act out" versus "work through" his actions online. Turkle defines "acting out" as occurring when "we stage our old conflicts in new settings, we reenact our past in fruitless repetition" (p.200). Acting out perceived hierarchies in digital spaces gets tricky, as it can be considered a new setting, especially one where the public nature is always apparent to users. When considering public versus private, I look at how Aristotle considers the concept of home as a space. Aristotle notes how the private home (*oikos)* is a different space than the public one of politics (*polis)* and as such, conversations that exist within certain contexts are always public. In their argument, the Knight Institute made a compelling argument for social media as a public space when they noted that social media platforms, such as Facebook and Twitter are "perhaps the most powerful mechanisms available to a private citizen to make his or her voice heard." This supports Aristotle's view by claiming that as long as conversations are political, they will always be public and subjected to the norms established by society.

Conclusion and Future Implications

As the world continues to shift in the definition of public and private spaces there needs to be more clear recommendations for how users engage online with one another, specifically when users hold a higher governmental status that gives them influence in online conflict. Prior to the banning of Trump's Twitter account, all seven plaintiffs were unblocked from Trump's Twitter account but there were still almost 50 users (if not more) who remained banned. Part of this reasoning may relate to the idea of "thin trust" put forward by Robert Putnam or a "generalized trust in others to do what they are supposed to do" (de Souza e Silva & Frith, 2012, p.73). Within the gray area of social media there is not an explicit rule for how individuals within public governmental offices should engage in conflict in an online public space. As such there may not be a solution for how public versus public spaces are navigated in terms of social media and physical differences of influence, political or otherwise.

Until recently, social media platforms like Twitter loosely addressed conflict by reinforcing their support of the freedom of speech of their users. With the transition to current President Joe Biden's presidency and subsequent social media identity, the role of government and conflict in social media spaces remains as uncertain as ever. Twitter has shown that they have taken a stance on the conflict, affirming that in the private/public dichotomous spaces of social media, Twitter retains control of how conflict is mitigated online. Whether this stance will remain the same for future governments will have to be determined, especially when it comes to conflict between governmental entities and public citizens. Looking at cases like the *Knight First Amendment Institute at Columbia University vs. Trump* (2018) and considering the events of January 2021 remain crucial in our efforts to understand how we as a society change to adapt to the spaces in which we engage.

References

Acker, A., & Kriesberg, A. (2017). Tweets may be archived: Civic engagement, digital preservation and Obama white house social media data. Proceedings of the Association for Information Science and Technology, 54(1): 1–9. DOI:10.1002/pra2.2017.14505401001

Baym, N. K., & boyd, d. (2012). Socially Mediated Publicness: An Introduction. *Journal of Broadcasting & Electronic Media, 56*(3): 320–329. DOI:10.1080/08838151.2012.705200

Hiltz, S. R., & Turoff, M. (1978). The network nation: Human communication via computer. Mit Press.

Hong, S. (2013). Who benefits from twitter? social media and political competition in the U.S. house of representatives. *Government Information Quarterly, 30*(4): 464–472. DOI:10.1016/j.giq.2013.05.009

Jensen, E. (2016, August 17). *NPR website to get rid of comments*. NPR. Retrieved September 1, 2021, from https://www.npr.org/sections/publiceditor/2016/08/17/489516952/npr-website-to-get-rid-of-comments.

Knight Institute v. Trump – Lawsuit Challenging President Trump's Blocking of Critics on Twitter. (n.d.). Retrieved from https://knightcolumbia.org/content/knight-institute-v-trump-lawsuit-challenging-president-trumps-blocking-critics-twitter

Kruikemeier, S. (2014). How political candidates use twitter and the impact on votes. *Computers in Human Behavior, 34*: 131–139. DOI:10.1016/j.chb.2014.01.025

Lee, E. (2013). Effectiveness of politicians' soft campaign on twitter versus TV: Cognitive and experiential routes. *Journal of Communication, 63*(5): 953–974. DOI:10.1111/jcom.12049

Marwick, A. E., & boyd, D. (2011). I tweet honestly, I tweet passionately: Twitter users, context collapse, and the imagined audience. *New Media & Society, 13*(1): 114–133. https://doi.org/10.1177/1461444810365313

Putnam, R. D. (2000). *Bowling alone: The collapse and revival of American community*. New York: Simon & Schuster.

Reid, E. (1999). Hierarchy and power: Social control in cyberspace. In M. A. Smith & P. Kollock (eds.), *Communities in Cyberspace* (107–134). New York: Routledge.

Ribke, N. (2015). Entertainment politics: Brazilian celebrities' transition to politics, recent history and main patterns. *Media, Culture & Society, 37*(1): 35–49. DOI:10.1177/0163443714549087

Silva, A. D., & Frith, J. (2012). *Mobile Interfaces in Public Spaces: Locational Privacy, Control, and Urban Sociability*. New York: Routledge.

Turkle, S. (1995). *Life on the Screen: Computers and the Human Spirit*. Chapter Seven: Aspects of the self (177–209). Cambridge, MA: MIT Press. Retrieved from https://about.twitter.com/en_us/values/civic-engagement.html

Ioana A. Cionea & Amy Janan Johnson

Chapter 8
Conflict Management on Facebook: Relationships between Conflict Styles, Incivility, Conflict Tactics, and Outcomes

Abstract: This chapter reports the results of a quantitative study (*N* = 417) examining conflict management on Facebook during the latter part of 2020 in the United States. Specifically, the study investigated how individuals' conflict styles related to their use of integrative or distributive conflict management tactics as well as the conflict's level of incivility. Furthermore, tactics and incivility were connected to the conflict's perceived resolvability and satisfaction with how the conflict was managed. Results revealed that conflict was managed in two main ways. First, collaboration and compromise predicted integrative tactics, which predicted resolvability and satisfaction positively. The conflict's perceived level of incivility made a significant impact in participants' perceptions about the conflict's outcomes. Second, accommodation, competition, and avoidance predicted distributive tactics, which predicted satisfaction with conflict management negatively. These results are discussed in the context of conflict on social networking sites and online incivility.

Keywords: Facebook, conflict management, conflict resolution, conflict styles, incivility

Introduction

Interpersonal conflict (conflict hereafter) occurs frequently on social networking sites (SNS), such as Facebook (Cionea et al., 2017; Halpern & Gibbs, 2013), where disagreements are commonplace (Sveningsson, 2014). Facebook is the most popular social media site, with more than 190 million users and roughly 60% of all social media traffic (Tankovska, 2021a, 2021b), and about 2.8 billion worldwide users (Facebook, Inc., 2021). "Facebook is well known, used frequently, and permits argumentative exchanges between individuals in the form of status updates, comments to other people's posts (or one's own), private messaging, or group discussions" (Cionea et al., 2017, p. 438). This ubiquitous social network has permeated many areas of people's personal lives. During the COVID-19 pandemic, as individuals sought connections with others, Facebook witnessed a significant increase in usage (Koeze & Popper, 2020). In the United States (U.S.) during 2020, this health crisis, coupled with Presidential elections, rising unemployment, and social protests, created a charged sociopolitical context

https://doi.org/10.1515/9783110687262-009

that, without a doubt, affected how individuals engaged with others on Facebook, including how conflicts emerged and unfolded.

The goal of this chapter is to examine conflict on Facebook between individuals in the U.S. during the latter part of 2020. Specifically, we investigate the relationships between individuals' conflict styles and the tactics they used during a conflict on Facebook, and whether these tactics related to how resolvable individuals perceived the conflict to be and how satisfied they were with how they managed the conflict. Numerous scholars have argued that online discussions are rife with incivility, which has become "a toxic feature of online political talk" (Rossini, 2020, p. 161). Therefore, we also investigate the relationships among incivility, tactics, and outcomes of conflict on Facebook to untangle further the role of incivility on SNS. This overall focus can enhance our knowledge about conflict management on SNS, which can yield useful information about how to engage in more constructive exchanges on social media.

Conflict and Incivility on Facebook

Conflict has been defined as "an interactive process manifested in incompatibility, disagreement, or dissonance within or between social entities" (Rahim, 2001, p. 18) or as "a situation in which interdependent people express (manifest or latent) differences in satisfying their individual needs and interests, and they experience interference from each other in accomplishing these goals" (Donohue & Kolt, 1992, p. 4). Despite a variety of definitions, Putnam (2006) summarizes the common components of conflict: 1) a focus on incompatible interests or goals; 2) some type of expressed or unexpressed struggle; 3) some degree of interdependence between parties; 4) potentially verbal and nonverbal communication between parties; and 5) often limited or scarce resources. In this study, we conceptualize conflict as an interaction between parties who have (perceived) incompatible beliefs, values, or goals.

How conflict occurs on social media is influenced by the features of platforms such as Facebook. Treem and Leonardi (2012) discuss certain features that distinguish how interactions progress. For example, messages are persistent on these channels, rather than quickly disappearing (except for Snapchat). Individuals have high visibility on social media, with the ability to fashion the impressions they send by sharing or not sharing certain personal information. Furthermore, asynchronicity means that people can leave comments or respond to messages at their leisure, providing a way for individuals to conduct research on the topics discussed or cool down between comments, options that might not exist in face-to-face contact. However, social media also has spreadability, which means that messages can spread quickly and that individuals may lose control over their content once they have published it on a SNS (boyd, 2014).

Although different types of SNS have commonalities, as discussed above, they also differ in factors that may affect how conflict occurs in these settings. For instance,

Facebook tends to connect individuals who know each other to a certain degree offline as well, which could affect how individuals choose to engage in conflict, given that their social networks could see their comments. Cionea et al. (2017), for instance, found that about two-thirds of those who argued online had also argued about the same topics in person. Roughly half of these participants also expected to interact in person in the future with the other individuals involved in the Facebook argument they described.

There is a limited body of research that has examined how individuals engage in conflict on Facebook. An early study found that 30% of individuals claimed to have had a conflict on a social media site. Conflicts on Facebook may be particularly relevant to individuals because Facebook's newsfeed leads to context collapse (boyd, 2008), meaning people who are usually separated in their social lives are all gathered in one space and can be contacted easily through Facebook (Kim & Ahn, 2013). Due to this context collapse, issues of self-presentation tend to be particularly relevant to Facebook conflict. For example, Kim and Ahn found that conflict resulted when people's self-presentation behaviors were disrupted by other Facebook friends. Similarly, Chen (2015) found that threats to one's positive face on Facebook brought on by others' insults led individuals to retaliate. Several authors have noted, however, that conflicts on Facebook tend to revolve around public issues (i.e., general topics of interest that could be discussed with anyone, as they do not pertain to a specific interpersonal relationship; A. Johnson, 2002), such as religion or politics. Cionea et al. (2017) reported that most arguments on Facebook were, indeed, about such topics. How individuals engage in conflicts about these topics on Facebook can differ, though. Sleeper et al. (2013) found that people reported avoiding topics they believed were controversial. Individuals with higher levels of political interest were more likely to engage in conversations about politics with those who disagreed with them (Lu & Lee, 2021). Thus, the topics that spark conflict and how individuals behave in such conflicts on Facebook vary somewhat, which can further affect social media users' approaches to such conflicts.

A major concern in online discussions on SNS is incivility, which has been defined in various ways, ranging from profanity, crude language, and foul language to unnecessarily disrespectful discussion tones, impoliteness, or intolerance (Chen et al., 2019; Coe et al., 2014). Scholars have pointed out that features of mediated communication that encourage communication can also function to increase aggressive behavior, flaming, and enraged discussions (Coe et al., 2014; Papacharissi, 2002). Previous research has confirmed these predictions, finding that online discussions are rife with incivility. For instance, Coe and colleagues (2014) analyzed comments posted during a three-week period on a local newspaper website. Of the total 6,400 comments examined, "more than one out of every five comments was uncivil" (p. 673). Heavy topics with clear sides stirred more incivility, whereas those involving "a high-profile source with an identifiable partisan leaning (i.e., President Obama) generated the most incivility" (Coe et al., 2014, p. 673). In another instance, Weber Shandwick, Powell Tate, &

KRC Research found in their 2018 yearly survey that people from the U.S. experienced an average of 5.4 incivility encounters weekly on social media. Thus, incivility is widespread online, including on SNS such as Facebook, and situations of conflict are likely to elicit incivility.

Moreover, incivility has negative consequences. For instance, Sveningsson (2014) found that individuals were reluctant to argue with others about politics on Facebook as they feared being verbally abused, whereas Cionea et al. (2017) found that arguing on Facebook damaged individuals' relationship with those involved in the argument in about 20% of cases. Thus, incivility is likely to influence the way conflict evolves and its outcomes, fostering a climate of negativity and uncivil commentary, while also suppressing constructive discourse. We examine these possibilities further in this chapter.

Conflict Styles, Tactics, and Outcomes

Another important area of study pertains to how conflict is managed. The dual concern model of conflict proposes that individuals have relatively stable conflict styles, rooted in two overriding concerns: concern for the self and concern for the other (Blake & Mouton, 1964; Kilmann & Thomas, 1977). When considered together, these concerns yield five types of conflict styles: collaborating, accommodating, competing, avoiding, and compromising, which we examine to understand how individuals manage conflicts on Facebook.

A high concern for both the self and the other results in a *collaborating* conflict style. Known as a win-win approach, collaborating often requires effort from both parties to be enacted. A high concern for the other but not for the self results in an *accommodating* conflict style, in which the other person's wishes often determine the conflict's outcome. A *competing* conflict style involves the combination of high concern for the self and low concern for the other. Individuals who have this conflict style often see conflict as a win-lose situation, in which only one person can obtain what they want. A low concern for both the self and the other results in an *avoiding* conflict style, where individuals withdraw from the conflict. Finally, a mid-range on both self and other concerns results in a *compromising* conflict style, where individuals try to find middle ground, meaning neither individual obtains their ideal outcome from the conflict (Rahim, 1983a; Kilmann & Thomas, 1977). How one approaches conflict can be predicted by considering a person's conflict style.

The behaviors that individuals engage in during conflict revolve around different tactics that people use during such interactions. Cupach et al. (2010) define conflict tactics as, "an individual's specific action at a specific moment in the [conflict] interaction" (p. 46). Two types of commonly examined tactics are integrative and distributive, which we also focus on in this study to understand how individuals manage their Facebook conflicts.

Ohbuchi and Tedeschi (1997) define integrative tactics as "attempts to negotiate with the other, taking into account both parties' concerns," whereas distributive tactics are defined as "attempts to strongly assert one's own requests" (p. 2185). Canary et al. (2010) further assert that integrative tactics involve, "working *with* other people," whereas distributive tactics involve, "working *against* other people" (italics in original; p. 50). Therefore, we expect the conflict styles that focus on higher concern for the other person (i.e., collaborating, accommodating, compromising) or potentially a higher concern for relational maintenance (i.e., avoiding) to predict reported integrative tactic use, whereas the conflict style that is high on concern for the self but low on concern for the other (i.e., competing) to predict distributive tactics. In conjunction with the considerations about incivility explained previously, the following hypotheses are proposed:

H1: *Integrative tactics are predicted positively by the a) collaborating, b) accommodating, c) compromising, and d) avoiding conflict styles and negatively by the e) competing conflict style and f) incivility.*

H2: *Distributive tactics are predicted negatively by the a) collaborating, b) accommodating, c) compromising, and d) avoiding conflict styles and positively by the e) competing conflict style and f) incivility.*

It is not surprising that prior research has found integrative tactics were associated with positive outcomes, whereas distributive tactics were related to negative outcomes (e.g., Bevan et al., 2007). Research on serial arguments (i.e., repetitive conflicts about the same topic with the same person; K. Johnson & Roloff, 1998) has found consistent associations between the tactics arguers use and the outcomes these tactics (in combination with the goals pursued) have for variables such as the perceived resolvability of the argument or relational satisfaction (e.g., Bevan, 2014; Cionea, A. Johnson, & Bostwick, 2019; Hample et al., 2012). Perceived resolvability is an important variable to examine; it has been found to be a better predictor of relational quality than the frequency of a serial argument conflict (K. Johnson & Roloff, 1998). High levels of perceived resolvability can function as a buffer for the negative effects of conflict on relational quality (Roloff, 2009). Furthermore, conflict management has been associated with satisfaction in interpersonal relationships. Integrative approaches have been found to correlate positively with satisfaction, whereas distributive approaches have been associated with lower satisfaction (Cupach, 1982; Cionea, A. Johnson, & Bostwick, 2019). In light of these considerations, we examine whether conflict management tactics and incivility predict perceived resolvability of a Facebook conflict and satisfaction with the way one manages the conflict. The following hypotheses are proposed:

H3: *Perceived resolvability is predicted a) positively by integrative tactics and b) negatively by distributive tactics and c) incivility.*

H4: *Conflict management satisfaction is predicted a) positively by integrative tactics and b) negatively by distributive tactics and c) incivility.*

Method

Participants

Participants in the study were 417[1] adults from across the United States, aged 18 to 78 ($M = 33.59$, $SD = 15.90$). One hundred and thirty-eight were male, 271 were female, two indicated intersex, and six preferred not to answer the question. Most identified as White ($n = 298$), had a four-year college degree ($n = 120$) or some college education ($n = 144$), and lived in the West South-Central region of the United States (Arkansas, Louisiana, Oklahoma, and Texas, $n = 332$). One hundred and sixty-nine participants identified as Republican, 130 indicated Democrat, and 58 identified as Independent. Finally, participants reported varied occupations, such as analyst, business owner, dentist, engineer, nurse, student, teacher, or real estate agent.

Procedures

Participants were recruited via snowball sampling by soliciting undergraduates in the Communication introductory course at the authors' university to share the survey with members of their networks. Eligibility included living in the U.S., being 18 or older, and having engaged in a conflict on Facebook with someone since August 1, 2020. This engagement was defined for them as "interacting with someone on Facebook about differences in [their] beliefs, values, or goals that seemed incompatible." Potential participants accessed an online survey open between November 4 and December 11, 2020. Those who passed eligibility questions and consented to participate then completed scale items assessing the variables of interest in this study and provided demographic information. When finished, participants could enter a drawing for one of four $25 Amazon gift cards. Median survey completion time was 15 minutes. The research was approved by the Institutional Review Board at the authors' university.

1 This is the final sample size, after data cleaning, which eliminated responses with less than 93% data, those that failed attention verification questions, or finished under five minutes.

Measures

All study variables were measured on a 7-point Likert type scale ranging from 1 = *strongly disagree* to 7 = *strongly agree*. Reliability coefficients, means, and standard deviations are included in Table 8.1.

Conflict Styles. How individuals handled disagreements with other people, in general, was assessed with Rahim's conflict style inventory ROCI-II (1983b), whose wording was adapted to reference other people. Twenty-eight items assessed the five styles: *collaborating* (seven items, e.g., "I try to investigate an issue with the other people to find a solution acceptable to us"), *accommodating* (six items, e.g., "I generally try to satisfy the needs of the other people"), *competing* (five items, e.g., "I use my influence to get my ideas accepted"), *avoiding* (six items, e.g., "I usually avoid open discussion of my differences with other people"), and *compromising* (four items, e.g., "I try to find a middle course to resolve an impasse").

Incivility. Incivility of the Facebook conflict was measured with seven items (those applicable to an online conflict) from Hample et al.'s (2009) measure of civility. Example items include, "The conflict involved negativity" or "The conflict involved successful problem-solving" (reverse-coded). Higher scores indicate more incivility.

Conflict Tactics. Eleven items adapted from Hample and Kruger's (2011) serial argument measure were used to capture conflict tactics. Six items assessed distributive tactics (e.g., "I wanted to win" or "I tried to defeat the other people involved in the conflict") and five items assessed integrative tactics (e.g., "I acknowledged and respected the needs and goals of the other people involved in the conflict" or "I aimed at a mutually beneficial solution").

Conflict Outcomes. *Perceived resolvability* of the conflict was assessed with six items from K. Johnson and Roloff's (1998) work on serial arguments, reworded for conflict. Items included, "I didn't think we would ever agree on the issue that sparked the conflict" or, "I thought that a productive solution for the conflict could occur." Higher scores indicate higher perceptions of resolvability. *Conflict management satisfaction* was measured by adapting five items from K. Johnson and Roloff (1998) and Cionea, A. Johnson, and Bostwick (2019). Examples include, "I was satisfied with how I managed the conflict" and "I felt bad about the things I said to the other people during the conflict." Higher scores indicate higher conflict management satisfaction.

Results

H1 proposed that integrative tactics would be predicted positively by the collaborating (H1a), accommodating (H1b), compromising (H1c), and avoiding (H1d) conflict styles and negatively by the competing (H1e) conflict style and incivility (H1f). A hierarchical

Table 8.1: Descriptive Statistics and Reliability Scores for Study Variables.

Variable	Cronbach's alpha	M	SD
Collaborating conflict style	.79	5.43	0.80
Accommodating conflict style	.78	4.22	1.01
Competing conflict style[a]	.80	4.20	1.25
Avoiding conflict style	.84	4.45	1.25
Compromising conflict style	.75	5.13	0.95
Incivility	.79	4.80	1.11
Integrative tactics[b]	.76	3.84	1.42
Distributive tactics[c]	.87	4.77	1.25
Perceived conflict resolvability	.82	3.51	1.28
Conflict management satisfaction	.82	4.28	1.19

Notes:
[a]Item 21 in the inventory (item 4 in this sub-scale) dropped.
[b]Item 5 dropped.
[c]Items 4 and 5 dropped.

regression was conducted with conflict styles entered in the first step, then incivility added in the second step. Results offered support for H1a, H1c, and H1f (see Table 8.2). The collaborating and compromising conflict styles predicted integrative tactics positively, as hypothesized. Incivility predicted integrative tactics negatively, as hypothesized. The addition of incivility as a predictor beyond conflict styles yielded a significant change in the percentage of explained variance in integrative tactics, adjusted R^2 change = .10, F-test change = 51.72, $p < .001$.

Table 8.2: Hierarchical Regression Results for Integrative Tactics.

Variable	Model 1			Model 2		
	B	SE	β	B	SE	β
Collaborating conflict style	0.26*	0.11	.17*	0.25*	0.10	.16*
Accommodating conflict style	−0.04	0.07	−.03	−0.05	0.07	−.04
Competing conflict style	−0.08	0.05	−.08	−0.08	0.05	−.08
Avoiding conflict style	0.08	0.06	.08	0.05	0.05	.05
Compromising conflict style	0.19*	0.09	.15*	0.21*	0.09	.15*
Incivility				−0.36***	0.05	−.32***
Adjusted R^2		.08		.18		
F-test value		8.24***		16.33***		

Note: *$p < .05$; ***$p < .001$.

Similarly, H2 proposed that distributive tactics would be predicted negatively by the collaborating (H2a), accommodating (H2b), compromising (H2c), and avoiding (H2d) conflict styles, and positively by the competing (H2e) conflict style and incivility (H2f). Results of a second hierarchical regression (conducted similarly to the one for H1) offered support for H2d, H2e, and H2f (see Table 8.3). The competing conflict style predicted distributive tactics positively and the avoiding conflict style predicted distributive tactics negatively, as hypothesized. Results for H2b were significant but in the opposite direction than predicted. The accommodating conflict style predicted distributive tactics positively rather than negatively. Incivility also predicted distributive tactics positively, as hypothesized. Adding incivility as a predictor in addition to conflict styles yielded a significant but small change in the percentage of explained variance in distributive tactics, adjusted R^2 change = .03, F-test change = 14.06, $p < .001$.

Table 8.3: Hierarchical Regression Results for Distributive Tactics.

Variable	Model 1			Model 2		
	B	SE	β	B	SE	β
Collaborating conflict style	−0.16	0.11	−.09	−0.15	0.11	−.08
Accommodating conflict style	0.29***	0.07	.21***	0.29***	0.07	.21***
Competing conflict style	0.49***	0.05	.43***	0.49***	0.05	.43***
Avoiding conflict style	−0.23***	0.06	−.20***	−0.21***	0.06	−.19***
Compromising conflict style	−0.15	0.09	−.10	−0.16	0.09	−.11
Incivility				0.20***	0.05	.16***
Adjusted R^2		.25		.27		
F-test value		28.01***		26.43***		

Note: ***$p < .001$.

H3 proposed that perceived resolvability of the conflict would be predicted positively by integrative tactics (H3a) and negatively by distributive tactics (H3b) and incivility (H3c). A hierarchical regression was conducted with tactics in the first step and incivility added in the second step (see Table 8.4). H3a was supported, whereas H3b was not. The addition of incivility offered support for H3c and also resulted in a significant and substantial change in the percentage of explained variance in perceived resolvability, adjusted R^2 change = .20, F-test change = 112.34, $p < .001$.

Finally, H4 proposed that conflict management satisfaction would be predicted positively by integrative tactics (H4a) and negatively by distributive tactics (H4b) and incivility (H4c). A hierarchical regression similar to the one employed for H3 was conducted. Results offered full support for H4 (see Table 8.5). The addition of incivility resulted in a very small but significant change in the percentage of explained variance in conflict management satisfaction, adjusted R^2 change = .01, F-test change = 5.64, $p < .05$.

Table 8.4: Hierarchical Regression Results for Perceived Resolvability.

Variable	Model 1			Model 2		
	B	SE	β	B	SE	β
Integrative tactics	0.29***	0.05	.28***	0.14**	0.05	.14**
Distributive tactics	−0.02	0.05	−.03	.00	0.04	.00
Incivility				−0.54***	0.05	−.47***
Adjusted R^2		.08				.28
F-test value		19.42***		53.89***		

Note: $^{**}p < .01$; $^{***}p < .001$.

Table 8.5: Hierarchical Regression Results for Conflict Management Satisfaction.

Variable	Model 1			Model 2		
	B	SE	β	B	SE	β
Integrative tactics	0.25***	0.05	.27***	0.22**	0.05	.23***
Distributive tactics	−0.13**	0.04	−.15**	−0.12**	0.04	−.14***
Incivility				−0.12*	0.05	−.12*
Adjusted R^2		.12			.13	
F-test value		28.72***			21.24***	

Note: $^{*}p < .05$; $^{**}p < .01$; $^{***}p < .001$.

Discussion

The goal of this study was to examine conflict on Facebook during the latter part of 2020, a unique time in the United States with the convergence of the COVID-19 pandemic, Presidential elections, and social protests which created a ripe environment for conflict on Facebook. We investigated whether individuals' general conflict styles predicted the tactics they used during conflict, as well as the relationship that incivility had with these tactics. We also examined the connections that conflict tactics and incivility had on outcomes of conflict, specifically perceived resolvability of that conflict and individuals' satisfaction with how the conflict was managed. Our results confirm previous research on conflict in interpersonal relationships and contribute new knowledge regarding conflict management on Facebook.

There are two different routes for conflict management on Facebook that became apparent from our data. On the one hand, an orientation towards the collaborating and compromising conflict styles positively predicted the use of integrative tactics. These tactics predicted higher perceptions of resolvability and higher conflict management satisfaction. These results echo the findings of serial argument process models. For example, Cionea, Wilson Mumpower, and Bassick (2019) modeled the connections between positively-valenced goals that were associated with integrative tactics, which related to positive outcomes on arguers' satisfaction following a serial argument episode. Although this study cannot support a causal chain process given the cross-sectional nature of our data, we uncovered patterns of positive relationships between conflict styles reflecting concern for both the self and the other and tactics, with further associations between these tactics and outcomes. That is, collaborating and compromise conflict styles related to integrative tactics, which predicted satisfaction and resolvability, creating a constructive conflict context. Results of the hierarchical regressions showed that incivility made a significant difference in these circumstances. When the conflict involved negativity, closed-mindedness, and hostility, the use of integrative tactics, such as acknowledging and respecting the needs and goals of other participants or working towards cooperative outcomes, decreased. Furthermore, participants perceived conflicts that involved incivility to be less resolvable. In both cases adding incivility into the regression models yielded significant changes in the percentage of explained variance in tactics (10%) and perceived resolvability (20%), respectively. The exception here was conflict management satisfaction, in which case adding incivility made only a small difference. Although incivility was a significant predictor, the percentage of explained variance changed by a minuscule 1% for conflict management satisfaction. In this case, then, conflict management satisfaction appears to be predicted best by the tactics one uses in the conflict, not by the general climate of the exchange.

On the other hand, a different route of conflict management involved the use of distributive tactics, which were predicted positively by the competing conflict style and negatively by the avoiding conflict style. Thus, individuals sought to dominate how the conflict worked out, wanted to win, and come out ahead of the other person when they also reported their conflict style, in general, was a dominating, competing one. Individuals who reported an avoiding conflict style indicated they used distributive tactics less, suggesting that such individuals may shy away from trying to take charge and control the interaction in their overall approach to conflict situations. That is, if individuals usually try to stay away from conflict, avoid conflict with their peers, or try not to ruffle any feathers, it is not likely that they would be the type of person to attempt to dominate a situation of conflict on Facebook, either.

Surprisingly, the accommodating conflict style also predicted the use of distributive tactics positively. Individuals who usually gave in to others' wishes and tried to fulfill others' needs when in conflict relied on more distributive tactics when engaging in conflict with others on Facebook. A possible explanation here is that Facebook conflicts may have surpassed some acceptability threshold beyond which individuals did not accommodate any further but rather tried to take control of the exchange. For example, given the strong polarization of political opinions regarding the 2020 Presidential election, we can imagine that people who usually would be willing to accommodate differing viewpoints about political candidates may have been sick and tired of listening to the other side's arguments, and became dominant when engaging for the umpteenth time in the same political debate. Ting-Toomey and Oetzel (2001) offer some support for this idea as they explain conflict styles can be situational responses. Thus, how effective accommodation is in conflict could be dependent, at least in part, on situational exigencies, which could be examined further in future research.

Distributive tactics predicted conflict management satisfaction negatively, which confirms previous research that competitive, destructive strategies tend to be associated negatively with satisfaction (Cionea, Wilson Mumpower, & Bassick, 2019; Cupach, 1982). Interestingly, the contributions of incivility along this route of conflict management involving distributive tactics were minimal. Although incivility predicted the use of distributive tactics positively, the change in explained variance was a minimal 2% when adding incivility in the regression equation, along with conflict styles. Similarly, as previously mentioned, adding incivility to explain conflict management satisfaction made a minor difference. This suggests incivility may not carry a lot of weight in a conflict situation that is already infused with negativity based on individuals' approaches and strategies used during the conflict; these latter considerations are the ones to shape the conflict's outcome in terms of conflict management satisfaction. Another possibility is that negative, destructive conflict approaches presuppose incivility already. Participants expect it; hence, this variable does not have as great of an impact as it does when the conflict is framed in positive, constructive terms. It is also possible that incivility is a function of certain topics, such as highly charged disagreements of opinion or those in which individuals are highly invested, as Coe and colleagues (2014) have suggested. Thus, future research should seek to disentangle the expectations that individuals have regarding incivility in conflict situations and further delineate how incivility works with other constructive or destructive conflict behaviors in situations of conflict on SNS and beyond.

Another direction for future research consists of identifying ways to cultivate constructive discussions on Facebook specifically and in online settings in general. Coe et al. (2014) found that incivility did not increase as exchanges progressed; it was possible to have actual discussions with others online without degenerating into incivility. Our results add more information concerning what such fruitful discussions may look like. In the case of Facebook conflicts, our findings suggest that individuals' own approaches to conflict, and the extent to which they are willing to use integrative tactics to engage in a conflict, matter. This further suggests that individuals need to think carefully about when and how they engage in conflict on Facebook. They should consider more strategically their goals when engaging in a conflict on Facebook (or any discussions on a SNS) and the tactics they have available. A. Johnson and Cionea (2020), for instance, found that people often argued with others on Twitter to release frustration, which would set a negative tone for the exchange. However, both A. Johnson and Cionea (2020) and Cionea et al. (2017) also found that individuals engaged in arguments because they wanted to persuade others, which would have better chances of occurring, our study suggests, with an integrative approach in mind. The challenge, then, is to motivate people to adopt constructive approaches, with a genuine orientation towards conflict resolution, even when they hold incompatible beliefs and goals.

Our study is not without limitations. Our sample came primarily from the South-Central U.S., was White, and was at least partially college-educated. Thus, our results are not generalizable to Facebook users across the United States, or users of different ethnic backgrounds and varying education levels. Furthermore, we asked participants to report on a conflict that occurred in the past three to four months. For some, recall and memory may have posed challenges when responding to study materials. Finally, participants reported on conflicts with a variety of others, from strangers to friends to family members. Relationships with others involved in the conflict may affect goals, tactics, and outcomes. Despite these limitations, this study offers valuable knowledge about the management of conflicts on Facebook during a tumultuous time in the U.S. We identified key associations between conflict styles, conflict tactics, and outcomes of conflict that can be further explored in experimental settings or everyday conflict interactions on SNS to help delineate constructive conflict management behaviors that could allow individuals to discuss opposing viewpoints online in fruitful ways.

References

Bevan, J. L. (2014). Dyadic perceptions of goals, conflict strategies, and perceived resolvability in serial arguments. *Journal of Social and Personal Relationships*, *31*(6), 1–23. https://doi.org/10.1177/0265407513504653

Bevan, J. L., Tidgewell, K. D., Bardull, K. C., Cusanelli, L., Hartsern, M., Holbeck, D., & Hale. J. L. (2007). Serial argumentation goals and their relationships with perceived resolvability and choice of conflict tactics. *Communication Quarterly*, *55*(1), 61–77. https://doi.org/10.1080/01463370600998640

Blake, R. R., & Mouton, J. S. (1964). *The managerial grid: The key to leadership excellence*. Houston, TX: Gulf.

boyd, d. m. (2008). *Taken out of context: American teen sociality in networked publics*. [Doctoral dissertation, University of California-Berkeley, School of Information]. Retrieved from https://www.danah.org/papers/TakenOutOfContext.pdf

boyd, d. m. (2014). *It's complicated: The social lives of networked teens*. New Haven, CT: Yale University Press.

Chen, G. M. (2015). Losing face on social media: Threats to positive face lead to an indirect effect on retaliatory aggression through negative affect. *Communication Research*, *42*(6), 819–838. https://doi.org/10.1177/0093650213510937

Chen, G. M., Muddiman, A., Wilner, T., Pariser, E., & Stroud, N. J. (2019). We should not get rid of incivility online. *Social Media + Society*, *5*(3), 1–5. https://doi.org/10.1177/2056305119862641

Cionea, I. A., Johnson, A. J., & Bostwick, E. N. (2019). Argument interdependence and its effects on serial argument goals and tactics in romantic relationships. *Journal of Social and Personal Relationships*, *36*(7), 1975–1995. https://doi.org/10.1177/0265407518774933

Cionea, I. A., Piercy, C. W., Bostwick, E. N., & Wilson Mumpower, S. (2019). Argumentative competence in friend and stranger dyadic exchanges. *Argumentation*, *33*, 465–487. https://doi.org/10.1007/s10503-019-09487-x

Cionea, I. A., Piercy, C. W., & Carpenter, C. J. (2017). A profile of arguing behaviors on Facebook. *Computers in Human Behavior*, *76*, 438–449. https://doi.org/10.1016/j.chb.2017.08.009

Cionea, I. A., Wilson-Mumpower, S. V., & Bassick, M. (2019). Serial argument goals, tactics, and outcomes in long distance and geographically close romantic relationships. *Southern Communication Journal*, *84*(1), 1–16. https://doi.org/10.1080/1041794X.2018.1531915

Coe, K., Kenski, K., & Rains, S. A. (2014). Online and uncivil? Patterns and determinants of incivility in newspaper website comments. *Journal of Communication*, *64*(4), 658–679. https://doi.org/10.1111/jcom.12104

Cupach, W. R. (1982, May). *Communication satisfaction and interpersonal solidarity as outcomes of conflict message strategy use* [Conference presentation]. Annual meeting of the International Communication Association, Boston, MA. Retrieved from https://files.eric.ed.gov/fulltext/ED217510.pdf

Cupach, W. R., Canary, D. J., & Spitzberg, B. H. (2010). *Competence in interpersonal conflict* (2nd edition). Long Grove, IL: Waveland Press.

Donohue, W. A., & Kolt, R. (1992). *Managing interpersonal conflict*. Thousand Oaks, CA: Sage.

Facebook, Inc. (2021). *Facebook reports fourth quarter and full year 2020 results*. Facebook Investor Relations. https://investor.fb.com/investor-news/press-release-details/2021/Facebook-Reports-Fourth-Quarter-and-Full-Year-2020-Results/default.aspx

Halpern, D., & Gibbs, J. (2013). Social media as a catalyst for online deliberation? Exploring the affordances of Facebook and YouTube for political expression. *Computers in Human Behavior*, *29*(3), 1159–1168. https://doi.org/10.1016/j.chb.2012.10.008

Hample, D., & Krueger, B. (2011). Serial arguments in classrooms. *Communication Studies*, *62*(5), 1–21. https://doi.org/10.1080/10510974.2011.576746

Hample, D., Richards, A. S., & Na, L. (2012). A test of the conflict linkage model in the context of serial arguments. *Western Journal of Communication*, *76*(5), 459–479. https://doi.org/10.1080/10570314.2012.703361

Hample, D., Warner, B., & Young, D. (2009). Framing and editing interpersonal arguments. *Argumentation*, *23*, 21–37. https://doi.org/10.1007/s10503-008-9107-x

Johnson, A. J. (2002). Beliefs about arguing: A comparison of public issue and personal issue arguments. *Communication Reports*, *15*(2), 99–112. https://doi.org/10.1080/08934210209367757

Johnson, A. J., & Cionea, I. A. (2020). An exploratory mixed-method analysis of interpersonal arguments on Twitter. In J. Rosenbaum-Andre & G. Bouvier (Eds.), *Twitter, the public sphere and the chaos of online deliberation* (pp. 205–231). London, UK: Palgrave Macmillan.

Johnson, K. L., & Roloff, M. E. (1998). Serial arguing and relational quality: Determinants and consequences of perceived resolvability. *Communication Research*, *25*(3), 327–343. https://doi.org/10.1177/009365098025003004

Kilmann, R. H., & Thomas, K. W. (1977). Developing a forced-choice measure of conflict-handling behavior: The "MODE" instrument. *Educational and Psychological Measurement*, *37*(2), 309–325. https://doi.org/10.1177/001316447703700204

Kim, J., & Ahn, J. (2013). The show must go on: The presentation of self during interpersonal conflict on Facebook. *Proceedings of the American Society for Information Science and Technology*, *50*(1), 1–10. https://doi.org/10.1002/meet.14505001056

Koeze, E., & Popper, N. (2020, April 7). *The virus changes the way we Internet*. The New York Times. https://www.nytimes.com/interactive/2020/04/07/technology/coronavirus-internet-use.html

Lu, Y., & Lee, J. K. (2021). Determinants of cross-cutting discussion on Facebook: Political interest, news consumption, and strong-tie heterogeneity. *New Media & Society*, *23*(1), 175–192. https://doi.org/10.1177146144819899879

Ohbuchi, K. I., & Tedeschi, J. T. (1997). Multiple goals and tactical behaviors in social conflicts. *Journal of Applied Social Psychology, 27*(24), 2177–2199. https://doi.org/10.1111/j.1559-1816.1997.tb01647.x

Papacharissi, Z. (2002). The virtual sphere: The Internet as a public sphere. *New Media & Society, 4*(1), 9–27. https://doi.org/10.1177/14614440222226244.

Papacharissi, Z. (2004). Democracy online: Civility, politeness, and the democratic potential of online political discussion groups. *New Media & Society, 6*(2), 259–283. https://doi.org/10.1177/1461444804041444

Putnam, L. L. (2006). Definitions and approaches to conflict and communication. In J. G. Oetzel & S. Ting-Toomey (Eds.), *The SAGE handbook of conflict communication* (pp. 1–32). Thousand Oaks, CA: Sage.

Rahim, M. A. (1983a). A measure of styles of handling interpersonal conflict. *Academy of Management Journal, 26*(2), 368–376. https://doi.org/10.2307/255985

Rahim, M. A. (1983b). *Rahim organizational conflict inventory-II: Forms A, B, and C.* Palo Alto, CA: Consulting Psychologists Press.

Rahim, M. A. (2001). *Managing conflict in organizations* (3rd edition). Westport, CT: Quorum Books.

Roloff, M. E. (2009). Links between conflict management research and practice. *Journal of Applied Communication Research, 37*(4), 339–348. https://doi.org/10.1080/00909880903233200

Rossini, P. (2020). Beyond toxicity in the online public sphere: Understanding incivility in online political talk. In W. H. Dutton (Ed.), *A research agenda for digital politics* (pp. 160–171). Cheltenham, UK: Elgar Publishing.

Sleeper, M., Balebako, R., Das, S., McConahy, A. L., Wiese, J., & Cranor, L. F. (2013). The post that wasn't: Exploring self-censorship on Facebook. In A. Bruckman & S. Counts (Chairs), *Proceedings of the 2013 ACM Conference on Computer Supported Cooperative Work Companion* (pp. 793–802). New York, NY: Association for Computing Machinery.

Sveningsson, M. (2014). "I don't like it and I think it's useless, people discussing politics on Facebook": Young Swedes' understandings of social media use for political discussion. *Cyberpsychology: Journal of Psychosocial Research on Cyberspace, 8*(3). http://dx.doi.org/10.5817/CP2014-3-8.

Tankovska, H. (2021a, February 2). *Number of monthly active Facebook users worldwide as of 4th quarter 2020.* https://www.statista.com/statistics/264810/number-of-monthly-active-facebook-users-worldwide/

Tankovska, H. (2021b, February 9). *Leading countries on Facebook audience size as of January 2021.* https://www.statista.com/statistics/268136/top-15-countries-based-on-number-of-facebook-users/

Ting-Toomey, S., & Oetzel, J. G. (2001). *Managing intercultural conflict effectively.* Thousand Oaks, CA: Sage.

Treem, J. W., & Leonardi, P. M. (2012). Social media use in organizations: Exploring the affordances of visibility, editability, persistence, and association. *Communication Yearbook, 36*(1), 143–189. https://doi.org/10.2139/ssrn.2129853

Weber Shandwick, Powell Tate, & KRC Research (2018). *Civility in America 2018: Civility at work and in our public squares.* https://www.webershandwick.com/wp-content/uploads/2018/06/Civility-in-America-VII-FINAL.pdf

R. Tyler Spradley & Elizabeth Spradley

Chapter 9 Best Practices for Navigating Escalatory Messages in YouTube Comments: Synthesizing Conflict and Crisis Communication to Address Resistance to Risk Messages

Abstract: The COVID-19 superpandemic has demonstrated how crisis and risk communication practices, even with public well-being in mind, can create or escalate conflict pertaining to risk mitigation. Given that organizations and content creators may be more attuned to content and media strategies for risk messages than to dispute resolution, conflict studies' perspectives are needed to examine how stakeholders react to, dispute with, and escalate organizational risk messages through social media. This chapter examines specific, escalatory disputes associated with organizational mask and safety messages on YouTube using Amtrak's mask messaging from June 2020–February 2021. Amtrak's stakeholders accept and resist the mask policy through their comments on video posts, which are contextualized by broader social discourse about masks, public health, and viral risks. Stakeholder comments function to support or dispute with the organization and with other stakeholders. The chapter culminates in practice-based recommendations for the concurrent management of conflict and risk communication including: anticipate conflict, contextualize with broader issue-specific discourse, de-escalate conflict, form interprofessional teams, partner with public health to promote health literacy, and respond to stakeholders.

Keywords: organizational communication, conflict escalation, social media, crisis communication, pandemic

Introduction

In 2020, the Centers for Disease Control and Prevention (CDC) and the World Health Organization (WHO) recommended organizations promote mask-wearing to increase stakeholder safety and mitigate the spread of COVID-19. Since the dissemination of COVID-19 risk messages regarding mask usage, these seemingly benign safety messages have morphed into controversy (Eikenberry et al., 2020; Lyu & Wehby, 2020; Spradley & Spradley, 2020a) even denoting political affiliation in the United States (Ike et al., 2021). Initial face mask recommendations were inconsistent and ambiguous (Tso & Cowling, 2020). One source of ambiguity is attributed to the

https://doi.org/10.1515/9783110687262-010

variety of masks with variations in material construction and design ranging from homemade cloth coverings, disposable masks, KN95 and N95 masks, and reserve N95 respirators for healthcare workers (CDC, 2021 Feb. 23). Additionally, public health organizations were inconsistent with one another and their own recommendations for covering guidelines from March through May of 2020 (Spradley & Spradley, 2020a). Initially, medical masks were recommended for healthcare workers, and cloth face coverings and disposable masks were only recommended for symptomatic members of the public or when caring for an ill person. The CDC and WHO's messages during this time emphasized the lack of evidence for face-covering recommendations for the public to reduce the risk of contracting or spreading COVID-19 (Tso & Cowling, 2020). Feng et al. (2020) trace early face mask recommendations as they vary across health organizations, countries, and regions up until mid-March of 2020. Nevertheless, health experts reached consensus in early April to early May of 2020 resulting in the recommendation for the public to use cloth face-coverings and disposable masks, and in relation to this chapter, face masks were also recommended for the entirety of long-distance public travel (Liu & Zhang, 2020). Given these noted shifts and tensions around face mask recommendations, there is little surprise that stakeholders vary with regard to their acceptance and resistance to organizational mask policies.

The COVID-19 superpandemic has demonstrated how crisis and risk communication practices, even with public well-being in mind, can create or escalate conflict pertaining to risk mitigation. Risk communication messages advocating the use of face masks stem from governing bodies mandating mask-wearing, expectations of those advocating mask-wearing, and the prophylactic effectiveness of mask wearing. Ensuing intractable conflicts bifurcate the population along social, political, and philosophical perspectives. News chronicles incident after incident of airline passengers ejected for mask noncompliance, service industry workers mediating mask arguments between customers, and security guards and police attacked for mask enforcement (Hutchinson, 2020 May 7; Zdanowicz & Hunter, 2020 June 18). Viral videos of mask altercations riddle social media (Bromwich, 2020 July 21). A quick search of "mask fights" on YouTube results in seemingly endless scrolling of disturbing verbal and physical altercations over mask-wearing caught on video and uploaded. Verbal disputes escalate, and violence is feared after physical confrontations, even attempted murder (Riess & Silverman, 2020 Aug. 4). Active resistance to mask-wearing contributes to risk communication conflict, especially as organizations have taken to social media to promote perceptions, intentions, policies, and behaviors. Such resistance is evident as stakeholders refuse to comply with mask mandates, citing liberty over safety, and confront organizations about their policies.

Given that organizations and content creators may be more attuned to content and media strategies for risk messages than to dispute resolution, conflict studies should consider how stakeholders react to, dispute with, and escalate organizational risk messages through social media. Organizations and risk and crisis communication practitioners need guidance to prevent and manage conflicts that stem from their risk communication messages. This chapter examines specific, escalatory disputes associated with organizational mask safety messages on YouTube. Using an exemplary case of organizational mask audiovisual content on YouTube produced by Amtrak, the chapter examines the stakeholder comments in response to the organizational messages that comprise the dispute between stakeholders and the organization and between stakeholders. Amtrak's mask safety messages do not anticipate stakeholder resistance nor actively avoid conflict escalation. The chapter culminates in best practices for organizations creating audiovisual content to communicate risk messages whilst de-escalating conflict.

Risk and Crisis Communication: Conflict Within Crisis and in Response to Risk and Crisis Messages

Arguably an undercurrent in the study of conflict is its organic occurrence in communication, and with regard to this chapter, its occurrence in risk and crisis communication. Despite its applicability, conflict literature is scantily applied to the study and practice of risk and crisis communication. This chapter aims to do just that – put conflict literature in direct conversation with risk and crisis communication literature to demonstrate a symbiotic relationship and interdisciplinary opportunities. To begin, consider this orienting definition to conflict, "Conflict centers on incompatibilities, an expressed struggle, and the interdependence among two or more parties" (Putnam, 2006, p. 5). Because interdependent parties perceive incompatibilities and interference toward reaching a goal, an expressed struggle ensues (Folger, Poole, & Stutman, 2021). Terms like argument, conflict, dispute, struggle, and tension connote subtle differences but insinuate a similarly expressed disagreement related to perceived dissimilarities. Conflict is oft characterized by uncertainty, ambiguity, emotions, and power (Bodtker & Jameson, 2001; Folger, Poole, & Stutman, 2021; Nair, 2008), which contribute to the complexity of its expression in both face-to-face and mediated contexts.

Conflict Communication and Social Media

Research examining conflict communication through technology, specifically social media, demonstrates how the medium impacts the conflict, often through escalation. Social media is technologically mediated communication that affords networking between users presenting them opportunities to follow one another, share content, and voice ideas (Trottier & Fuchs, 2015; Zeitzoff, 2017). Because of the various features and user motivations, social media is used differently by different users (Khan, 2017), but the proliferation of social media allows for dissemination and user engagement in real time (Zeitzoff, 2018). Of note, research on social media conflict ranges in scope from nation-state political conflicts (e.g. Makhortykh & Sydorova, 2017; Zeitzoff, 2017; 2018) to interpersonal conflicts (e.g. Fox & Moreland, 2015). While there are many different strands of social media and conflict research, one such strand examines the social identity model of deindividuation effects (SIDE) that explains individual and group polarization based on identification with a group over the self (Lee, 2007; Postmes, Spears, & Lee, 1999). Applied to mediated communication, research using the SIDE model posits that individuals will polarize their argumentation to identify more with those they deem as in-group members and contrast their argumentation with those they deem as out-group members, thus making resolution between polarized arguments challenging. Another and sometimes linked strand of research on mediated conflicts is flaming. Flaming, while a disputed term, is associated with uninhibited, verbal communication characterized by cursing, hostility, insults, name-calling, and threats online (O'Sullivan & Flanagin, 2003). Disinhibition, lack of social cues, and depersonalization are partial causal explanations for online behavior labeled flaming (Lea et al., 1992). Such strands of social media and conflict research underscore the interest in better understanding the role of social media in conflicts and developing ways to address it. More research is needed to understand how social media conflict, escalation, and flaming apply to organizational communication with stakeholders. This chapter extends social media and conflict research by examining its concurrence with organizational risk and crisis communication. To do so, the next section begins to unpack what is meant by risk and crisis communication and how risk and crisis communication intersect with conflict studies.

Risk and Crisis Communication

Risk and crisis communication emanate from the need to prevent, manage, mitigate, and recover from a crisis. Crises are characterized by specific, non-routine events and the uncertainty, intensity, and outcomes surrounding those events (Sellnow & Seeger, 2013; Ulmer, Sellnow, & Seeger, 2019). As such, crises are often associated with disorganization, disruption, and chaos (Weick & Sutcliffe, 2015). Organizations must anticipate crises through strategic crisis planning, manage crises through risk and crisis communication and response, and recover from crises by learning, adapting, and innovating. Strategic communication efforts in organizations have long employed crisis and risk communication practices to provide relevant information to stakeholders and to the public regarding sensemaking, efficacy, response, and renewal (Ulmer, Sellnow & Seeger, 2019). However, these strategic efforts bend to public relations and managerial interests when organizational crises are perceptually or actually the fault of organizational ethical violations, illegality, or privileging (Seeger, Sellnow & Ulmer, 2003). For example, image restoration strategies are often employed by organizations to bolster the tarnished star, as can be seen in when Texaco board members were recorded making racist comments (Brinson & Benoit, 1999). Simply, crises and risks identify a massive umbrella of potential unexpected, extreme contexts that are imbued with organizational conflicts more akin to strikes, layoffs, and ethical and abusive management behaviors. Enron's collapse provides a great example of how unethical organizational behavior escalates into a crisis event that impacted the corporation and the economy (Seeger & Ulmer, 2003). The escalatory nature of crisis, often termed ripple effects, can have widespread repercussions that transcend the organization and the crisis event. Considering risk messages will be interpreted through the perceptions and expectations of stakeholders, making sense of conflicts that arise out of these ripple effects is a significant endeavor.

Conflict in Risk and Crisis Communication

There are points of intersection with conflict and risk and crisis communication. As this section unfolds, a point of clarification is needed. First, the conflict constitutes the risk and/or crisis. While such is evident in hostage negotiation and nation-state disputes with the threat of violence in the absence of resolution, less violent contexts in which conflict constitutes crisis is evident when organizational conflicts threaten the vitality and perpetuation of organizing as with labor strikes or organizational dissolution. Second, the risk or crisis may constitute a conflict. In these conflicts, the tensions stem from characteristics of, responses to, or complexities within the risk and crisis communication. When citizens resist mandatory hurricane evacuations or when the organization is found culpable for the crisis, conflict is constituted. To illustrate how these two approaches to conflict and risk/crisis relationships are studied, see Table 9.1: Conflict Constitutes Risk/Crisis and Risk/Crisis Constitutes Conflict.

Table 9.1: Conflict Constitutes Risk/Crisis and Risk/Crisis Constitutes Conflict.

	Exemplary Cases
Conflict constitutes the risk and/or crisis.	*Hostage negotiation* (Agne, 2007; Rogan & Hammer, 2006) *Intractable negotiations such as labor strikes or community resource allocation* (Brummans et al., 2008; Godard, 1992) *Organizational dissolution* (Spradley & Spradley, 2020b) *Viral videos of conflicts* (Benoit, 2018) *War* (Gleditsch, Salehyan, & Schultz, 2008)

Table 9.1 (continued)

	Exemplary Cases
The Risk And/Or The Crisis Constitutes The Conflict	*Failure to comply with risk/crisis activity* (Sorensen & Sorensen, 2007) *Image threat and repair and attribution of risk/crisis blame* (Brinson & Benoit, 1999; Harlow, Brantley, & Harlow, 2011)

Loci of Tensions in Risk and Crisis Communication

What are loci of tensions in risk and crisis? Identifying or locating tensions central to conflict in risk and crisis communication exposes the entry points of interdisciplinary work. Risks and crises are emergent, socially constructed, complex constellations of organizations and stakeholders anticipating, responding, and rebuilding across stages of crises. Consider this concise list that identifies loci of tensions in risk and crisis communication: 1) uncertainty, 2) ambiguous messages, 3) severity/cost, 4) stakeholder relationships, 5) resource allocation, and 6) resistance. Considering these inherent tensions in risk and crisis communication, much attention is needed to inquiry that explores the role of conflict in risk and crises.

High Stakes: Confluence of Risk, Crisis, and Conflict

If conflict escalation ensues and intractability forms, resolution is difficult. Conflict escalation is characterized by a number of factors including aggression, blaming/counter-blaming, change in view of the other, identity or face threats, polarization, rigidification or dogmatism, and more (Friedman & Currall, 2003; Jameson, 2003), and as conflict includes more identity threats than support, more separation than unity, more escalation than de-escalation, then intractability is more likely (Jameson, 2003). Intractable conflicts mean there is a failure to resolve the conflict, and when stakes are high as in water rights (Brummans et al., 2008; Putnam & Shoemaker, 2007) or border/sovereignty recognition (Coleman, 2003), intractability impacts quality of life and mortality. When overlaying escalation and intractability onto a crisis, possibly in extreme contexts like a pandemic, the impact becomes high stakes to risk mitigation, public outrage, emergency and crisis response, and recovery/renewal. Disaster diplomacy studies (Kelman, 2012) forge an interesting ground to better unpacking the high stakes confluence of risk, crisis, and conflict. "Disaster diplomacy examines how and why disaster-related activities do and do not reduce conflict and induce cooperation" (Kelman, 2012, p. 4). Work in this area has been applied to a wide array of disaster types and locales primarily using case study methodology with implications for nation-state disputes and violence. Overall, extreme contexts like crises pose high stakes for the confluence of conflict and risk and crisis communication.

Social Media in Conflict and Risk and Crisis Communication Research

Before moving on, there a few studies that seemingly pull together social media, conflict, and risk and crisis communication, albeit in a very different vein than this chapter. Research examining social media's role in nation-state conflicts and terrorism illustrate how social media is used in collective action, influencing public opinion, and organizing responses (Makhortykh & Sydorova, 2017; Zeitzoff, 2017; 2018). Research examining emergency response in crisis in tandem with conflict and social media is emerging. In a special issue of *Behavior & Information Technology*, six different articles demonstrated different ways of studying and conceptualizing the confluence of social media, conflict, and risk and crisis communication (Reuter, Stieglitz, & Imran, 2020). Despite noted scholarly interest, there is much to be learned.

Electronic connectivity has been championed as a means of coping with physical dysconnectivity during the coronavirus pandemic, but concerns arise from plausible challenges of social media's role in connectivity to risk communication fatigue, overload, and stress (O'Brien, Moore, & McNicholas, 2020). Moving forward in this chapter, the interests in conflict, social media, and risk and crisis communication comes to bear on the pandemic by overlaying these interests onto an organization's risk communication with stakeholders. The overarching question driving this chapter and case study is: how do organizations manage conflict during a crisis when tensions escalate from or around advocated risk and crisis communication messages? To address this question, attention turns to a case of risk and crisis communication through YouTube videos that resulted in stakeholder conflict.

Methods

When considering how organizations manage conflict in response to their risk messages, the study of Amtrak's YouTube videos and user comments is presented as a case study. Amtrak, and other businesses, face a steep learning curve with regard to the way their stakeholders – consumers and the general public – research and evaluate their products and services by sharing and commenting on social media content (Hudson & Hudson, 2013). Because conflict and negative user comments on YouTube video posts impact engagement with YouTube videos (Khan, 2017), studies, like this one, are needed to enhance understanding of stakeholder conflict through YouTube.

YouTube

YouTube debuted in 2005 but quickly rose to become a top social media platform (Burgess & Green, 2018). YouTube, closely followed by Facebook, is US adults' social media platform of choice with 73% using YouTube and 90% of 18–24 year-olds using YouTube in a 2019 survey conducted by Pew Research (Auxier, Anderson, & Kumar, 2019). With its impressive influence as a social media site, YouTube is generating academic interest in algorithm, content, function, production, and effect (Arthurs, Drakopoulou, & Gandini, 2018). Pihlaja (2014) explains, "YouTube pages are complex sites of interaction, with different elements (such as comments, description boxes, keyword 'tags,' and the video) contained on the page, all with different features of text production" (p. 2). As a social media site, YouTube's comment section enables interactivity among peer users with high degrees of anonymity (Walther et al., 2010). Web activity through user comments enhances perceptions of interactivity and credibility (Khan, 2017) and results in the co-creation of value between users (Brodie et al., 2013). Honing in on the comment, description boxes, and the video elements of YouTube, this chapter examines the development of conflict. Extant research indicates that comments tend to relate to content in videos and that incivility and hostility increase from the video to the comments (Edgerly et al., 2013). Coding YouTube comments led Madden, Ruthven, and McMenemy (2013) to develop a classification scheme. Their categories expanded on original work by Jansen et al. (2009) to ensure that the content analysis of comments demonstrated how YouTube users interacted with one another with their comments. Within their extensive classification scheme, Madden, Ruthven, and McMenemy (2013) response types are useful for coding conflict interaction, which was applied to this case study.

Amtrak: Case in Audiovisualizing Risk Disputes and Paradoxes on YouTube

Amtrak's service debuted on May 1, 1971, following the Rail Passenger Service Act of 1970. The act provides "financial assistance for and establishment of a national rail passenger system, to provide for the modernization of railroad passenger equipment." Enacted to modernize rail transportation for efficient intercity and interstate travel, the bill set in motion the creation of Amtrak. At the time of its inaugural service, Amtrak had 21 routes servicing 43 of the 48 states in the continental United States (Amtrak, 2020a). Over five decades, Amtrak experiences an ebb and flow of support from federal and state governments, undertakes massive infrastructure projects and rail improvements, and extends rail service to both rural and urban areas. In 2019, Amtrak has its best fiscal year and boasts a record 32.5 million trips by passengers. Like other transportation companies, Amtrak's 2019 performance will dramatically shift in 2020 (Amtrak, 2020b).

The transportation company, Amtrak, experienced disruption in their train operations and services during the COVID-19 pandemic and decreased demand for long-distance travel (Magliari, 2020 Aug. 17). To adapt to and comply with public health safety, Amtrak implemented a mandatory facial covering policy as of May 11, 2020 (Abrams, 2020 May 7; Lazo, 2020 May 7). As the company communicated with stakeholders about their response to reduce employees' and travelers' risk of contracting or spreading the coronavirus, Amtrak produced a series of videos released on YouTube. While not all of Amtrak's video-based risk messages were released on YouTube (some were officially released on their website), Amtrak used their YouTube channel to communicate changes in Amtrak's policies and services to improve customer and employee safety.

Four mask-related videos and their public comments were selected for analysis based on the following two criteria: 1) video is produced and posted by Amtrak to their official YouTube channel and 2) video content expressly communicates Amtrak's mask policy. See Table 9.2: Amtrak's YouTube Passenger Safety Messages. This data reflects views and comments up until February 17, 2021. In sum, the videos' risk messages functioned to demonstrate safety, demonstrate mask policy, instruct passengers, reassure stakeholders, redirect customers to other information sources, use credible messengers, and visualize Amtrak travel and mask-wearing.

Table 9.2: Amtrak's YouTube Passenger Safety Messages.

Amtrak Video	Date Posted	Length	Purpose	Views	Comments
Amtrak's Medical Services Team: Delivering a New Standard of Travel	June 26, 2020	2:37	Demonstrate safety Instruct passengers Use credible messengers Visualize Amtrak travel	411,612	64
Did You Know? Learn About Our Mask Policy	July 24, 2020	0:46	Demonstrate mask policy Inform about mask policy Visualize mask wearing	6,091	32
Delivering a New Standard of Travel: Our Commitment to Safety	October, 5, 2020	3:28	Demonstrate safety Reassure stakeholders Visualize Amtrak travel	47,358	120
Did You Know? Mask Policy	February 17, 2021	0:45	Clarify mask policy Redirect customers to other information sources Visualize mask wearing	577	49

Amtrak's Risk Communication Videos Communicate Mask Safety Messages

Within the following section, we outline each of the four videos and their risk messaging. To begin, "Amtrak's Medical Services Team: Delivering a New Standard of Travel" was posted on June 26, 2020. Dr. Ann Kuhnen, Amtrak's corporate medical director, narrates the video with images of a sparsely populated Amtrack station as her backdrop. As a medical doctor and corporate medical director, Dr. Kuhnen is a credible messenger for the health-related risk messages. The video mentions Amtrak's mask policy at two points. First, Dr. Kuhnen explains how Amtrak addresses safety for booking travel and arriving in an Amtrack station. With regard to masks, Dr. Kuhnen explains, "For your well-being and ours, Amtrak is requiring all customers and employees to wear facial coverings while in stations." Framing mask wearing as altruism, Amtrak uses both self and other-centered altruistic messaging to persuade stakeholders that the policy is in their best interest. Compassionate messages such as altruism tend to resonate with stakeholders unless those stakeholders are antagonistic (Blagov, 2020). Next, Dr. Kuhnen explains how mask wearing affects Amtrak travel. "All customers and employees are required to wear facial coverings on board our trains and thruway buses. Facial coverings can be removed when customers are in their private rooms." This part of the message frames risk messages as instructive and demonstrative as the policy is verbalized by the narrator while mask-wearing is visualized with images of employees and travelers in facial coverings. Thus, the first video appealed to stakeholders by framing mask-wearing and Amtrak's policies as altruistic and by framing risk messages as instructive and demonstrative.

Next, a more comprehensive yet similar video, "Did You Know? Learn About Safe Traveling on Amtrak" was posted on July 24, 2020, which was four to five months after the pandemic began affecting transportation. The video features a series of Amtrak employees wearing masks and explaining new policies and processes to travel with Amtrak. In actuality, this video is several smaller videos compiled together with uniform graphics and transitions, one of which explains how Amtrak approaches face coverings. This is the video entitled "Did You Know? Amtrak's Mask Policy" and touts 6,091 views. Nick, the director of long distance service, is the featured employee in the video and explains Amtrak's mask policy,

> Masks and facial coverings are a hot topic right now. We want to make sure that you're clear about our policy. To ensure everyone's safety, Amtrak is requiring customers in stations, on trains, and thruway buses to wear facial coverings throughout their trip. Don't worry, you're not alone. Our employees are wearing facial coverings too. There is one exception, facial coverings can be removed when customers are in their private rooms. Safe travels.

Then, a follow up video is the third video entitled, "Did You Know? Mask Policy," and it was posted on February 17, 2021 and has 577 views with 49 comments. The video is slightly different than its predecessor through its references to federal law, clarifications to Amtrak's mask policy, and redirection to Amtrak's other social media accounts with information on the mask policy. Otherwise, the second and third videos are almost identical.

Fourth, "Delivering a New Standard of Travel: Our Commitment to Safety" was posted seven to eight months into the COVID-19 pandemic on October 5, 2020. The video features Roger Harris, Amtrak's executive vice president and chief marketing and revenue officer, as the narrator. This video moves seamlessly between the narrator's verbal text explaining safety measures in the chronology of a passenger booking and traveling with Amtrak. The visual text parallels the verbal text illustrating Amtrak's trains, services, and safety measures. The mask policy is explicitly stated.

> We all need to look out for each other. While in stations, onboard and in all public places, Amtrak requires customers and employees wear a face mask that fully covers the entire mouth and nose.

Harris' mask message evokes Dr. Kuhnen's altruistic appeals. By looking out for one another, personal and public safety are achieved. Adding credibility to the mask policy and other safety messages within the video, Harris ends the video with, "Leveraging our full-time medical director, CDC guidance, and public health and safety experts, we continue to assess and improve our procedures so that you can travel with us safely." Harris' final comment reminds the audience that Amtrak's mask policy is not an arbitrary policy by a sole organization. Instead, Amtrak's mask policy is enmeshed in a public health effort supported by governmental agencies and experts.

Overall, each of the four videos consistently communicate the same policy regarding employee and customer mask usage and risk-related messages. While they vary slightly in verbal and visual texts, the videos rely on appeals to altruism and credibility of messengers and/or external organizations. One interesting consistency across the four videos was the moderate use of the video description. The description can be used to link stakeholders to additional sources of information or elaborate on arguments in the video, but Amtrak limited descriptions to one sentence. In the next section, attention turns to the stakeholders' use of the comment function on YouTube to interact with Amtrak, the mask policy, and other stakeholders.

Amtrak's Risk Communication Video Comments Reveal Stakeholder Acceptance and Resistance of Mask Safety Messages

Stakeholder comments on the four aforementioned Amtrak videos were coded using Jansen et al.'s (2009) classification scheme for YouTube video comments: announcement, answer, chitchat, comment, confirmation, consuming, expecting, forwarding, maintenance, missing, negative comment, notification, order via Twitter, patronizing, positive comment, question, recommendation, recommendation request, request, research, response, suggestion, and supplement. In doing so, the schema was helpful for understanding the stakeholder's function of the comment, but many of the functions were not relevant to mask-specific comments. We narrowed comments based on general references to masks, negative comments resistant to masks, and positive comments accepting of masks. Table 9.3: Public Comments to Amtrak's YouTube Passenger Safety Messages breaks down the comments. While considering Madden, Ruthven, and McMenemy's (2013) classification scheme, the most applicable response types were: agree, confirm, disagree, and challenge. Inevitably, Madden, Ruthven, and McMenemy's response types were most helpful in untangling escalating disputes between stakeholders posting mask-accepting and mask-resistant comments. Overall, mask-resistant comments were more frequent than mask-accepting comments, and the mask comments illustrate escalating mask-disputes.

Table 9.3: Public Comments to Amtrak's YouTube Passenger Safety Messages.

Amtrak Video	Comments	Mask Comments	Mask Accepting Comments	Mask Resistant Comments
Amtrak's Medical Services Team: Delivering a New Standard of Travel	64	6	3	3
Did You Know? Learn About Our Mask Policy	32	21	7	10
Did You Know? Mask Policy	49	9	5	4
Delivering a New Standard of Travel: Our Commitment to Safety	120	6	2	4

Mask-accepting comments tended to focus on concerns for personal and public safety. Comments like "Thank you for keeping passengers safe" and "that's a great video, thank you" are positive comments, but they are not specific to Amtrak's mask policy. These ambiguous positive comments were more typical in response to the first and fourth videos that were not solely focused on the mask policy. Positive comments that were sub-categorized as mask accepting were more typically in response to the second and third videos that solely focused on the mask policy. Keith Matthews comments, "Thank you Amtrak 😷 Honestly, I just can't wait for this Pandemic to be over. Hopefully soon 😱." Mask-accepting comments were also posted in response to mask-resistant comments. In response to a number of negative mask-resistant comments to the "Did You Know? Learn About Our Mask Policy" video, SMW writes, "An remember, everybody; If you think wearing a mask is uncomfortable, you really won't like wearing a ventilator." While mask-supportive comments were made, mask-resistant comments were more common.

Mask-resistant comments varied but typically echoed mask objections circulating in the US including personal freedom, politicization, and skepticism of effectiveness (Halpern, 2020). These comments represent objections based on sociocultural meanings associated with face masks (Ike et al., 2021). Valerie Gilbert's comment to the "Did You Know? Learn About Our Mask Policy?" video encapsulates a variety of mask resistance justifications.

> Love Amtrak. Hate masks. They don't work, they're bad for you, and enforcing their usage is unconstitutional. Won't be taking Amtrak until they act American. If you want a mask, wear one. This is not Iran. No Burka for me.

Like Valerie Gilbert, other mask-resistant comments tend to provide a modicum of justification for their positions on Amtrak's policy. With reference to personal freedom and politicization justifications, they tap into what Brehm (1966) asserts in psychological reactance theory – "that messages attempting to elicit an attitudinal or behavioral change may inadvertently create a threat to an individual's autonomy to hold attitudes or enact behaviors (Richards, et al., 2020, p. 1). Scheid et al. (2020) explain that autonomy is a psychological need, and public deliberation is a democratic ideal, both of which were arguably perceived by certain populations in the US as threatened by mask policies.

There were two distinct variations from the sociocultural meanings associated with masks explaining resistance – difficulty breathing because of a health condition and physical discomfort from prolonged mask wearing. For example, Buck Kite posted this in reply to the "Did You Know? Learn About Our Mask Policy" video:

> If you require masks on coach for a 12 [hour] and over trip . . . there needs to be a discount. I am NOT against masks at all but, having on for a 3 day trip maybe too much for people. Just sayin'

The mask-resistant comments related to physiological discomfort were typically more concerned about the logistics of mask-wearing for long-distance travel in coach. This is evident for travelers like Mary S, who writes, "Nice to hear and thanks, Amtrak, but I won't be traveling for a while. Do not like wearing a mask as I have breathing problems . . . " In this case and others, the objection to mask wearing is not intended as a negative comment or to be antagonistic to Amtrak's mask policy. Comments like Buck Kite and Mary S.'s are more akin to announcements to make Amtrak aware that some stakeholders have non-sociocultural justifications for refraining from mask wearing. Of interest, there are studies that support such concerns despite Amtrak's silence on this issue in their videos. While extant research does not support oxygen shortage due to mask wearing, there are some studies that suggest prolonged wearing may increase headaches, generate light-headedness (dizziness), or cause discomfort where the mask wearing rubs against the skin (Scheid, 2020). It is challenging to untangle other factors contributing to these discomforts such as changes in drinking and eating that contribute to increased headache occurrence. Nevertheless, there is early support to suggest that prolonged mask wearing may have some negative physiological effects on even healthy wearers. This is the case with early studies on frontline healthcare workers wearing masks continuously at work and when out in public (Rosner, 2020). Of note in the case of Amtrak's mask-resistant comments, some comments are physiologically-oriented rather than socioculturally-oriented.

With regard to the interactive dynamic of stakeholder acceptance and resistance to mask safety messages, this chapter makes two important observations to the concurrent study of conflict and crisis. First, acceptance-resistant comments constituted disputes between stakeholders and with Amtrak. Disputes are conflicts characterized by win-lose hostility (Keltner, 1987), and although YouTube comments were not initially conceived of in terms of dispute, their content and quality directed the case analysis toward dispute. At the outset, YouTube comments were coded using the Jansen et al. (2009) scheme and Madden, Ruthven, and McMenemy's (2013) response types, and while helpful to understand positive and negative comments and interactivity, even when further specifying positive comments as mask accepting and negative comments as mask resistant, the scheme did not capture the escalatory nature of these positive and negative comments.

Amtrak stakeholders were disputing with one another, not just disputing Amtrak because of the organization's mask policy. Consider this dispute exchange to the "Did You Know? Mask Policy" video. The dispute begins with Kenny G and includes three additional stakeholders replying to the original comment or to one another's comments.

> **Kenny G:** Yeah? Guess you don't care about people with debilitating ptsd or other medical issues that prevent face covering.
>
> **Mardasee:** I have PTSD. I haven't checked it but I think we get waivers.
>
> **EUDashLPs:** I live with someone who has PTSD and loves wearing face masks so your argument makes no sense.
>
> **Mardasee:** @EUDashLPs that someone you know does not have severe PTSD. Probably witnessed a car wreck let's say and still whines to this day saying "I have PTSD".
>
> **EUSashLPs:** @Mardasee rape trauma PTSD
>
> **Mardasee:** @EUDashLPs repeated trauma produces severe PTSD
>
> **Kenny G:** Ok to put this stupid argument to bed not all ptsd is the same and affects everyone the same everyone needs to educate themselves on that when someone says I have ptsd and cannot wear a mask take their word for it don't be an ass a lady screamed at me because of it and I had to isolate myself to come down because of it
>
> **CalRailFan90208:** But at the same time they are caring for thousands of Americans that use Amtrak every day to ensure they are safe as possible. And there are many people with medical issues who still wear masks. However I am sorry about those who cannot and aren't overreacting.

The responses to Kenny G could be classified as negative comments, patronizing, or responses, but to classify them as such would miss their express dispute function. Kenny G, Mardasee, EUSashLPs, and CalRailFan90208 are presenting arguments and counter-arguments to dispute the claims and make rebuttals presented in the interaction.

In addition to the dispute function of YouTube comments, analysis of comments demonstrated that disputes escalated rather than de-escalated. Conflict escalation occurs when there are increases in intensity or degeneration of the conflict that moves parties closer to intractability (Wall & Callister, 1995). Consider the following original comment and replies that ensue to the "Did You Know? Learn About Our Mask Policy" video.

> **Valerie Gilbert:** Love Amtrak. Hate masks. They don't work, they're bad for you, and enforcing their usage is unconstitutional. Won't be taking Amtrak until they act American. If you want a mask, wear one. This is not Iran. No Burka for me.
>
> **Jon Jackson:** @Valerie Gilbert It only works if we ALL WEAR ONE. You wear a mask to protect me; I wear a mask to protect you. Once you get that, you'll understand why WE insist that YOU wear a mask. Your choice is to wear it or don't come out in public.
>
> **Valerie Gilbert:** @Jon Jackson Then clearly you're proved my point. Masks do NOT work. If they did, the person wearing would be safe. It's the same BS argument about vaccines. Want one? Get one. I am not vaccinated. You need to read the Constitution. No one tells me what to put ON (masks/muzzles) or IN my body. Your job is to take care of you. Case . . .
>
> **Jon Jackson:** @Valerie Gilbert Don't be obtuse. Simple cloth masks DO work to contain virus particles coming out of our nose and mouth. Be sure, you're an anti-vax'er too. How predictable. I'm not a nice guy – I pray you get . . .
>
> **Sage Wisdom:** @Jon Jackson Masks diapers DO NOT protect anyone. You're a lying fraud, or just trying to control others. Wear ur diaper & stfu. Not your business WHAT others are doing, or what their health issues are. Never in American history have HEALTHY people been ordered to wear a mask during flu seasons.
>
> **Jon Jackson:** @Sage Wisdom Masks DO WORK when we all wear them. Keep the virus out of the air and it does not spread. How thick-headed do you need to be to not understand something as simple as this? . . .
>
> **MrRussell86:** @Jon Jackson Go fly a kite with your Fauci propaganda, bozo.
>
> **Jon Jackson:** MrRussell86 You sound like the very blissful type.

This dispute evolved from the original comment by Valerie Gilbert, who is the only one to even reference Amtrak in the comments, to be less about an organization's mask policy to be more about societal mask disputes. This mediated exchange is not commensurate with the properties and relational contexts of email conflict escalation, but it does reflect Friedman and Currall's (2003) description of mediated conflict escalation and reciprocity and is consistent with descriptions of flaming (Jane, 2015). The interaction demonstrates polarization (e.g. WE versus YOU), dehumanization (e.g. "I pray you get . . . "), name calling (e.g. "fool," "lying fraud," and "bozo"), aggressive capitalization (e.g. "DO WORK") and language (e.g. "BS argument"), and dogma (intractability of comments). In other words, the dispute demonstrated flaming typified by such qualities as aggression, hostility, inhibition, intimidation, insults, offensiveness, and profanity (O'Sullivan & Flanagin, 2003; Turnage, 2008). Because flaming behaviors on YouTube tend to express disagreement or a response to a perceived offense (Moor, Heuvelman, & Verleur, 2010) consistent with dispute attributes, conflict escalation in YouTube comments is further support for coding disputes.

In addition to adding dispute-related categories to YouTube comment classifications, there is also value in a sub-classification of escalatory or flaming comments to better understand how escalation is constituted through the comment patterns. Lingam and Aripin's (2017) classification of YouTube comment flaming demonstrates the value of a sub-classification system. Their work identifies political attack, racial attack, stereotypes, speculation, comparison, degradation, slander/defamation, sedition, sarcasm, threat, challenge, criticism, name-calling and sexual harassment. However, the Amtrak escalating dispute also notes polarization, dogma, dehumanization, and aggressive capitalization. Thus, further work is needed to develop a more comprehensive sub-classification of dispute escalation and flaming in YouTube comments. Madden, Ruthven, and McMenemy's (2013) classification should add a categories for YouTube video comments that flame and escalate conflicts, and while Lingam Aripin's (2017) is a good place to start, the classifications did not wholly represent the types of escalation noted in the Amtrak case study.

Second, acceptance-resistant comments reify the sociocultural variations in mask meaning. Ike et al. (2021) historically explore the sociocultural meanings of face masks, and with regard to COVID-19, they remark, "In the current polarized political and social climate in the United States, masks reflect both individual and societal values" (p. 4). Explaining the divisiveness of mask wearing in the coronavirus pandemic in the US, Ike et al. (2021) juxtapose the mask wearer with the mask resister. Mask wearers embrace medical science, public health experts, and altruistic motives for personal and public safety. Mask resisters demonstrate concern over authoritarian rule and individual liberty. Because political leaders of the Democratic and Republican parties exuded the social and personal values associated with mask acceptance and resistance, Democrats became synonymous with mask acceptance, and Republicans became synonymous with mask resistance.

Summarizing the Amtrak Case: Crisis and Conflict Confluence

In sum, the public health conditions brought about by COVID-19 in 2020 and continuing into 2021 caused wide-spread and large-scale changes to mitigate the risks of contracting and spreading the coronavirus. As a transportation company, Amtrak enacted new policies and services to maintain their operations whilst adhering to safety recommendations including face mask usage by employees and travelers. From a crisis communication lens, Amtrak's policy change on masks may be looked at differently than from a conflict communication lens; yet, Amtrak's YouTube videos and stakeholder comments illustrate a confluence of crisis and conflict communication. In other words, Amtrak's communication exemplified risk and crisis communication, and stakeholders' communication exemplified conflict.

Specifically, Amtrak used YouTube videos to communicate its mask policy with stakeholders, and stakeholders used YouTube comments to accept and resist the mask policy. The divergent uses of YouTube between Amtrak and stakeholders demonstrate Amtrak's non-interactive approach to mask disputes and stakeholders' interactive approach to mask disputes. A series of questions are posed regarding the level of involvement organizations should or should not have in YouTube comments resulting in disputes. What role do organizations that sponsor or release videos on YouTube have in mediating and resolving disputes that transpire in the comment section? What type of meta-messages do organizational replies to YouTube comments communicate (e.g., the organizational cares about the concern, the organization is taking sides, the organization is self-interested)? Will an official organizational reply to a dispute in YouTube comments amplify the dispute? What are the legal ramifications of organizational replies in YouTube comments?

Additionally, mask resistant comments demonstrated that resistance justifications could be sub-categorized into socioculturally-oriented or physiologically-oriented resistance. Sociocultural meanings associated with Amtrak's mask policy reify the sociocultural meanings associated with mask wearing in society. Thus, mask acceptance-resistance may be less about Amtrak's policy, and more about societal discourses that contest the meanings of masks. Furthermore, mask resistance constituted mask disputes that escalated conflict through flaming, which underscores the need for codification of YouTube comments to include disputes.

Implications for Practitioners

Following this case analysis, the chapter turns to how companies like Amtrak could approach conflict and crisis concurrently, specifically with regard to organizational videos. As organizations respond to crises with risk and crisis messages, stakeholders may dispute organizational efforts to mitigate risk and manage the crisis. What are best practices that organizations can use to guide their risk and crisis communication that will address emerging conflict? The following section proposes a set of six best practices that stem from the Amtrak case analysis of the organization's risk and crisis and stakeholder comments on YouTube. See Table 9.4: Best Practices to Manage Conflict in Response to Risk and Crisis YouTube Messages for an outline of the six best practices highlighted in this section.

Table 9.4: Best Practices to Manage Conflict in Response to Risk and Crisis YouTube Messages.

Best Practice	Practice Defined
Anticipate Conflict	Anticipate stakeholder conflict and use refutational two-sided argumentation to address common tensions related to recommended safety behaviors.
Contextualize with Broader Issue-Specific Discourse	Contextualize recommended safety behaviors that stakeholders are being asked to perform by the organization. Contextualization should include references to broader discourse about the safety issue and appeal to stakeholders' autonomy.
De-escalate Conflict	As stakeholders escalate, organizational messages should de-escalate.
Form Interprofessional Teams	Include conflict experts on interprofessional risk and crisis management teams.
Partner with Public Health to Promote Health Literacy	Health literacy may be an underlying factor in resistance to risk messages, but organizations can partner with public health to increase health literacy and risk message acceptance.
Respond to Stakeholders	Responsiveness to stakeholders will vary, but organizations should respond to contentious issues important to stakeholders.

Best Practice 1: Anticipate Conflict

Anticipate stakeholder conflict and use strategies like refutational two-sided arguments to address common tensions related to recommended safety behaviors. Based on the Amtrak case study, stakeholder mask-resistant comments were not addressed in the videos. One-sided arguments ignore opposing points of view or counter arguments (O'Keefe, 1999), and this is precisely what Amtrak did in their mask safety messages. One-sided arguments are found to be most persuasive in political, satirical, and advertising contexts (Becker & Anderson, 2019; Kim, 2020; O'Keefe, 1999), but little is known about these types of arguments in risk and crisis communication contexts. Amtrak presented one-sided arguments to appeal to altruism and credibility to persuade stakeholders to travel with Amtrak and wear masks. Stakeholders used the comments section to voice resistance, which is a counter argument to Amtrak's original one-sided arguments. Arguably a more proactive strategy, Amtrak could have constructed two-sided arguments in their videos anticipating stakeholder resistance. Two-sided arguments present the organization's risk message claims but also present counter or oppositional claims. Non-refutational two-sided arguments acknowledge the counter claim but do not present evidence to refute it; whereas refutational two-sided arguments both acknowledge and refute the counter claim (Allen, 1991). Studies on argumentation support the use of refutational two-sided arguments over non-refutational two-sided arguments (O'Keefe, 1999). Thus, Amtrak could have used refutational two-sided arguments to acknowledge the contestation of mask wearing, present evidence to counter unmasked travel, and present evidence supporting masked travel.

Best Practice 2: Contextualize with Broader Issue-Specific Discourse

Contextualize recommended safety behaviors that stakeholders are being asked to perform by the organization. The organizational safety policies are not constructed or enforced in isolation from larger discourses of safety, and these discourses of safety are being negotiated in public dialogue as meanings are contested. Amtrak's mask safety policies are contextualized in the transportation industry and public health response to COVID-19. Of particular interest to Amtrak, misinformation and conspiracy theories circulating in and around COVID-19 and face masks affect how Amtrak's stakeholders interpret and respond to the organization's mask safety messages. As Malecki, Keating, and Safdar (2021) describe public information regarding risk evolves, and public perceptions of risk are impacted by numerous factors including trustworthiness of sources, misinformation, immediacy, cultural factors, uncertainty, familiarity, personal control, and scientific uncertainty. YouTube commenters demonstrate the way these factors impacted perceptions of masks – whether comments were mask accepting or resistant. Amtrak's YouTube videos do not explicitly contextualize the organization's mask safety messages in the larger discourses of safety nor address the nuances of these factors that affect public perceptions of risk. Contextualization should include references to broader discourse about the safety issue and appeal to stakeholders' concerns and misinformation.

Best Practice 3: De-escalate Conflict

As stakeholders escalate conflict, organizational messages should de-escalate. When conflicts cyclically escalate, the conflict is rooted in a destructive cycle (Jeong, 2008).

Conflict escalation can result in intractable conflicts, in which stakeholders and organizations sever ties with one another. In the case of Amtrak, the transportation organization wants to retain existing passengers and recruit new passengers, which is threatened by escalating and intractable conflict. Conflict de-escalation is complex given that the organization has likely not participated in the YouTube comments constituting escalation. Lessons from conflict negotiation and dispute resolution come to bear on de-escalation and could be applied to organizations' YouTube content creation. Consider the following practices that de-escalate and prompt constructive communication.

- Demonstrate care for the resistant stakeholders and their interests, identity, and goals (Jameson, 2003; Janseen & van de Vliert, 1996), which can come through listening (Elliott, Gray, & Lewicki, 2003).
- Reframe conflicts by emphasizing unity and similarity rather than separation and difference (Jameson, 2003; Shmueli, Elliot, & Kaufman, 2006).

Best Practice 4: Form Interprofessional Teams

Interprofessional crisis management teams and cross-training in risk and crisis is commonplace (Lindell, Prater, & Perry, 2007; McEntire, 2007), especially in medicine (Bridges et al., 2011; Molyneux, 2001), but the literature in this area does not indicate the need for conflict experts or cross-training in dispute resolution. However, conflict experts should be included on interprofessional risk and crisis management teams and/or cross-training in dispute resolution should bolster the conflict skills of risk and crisis managers. With managerial support, there are different avenues for interprofessional teams to develop experience working as a team and responding to unique circumstances such as socially mediated conflict in risk and crisis situations. Exercises, simulations, trainings with interprofessional teams' function to achieve this aim (Bridges et al., 2011; Truta et al., 2018) as do cross-training professionals and action teams to perform roles and skills associated with another professional or action team (Marks et al., 2002).

Best Practice 5: Partner with Public Health to Promote Health Literacy

Disputes may arise between stakeholders and organizations related to organizational policies that adhere to public health guidelines, in part, due to health and media illiteracy. Ratzan, Sommariva, and Rauh (2020) explain one of the lessons from the COVID-19 superpandemic is the lack of health and media literacy that generates skepticism of public health recommendations like mask wearing. In the Amtrak case that analyzes YouTube videos and comments, concern arises related to possible misinformation about the COVID-19 crisis and related risks for contracting it that stakeholders could have been exposed to through other YouTube content. Pew Research indicates that most Americans, 64%, report encountering videos that seem false or misleading while on YouTube (Van Kessel, 2019 Dec. 4). Despite YouTube's medical misinformation policies, videos with medical misinformation and falsehoods may have high numbers of views prior to their deletion from the site (Ohlheiser, 2020 May 7). Is it possible that some of the stakeholders' mask resistant comments were due to false or misleading information on the social media platform that they used to access information about Amtrak? Given the need for health and media literacy to affect attitudes and behaviors toward personal and public safety in a superpandemic, organizations should partner with public health agencies in their local municipalities, regions, states, and/or nation to develop YouTube videos that not only communicate organizational policy but increase the public's health and media literacy.

Best Practice 6: Respond to Stakeholders

Responsiveness to stakeholders will vary, but organizations should respond to contentious issues important to stakeholders. Responsiveness should consider how future YouTube content will address stakeholder concerns. The video directs the focus and tone of comments (Edgerly et al., 2013), which positions new videos as strategic dispute resolution responses to the counter arguments in comments. This type of response is indirect and does not single out stakeholders or their comments.

Conclusion

In sum, the case demonstrates a myriad of stakeholder reactions to risk communication aimed at enhancing stakeholder safety. Stakeholders accept and resist Amtrak's mask policy through their YouTube comments directed at Amtrak and one another. Acceptance user comments bolster the claims of Amtrak and public health officials that are linked or cited within the comments section, whereas resistance comments dispute the underlying values or health information behind Amtrak's mask policy. The acceptance-resistance tension resonates with paradoxes and tensions that discourse scholars like Fairhurst and Endres relate to the coronavirus pandemic, who introduce the ways media translate risk discourse to the public (Sharma et al., 2021):

> These translations show us that conditions are ripe for paradox when we come to the medical community for answers but excoriate them when they are not perfect and in unison. The conditions are ripe for paradox when business and government impose preexisting standards of competition and regulation on the helping professions who must improvise on the front lines to fight the pandemic's extreme novelty. Paradox is likely when the political arena is no longer

> a way to come together to solve problems, but a means of exclusion based on carefully drawn boundary lines reinforced by media choices. Finally, conditions are ripe for paradox when a U.S. president who is supposed to bolster the public's trust in government ironically erodes it by attacking or sidestepping the government's extant science and public health infrastructures. (p. 125)

Subsequently, at the crossroads of conflict, risk, and crisis communication scholarship, researchers and practitioners alike should consider the value of paradox and tensions as a means to conceptualize, study, and interpret stakeholders' responses to risk messages on social media.

This chapter culminates in a number of takeaways relevant to the concurrent practice and study of conflict and risk and crisis communication. First, the acceptance-resistance of mask safety messages in YouTube comments is exemplary of the broader mask discourse. As if a microcosm of mask disputes, the YouTube comments accompanying Amtrak's mask safety videos function as a window into the mask disputes that have unfolded in the United States and elsewhere. Disputes in comments demonstrate the varied sociocultural meanings that stakeholders are attributing and negotiating related to masks. Masks are not symbolically neutral objects; masks' complex, contested, and contradictory meanings are emotionally charged (Ike et al., 2021; Spradley & Spradley, 2020a). Furthermore, mask dispute messages reverberate with distrust of the scientific community and public health, at the very least, and with disinformation, at the very worst. Given that COVID-19 disinformation circulating in social media through messages like those in the YouTube chat fan the flames of what some call an "infodemic" (O'Brien, Moore, & McNicholas, 2020). This begs the question as to the role of organizations who are not connected to public health in addressing distrust and disinformation. Distrust and disinformation affect organizational practices, reputation, and relationships with stakeholders, such as members, customers, and the community. While masks are the subject of this chapter, the chapter could have analyzed social distancing, hand sanitizing, sheltering-in-place, or a number of other public health issues that organizations enact safety policies with regard to, post safety videos on YouTube about, and invite stakeholders to comment on. Therefore, YouTube is a *site par excellence* for studying cases of dispute embedded in broader discourses over tensions and paradoxes emerging from sociocultural assumptions toward the variant of risk and safety messages.

Second, YouTube comment classification schemes need to reflect disputes that unfold through the public comments, and a sub-classification scheme should be refined for YouTube flaming that escalates conflict. Building on the works of Jansen et al. (2009), Madden, Ruthven, and McMenemy (2013), and Lingam and Aripin (2017), a sub-classification scheme for studying conflict in YouTube comments should consider the types of escalation noted in this chapter as well as in other cases. Additional research with a greater variety of YouTube content and communities should aim to develop and test an escalation or flame classification scheme.

Third, the practice-based recommendations in this study are a start for the development of risk and crisis communication practices designed to navigate escalatory conflicts and polarizations through social media; however, additional case studies and data are needed to advance understanding related to organizational responsiveness to disputes with and between stakeholders during risk and crisis management. Amtrak assumes a non-interactive, unresponsive position in the mask dispute in YouTube comments. Considering the limited number of YouTube comments despite the escalating dispute over the mask policy, Amtrak's silence may be warranted and advisable to other organizations facing similar situations. However, if there had been more negative and mask-resistant comments, would a non-interactive, unresponsive position be advisable? What is the threshold of resistance commentary that should move organizations to respond? Does responding lend credibility to the resistance commentary? If so, is response advisable if the resistance is contention with science, public health, and regulation? YouTube comments invite flaming and dispute, and additional studies are needed to examine how organizations should approach stakeholder disputes on social media.

One final thought in summation, social media creates a myriad of organizational and stakeholder relationships that paradoxically enable conflict communication and stakeholder voice as they network, share, and comment. This interconnectivity may both help organizations craft responsive risk and safety messages and estrange stakeholders entrenched in polarized perceptions of those messages. Considering the microcosm of intractable, polarizing positions tied to stakeholders' sociocultural meanings and identities of mask-wearing, Amtrak's case of mask accepting-rejecting YouTube comments demonstrate the challenges that organizations face in developing effective risk communication. In Amtrak's case, their one-sided argumentation did little to address the characteristics of intractable conflicts: paradoxical structure, depth of meaning, emotionality, complexity, trauma, and identity (Coleman, 2003; Jameson, 2003). With interprofessional collaborations between experts in conflict, social media, and risk and crisis communication, the complexity of the communication team and their strategies should match the complexity of situation.

References

Abrams, J. (2020 May 7). *Amtrak requires facial coverings as added measure of protection.* Retrieved from https://media.amtrak.com/2020/05/amtrak-requires-facial-coverings-as-added-measure-of-protection/

Agne, R. R. (2007). Reframing practices in moral conflict: Interaction problems in the negotiation standoff at Waco. *Discourse & Society, 18*(5): 549–578. DOI: 10.1177/0957926507079634

Allen, M. (1991). Meta-analysis comparing the persuasiveness of one-sided and two-sided messages. *Western Journal of Speech Communication, 55*(3): 30–404.

Amtrak. (2020a). *1970's-The journey forward.* Retrieved from https://history.amtrak.com/amtraks-history/1970s

Amtrak. (2020b). *Historic timeline.* Retrieved from https://history.amtrak.com/amtraks-history/historic-timeline

Amtrak. (2020 Oct. 5). *Delivering a new standard of travel: Our commitment to safety* [YouTube]. Retrieved from https://www.youtube.com/watch?v=m-5jyObKFsk

Amtrak. (2020 July 24). *Did you know? Learn about our mask policy* [YouTube]. Retrieved from https://www.youtube.com/watch?v=0lT76x3gpxc

Amtrak. (2021 Feb. 17). *Did you know? Mask policy* [YouTube]. Retrieved from https://www.youtube.com/watch?v=iRWJlCOQhlY

Amtrak. (2020 June 26). *Amtrak's Medical Services Team: Delivering a New Standard of Travel* [YouTube]. Retrieved from https://www.youtube.com/watch?v=IzslbGbxDjk

Arthurs, J., Drakopoulou, S., & Gandini, A. (2018). Researching YouTube. *Convergence: The International Journal of Research into New Media Technologies, 24*(1): 3–15. DOI: 10.1177/1354856517737222

Auxier, B., Anderson, M., & Kumar, M. (2019 Dec. 20). 10 tech-related trends that shaped the decade. *Pew Research Center.* Retrieved from https://www.pewresearch.org/fact-tank/2019/12/20/10-tech-related-trends-that-shaped-the-decade/

Becker, A., & Anderson, A. A. (2019). Using humor to engage the public on climate change: The effect of exposure to one-sided vs. two-sided satire on message discounting, elaboration and counterarguing. *Journal of Science Communication, 18*(4): 1–18. DOI: 10.22323/2.18040207

Benoit, W. L. (2018). Crisis and image repair at United Airlines: Fly the unfriendly skies. *Journal of International Crisis and Risk Communication Research, 1*(1): 11–26. DOI: 10.30658/jicrcr.1.1.2

Blagov, P. S. (2020). Adaptive and dark personality in the COVID-19 pandemic: Predicting health-behavior endorsement and the appeal of public-health messages. *Social Psychological and Personality Science, 12*(5): 697–707. DOI:10.1177/1948550620936439

Bodtker, A. M., & Jameson, J. K. (2001). Emotion in conflict formation and its transformation: Application to organizational conflict management. *The International Journal of Conflict Management, 12*(3): 259–275.

Brehm, J. W. (1966). *A theory of psychological reactance.* Academic Press. New York.

Bridges, D. R., Davidson, R. A., Odegard, P. S., Maki, I. V., & Tomkowiak, J. (2011). Interprofessional collaboration: Three best practice models of interprofessional education. *Medical Education Online, 16*(1): 1–10. DOI: 10.3402/meo.v16i0.6035

Brinson, S. L. & Benoit, W. L. (1999). The tarnished star: Restoring Texaco's damaged public image. *Communication Quarterly, 44:* 416–433.

Brodie, R. J., Ilic, A., Juric, B., & Hollebeek, L. (2013). Consumer engagement in a virtual brand community: An exploratory analysis. *Journal of Business Research, 66*(1): 105–114. DOI: 10.1016/j.jbusres.2011.07.029

Bromwich, J. E. (2020 July 21). Fighting over masks in public is the new American pastime. *The New York Times*, Retrieved from https://www.nytimes.com/2020/06/30/style/mask-america-freedom-coronavirus.html

Brummans, B. H. J. M., Putnam, L. L., Gray, B., Hanke, R., Lewicki, R. J., & Wiethoff, C. (2008). Making sense of intractable multiparty conflict: A study of framing in four environmental disputes. *Communication Monographs, 75*(1): 25–51. DOI: 10.1080/03637750801952735

Burgess, J. & Green, J. (2018). *YouTube: Online video and participatory culture* (2nd ed.). Polity. Cambridge.

Centers for Disease Control and Prevention (CDC). (2021 Feb. 23). *Types of masks.* Retrieved from https://www.cdc.gov/coronavirus/2019-ncov/prevent-getting-sick/types-of-masks.html

Coleman, P. T. (2003). Characteristics of protracted, intractable conflict: Toward the development of a metaframework-I. *Peace and Conflict: Journal of Peace Psychology*, *9*(1): 1–37.

Edgerly, S., Vraga, E. K., Dalrymple, K. E., Macafee, T., & Fung, T. K. F. (2013). Directing the dialogue: The relationship between YouTube videos and the comments they spur. *Journal of Information Technology & Politics*, *10:* 276–292. DOI: 10.1080/19331681.2013.794120

Eikenberry, S. E., Mancuso, M., Iboi, E., Phan, T., Eikenberry, K., Kuang, Y., Kostelich, E., & Gumel, A. B. (2020). To mask or not to mask: Modeling the potential for face mask use by the general public to curtail the COVID-19 pandemic. *Infectious Disease Modelling*, *5:* 293–308. DOI: 10.1016/j.idm.2020.04.001

Elliott, M., Gray, B., & Lewicki, R. (2003). Lessons learning about the framing of intractable environmental conflicts. In R. Lewicki, B. Gray, and M. Elliott (Eds.), *Making sense of intractable environmental conflicts: Concepts and cases.* Island Press. Washington.

Feng, S., Shen, C., Xia, N., Song, W., Fan, M., & Cowling, B. J. (2020). Rational use of face masks in the COVID-19 pandemic. *The Lancet: Respiratory Medicine*. DOI:10.1016/S2213-2600(20)30134-X

Folger, J. P., Poole, M. S., & Stutman, R. K. (2021). *Working through conflict: Strategies for relationships, groups, and organizations* (9th ed.). New York: Routlege.

Fox, J. & Moreland, J. J. (2015). The dark side of social networking sites: An exploration of the relational and psychological stressors associated with Facebook use and affordances. *Computers in Human Behavior*, *45:* 168–176. DOI: 10.1016/j.chb.2014.11.083

Friedman, R. A. & Currall, S. C. (2003). Conflict escalation: Dispute exacerbating elements of e-mail communication conflict. *Human Relations*, *56*(11): 1325–1347.

Gleditsch, K. S., Salehyan, I., & Schultz, K. (2008). Fighting at home, fighting abroad: How civil wars lead to international disputes. *Journal of Conflict Resolution*, *52*(4): 479–506. DOI: 10.1177/0022002707313305

Godard, J. (1992). Strikes as collective voice: A behavior analysis of strike activity. *ILR Review*, *46* (1): 161–175.

Halpern, L. W. (2020). The politicization of COVID-19. *American Journal of Nursing*, *120*(11): 19–20. DOI: 10.1097/01.NAJ.0000721912.7481.d7

Harlow, W. F., Brantley, B., & Harlow, R. M. (2011). BP initial image repair strategies after the *Deepwater Horizon* spill. *Public Relations Review*, *37:* 80–83. DOI: 10.1016/j.pubrev.2010.11.005

Hudson, S. & Hudson, R. (2013). Engaging with consumers using social media: A case study of music festivals. *International Journal of Event and Festival Management*, *4:* 206–223. DOI: 10.1108/IJEFM-06-2013-0012

Hutchinson, B. (2020 May 7). 'Incomprehensible': Confrontations over masks erupt amid COVID-19 crisis. *ABC News*. Retrieved from https://abcnews.go.com/US/incomprehensible-confrontations-masks-erupt-amid-covid-19-crisis/story?id=70494577

Ike, J. D., Bayerle, H., Logan, R. A., & Parker, R. M. (2021). Face masks: Their history and the values they communicate. *Journal of Health Communication*, *25*(12): 990–995. DOI: 10.1080/10810730.2020.1867257

Jameson, J. K. (2003). Transcending intractable conflict in health care: An exploratory study of communication and conflict management among anesthesia providers. *Journal of Health Communication*, *8:* 563–581. DOI: 10.1080/10810730390250344

Jane, E. A. (2015). Flaming? What flaming? The pitfalls and potentials of researching online hostility. *Ethics and Information Technology*, *17:* 65–87. DOI: 10.1007/s10676-015-9362-0

Jansen, B. J., Zhang, M., Sobel, K., & Chowdury, A. (2009). Twitter power: Tweets as electronic word of mouth. *Journal of the American Society for Information Science and Technology*, *60*(11): 2169–2188.

Janssen, O. & van de Vliert, E. (1996). Concern for the other's goals: Key to (de-)escalation of conflict. *International Journal of Conflict Management*, *7*(2): 99–120. DOI: 10.1108/eb022777

Jeong, H. (2008). *Understanding conflict and conflict analysis*. Los Angeles Sage.

Kelman, I. (2012). *Disaster diplomacy: How disasters affect peace and conflict*. London: Routledge.

Keltner, J. W. (1987). *Mediation: Toward a civilized system of dispute resolution*. Urbana, IL: ERIC Clearinghouse on Reading and Communication Skills.

Khan, M. L. (2017). Social media engagement: What motivates user participation and consumption on YouTube. *Computers in Human Behavior*, *66:* 236–247. DOI: 10.1016/j.chb.2016.09.024

Kim, K. (2020). Stealing thunder in negative political advertising: The persuasive impact of one-sided and two-sided negative messages on partisan individuals. *Journal of Creative Communications*, *15*(1): 7–18. DOI: 10.1177/0973258619876222

Lazo, L. (2020 May 7). Amtrak to require all passengers to wear masks. *The Washington Post*. Retrieved from https://www.washingtonpost.com/transportation/2020/05/07/amtrak-require-all-passengers-wear-masks/

Lea, M., O'Shea, T., Fung, P., & Spears, R. (1992). "Flaming" in computer-mediated communication: Observations, explanations, implications. In M. Lea (Ed.), *Contexts of computer-mediated communication* (pp. 89–112). New York: Harvester Wheatsheaf.

Lee, E. J. (2007). Deindividuation effects on group polarization in computer-mediated communication: The role of group identification, public-self-awareness, and perceived argument quality. *Journal of Communication*, *57:* 385–403. DOI: 10.1111/j.1460-2466.2007.00348.x

Lindell, M. K., Prater, C., & Perry, R. W. (2007). *Introduction to emergency management*. United States of America, Wiley.

Lingam, R. A. & Aripin, N. (2017). Comments on fire! Classifying flaming comments on YouTube videos in Malaysia. *Malaysian Journal of Communication*, *33*(4): 104–118. DOI: 10.17576/JKMJC-2017-3304-07

Liu, X. & Zhang, S. (2020). COVID-19: Face masks and human-to-human transmission [Letter to the Editor]. *Influenza and Other Respiratory Viruses*, *14:* 472–473. DOI: 10.1111/irv.12740

Lyu, W. & Wehby, G. L. (2020). Community use of face masks and COVID-19: Evidence from a natural experiment of state mandates in the US. *Health Affairs*, *39*(8): 1419–1425. DOI: 10.1377/hlthaff.2020.00818

Madden, A., Ruthven, I., & McMenemy, D. (2013). A classification scheme for content analysis of YouTube video comments. *Journal of Documentation*, *69*(5): 693–714. DOI: 10.1108/JD-06-2012-0078

Magliari, M. (2020 Aug. 17). *Amtrak statement: Aligning services to current travel needs*. Retrieved from https://media.amtrak.com/2020/08/amtrak-statement-aligning-services-to-current-travel-needs/

Makhortykh, M. & Sydorova, M. (2017). Social media and visual framing of the conflict in Eastern Ukraine. *Media, War & Conflict*, *10*(3): 359–381. DOI: 10.1177/1750635217702539

Malecki, K. M. C., Keating, J. A., & Safdar, N. (2021). Crisis communication and public perception of COVID-19 risk in the era of social media. *Clinical Infectious Diseases*, *72*(4): 699–704. DOI: 10.1093/cid/ciaa758

Marks, M. A., Sabella, M. J., Burke, C. S., & Zaccaro, S. J. (2002). The impact of cross-training on team effectiveness. *Journal of Applied Psychology*, *87*(1): 3–13. DOI: 10.1037//0021-9010.87.1.3

McEntire, D. A. (2007). *Disaster response and recovery*. Hoboken, New Jersey: Wiley.

Molyneux, J. (2001). Interprofessional teamworking : What makes teams work well? *Journal of Interprofessional Care*, *15*(1): 29–35. DOI: 10.1080/13561820020022855

Moor, P. J., Heuvelman, A., & Verleur, R. (2010). Flaming on YouTube. *Computers in Human Behavior, 26*(6): 1536–1546. DOI: 10.1016/j.chb/2010.05.023

Nair, N. (2008). Towards understanding the role of emotions in conflict: A review and future directions. *International Journal of Conflict Management, 19*(4): 359–381. DOI: 10.1108/10444060810909301

Ohlheiser, A. (2020 May 7). How COVID-19 conspiracy theorists are exploiting YouTube culture. *MIT Technology Review.* Retrieved from https://www.technologyreview.com/2020/05/07/1001252/youtube-covid-conspiracy-theories/

O'Brien, M., Moore, K., McNicholas, F. (2020). Social media spread during Covid-19: The pros and cons of likes and shares. *Irish Journal of Medicine, 113*(4): 52.

O'Keefe, D. J. (1999). How to handle opposing arguments in persuasive messages: A meta-analytic review of the effects of one-sided and two-sided messages. *Annals of the International Communication Association, 22*(1): 209–249. DOI: 10.1080/23808985.1999.11678963

O'Sullivan, P. B. & Flanagin, A. J. (2003). Reconceptualizing "flaming" and other problematic messages. *New Media & Society, 5*(1): 69–94.

Pihlaja, S. (2014). *Antagonism on YouTube: Metaphor in online discourse.* London: Bloomsbury.

Postmes, T., Spears, R., & Lea, M. (1999). Social identity, normative content and 'deindividuation' in computer-mediated communication. *Communication Research, 25:* 689–715.

Putnam, L. L. & Shoemaker, M. (2007). Changes in conflict framing in the news coverage of an environmental conflict. *Journal of Dispute Resolution, 1:* 167–175.

Putnam, L. L. (2006). Definitions and approaches to conflict and communication. In J. G. Oetzel & S. Ting-Toomey [Eds.], *The sage handbook of conflict communication: Integrating theory, research, and practice* (pp. 1–32). Thousand Oaks, CA: Sage.

Rail Passenger Service Act, H.R. act 17949 Cong. (1970). https://www.govinfo.gov/content/pkg/STATUTE-84/pdf/STATUTE-84-Pg1327.pdf

Ratzan, S. C., Sommariva, S., & Rauh, L. (2020). Enhancing global health communication during a crisis: Lessons from the COVID-19 pandemic. *Public Health Research & Practice, 30*(2): 1–6. DOI: 10.17061/phrp3022010

Reuter, C., Stieglitz, & Imran, M. (2020). Social media in conflicts and crises. *Behavior & Information Technology, 39*(3): 241–251. DOI: 10.1080/0144929X.2019.1629025

Richards, A. S., Bessarabova, E., Banas, J., & Bernard, D. R. (2020). Reducing psychological reactance to health promotion messages: Comparing preemptive and postscript mitigation strategies. *Health Communication*, Oct 27: 1–9. DOI: 10.1080/10410236.2020.1839203

Riess, R. & Silverman, H. (2020 Aug. 4). Man charged with shooting at an employee after being asked to wear a mask in a Pennsylvania cigar shop, police say. *CNN.* https://www.cnn.com/2020/08/04/us/man-gun-pennsylvania-cigar-shop-masks/index.html

Rogan, R. G. & Hammer, M. R. (2006). The emerging field of crisis/hostage negotiation: A communication-based perspective. In J. G. Oetzel & S. Ting-Toomey [Eds.], *The sage handbook of conflict communication: Integrating theory, research, and practice* (pp. 451–478). Thousand Oaks, CA: Sage.

Rosner, E. (2020). Adverse effects of prolonged mask use among healthcare professionals during COVID-19. *Journal of Infectious Diseases and Epidemiology, 6*(3): 1–5. DOI: 10.23937/2474-3658/1510130

Scheid, J. L., Lupien, S. P., Ford, G. S., & West, S. L. (2020). Commentary: Physiological and psychological impact of face mask usage during the COVID-19 pandemic. *International Journal of Environmental Research and Public Health, 17*: 1–12. DOI: 10.3390/ijerph17186655

Seeger, M. W., Sellnow, T. L., & Ulmer, R. R. (2003). *Communication and organizational crisis.* Westport, CT: Greenwood Publishing Group.

Sellnow, T. L., & Seeger, M. W. (2013). *Theorizing crisis communication.* Oxford: John Wiley & Sons.

Sharma, G., Bartunek, J., Buzzanell, P. M., Carmine, S., Endres, C., Etter, M., Fairhurst, G., Hahn, T., Le, P., Li, X., Pamphile, V., Pradies, C., Putnam, L. L., Rocheville, K., Schad, J., Sheep, M., & Keller, J. (2021). A paradox approach to societal tensions during the pandemic crisis. *Journal of Management Inquiry*, *30*(2): 121–137. DOI: 10.1177/1056492620986604

Shmueli, D., Elliott, M., & Kaufman, S. (2006). Frame changes and the management of intractable conflicts. *Conflict Resolution Quarterly*, *24*(2): 207–218. DOI: 10.1002/crq.169

Sorensen J.H., Sorensen B.V. (2007) Community Processes: Warning and Evacuation. In H. Rodríguez, E. L. Quarantelli, & R. R. Dynes (Eds.), *Handbook of Disaster Research. Handbooks of Sociology and Social Research* (pp. 183–199). New York: Springer. DOI: 10.1007/978-0-387-32353-4_11

Spradley, R. T. & Spradley, E. L. (2020a). Contradiction and double binds in COVID-19 face covering recommendations. *International Research Journal of Health Education, 3(13):* 1–6. DOI: 10.28933/irjhe-2020-09-1205

Spradley, R. T. & Spradley, E. (2020b). The case of toxic leadership on Mars Hill: Conflict framing and image restoration strategy in the devolution and dissolution of a megachurch. *Journal of Leadership Accountability and Ethics*, *17*(6): 73–87. DOI: 10.33423/jlae.v17i6.3797

Trottier, D. & Fuchs, C. (2015). Theorizing social media, politics, and the state. In D. Trottier & C. Fuchs (Eds.), *Social media, politics and the state: Protests, revolutions, riots, crime and policing in the age of Facebook, Twitter, and YouTube*. (pp. 3–38). New York: Routlege.

Truta, T. S., Boeriu, C. M., Copotoiu, S. M., Petrisor, M., Turucz, E., Vatau, D., & Lazarovici, M. (2018). Improving nontechnical skills of an interprofessional emergency medical team through a one day crisis resource management training. *Medicine (Baltimore)*, *97*(32): 1–7. DOI: 10.1097/MD.0000000000011828

Tso, R. V., & Cowling, B. J. (2020). Importance of face masks for COVID-19: A call for effective public education. *Clinical Infectious Disease*, *71*(16): 2195–2198. DOI: 10.1093/cid/ciaa593

Turnage, A. K. (2008). Email flaming behaviors and organizational conflict. *Journal of Computer-Mediated Communication*, *13:* 43–59. DOI: 10.1111/j1083-6101.2007.00385.x

Ulmer, R. R., Sellnow, T. L., & Seeger, M. W. (2019). *Effective crisis communication: Moving from crisis to opportunity* (4th ed.). Los Angeles, CA: Sage.

Van Kessel, P. (2019 Dec. 4). 10 facts about Americans and YouTube. *Pew Research*. Retrieved from https://www.pewresearch.org/fact-tank/2019/12/04/10-facts-about-americans-and-youtube/

Wall, J. A., Jr. & Callister, R. R. (1995). Conflict and its management. *Journal of Management*, *21*(3): 515–558. DOI: 10.1177/014920639502100306

Walther, J. B., DeAndrea, D., Kim, J., & Anthony, J. C. (2010). The influence of online comments on perceptions of antimarijuana public service announcements on YouTube. *Human Communication Research, 36:* 469–492.

Weick, K. E. & Sutcliffe, K. M. (2015). *Managing the unexpected: Sustained performance in a complex world* (3rd ed.). Hoboken, New Jersey: John Wiley & Sons.

Zdanowicz, C. & Hunter, M. (2020 June 18). Passenger removed from American Airlines flight has been temporarily banned by the airline. *CNN*. Retrieved from https://www.cnn.com/travel/article/passenger-removed-flight-for-refusing-to-wear-mask-trnd/index.html

Zeitzoff, T. (2017). How social media is changing conflict. *Journal of Conflict Resolution*, *61*(9): 1970–1991. DOI: 10.1177/0022002717721392

Zeitzoff, T. (2018). Does social media influence conflict? Evidence from the 2012 Gaza conflict. *Journal of Conflict Resolution*, *62*(1): 29–63. DOI: https://10.1177.0022002716650925.

Ekaterina Bogomoletc

Chapter 10
Normalizing the New Reality: Newsjacking or Brand Activism?

Abstract: With the COVID-19 pandemic becoming part of our lives, brands are facing the challenge of figuring out appropriate ways to build relationships with their publics as well as to promote their products and services. Drawing upon research on brand activism and newsjacking, this chapter examines public reactions to three campaigns, *You Can't Stop Us* by Nike, *Socialize Responsibly* by Heineken, and *Open Like Never Before* by Coca Cola. The research is done by analyzing YouTube comments using computational text analysis (N = 4979) and thematic analysis (N = 600). The analysis demonstrated that brands' publics were more concerned about the political side of the campaigns which might indicate publics' readiness to negotiate brands' place in the new reality without viewing their actions as opportunistic. At the same time, the campaigns were perceived as brand activism which brings additional concerns when it comes to the authenticity of companies' COVID-19 responses. Overall, the chapter explores the broader questions of brands negotiating their place in the new, post-pandemic, world.

Keywords: COVID-19, brand activism, newsjacking, social media, sentiment analysis, thematic analysis

Introduction

With the COVID-19 pandemic lasting for more than a year, brands are facing the challenge of building relationships with their publics as well as promoting their products and services. As mentioned by experts, today, "some viewers expect to see cues about current events on the screen, such as actors practicing social distancing, while others want to escape from reality" (Vranica, 2020, para. 6). A number of companies approached this challenge by launching "life after the pandemic" kinds of

Acknowledgements: I would like to thank Dr. Steve McDonald, Dr. Sergei Samoilenko, and Jessica Carter for their helpful feedback on this piece.

Note: This study previously appeared in Birmingham, B., Yook, B., Chen, Z.F. (2021). Contributing at the top and throughout an organization: research and strategies that advance our understanding of public relations. Proceedings of the 24th International Public Relations Research Conference, USA, Retrieved November 8, 2021, from: https://bit.ly/3wqmorh.

https://doi.org/10.1515/9783110687262-011

campaigns. In these campaigns, brands would usually discuss the new habits and life adjustments that people are getting used to in the post-pandemic world, such as contactless delivery or cooking at home (Vranica, 2020). However, companies' attempts to navigate the new environment did not always work well, and some of the campaigns received controversial feedback from their audience.

Drawing upon research on brand activism (Manfredi-Sánchez, 2019) and newsjacking (Angell et al., 2019), this chapter examines public reactions to three campaigns, *You Can't Stop Us* by Nike, *Socialize Responsibly* by Heineken, and *Open Like Never Before* by Coca Cola. These campaigns were launched several months after the beginning of the pandemic. They all communicated brands' vision of going back to a "normal" life. More interestingly, all of them got massive, conflicted responses from their publics online.

In the next sections, I first describe the case studies and the theoretical framework of the project. Then, using computational text analysis, I conduct sentiment analysis of the public reactions to the campaigns. Finally, I conduct qualitative thematic analysis of the reactions to uncover the meanings behind the sentiments.

Normalizing the New Reality

The campaigns by Nike, Heineken, and Coca Cola were launched at the end of July and beginning of August 2020. Nike's commercial was created by Wieden+Kennedy agency and communicated the idea of coming "back stronger, together" after the pandemic and civil unrest in the U.S., underlining the power of sports in bringing people together and "pushing [them] ahead" (Dan, 2020; Nike Youtube, 2020, para. 3). The ad is an impressive compilation of video recordings from sport events with videos of athletes training at home during the pandemic. Through the campaign, Nike addresses the issues of COVID-19, racial and social justice, and inclusivity. The commercial was posted on social media platforms and received almost 60 million views on YouTube (Nike YouTube, 2020), 40 million views on Twitter (Nike Twitter, 2020), and hundreds of thousands of reposts and thousands of likes across platforms. The commercial also received a lot of attention from popular media with some outlets praising the video and the team behind it (Dan, 2020).

Coca Cola's ad was created together with George the Poet. The implied message was to encourage people to "start over" and come back to a new, better reality after the lockdown (Coca Cola YouTube, 2020). The commercial addresses not only the issue of COVID-19 but also the pressing issue of social justice. The ad received more than 200,000 views on YouTube and hundreds of comments. The commercial also got covered by popular and professional media (see, e.g., Marketing Week, 2020).

Finally, the ad by Heineken depicts post-pandemic life from the perspective of those going to bars (Heineken YouTube, 2020). In the video, people wear masks at a bar, keep six feet distance when going to a bathroom, blow birthday candles with a napkin, and find creative ways to keep their hands clean. The ad has received more than 200 thousand views and hundreds of comments on YouTube (Heineken YouTube, 2020). It also received media coverage by professional and popular media with some outlets calling the ad "100% relatable" and suggesting that the video "captures the joy and awkwardness of the new normal" (Spary, 2020, para. 3).

Overall, the ads were part of a trend where brands tried imagining and normalizing the new reality, whether it was the "new normal" related to COVID-19 safety measures or the idea of a better world without the virus and racism. While companies have been responding to relevant news and societal issues in the past, the COVID-19 situation seems to be unusual. First, due to the scale of the crisis, companies seem to have no choice but to react to the pandemic in some way. At the same time, with hundreds of thousands of people dying from the virus, there is a risk of looking tone-deaf and being accused of opportunistic behavior. To account for these aspects of strategic communication during the pandemic, the current study draws upon research on newsjacking and brand activism. In the next sections, through the lenses offered by these approaches, I explore public reactions to brands' attempts to normalize a new reality and negotiate brands' place in the new, post-pandemic, world.

Responding to the Current Events: Newsjacking and Brand Activism

Newsjacking is the strategy of "referencing of topical news stories in marketing communications" (Angell et al., 2019, p. 756). This is an increasingly popular practice among communication professionals, especially those working in digital PR and marketing, who see it as a way to get free publicity and/or better social media engagement (Scott, 2012; Sprout Social, 2020). The strategy is also called real time marketing (RTM) suggesting that marketing materials are being designed in real time, thus becoming "part of the ongoing conversation" (Willemsen et al., 2018, p. 830). Despite the growing popularity of this strategy among communication professionals in the industry, research on the topic of newsjacking is scarce. Existing studies show that newsjacking positively affects attitudes towards brands' content (Angell et al., 2019), increases content shareability on Twitter (Willemsen et al., 2018), and negatively affects public responses to brands' communication on Instagram (Mazerant et al., 2021). Research by Willemsen and colleagues (2018) also demonstrated that using unpredictable events (e.g., news) for newsjacking is more efficient than using predictable events (e.g., holidays) in terms of content shareability. Interestingly, scholars suggested that in situations when "newsjacking is perceived as opportunistic or trivializing grave matters, it could prove counterproductive" (Angell et al., 2019, p. 769). Similar concerns were voiced in the community of marketing practitioners discussing whether some newsjacking practices might be "in poor taste" (see, e.g., Volpe, 2012, para. 1).

Brand Activism

A different way for companies to address pressing issues is through brand (or corporate) activism. Brand activism is defined as "the act of taking a stand on controversial social or political issues for which society has yet to reach consensus" (Mukherjee & Althuizen, 2020, The Asymmetric Effect of Brand Activism section, para. 1). When conceptualizing brand activism, some scholars also highlight companies' responsibility to contribute to the good of the society. For example, Eilert and Cherup (2020) define corporate activism as "a company's willingness to take a stand on social, political, economic, and environmental issues to create societal change by influencing the attitudes and behaviors of actors in its institutional environment" (p. 461). In addition, some also discuss pragmatic benefits of such communication moves. Vredenburg et al. (2020) argue that brand activism allows companies to "stand out in a fragmented marketplace" (p. 444).

Unlike traditional corporate social responsibility initiatives, brand activism is oftentimes related to controversial issues (Vredenburg et al., 2020). In addition, brand activism "involves both intangible (messaging) and tangible (practice) commitments to a sociopolitical cause" (Vredenburg et al., 2020, p. 448). As a result, some scholars and marketing practitioners suggest that brand activism might bring risks for a company (Moorman, 2020). Some scholars also argue that the success of brand activism depends a lot on its authenticity, i.e., how well it aligns with a company's reputation and behavior (Moorman, 2020). The brands that do not demonstrate genuine commitment to the declared views and values might be accused of "woke washing" or the practice of capitalizing on societal issues (see, e.g., Mahdawi, 2018). Among the possible strategies to evoke positive response to brand activism, researchers list using specific language when articulating brands' position and communicating its actions, having third parties confirm their commitment to societal good, and engaging with local organizations that influence policies of social interest (Vredenburg et al., 2020).

Based on the two approaches described above, this study seeks to answer the following questions:

RQ1: What public reactions did the brands' COVID-19 responses evoke?

RQ2: To what extent do public reactions to the brands' ads reflect the perception of the brands' COVID-19 efforts as newsjacking or brand activism?

Methods

In order to answer the research questions, YouTube comments under the brands' commercials were analyzed. The comments were collected on October 6, 2020, using the Coberry tool (Coberry, 2020) which allows exporting YouTube comments. The dataset includes user responses to the videos by Nike (N = 4400), Coca Cola (N = 263), and Heineken (N = 316).

The YouTube comments were analyzed in two stages using computational text analysis and thematic analysis. First, the computational text analysis was performed using the *tidyverse* R package. At this stage of the analysis, the comments for each campaign were broken down into single words ("tokenized"). After that, "stop words" (popular yet meaningless in the context of the study words, i.e., articles) were removed. Then, the most frequent words among the responses to each ad were identified. At this stage, the analysis was conducted using stemming technique, i.e., words with the same roots were counted as one word (e.g., "meet" and "meeting"). Finally, the sentiment analysis using the *bing* lexicon was performed. The top ten words with the highest frequency contributing to the negative and positive sentiments were identified for each campaign.

At the second stage, thematic analysis of the comments was conducted. For each campaign, 200 random posts were selected for analysis (N = 600). The comments were selected using the random number generator in Excel spreadsheets. The comments that were not in English, blank comments, or comments consisting of emojis were replaced by the next comment in line. The thematic analysis was based on the approach described by Braun and Clarke (2006). This approach consists of six rounds of data examination that involve getting familiar with the data as well as identifying key themes. First, the themes were identified for each case study separately. Then, common trends across the case studies were identified.

Overall, combining computational text analysis with thematic analysis allows for identifying underlying trends in the data and a deeper "immersion" into people's conversations at the same time (see, e.g., Light & Roscigno, 2020). By adding thematic analysis to the sentiment analysis, I was able to uncover reasons behind the trends manifested through the negative and positive sentiments expressed by the brands' publics.

Results

Overall Trends

Public reactions to Nike's and Heineken's campaigns demonstrated the predominance of negative polarity words over positive polarity words (4083 vs. 2183 words and 278 vs. 96 words respectively) while the ad by Coca Cola received almost equal number of negative and positive polarity words as a reaction to the campaign (99 vs. 103 words).

Nike's Campaign

The top ten words in the public reactions to Nike's campaign include "Nike," "Muslim," "Islam," "people," "sport," "change," "religion," "buy," "video," "ad," and "woman" (See Figure 10.1). Based on the list of the most frequent words, the discussion revolved around religion and women.

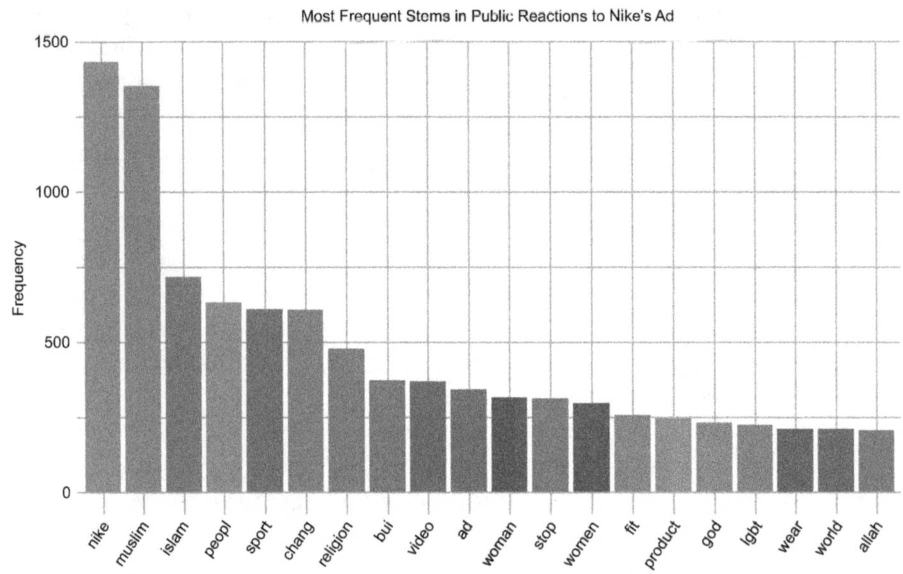

Figure 10.1: Top Frequent Words in Public Reactions to Nike's Campaign.

The top ten words contributing to the negative sentiment in the discussion of Nike's campaign were the words *wrong, boycott, bad, shame, hate, disgusting, offensive, racist, slave, and disrespectful* (See Figure 10.2). The top words contributing to positive sentiment were *respect, love, support, freedom, peace, free, supporting, nice, wow, proud, and faith.* Interestingly, none of these words directly relate to COVID-19 or the idea of the new reality. It is also interesting how a number of words on both sides relate to respect and strong feelings regarding either supporting or boycotting the brand. Also, one can see that while the original intention behind the campaign was to bring people together, some of the popular sentiments relate to racism, slavery, and hatred.

The thematic analysis helps examine what stands behind these public reactions. Based on the analysis of a random sample of comments (n = 200), several key themes emerge. First, the biggest theme seems to be *Anti-Islam Ad.* The comments under this theme accused the brand of promoting anti-Muslim ideas both through the visual part of the commercial and through the narration. It seems that this theme stands behind

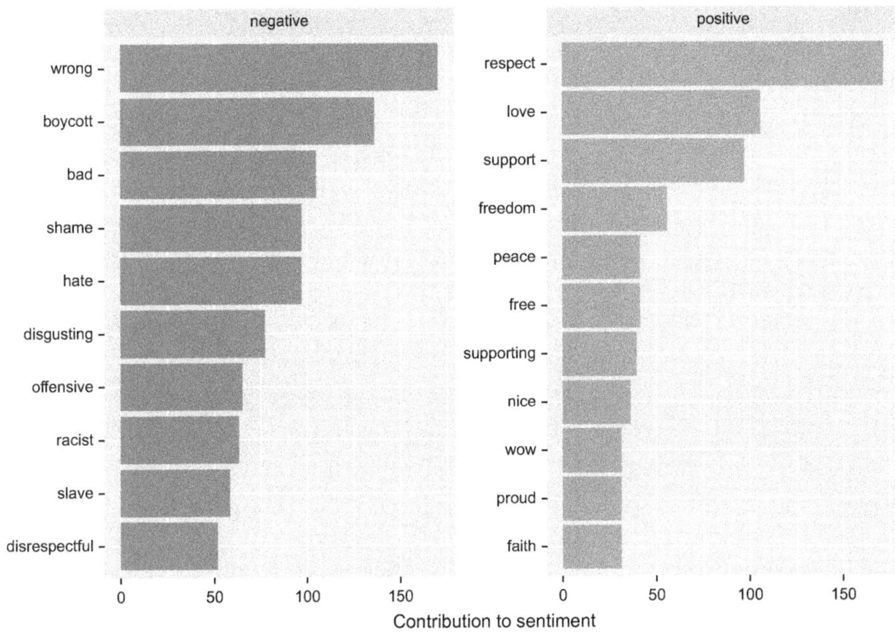

Figure 10.2: Sentiment Analysis of Nike's Campaign.

the trends manifested through some of the frequent words contributing to the negative sentiment including *wrong, shame, hate, disgusting, offensive, racist,* and *disrespectful.* The outrage related to this theme might be seen in such comments as, "*We don't fit ????? as a Muslim woman I don't want to fit on your version*" (User_18) and "*I am a Muslim and seeing this ad makes mc really offended and uncomfortable. Good job Nike, good job . . . " (User_109).*

The second theme stems from the first one, and this is the theme of *Boycotting* Nike. This theme manifested through declarations of one's intentions to stop buying Nike's products, suggestions to join the boycott, and suggestions to report the video. This is the theme that might explain the frequency of the word *boycott* in the sentiment analysis. For example, the theme is manifested through such comments as, "*I'm a Muslim and I'm never buying ur products again*" (User_49).

The company was also reminded of its *Past Missteps.* The comments falling under this theme discuss Nike's hiring practices in China as well as refer to a negative reputation of the company in general. This is the theme that might explain the "slave" portion of the negative sentiments. For example, one comment stated, "*Nike has always been shady, but d*mn you guys are the worst. Boycott all major fashion corporations that benefit from illegal child and slave labour!!*" (User_73).

Another interesting theme that emerged during the analysis was the theme of *Propaganda.* Users accused Nike of promoting "leftists" views through their commercial. This theme might be seen in such comments as "*New Wolrd Agenda Advertisment*"

(User_38), and "*the liberals & feminists will you use any tactics for their agenda.*" (User_197). Interestingly, some users also questioned the sincerity of Nike's position by calling it "woke".

Finally, some users tried *Supporting Nike*. They expressed admiration for the quality of the video production and editing skills of those behind the campaign. They also tried defending the implied message bringing the discussion back to the idea of the unifying power of sports. For example, this theme was manifested through such comments as, "*Wow why does such a nice message have to offend so many people.*" (User_43) and "*Seriously This is sooo satisfying for a sports person like me*" (User_79). This is the theme that might explain some of the words that contributed to the positive sentiment of the discussion. However, in most cases, the positive words were related not to the brand but to one's religion and views.

Coca Cola's Campaign

The top ten words in the public reactions to Coca Cola's campaign include "coca", "cola," "song," "ad," "drink," "normal," "people," "background," "coke," and "music" (See Figure 10.3). These words are not very informative, and overall, look like a neutral conversation about the ad and the music that was used in the video.

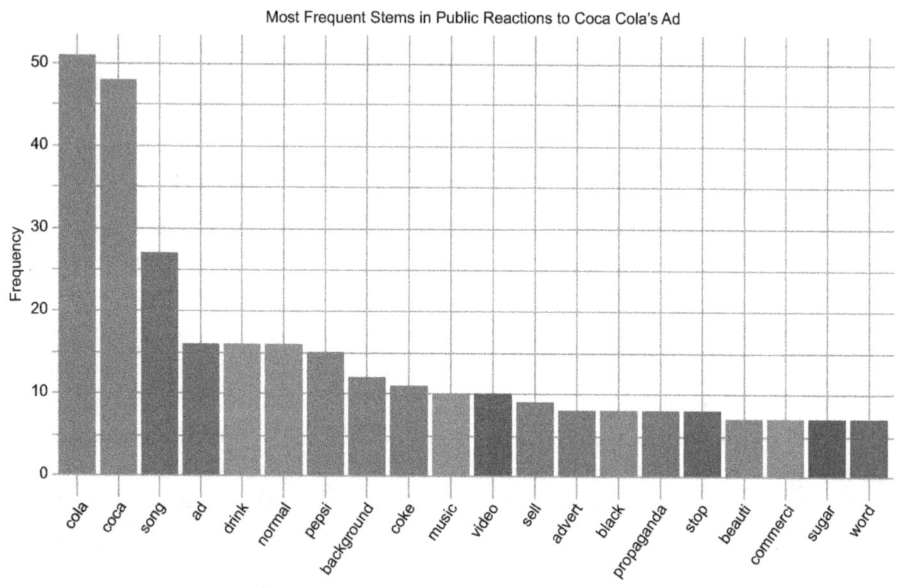

Figure 10.3: Top Frequent Words in Public Reactions to Coca Cola's Campaign.

The top ten words contributing to the negative sentiment in the discussion of Coca Cola's campaign were the words *propaganda, worst, die, bad, stole, poison, disgusting, cringe, broke, and uncomfortable* (See Figure 10.4). The top words contributing to positive sentiment were *beautiful, lead, love, positive, masterpiece, awesome, wow, supports, pure, and pretty*. Some of these words overlap with the public reaction to Nike's campaign. For example, one might see similarities when it comes to the idea of propaganda and brainwashing on the negative side of the discussion.

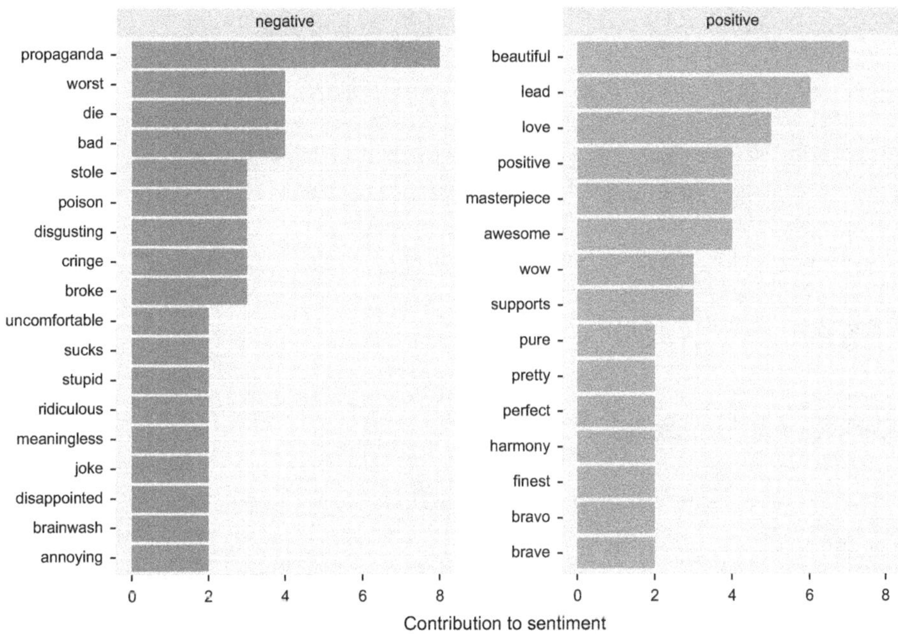

Figure 10.4: Sentiment Analysis of Coca Cola's Campaign.

The thematic analysis revealed several key themes in the discussion. One of the biggest themes was *Propaganda*. The comments under this theme accused Coca Cola of *propaganda* and *brainwashing*. For example, User_118 wrote, "*This Ad/ Spot/ Clip is disgusting. I've changed to organic coke by opponents. Better stuff, better taste, no brainwash. Thanks for makin goodbye this easy!* 👋🏻". Users also argued that the ad was overly political for a soft drink. Several users commented using a popular expression "*Go Woke Go Broke*." (e.g., User_63) referring to the idea that taking political stands might bring companies loss of revenue.

Another theme was related to *Health*. This is the theme that might explain the negative sentiments brought by the word "*poison*". People commented on the amount of sugar in Coke drinks and health risks associated with drinking soda including obesity and diabetes. The theme was manifested through such comments as "*and then we all get obese and diabetic.:)*" (User_60) and "*What if Coca-Cola stopped producing poison that it markets through flat, supposedly emotional engaging, content. Your intentions are transparent and you do not deserve the right to be a part of the new normal.*" (User_74).

Some users shared their intentions of *Boycotting* Coke. Interestingly, in this case, a boycott was suggested in the form of buying from the brand's competitors, Pepsi. As it is seen from the examples below, oftentimes, users would not even explain their motivations behind such a move simply suggesting switching to another drink: "*Yeah, what if we are #OpenLikeNeverBefore and actually start drinking Pepsi! I hope we don't go back to Coca-Cola.*" (User_4); "*I will never buy coca cola again in my life. From now on i will only buy Pepsi or something else.*" (User_40).

Finally, a number of people discussed the *Quality of the Ad*. Just like in Nike's case, users discussed whether they liked the quality of the video, music, and text. However, in the case of Coke, users had polar opinions regarding everything but the music. An example of comments supporting the ad would be "*Great emotional Video! BRAVO COCA COLA!! Can someone tell me wich song plays in the backround?*" (User_191). Those who disliked the video, would comment "*worst and most annoying ad ever*" (User_15).

Heineken's Campaign

The top ten words in the public reactions to Heineken's campaign include "people," "mask," "wear," "Heineken," "death," "covid," "flu," "virus," "life," and "Sinatra" (See Figure 10.5). This list suggests that the public responses to the ad are focused on issues of the pandemic and the new reality that includes mask wearing, death, and the virus.

The top ten words contributing to the negative sentiment in the discussion of Heineken's campaign were the words *virus, sad, die, disgusting, stupid, fake, died, geezer, fear, and propaganda* (See Figure 10.6). The top words contributing to positive sentiment were *love, safe, protection, prefer, nice, healthy, wow, top, super,* and *rich*. As is evident from the frequency count, this is the first ad that provoked a discussion regarding the virus itself. One might also see overlaps with the previous case studies when it comes to the topics of propaganda on the negative side and love on the positive one.

One of the key themes that emerged during the thematic analysis was *Science*. People shared statistics about the virus, expressed their support towards doctors' recommendations, and argued about the risks of the pandemic. The theme also includes comments arguing for or against masks, sharing links to research, and discussing trustworthiness of scientists. For example, this theme was manifested through such comments as "*@HetFloortje: Do you really think everybody will die of covid? There' s a new study in Germany from the DIW (german institute of economy) that shows, most*

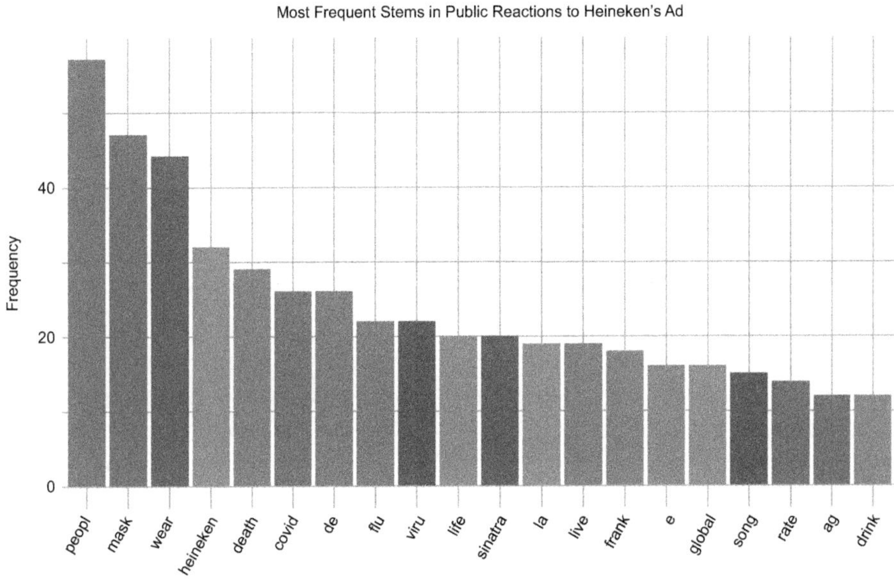

Figure 10.5: Top Frequent Words in Public Reactions to Heineken's Campaign.

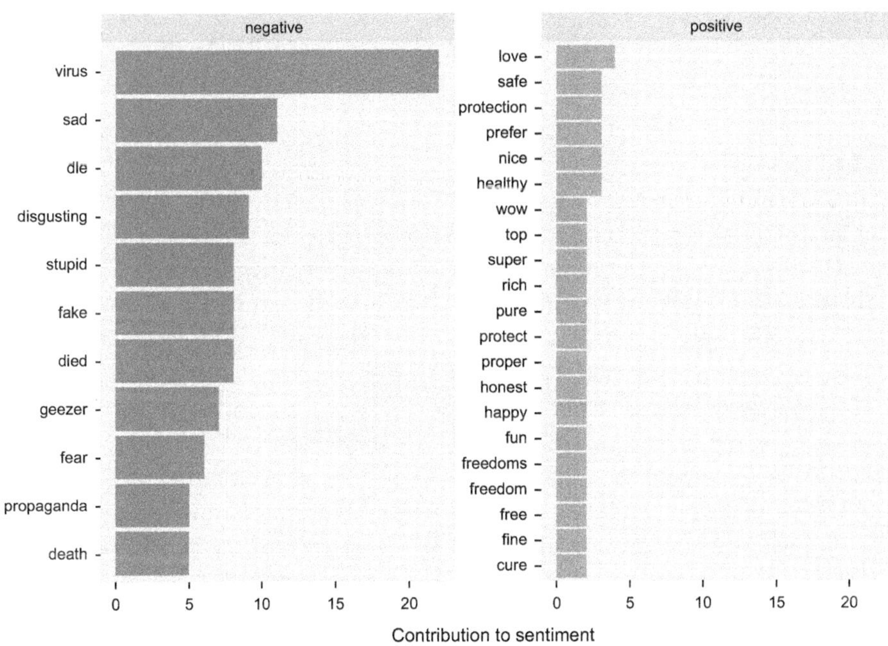

Figure 10.6: Sentiment Analysis of Heineken's Campaign.

people overestimate by fare the chance of getting so ill by covid one may die." (User_21). This is the theme that explains the negative sentiments behind the words *virus, die,* and *death.*

Another theme that emerged at this stage of the analysis is *Propaganda.* The brand was accused of brainwashing its publics. Interestingly, Heineken's comments included claims regarding the brand getting money from the World Health Organization (User_182) and supporting the New World Order[1] (User_13). These comments explain the sentiments brought by the words *propaganda, disgusting, and stupid.* The theme manifested through such comments as "*Absurd sad sick world. Pure brainwashing and propaganda.*" (User_171).

Some of the comments discussed the *New Reality* depicted by the ad. In most cases, the offered vision of the new normal was not received well. People even called the suggested way of going back to bars "*the new abnormal*" (User_81). Users pointed out that the suggested safety measures would ruin all the fun, and the attempt to normalize it is "totally absurd" (User_18). The theme got manifested through such comments as "*This is why I'm not going to the pub etc., until the world regains its sanity. That is not a good night out. It's a dystopian purgatory.*" (User_17).

Finally, some people argued for *Boycotting* Heineken. The theme of boycott appeared in the comments related to the new reality, propaganda, and also without any explanation: "*Scr*w u heineken!!! U KNOW WHY!!*" (User_40), "*what a shame I love Heineken but I will never drink it ever again after this advert it is disgusting that's abnormal you should be very ashamed of yourselves.*" (User_126).

Discussion

This study explored reactions to brands' attempts to reconsider the new reality after the COVID-19 pandemic. The analysis demonstrated that while some of the reactions to the companies' campaigns were unique to the brands, a number of comments conveyed similar public reactions across the case studies. First, the publics seemed to be more concerned with the political side of the brands' responses to the pandemic rather than with the newsjacking aspect of the campaigns. This might be seen both through the sentiment analysis and through thematic analysis. The comments focused more on the values promoted by the companies than on the brands capitalizing on public interest to COVID-19. This is an interesting take-away from this study as previous research raised questions about the benefits of newsjacking negative events (Angell et al., 2019). A different reaction in the case of COVID-19 might be due to the shared understanding that the pandemic is affecting everyone's lives, including brands'.

1 A famous conspiracy theory suggesting the existence of one global government.

At the same time, all three campaigns were accused of promoting a certain political agenda and propaganda. This demonstrates that the campaigns were perceived as part of brand activism efforts. This is not as surprising in the cases of Nike and Coca Cola since they explicitly addressed the issues of social and racial justice. However, this is rather unexpected in the case of Heineken as the campaign focused specifically on COVID-19 safety. The perceptions of brands' COVID-19 responses as brand activism bring extra expectations in terms of authenticity of companies' efforts which might be seen through some of the comments accusing the brands of woke washing. It might also mean that brands' reactions to COVID-19 might be perceived as taking a political stand, whether companies want it or not. This finding raises questions about how companies might react to the increasing politicization of various topics, including public health issues and the new, post-pandemic, etiquette. When does a company decide that an issue gets political and requires the company not only to address it but also to take a stand? When do companies' actions stop being perceived as newsjacking and become brand activism?

Second, as a result of negative reactions to such "propagandistic" efforts, publics suggested boycotting the brands. This included reporting the ads, buying from competitors, or not buying from the brands themselves. Such a reaction reflects the trends highlighted in scholarship on brands' activism suggesting that by taking a stand, a company might lose some of its customers who might not share the declared views of the organization (see, e.g., Moorman, 2020).

Finally, the case studies demonstrate that organizations' past missteps or the negative aspects of products might become an unintended part of the public discussion of brands' activism. In other words, when reacting to brands' activism, not only would publics criticize the companies for their stances but also for other actions or products that reflect negatively on their reputation in general. Similar phenomena are well-known in crisis communication scholarship which suggests that *crisis history* and *prior reputation* would affect public reactions to new crisis situations (Coombs, 2007). This is due to the fact that publics interpret new crises as part of the pattern demonstrating organizations' approach to building relationships with their publics (Coombs, 2007). I would suggest that in the case of brand activism, negatively perceived activism also becomes a part of "the company's character".

Implications For Communication Practitioners

The findings offer several implications for communication practitioners. First, the results of the study might mean that several months after the beginning of the pandemic, publics were open to negotiating brands' place in the new reality without viewing their actions as opportunistic. This might be encouraging news for companies willing to engage in "post-pandemic" promotion of their products and services as well as in relationship building with their publics.

Second, the reactions to the advertisements raise questions about possible ways to navigate public health crises for brands. When an issue is happening at the scale of the global pandemic, is it possible for a company to ignore it? Is it possible for a company to take a "neutral" stand when negotiating the company's place in the new reality? How can a company ensure that its actions are socially responsible and are not contributing to the growing polarization of the society? Based on the case studies in this chapter, I would suggest that being "neutral" is becoming less of an option once a public health topic becomes political. For brands, this might mean that they would need to craft their responses to such health crises as if the organizations were engaging in brand activism. Among other implications of this shift, the brands would need to make sure that the company's position on a public health issue aligns with core organizational values and fits a bigger communication strategy. The organizations would also need to be ready to engage with local organizations to address the public health issue and prepare to lose some of the brand's audience due to a mismatch in perspectives on the given topic.

Finally, organizations engaging in such "unintended" activism might receive negative reactions related not only to the campaign itself but to the organizations' past missteps. With this possibility in mind, brands could benefit from prioritization of their publics and an analysis of the perceived "character" of the organization. Would responding to a public health crisis add to the negative perception of the company among publics with a higher priority? If so, would the benefits of such campaigns outweigh the losses, including financial and reputational damage? Is it possible to prevent such reactions? These are the questions that would need to be addressed at the stages of analysis and planning when designing the campaign.

Limitations

While this chapter provides valuable insights regarding public reactions to brands' COVID-19 responses, it has certain limitations. The biggest limitation of the study is that it only relies on YouTube data thus omitting other social media platforms. Also, the study treats threads and replies equally thus omitting the dynamics of the conversations between users.

References

Angell, R., Gorton, M., Bottomley, P., Marder, B., Bhaskar, S., & White, J. (2019). News you can use! Evaluating the effectiveness of newsjacking based content on social media. *Information Technology & People*, *33*(3), 755–773.

Braun, V., & Clarke, V. (2006). Using thematic analysis in psychology. *Qualitative Research in Psychology*, *3*(2), 77–101. DOI:10.1191/1478088706qp063oa

Coberry (2020). *Export YouTube video comments to CSV*. https://coberry.com/youtube

Coca Cola Youtube. (2020). *Coca-Cola & George the Poet present: Open like never before*. YouTube. https://www.youtube.com/watch?v=SukwNeHMMhQ

Coombs, T. (2007). Protecting organization reputations during a crisis: the development and application of situational crisis communication theory. *Corporate Reputation Review*, *10*(3), 163–176. DOI:10.1057/palgrave.crr.1550049

Dan, A. (2020). *This Nike ad took 4000 hours of sports footage to make. the result is stunning*. Forbes. https://www.forbes.com/sites/avidan/2020/08/07/this-nike-ad-took-4000-hours-of-sports-footage-to-make-the-result-is-stunning/?sh=2017e25d21f4

Eilert, M., & Cherup, A. N. (2020). The activist company: examining a company's pursuit of societal change through corporate activism using an institutional theoretical lens. *Journal of Public Policy & Marketing*, *39*(4), 461–476. DOI: 10.1177/0743915620947408

Heineken Youtube. (2020). *Heineken – back to the bars*. YouTube. https://www.youtube.com/watch?v=XDD2Xhdq_Ds

Light, R., & Roscigno, V. J. (2020). *Power, resistance, and slavery in the United States*. https://doi.org/10.31235/osf.io/wx26a

Mahdawi, A. (2018). *Woke-washing brands cash in on social justice. It's lazy and hypocritical*. The Guardian. https://www.theguardian.com/commentisfree/2018/aug/10/fellow-kids-woke-washing-cynical-alignment-worthy-causes

Manfredi-Sánchez, J. L. (2019). Brand activism. *Communication & Society*, *32*(4), 343–359. DOI: 10.15581/003.32.4.343-359

Marketing Week. (2020). *Coca-Cola, McDonald's, junk food ad ban: 5 things that mattered this week and why*. Marketing Week. https://www.marketingweek.com/coca-cola-mcdonalds-junk-food-ad-ban-5-things-that-mattered-this-week-and-why/

Mazerant, K., Willemsen, L. M., Neijens, P. C., & van Noort, G. (2021). Spot-on creativity: creativity biases and their differential effects on consumer responses in (non-)real-time marketing. *Journal of Interactive Marketing*, *53*, 15–31. https://doi.org/10.1016/j.intmar.2020.06.004

Moorman, C. (2020). Commentary: Brand Activism in a Political World. *Journal of Public Policy and Marketing*, *39*(4), 388–392. DOI:10.1177/0743915620945260

Mukherjee, S., & Althuizen, N. (2020). Brand activism: Does courting controversy help or hurt a brand? *International Journal of Research in Marketing*. DOI:10.1016/j.ijresmar.2020.02.008

Nike Youtube. (2020). *You can't stop us / Nike*. Youtube. https://www.youtube.com/watch?v=WA4dDsOT7sM

Nike Twitter (2020). *Nothing can stop what we can do together*. Twitter. https://twitter.com/Nike/status/1288845608694902786

Scott, D. M. (2012). *Newsjacking: How to inject your ideas into a breaking news story and generatetons of media coverage. John Wiley & Sons*, Hoboken, New Jersey. (Kindle Edition).

Spary, S. (2020). *As the world's bars reopen, Heineken's ad about social distancing is 100% relatable*. AdWeek. https://www.adweek.com/brand-marketing/as-the-worlds-bars-reopen-heinekens-ad-about-social-distancing-is-100-relatable/

Sprout Social. (2020). *Newsjacking*. Sprout Social. https://sproutsocial.com/glossary/newsjacking/

Volpe, M. (2012). *Is newsjacking hurricane sandy right or wrong?* Hubspot. https://blog.hubspot.com/blog/tabid/6307/bid/33771/is-newsjacking-hurricane-sandy-right-or-wrong.aspx?fbclid=IwAR2-IxpzLIpeU_Taq3UZbfxcUTTQpJJ946jKWA_8T_K3-usVyU8YsnCk24

Vranica, S. (2020). *Coronavirus upended advertising. Here's how brands from Progressive Insurance to Budweiser responded.* https://www.wsj.com/articles/coronavirus-upended-advertising-madison-avenue-wasnt-ready-11601697645

Vredenburg, J., Kapitan, S., Spry, A., & Kemper, J. A. (2020). Brands taking a stand: authentic brand activism or woke washing? *Journal of Public Policy and Marketing*, *39*(4), 444–460. DOI: 10.1177/0743915620947359

Willemsen, L. M., Mazerant, K., Kamphuis, A.-L., & van der Veen, G. (2018). Let's get real (time)! The potential of real-time marketing to catalyze the sharing of brand messages. *International Journal of Advertising*, *37*(5), 828–848.

Part III: **Online Conflict Management in Education, Training, and Practice**

Rachelly Ashwall-Yakar

Chapter 11 Resolving Digital Conflicts – Using Community Wisdom for Conflict Resolution Education and Practice in the Digital Era

Abstract: This chapter describes the Online Dispute Resolution (ODR) initiative 'Agree-Online,' which utilizes community wisdom to increase the possibilities for conflict resolution. Community Wisdom refers to the knowledge gained through sharing different perspectives within a community (identified as people who share a demographic category such as age range, gender, race, ethnicity, religion, or profession) "where greater value is placed on collective intelligence and collective problem solving" (Zoref, 2005, 5). Our study has revealed both digital conflict characteristics and the most common ways to overcome them, as suggested by the digital community of Generation-Z[1] in Israel. This new knowledge may contribute to both the field of Conflict Resolution Education (CRE) and the field of Online Dispute Resolution. Through this study, we can learn from the wisdom of digital natives, as well as equip future generations with relevant skills to deal with online conflict and become digital citizens who possess both social and emotional skills that fit their needs in the 21st century.

Keywords: conflict resolution education, community wisdom, cyberbullying, mediation skills, online dispute resolution

Introduction

This chapter presents a study exploring new knowledge about conflict resolution in the digital age. At the beginning of the chapter, I describe the impact of the transition of social interaction to the digital environment on children in our schools. I examine the disadvantages of digital interaction and the harmful consequences of using digital social communication without deep understanding of the differences between face-to-face (FTF) communication vis-à-vis social communication in the digital space. I also discuss the way technology may be harnessed to improve our skills and knowledge in general and, from the perspective of Conflict Resolution Education (CRE), address the social difficulties in the lives of the young population.

1 The generation of people born in the late 1990s and early 2000s. In Merriam-Webster's online dictionary, Retrieved from https://www.merriam-webster.com/dictionary/Generation%20Z.

https://doi.org/10.1515/9783110687262-012

The literature on CRE presents its positive impact, both on individual learners and the school environment (Jones, 2004). However, most of the research refers to FTF interactions. Due to the development of digital social life, there is a need to further investigate digital interactions, the conflicts that arise in these interactions, and the relevant skills needed to address them. The purpose of this chapter is to demonstrate an online conflict resolution tool that has been used for training and to show how examining student conflict resolution helps us understand the ways children deal with conflicts online and how we can better educate them to gain ODR competencies.

The Problem: Conflicts in the School Environment and Beyond

One of the primary social spaces of the young population is school. Conflicts are a natural part of social relations (Carter & Osler, 2000; Johnson & Johnson, 1994), yet many young people do not have the knowledge or skills to deal with conflict effectively. In fact, teasing, insulting others, or expressions of physical violence and aggression among children and teenagers are a symptom of their inability to cope properly with conflict situations (Carter & Osler, 2000; Johnson & Johnson, 1994).

In 2012–2013 in U.S. schools, there were 31 homicides among school children between the ages of 5–18, and studies examining safety in schools point to even higher rates of violence in the following years (Diliberti et al., 2017). The statistics also show an increase in the extent of bullying, derogatory exclamations, and other expressions of violence that have implications for the emotional and social development of the pupils involved. These findings have significant implications for each student's sense of personal security in a space that should be protected and designed for the purposes of acquiring knowledge, life skills, and enrichment.

Further, traditional educational punishment methods in response to conflict situations lead to the suspension, expulsion, or imprisonment of those involved, without allowing them the opportunity to learn how to prevent future conflict. Studies from the U.S. educational system indicate that a student who has been expelled three times no longer sees the educational system as a positive resource (Brooks, Schiraldi, & Ziedenberg, 2000).

The transition to social life in the digital space has exacerbated conflict within the school environment and other social difficulties experienced by children and teenagers (Brun, Ashwall, & Haimovich, 2017; Franco, Almog, & Genaim, 2019). We have learned that when not treated appropriately and in a timely manner, digital conflicts can easily escalate to violence and cyberbullying, an offensive behavior that makes social media an unsafe environment for its users (Dwyer & Easteal, 2013; Gefen, 2019). Digital conflicts and cyberbullying have significant implications for children's ability to concentrate on their education and to perceive the school environment as secure. Thus, if children can learn how to resolve online conflict effectively, it could have preventive benefits and possibly lead to more positive engagement in the educational system.

The pioneering research project described in this chapter has three main contributions:

(1) It defines the characteristics of interpersonal conflict in digital media;
(2) It uses both a conflict resolution model (Fisher, Ury, & Patton, 1991; 2011) and the advantages of community wisdom to expand creative thinking using an innovative online dispute resolution technology;
(3) It emphasizes how technology itself has enabled us to conduct this research and gain new knowledge coming from the wisdom of Generation Z.

Emergence of Digital Social Interaction

Ten years ago, the use of social media was not as widespread and global as it is today, where Facebook, Instagram, Twitter, YouTube, TikTok and WhatsApp provide a digital social environment and means of communication for children, teenagers, and adults (Anderson & Jiang, 2018; Statista, 2018b). Even before the COVID-19 pandemic so radically transformed our ways of communication, the World Economic Forum Report (2018) declared that digital accessibility was increasing by one percent each year, globally.

According to reports examining Generation Z screen behavior, children and teens spend a significant amount of time with screens, even at the expense of leading a substantive social life (Baron, 2008; Evans, 2017; Lenhart et al., 2007; Statista, 2018a). From the early days of the 21st century, Generation Z was described as composed of digital natives who live in the social media environment as if it were their natural playground (Palfrey & Gasser, 2008). Over a decade ago, Palfrey and Gasser (2008) described the 'Screen Generation' and pointed out a general phenomenon of attachment to electronic and digital tools as a trademark of global culture.

Based on a survey conducted in the USA, 95% of children aged 13–17 have access to a smartphone, 95% of them reported daily web surfing for gaming, knowledge, and fun, and 45% reported that they were almost constantly connected to the digital space (Anderson & Jiang, 2018). In a study of screen use among children, the average duration of computer, smartphones, and internet uses is estimated as four hours and upwards (Franco, Almog, & Genaim, 2019).

The age of children occupying the digital space keeps getting lower (Franco, Almog, & Genaim, 2019). Data from the U.S.A. shows that more than 50% of children get their first smartphone before they have reached the age of seven (Statista, 2018a). An American child under the age of eight spends an average of 5.5 hours in front of screens every day and 16% of children between ages 8–18 spend over 10.5 hours each day on social media platforms (boyd, 2014; Palfrey & Gasser, 2008). In Israel, 81% of children start using a smartphone before the age of 12, and this data has probably changed in the past few years due to the constant increase in usage of the digital space for social purposes (Mann & Lev-On, 2015).

In recent years, the way children use the internet has shifted from using digital media for content consumption to using it as a means of communication (Mann & Lev-On, 2015; Third et al., 2014). Nowadays, children manage their social lives in two parallel and complementary spaces (Franco, Almog, & Genaim, 2019): the tangible space and the virtual space, the latter especially in social networks that scholars describe as their main social environment (Aizenkot, 2017; boyd, 2014; Statista, 2018b). The internet serves not only as a parallel social space, it is also a generative medium that creates behavioral patterns, develops stances and values, models thinking and expression styles, and provides free learning of various content (Eshet, 2012; Evans, 2017).

There are, or course, also advantages of the digital age, such as removing geographical barriers to interaction, providing access to communication and services, and allowing for ongoing, asynchronous interaction (boyd, 2014; Eshet, 2012; Katsh & Rabinovich-Einy, 2017; Zoref, 2015). However, it is also impossible to ignore the challenges of conflicts that arise in online spaces, how quickly (and broadly) they can escalate, and the particularly significant consequences, such as increased distress and suicide attempts among the young population (Plemmons et al., 2018). In the next section, I will address some of the characteristics of online communication and their implications.

Characteristics and Consequences of Online Communication

One of the most noticeable effects of this transition from face-to-face to digital interaction is the crucial role of content on social media. Offering large and various tools of communication by the internet has empowered the young population to create content and invent ways of digital social communication, using the technology and the new abilities of digital networking. Spending time online includes social interactions mostly focused on creating content through writing messages and sending them to a person or a group, uploading pictures and distributing them, and creating videos and stickers using technologies that the internet offers. All are an integral part of children and teenagers' daily activities on social media networks.

Even 'visiting' profiles of other children in social media has replaced the visiting encounters in the physical life. Many children find it less intimidating and much easier to initiate interaction with others when it happens via screens (boyd, 2014). Yet online interactions have different characteristics than in FTF interaction. Researchers discuss four main aspects of the transition from FTF to online social communication and their implications: (1) communication style and content, (2) the phenomenon of social media influencers, (3) emotional effects, and (4) conflict and cyberbullying. A glimpse into each aspect is described in the following section.

Online Communication Styles and Expectations

Investigating communication on social media has shown that digital social communication has become flat and fosters misunderstanding, and the dynamics and speed of the internet impact communication styles and their outcomes (Baron, 2008; boyd, 2014; Evans, 2017). We expect instantaneous response to our communication, and those who are not connected online are left out of the social gathering – even when those are conducted in the physical space (boyd, 2014). In addition, in social media networks, everything occurs quickly, thus misunderstanding and digital conflicts might escalate in seconds to a violent action or cyberbullying.

Some of the implications of moving to online social interactions refer to the content that is created or distributed on the internet, and includes harmful content, or content that is created in order to harm others (Aizenkot, 2017; Franco, Almog & Genaim, 2019). In the literature regarding the consequences of online bullying, it is agreed upon that the intensity of the harm it causes is more severe than that of direct 'traditional' bullying (Aizenkot, 2018; Bastiaensens et al., 2014; Bryce & Fraser, 2013; Gefen, 2019; Lenhart et al., 2007). Moreover, the younger the person is when sustaining the abuse, the longer its consequences will last (Gefen, 2019).

The Phenomenon of Social Media Influencers

The role of the social media influencer has become profound and has a major impact on children's self-esteem, confidence, and desires. Social media influencers are social media users who attract large-scale followers by posting visual or textual content, share pieces of their daily lives, and communicate with their audience regarding those moments, often including responses from their followers (Hudders, De Jans, & De Veirman, 2021). In the literature, they are analyzed as marketing figures who influence consumption trends among the young population (Hudders, De Jans, & De Veirman, 2021; De Veirman, Cauberghe, & Hudders, 2017; Swant, 2016).

From the followers' social-emotional standpoint, the consequences of watching those influencers on social media, observing their success and wide audience, creates a fragile distinction between the potential online advantages of empowerment, large-scale learning opportunities, and admiration to a huge downside of frustration and despair. Social media influencers not only affect young people's consumption trends, they are influencing the population's self-esteem and evidence suggests the resulting social comparison may have negative impacts (Stapleton, Luiz, & Chatwin, 2017).

Emotional Effects

Some researchers claim that digital social communication is devoid of organized norms or familiar social barriers, due to the lack of eye contact that eliminates feelings of shame, shyness, and judgment (Barak, 2006; Barak & Dolev-Cohen, 2006). Other researchers argue that children develop digital social communication skills that include behavior that is faithful to the individual's own feelings (boyd, 2014; Suler, 2004).

Suler (2004) claims that the internet user feels free of any attributions or labels others may give him (even without having any apparent external characteristics). As such, teenagers feel free to express themselves more candidly and act according to their psychological wants and needs. Moreover, boyd (2014) states that there are children for whom social media is not merely a tool, but a literal social-life saver that allows them to feel safe and remain connected to people.

Screen use strengthens the feeling of freedom and the absence of examining eyes, which leads to the inhibition removal effect (Suler, 2004). Moreover, the user has an excessive illusion of security, stemming from the lack of clear visual signs of danger. For example, when the teenagers are sitting in the comfort of their home or their safe private room, they feel safe. The invisibility aspect contributes to personal empowerment and the confidence to state an opinion.

The lack of eye-contact, the illusive power of being behind the keyboard, and the inability to view emotions as they arise in an emotional situation all create a different kind of social communication, which has its own limitations and negative outcomes (Yavich, Davidovitch, & Frenkel, 2019).

The experience of isolation on the internet and the absence of immediate feedback in the form of facial expression, the tone of voice, and body language can lead to negative behaviors due to confusion, occasionally unintended. When interacting online, words that are negative and/or aggressive, are written, not necessarily considering the person sitting on the other side of the screen and the possible repercussions for him (Boniel-Nissim, 2013). At the same time, words on the internet can be negatively construed, without their author necessarily meaning to assign them that tone and/or meaning (Suler, 2004).

Thus, children, as well as adults, who try to cope with limitations of the digital space, might end up feeling frustrated, lonely, and with a sense of facing an impasse when confronting conflictual situations.

Online Conflict and Cyberbullying

As in any social interaction, online interaction has both strengths and weaknesses. For instance, the characteristics of digital communication create unique opportunities for resolving conflicts, especially in asynchronous platforms. The internet enables interpersonal communication in asynchronous writing (such as email, blog, forum), thus enabling re-reading and editing, which are absent in spoken communication (Boniel-Nissim & Barak, 2011). Reading also makes it possible to re-read the other's words, examine them closely, quote passages in answering them, and save messages on the computer. Many users tend to 'read themselves' later on, and this reflective reading allows for clearing up certain points and increases awareness and understanding (Suler, 2004). Thus, asynchronous written communication allows the disputants to linger in their writing or reading, tailoring their communication to their personal progress along the process.

However, in many online interactions, especially conflict situations, neither children nor adults take advantage of what asynchronous communication allows. They often react without being reflective and mindful first, which may lead to escalation and harmful consequences. Moreover, in some cases the fact that digital social communication is written and recorded can make the conflict more complex, because words said in the heat of the moment remain there forever.

The negative consequences of interacting via screens were examined in the last decade and include essential findings. One of the characteristics of social activity in the digital space relates to users who are watching social interactions from the sidelines and may be hurt even without taking actual action. Cyberbullying[2] is a negative, hurtful phenomenon, which involves an attacker (or attackers) against a victim. Cyberbullying occurs repeatedly, over time, and experts suggest it should be reported to an adult or someone with enforcement capabilities (Gefen, 2019). A study conducted in Israel found that out of 1101 participants, most of them (70%, N=771) had experienced cyberbullying: 30.7% of the participants (*n*= 338) experienced cyberbullying as victims and 39.3% (*n*= 433) experienced it as witnesses. More than half of the research participants experienced more than one shaming expression at a time. The offensive messages were insults (51.6%), swearing (47.1%), forced expulsion from the group (39.2% of the group), and even the uploading of embarrassing pictures to the group (28.8%) (Aizenkot, 2017, pp. 373).

The past decade has seen instances of conflicts joined by boycotts and expressions of violence on digital social media (Gefen, 2019). Examining the incidents reported, 15.5% of students in the U.S.A. suffered from harassment in the digital

2 Cyberbullying (2019): the electronic posting of mean-spirited messages about a person (such as a student) often done anonymously. **Merriam-Webster's online dictionary,** Retrieved from https://www.merriam-webster.com/dictionary/cyberbullying#h1

space[3] in the 12 months prior to the survey. This finding was particularly high among girls (21.7%) and lower among boys (9.7%) (Kann et al., 2016). In the age range of 10–15, the level of exposure and degree of vulnerability is the highest (Kowalski et al., 2014).

Most digital violence incidents occur among peers, when children are hurting other children by the content they have created, as opposed to hurting them by content created by an adult they do not know (Ringrose et al., 2012). In terms of age range and gender, in the United Kingdom 19% of teenagers aged 11–16 were exposed to offensive content created by their friends on social networks and among girls aged 14–16 this rate went up to 32% (Dwyer & Easteal, 2013).

One of the most harmful effects of moving our social lives to the digital space is the increase in suicide attempts, which several researches relate to the increase in access to the digital space and the use of digital communication tools (Chang et al., 2015; Plemmons et al., 2018). According to Plemmons and others (2018), suicide intentions and attempts among teenagers have nearly doubled since 2008. This data is attributed to the increase in internet use and connectivity through social networks (Chang et al., 2015) as well as feelings of loneliness and/or low self-esteem that may result from the daily exposure to internet influencers, as described above (Stapleton, Luiz, & Chatwin, 2017).

The findings regarding the deficiencies and dangers of online interactions highlight the need for tools and knowledge that would assist children to best deal with conflicts and prevent their escalation into cyberbullying, violence, and deep frustration. The appropriate approach to prevent cyberbullying is educating for safe and wise web surfing and to encourage children and teens to inform an adult or a responsible figure to stop its occurrence. Digital conflicts might escalate to cyberbullying if not treated appropriately and in a timely manner. However, conflict resolution skills, which can be taught, can be used to prevent the escalation of digital conflicts to a more severe outcome or to find a creative solution for the benefit of both parties.

A Solution: Conflict Resolution Education (CRE)

Teaching students how to manage conflict and avoid cyberbullying was found effective as an intervention educational model for dealing with cyberbullying and decreasing its occurrence (Aizenkot & Kashy-Rosenbaum, 2018). Thus, Conflict Resolution Education (CRE) is a particularly important component of a comprehensive violence prevention program and in intervention programs in the schools and in community life (Jones, 2004; Jones & Sanford, 2003; Olive, 2006). The next section of this chapter

3 Defined here as email, chat, various instant messaging apps, websites, blogs and other digital social networks.

describes CRE and then moves into a discussion of using community wisdom for CRE in the digital era and the details of our workshops and our research project.

CRE programs help the learners recognize that, while conflicts are an integral part of our lives and occur all the time, there are tools that could help overcome them independently. Among those abilities, researchers examined the benefit of problem solving and conflict resolution principles, listening as the basis for effective communication, creative thinking, the illustration of each individual's personal responsibility, and his/her capability of self-discipline (Jones, 2004; Jones, 2014; Olweus, 2006). The educational frameworks that have mediation, for example, as an integral part of their vision and curriculum, quickly become a positive anchor among their pupils (Jones, 2014).

Nowadays, CRE programs are combined with Social Emotional Learning (SEL). The field of SEL refers to skills such as perspective-taking, empathy, decision-making, managing emotions, respecting and accepting diversity and more. The combination of those two fields takes place not only in the U.S.A. and in Europe, but also in many other countries over the globe (Gullotta et al., 2016).

The literature in the field of CRE relates mainly to FTF encounters within the school framework (Barron, 2000; Bodine & Crawford, 1998; Jones, 2004; Jones & Kmitta, 2002; Olweus, 2006; Sherman et al., 2000). Although we understand that in the last two decades the social space has become largely digital and many of the conflicts are making their way to online interactions, the attitudes towards the digital space and the conflicts within it are not adequately addressed in the CRE programs. Therefore, addressing this issue in the face of the constant rise in digital connectivity and the transition to online space as a central channel of communication between people is of great importance.

In order to examine a Conflict Resolution Education program that addresses digital conflict phenomenon, I now present the Agree-online Educational Program. First, I describe the theoretical framework for the program, its methodological development, and the content provided to students who participate in Agree-Online workshops. Afterwards, I present a study that reveals some insights regarding the phenomena of communication and conflicts in social media, the program's suggestion for a digital way out of conflicts and cyberbullying, and its implications, limitations, and benefits.

Theoretical Grounds of the Agree-Online Educational Program

The *Getting to Yes* approach of Fisher, Ury, & Patton (1991; 2011) influences the concept of conflict resolution that I present in this chapter and that has shaped the development of the 'Agree Online' project. The authors presented several principles for success in negotiations, including the need to focus on interests rather than positions, the ability to brainstorm creative options for mutual benefit, the importance of managing emotions by separating the people from the problem, and the need to base the agreement on objective criteria.

Other important sources of the thinking behind the CRE workshops and Agree - Online's digital platform are "The Wisdom of the Crowd," as expressed in Surowiecki's approach (2005), and the impact of sharing ideas to improve decision-making processes and risk management (Zoref, 2015). According to Surowiecki, a random collection of people is more likely to solve problems and provide good and reliable answers than a single person, even if s/he is an expert.

Those scholars (Surowiecki, 2005; Zoref, 2015) present the *Crowd wisdom* notion as the *end result* when diverse and even conflicting viewpoints are generated by a large group of people of different ages, backgrounds, and areas of interest or expertise. Thus, community wisdom refers to the knowledge gain by different perspectives shared within a community which could be identified by the same age range, gender, background, area, religion, or profession. Zoref (2005) defines this end-result as "Mindsharing," which is "where greater value is placed on collective intelligence and collective problem solving" (5). When people share their thoughts and ideas regarding a relevant problem or for decision-making purposes, community wisdom is generated. The internet is an optimal arena for examining such use of community wisdom.

The educational model we have implemented in the CRE digital workshops utilizes peer-learning (Barron, 2000) and brainstorming for creative ideas (Fisher, Ury, & Patton, 2011) as factors that increase the confidence of finding a way out of the conflict situation. We apply these theoretical grounds as part of the Agree-Online technology design and conflict resolution methodological process.

Development of the Agree-Online Educational Program

The Agree-Online Educational Program adds a community-based component to Ury and Fisher's integrative model (1991; 2011) to create a digital platform that enables participants to produce innovative results. In recent years, we have used the digital platform[4] as an educational technology of ODRE (Online Dispute Resolution Education). Nearly 2,000 users (children and teens) have participated in workshops and used the ODRE platform to offer solutions to other children's conflicts.

4 Available for view: www.maskimim.com (the Hebrew version); www.agree-online.com (the English version).

In our workshops, we have focused mainly on communication skills, emotion management, problem solving, and creative win-win thinking. Our goal was to reduce and prevent situations of cyberbullying, violence, and conflict. Moreover, we wish to improve children's ability to cope positively and independently in conflict situations and to help them transform from digital natives to digital citizens.

The children who participated in the ODRE workshops reviewed conflict episodes, uploaded their own conflicts, and often became advisers. As "advisers," they could choose from the conflict episodes in the platform and offer possible solutions to other children's conflicts. When the advisers offer a solution in the platform, they get points and rewards in three tiers, based on the quality of their offer. If the solution they offered is later chosen by one of the disputants they get more points, and if the solution they offered is later chosen by both parties, they get double the points. Our goal was to educate the children to think creatively about the disputants' needs and to frame a win-win solution both parties would agree upon.

Due to the nature of social networks and the roles of influencers within them, as well as the significant part these influencers play in the lives of their followers, one of the goals was that workshop participants would become positive influencers in their social media surroundings, equipped with Alternative/Online Dispute Resolution skills. The workshops provide in-class lessons using a digital platform in a secure and trusted environment with their classmates. The ODRE platform has a gamified process and includes adult guidance: a teacher or a mediator who facilitates CRE workshops.

Besides educating children on how to resolve conflicts in a technology-based activity, the workshops helped us better understand the characteristics of digital conflicts on social media and the participants' attitudes toward online social difficulties. We also discovered their strategies for resolving both offline and online conflicts. The next section provides an overview of the research conducted between the years 2017–2020 using the ODRE platform, including the study sample, methodology, and main findings.

Research Design

In the past three years, we have implemented our beta-website[5] and curriculum in dozens of schools with the participation of nearly 2,000 children, teens, and teachers, who shared more than 200 disputes they have experienced.

In the current study, I examined three main research questions. Two of them are descriptive and aim to understand the characteristics of conflicts in the social

5 Maskimim.com is the Hebrew version of 'Agree-Online' initiative, which has served as the ODRE database for the described research.

media environment and their consequences and to discover the strategies children are using to resolve their conflicts, regardless of the knowledge they gain from the workshops. This will help us identify limitations in the field of conflict resolution education that need to be addressed for the digital age. The third question focuses on the ODRE workshop outcomes. I examine whether using the technology to focus on conflicts in social media helps children gain the relevant knowledge to be independent and confident in resolving conflicts.

Research Questions

RQ1*: What are the characteristics of the conflicts children experience online?* Here I examine the main ingredients of conflicts in social media: Who is involved in the online conflict among children? Where and when do those conflicts occur? Is there a difference between offline and online conflicts? What are the issues those conflicts address?

RQ2*: What types of strategies do children (aged 10–14) offer as solutions to online conflicts?* The community wisdom in the digital platform allows us to reveal the main strategies children are using in their attempts to resolve online and offline conflicts. The answer to this question could help us map the skills and knowledge children gain from conflict resolution education and aim our efforts in positive strategies that are not enough in use.

RQ3*: Do children (aged 10–14) report increased confidence in their conflict resolution competence after participating in an online dispute resolution workshop?* What are the benefits they report after experiencing the ODRE workshops? This question could help us understand the benefits and limitations of the workshop from the participants' point of view. This will allow us to improve the workshop and point to areas for further research.

Method

The methodology in the current research includes analyzing the data gathered in the maskimim.com database and performing content analysis of the solutions presented on this platform. This method helps reveal online and offline conflict characteristics among children, makes explicit the strategies they use to resolve and suggest a way out of the conflicts, and allows us to understand the weaknesses and strengths of using a digital tool for CRE purposes.

Sample Population

Pupils in Israel, ages 10–14 years, from various cities (1,437 pupils). We conducted the workshops between the years 2017–2020. The research was conducted before the global COVID-19 pandemic, when children could meet together on a daily basis.

Data Collection

In the current study, 75 conflicts and 1,345 solutions generated by the ODRE workshop participants were analyzed. The conflict situations in the workshop were real life dilemmas from children's and teachers' experiences. The data collection process was blind and we used only the uploaded content of conflicts and solutions, without users' identification.

Research Tools and Data Analysis

(1) The Maskimim database (www.maskimim.com) contains disputes, solutions, a popularity counter, and dispute categories (home, school, afterschool; interpersonal, social, family). The access to the platform data is part of the Agree-Online project permissions and licensing;
(2) Content analysis of digital conflicts, as presented in Agree-Online Platform (Hebrew version). The conflict episodes were gathered during the ODRE workshops. This analysis helps to study digital conflict characteristics (what are the tools used during the conflict and as result of it, where does the conflict take place, who are the disputants and other involved parties, and what are the issues they quarrel about);
(3) Content analysis of solutions by themes, patterns, and categories in an inductive approach. We reveal the categories of strategies children are using to manage conflicts, which were inductively derived from the data. We did not focus on specific categories prior to the study. Instead, we let the data emerge when one of our research questions was "What are the ways children are using to manage their conflicts?"

Our experience in the conflict resolution education workshops in schools in the past few years, with the focus upon conflicts in social media, and the ability to view children's behavior via the digital platform maskimim.com, has resulted in valuable findings, which expand our knowledge about communication and conflict resolution in the digital era.

Research Findings

Three main themes emerged through this analysis. These are defined below and followed by an elaboration of each theme.

1. Digital (online) conflicts among children ages 10–14 have unique characteristics: they differ from offline conflicts and they differ from cyberbullying. They disturb the children and have a negative influence on their digital and physical social lives.
2. Community Wisdom reveals 10 categories and 2 main patterns to solutions that children and teenagers (ages 10–14) offer for resolving their own conflicts. The categories differ in their frequencies, their consequences, and their focus: whether they are relationship-focused or concrete-outcome (task) focused.
3. There are major benefits of CRE using digital "Mindsharing" (Zoref, 2015). *Empowering students* and *contributing to their self-esteem*. It *improves social abilities* such as *creative thinking, problem solving, perspective taking,* and *detecting empathy*. Those four main abilities are central to social emotional learning (SEL) skills and there is strong evidence that teaching these skills improves CRE outcomes (Cohen, 2004; Jones & Sanford, 2003; Lane-Garon & Richardson, 2003).

The subsequent paragraphs describe these three research findings in more detail.

Theme #1: Digital Conflict Characteristics

Based on our study, we define *digital conflict* as a conflict which takes place, at least in part, in the digital space. Manifestations of digital conflict include:

- Conflicts from the physical space that reach the digital space, and/or
- Conflicts that emerge online that affect relationships outside of the digital space, and/or,
- Conflicts that have been resolved via the digital space.

Another main characteristic refers to digital conflicts as a social situation among peers who are on equal standing. Most of the digital conflicts which disturb the children in our study did not occur with a stranger or a person in a position of power. They were conflicts with their best friend, classmates, or even siblings who have a dispute that incorporates digital tools. There are digital conflicts with strangers they chat with online, in applications such as Instagram, Twitter, Tik-Tok or FB; however, those interactions were not in their focus and seem to be less disturbing from our workshop participants' perspectives.

Reviewing the conflicts that children are coping with during our research taught us about the dynamic and unique characteristics of digital conflicts: they flare up fast, take place in front of active members of digital groups, are preserved over time, and include the use of digital tools (Brun, Ashwall, & Haimovich, 2017). One of the characteristics of digital conflicts among children and teens concerns the rapid aspect of the digital medium. In social media networks, everything occurs quickly, and digital conflicts might escalate in seconds to a violent action or cyberbullying.

Often, digital conflicts take place in front of involved, active witnesses, who may contribute to the escalation of the conflict by either their responses or their silence. There are no time or place constraints (24/7), no boundaries: children can get messages well into the night; they communicate on WhatsApp while their parents are at work or even if the family is together at home. Either way, the parents will not necessarily notice that their child is in crisis because one of the kids at school, their classmates or even a close friend, wrote to them in public that they are losers, stupid, or ugly. Hence, this is one more characteristic of the digital conflict: there is no adult (parent, teacher, or guide) supervision that can get immediately involved when a conflict evolves, as used to be the case when children spent many hours at school or spent time together, face to face.

We identified that children are quarreling in every app they use, on WhatsApp, online net gaming platforms like Fortnight, Tik-Tok, and even in emails, mostly if they are related to joint school assignments. We identified the issues from which conflicts arise: they have conflicts regarding games (virtual and physical), parties, joint activities (social or educational), spending time outside, sitting arrangements or physical conditions, and even their digital social communication and behaviors.

From our participants' reports, digital conflicts create a feeling of helplessness. Due to difficulties in communication, the dispute is magnified and negative feelings intensify. In this digital space, such as in social media, even minor conflicts can easily escalate and end up in frustration or violence. The children who participated in the ODRE workshops reported situations such as removal from a WhatsApp group, creating a group against someone, sharing embarrassing pictures and videos, privacy issues, and the use of stickers and emoji to insult. They described those episodes as deadlock situations they could not resolve prior to the ODRE workshop.

Another claim among the students in our study was that there were no adults they could go to for support when online conflicts occur. Since their teachers or parents are not a part of their digital surrounding and "would not understand," they did not approach them for help, resulting in feelings of loneliness and helplessness following digital conflict.

Theme #2: Solutions to Conflict: The Value of 'Mindsharing'

Social life in the digital space involves much more than weaknesses and risks. In fact, the transition to the digital sphere seems to entail many opportunities and potential for learning and personal/educational development. The use of the digital platform enables us to identify not only the conflict characteristics, but also the suggested solutions that the children who participated in the ODRE workshops have offered, which reveals how they might manage those conflicts.

In the data-gathering process, we could recognize their intuitive suggestions prior to the educational program, which were mainly judgmental, including apologizing and taking turns, while creative solutions constituted only 8% of all suggestions. At the end of the educational program, we revealed an increase in the win-win solutions and decrease in judgmental statements, as well as an increase in the use of various fairness models (a raffle, creative division of time and resources, taking turns).

We identified the way that students internalized the lessons through a content analysis of their suggestions and due to an exam that they took using a digital platform.

In analyzing the participants' suggestions, we identified 10 recurring categories of offered solutions[6]: (1) Apology, (2) Creative Win-Win, (3) Explanatory and preventive suggestions (4) Fairness models (taking turns, a raffle, "first cuts, the other chooses," and more), (5) Judgmental (who's right), (6) Meet face-to-face, (7) No actual solution, (8) Part ways, (9) Talk, (10) Turn to a responsible adult (See Figure 11.1).

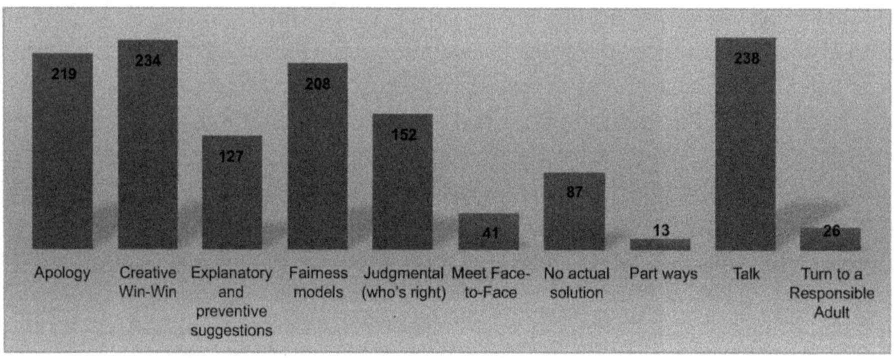

Figure 11.1: Ten Main Categories of Conflict Resolution Solutions from the Community Wisdom of Children in Agree-online ODRE Workshop.

We have noticed, too, an interesting phenomenon which emphasizes a communicative manifestation of the digital age. The participants made a distinction between "talk," by which they refer to conversation through screens (in apps such as WhatsApp and Instagram) and "meet," by which they refer to a face-to-face conversation in the classic sense.[7] Moreover, there is a difference in the frequency of the offer to

6 Listed in alphabetic order.

7 As I have mentioned in the methodology section, the research was conducted before the global COVID-19 pandemic, when children could meet each other on daily basis.

"talk" versus the offer to "meet": the scope of participants offering "talk to each other" was 238 proposals, which are 18% of the proposals, where the main reference is to a screen-based dialogue (WhatsApp/chat, textual conversation and not necessarily voice or frontal conversation). The scope of a solution proposal of "meet," where the intention is to face-to-face communication, stood at 41 out of 1,345 offers (only 3% of the total offers).

The need to turn to a responsible adult for resolving the conflict accounted for only 2% of all proposals (26 proposals out of 1,345). This finding could indicate that in such events, pupils estimate the involvement of a responsible adult as less appropriate and relevant. It may also be evidence of self-efficacy and independence of the participating pupils. However, those assumptions need further examination in future research.

Analyzing the data allows us to make an additional distinction between two main solutions patterns: "practical solutions" and "relationship-based solutions." Among the practical solutions we identified fairness models (208 proposals, 16%) and possible creative solutions tailored to the needs of the parties (234 proposals, 18%). The relationship-based solutions are recommendations to avoid abusive activity in order to preserve the relationship (540 proposals, about 40 % of solutions). In addition, digital conflicts which had more relationship-based suggestions were also characterized with explanatory and preventive solutions (127 proposal, 9.5% of solutions), pleading the disputants to be more aware of their offensive behavior consequences.

Here, too, it seems that the students attach importance to the relationship continuity and they are in no hurry to propose a 'severance of the relationship' following the conflict (proposals for severing the relationship were only about 1% of total proposals). Of the total proposals, the recommendation to apologize as a tool for reconciliation between the parties was seen in 17% of total proposals (219 proposals in total, some of which were part of the "talk to each other" proposals).

Theme #3: Participants' Perspectives on the Benefits of ODRE Workshops

We claim that conflict resolution knowledge among children and teens equips them with the relevant skills for dealing positively with their social challenges. In order to explore the benefits of using the digital tool and generate community wisdom from Generation Z regarding how they manage digital conflicts, we asked the workshop participants for their perspectives.

In general, the children who participated in the ODRE workshops perceived our discussions with them about their difficulties in the social media as unusual. They were grateful for having those discussions and an educational digital-based activity. From a 10-year-old student's point of view: "*This is the first time someone is talking with us about things that happen in our social lives, and not lecturing only to be safe and avoid the web.*" Another student pointed out: "*Instead of teaching us History or Chemistry which are general, you taught us how to cope with our own troubles.*"

Another feedback response emphasized the importance of perspective taking and complex thinking, in addition to the empathy needed in communication via screens. A 14-year-old student reported:

> I learned that I cannot pick a side whenever I see a digital conflict. I also learned that I need to look for more than one source of information before I make my own conclusion. I think it is very important to resolve digital conflicts because today all of our lives are on social media and on the internet and this area is very subjective. This area is also full of uncertainty and people just tend to hurt other people without actually noticing. Because they cannot really read their body language, facial expression, and just because they cannot feel them, it does not mean they can use harmful words, because it is not what is going to solve their problem.

One of the students, a 13-year-old, explained that she has learned about various ways to avoid deadlock feelings and find win-win solutions to social media conflicts:

> During the project, I learn about different ways and skills to approach digital conflicts. I think it is very important to know about resolving social media conflict, especially in times like this, when people are using their freedom in social media as a barrier between them and the people they talk about. When I saw the suggested resolutions, I took a minute to look at the situation I had and the ways I could approach it, along with finding a win-win solution.

A 12-year-old girl explained the complexity of online social communication. She describes how the ODRE lessons allow her to think about the disputants' needs:

> In this project, I learned how to solve problems on the Internet and reach a win-win situation. I think everyone should learn how to resolve a digital conflict because today everyone uses the Internet and social media to communicate for good and for bad. When I was asked to suggest a resolution for different conflicts in order to achieve a win-win situation, I needed to stop and think for a few minutes about how the two sides of the conflict can get the things that they wanted.

The workshop participants described the benefits they achieved from learning conflict resolution skills and knowledge using a social media based platform. However, further research should examine before- and after-workshop suggestions and check the complexity of solutions given by participants in comparison to children who do not participate in ODRE workshops. Further research should also examine whether the training translates to effective ODR outside the training environment, as well as the ways children of Generation Z versus Generation Alpha are feeling towards communication online and the ways they cope with digital conflicts.

Out of nearly 2,000 users who were involved in more than 200 conflicts, the sample of 1,345 suggestions for resolving 75 conflicts indicates a high level of pupil involvement. In the feedback given by the pupils at the end of the workshops, the participants addressed the sense of their capabilities and competence when coping with conflict on social media. It seems that their activities as "advisers" have empowered them. They were glad to influence positively the conflict solutions and to share their perspectives on how the dispute should be resolved.

Conclusion

Examining the development of technology and interaction in the digital space over the last two decades has taught us that relationships carried out through screens are different from FTF communication (Baron, 2008; Evans, 2017). Communication style and content, the phenomenon of social media influencers, and emotional effects of communicating online have various implications, including harmful ones. The continued increase in social interactions through screens is adding to the scope of our discussion.

However, not only the micro-level is at stake. A society of individuals deprived of a physical social life can result in the development of antisocial citizens who demonstrate an apathetic citizenship, unused to and unfamiliar with the contributive interactions which ought to build our society.

The increase in cases of low self-esteem among children and teens, the increasing rate of cyberbullying, an increase in suicide attempts among young children, and the significant increase in accessibility to the digital space indicate that we must pay attention to the phenomenon of online interaction and help provide children with the skills to manage interaction and relationships in this space.

Furthermore, we have learned that the evidence of digital conflict remains online for good (what happens online is permanent), which amplifies its consequences and negative feelings. Nowadays, even the social media companies themselves are struggling with the consequences of their own policies regarding these issues.

Understanding the digital space through the prism of conflict resolution is crucial for our future as parents, citizens, and practitioners and researchers in the conflict resolution field. According to the Annual Report of the World Economic Forum (2017–2018), conflict resolution skills such as problem solving, detecting empathy and managing emotions, and communicating and respecting diversity are identified as the main social and emotional skills needed in the 21st century.

Engaging with CRE training that focuses on online social communication provides skills that allow children to manage their emotions and other negative consequences of digital conflict. Equally important, the children of today are the citizens of the future. They already speak an emerging language that includes new meanings for words such as "block," "talk," "meet," and "follow." The establishment of a digital language and online behaviors requires conflict resolution skills.

With new knowledge regarding social media conflicts, we can help the young population deal more effectively with their social difficulties and develop the main social and emotional skills that CRE provides. The main advantages of online communication included our ability to examine the creativity of the student participants and the way they refer to the internet as a natural place to consult with others (Eshet, 2012; Palfrey & Gasser, 2008; Zoref, 2015). Another potential advantage might include the creation of social media influencers as digital peace ambassadors, with abilities and competencies that befit the 21st century.

Moreover, we found that solutions could be clustered into 10 main categories by their main outcomes and characteristics. This kind of knowledge could aid in preventing conflict escalation (Katsh & Rabinovich-Einy, 2017) and in educating young children to think about creative solutions to conflicts, reaching out to help others in need instead of being indifferent or, even worse, contributing to the escalation of conflicts.

In addition, we have also recognized a way to help children manage digital conflicts. We suggest two different methods of intervention: for cyberbullying, we must teach children to immediately report the event by providing a safe space and trusted adult; for digital conflict, we need to provide more widespread online dispute resolution education (ODRE) in order to equip the parties with the necessary skills and knowledge.

Should we expand our ODRE efforts, we could equip the children with the relevant skills to address the negative trends we identify in social media communication and avoid feelings of helplessness and cyberbullying, while using the advantages of community wisdom and positive influence online for the better. Yet, when we delve deeper into the current study findings, we realize that there are still a number of issues to investigate in further research. As long as digital accessibility continues to expand, we ought to respectively increase Online Dispute Resolution Education examination and effort.

References

Aizenkot, D. (2017). WhatsApp cyberbullying among children and adolescents in Israel: A pilot research. *Educational Counseling, 20*: 363–389. [Hebrew]. Retrieved from http://www.shaanan.ac.il/wp-content/uploads/2018/01/20-gilayon-male-1.pdf

Aizenkot, D. (2018). Cyberbullying in WhatsApp classroom croups among children and adolescents: Exposure and victimization. In M. Shelly, M. Ozaslan, & W. Wu (Eds.), *The International Conference on Research in Education and Science ICRES 2018 Proceeding Book*, Volume I (pp. 1–10). Iowa: ISRES Publishing.

Aizenkot, D., & Kashy-Rosenbaum, G. (2018). Cyberbullying in WhatsApp classmates' groups: Evaluation of an intervention program implemented in Israeli elementary and middle schools. *New Media & Society*, 20(12): 4709–4727. DOI:10.1177/1461444818782702

Anderson, M., & Jiang, J. (2018). Teens, social media & technology 2018. *Pew Research Center*, 31, 2018. Retrieved from http://publicservicesalliance.org/wp-content/uploads/2018/06/Teens-Social-Media-Technology-2018-PEW.pdf

Barak, A. (2006). Youngsters and the Internet: The psychology of "kind of" and "like". *Panim*, 37: 48–58. Retrieved from https://www.itu.org.il/?CategoryID=1035&ArticleID=7857

Barak, A. & Dolev-Cohen, M. (2006). Does activity level in online support groups for distressed adolescents determine emotional relief? *Counselling and Psychotherapy Research*. 6. 186–190. 10.1080/14733140600848203.

Baron, N. (2008). *Always On: Language in an Online and Mobile World* Oxford: Oxford University Press. Retrieved 15 Mar. 2022, from https://oxford.universitypressscholarship.com/view/10.1093/acprof:oso/9780195313055.001.0001/acprof-9780195313055.

Barron, L. (2000). *The Impact of peer mediation training on adolescents' problem-solving skills, perception of school climate, and attitudes toward conflict management*. Ph.D. Thesis, University of South Carolina, 2000.

Bastiaensens, S., Vandebosch, H., Poels, K., Van Cleemput, K., DeSmet, A., & De Bourdeaudhuij, I. (2014). Cyberbullying on social network sites. An experimental study into bystanders' behavioral intentions to help the victim or reinforce the bully. *Computers in Human Behavior*, *31*: 259–271. DOI:10.1016/j.chb.2013.10.036

Bodine, R., & Crawford, D. (1998). *The Handbook of Conflict Resolution Education: a Guide to Building Quality Programs in Schools*. Richard J. Bodine, Donna K. Crawford; foreword by Judith M. Filner. Jossey-Bass Publishers. San Francisco, California. : Jossey-Bass Publishers, c1998.

Boniel-Nissim, M. (2013). *Psychological Aspects of Internet Use. To Network – Implementation of Practical Procedures for the Correct and Safe Use of the Internet*. Rimon Internet Publishing, (18–26). Retrieved from http://www.mbnpsychonet.com/Default.asp?sType=0&PageId=98015

Boniel-Nissim, M., & Barak, P. (2011). The Internet for the help of individual adolescents: The therapeutic value of blogging. *Meeting for Social Educational Work*, *34*: 9–30.

boyd, D. (2014). *It's Complicated*. New Haven: Yale University Press books.

Brooks, K., Schiraldi, V., & Ziedenberg, J. (April 2000), *School House Hype: Two Years Later*, Washington, DC: Justice Policy Institute and Children's Law Center, Inc.

Brun, I., Ashwall, R., & Haimovich, M. (2017). Educating children to resolve their digital conflicts before escalating to violence and cyberbullying (Workshop), In: *13th Annual Conference Book for Research on Innovation and Learning Technologies by Chase: The Person Studying in the Truckee Era*. Y. Eshet-Elkayi, A. Blau, A. Caspi, S. Etgar, N. Gerry, J. Kalman, & V. Silver.), Ra'anana: The Open University (Hebrew).

Bryce, J., & Fraser, J. (2013). "It's common sense that it's wrong": Young peoples' perceptions and experiences of cyberbullying. *Cyberpsychology, Behavior and Social Networking*, 16(11): 783–787. DOI:10.1089/cyber.2012.0275

Carter, C. & Osler, A. (2000). Human rights, identities and conflict management: a study of school culture as experienced through classroom relationships, *Cambridge Journal of Education*, *30*(3): 335–356.

Chang, F.-C., Chiu, C.-H., Miao, N.-F., Chen, P.-H., Lee, C.-M., Chiang, J.-T., & Pan, Y.-C. (2015). The Relationship between parental mediation and Internet addiction among adolescents, and the association with cyberbullying and depression. *Comprehensive Psychiatry*, 57: 21–28. DOI:10.1016/j.comppsych.2014.11.013

Cohen, J. (2004). *Educating Minds and Hearts: Social Emotional Learning and the Passage into Adolescence*. Teachers College Press, Williston, VT. ISBN: 978-0807738382.

Cyberbullying (2019). *In Merriam-Webster's online dictionary*, Retrieved from https://www.merriam-webster.com/dictionary/cyberbullying#h1

De Veirman, M., Cauberghe, V., & Hudders, L. (2017), Marketing through Instagram influencers: The impact of number of followers and product divergence on brand attitude, *International Journal of Advertising*, *36*(5): 798–828. Williston, VT: Teachers College Press.

Diliberti, M., Jackson, M., Kemp, J. & Hansen, R. (2017). Crime, violence, discipline, and safety in u.s. public schools findings from the school survey on crime and safety: 2015–16. *Center for Education Statistics*, NCES 2017-122 U.S. Department of Education.

Dwyer, A., & Easteal, P. (2013). Cyberbullying in Australian schools: The question of negligence and liability: *Alternative Law Journal*, 38: 92. 10.1177/1037969X1303800206.

Eshet, Y. (2012). Thinking in the digital era: A revised model for digital literacy. *Issues in Informing* Science *and Information* Technology, *9*: 267–276. Retrieved from http://iisit.org/Vol9/IISITv9p267-276Eshet021.pdf

Evans, V. (2017). *The Emoji Code: How Smiley Faces, Love Hearts and Thumbs Up are Changing the Way We Communicate*. Picador: New York.

Fisher, R., Ury, U., & Patton, B. (1991). *Getting to Yes: Negotiating Agreement without Giving in*, (Second ed.). Harmondsworth: Penguin: New York

Fisher, R., Ury, W., & Patton, B. (2011). *Getting to yes : Negotiating Agreement without Giving in*. (Third ed.). Penguin Books: New York, NY.

Franco, L., Almog, S., & Ghanayim, K. (2019). *Childhood on a Social Network – A Lawless Distance* (November 21, 2019). Available at SSRN: https://ssrn.com/abstract=3491298 or http://dx.doi.org/10.2139/ssrn.3491298

Gefen, A. (2019). Cyberbullying among adolescents – Victims' characteristics and digital literacy, stress condition, and mediating resilience resources. School of Education *Ph.D. Thesis*. Bar-Ilan University.

Generation Z (1997). *In Merriam-Webster's online dictionary*, Retrieved from https://www.merriam-webster.com/dictionary/Generation%20Z.

Gullotta, T., Weissberg, R., Durlak, J., & Domitrovich, C. (2016). *Handbook of Social and Emotional learning: Research and Practice*. New York: The Guilford Press.

Hudders, L., De Jans, S., & De Veirman, M. (2021). The commercialization of social media stars: a literature review and conceptual framework on the strategic use of social media influencers, *International Journal of Advertising, 40*(3):327–375, DOI: 10.1080/02650487.2020.1836925

Jones, T. S., (2004). Conflict Resolution Education: The field, the findings, and the future. *Conflict Resolution Quarterly, 22*(1–2), 233–267. https://doi.org/10.1002/crq.100

Jones, T. S., (2014). Ethical Challenges and Suggestions for Conflict Resolution Education. *ACResolution, 13*(2): 14–18.

Jones, T. S., & Sanford, R. (2003). Building the container: Curriculum infusion and classroom climate. *Conflict Resolution Quarterly, 21*(1): 115–130.

Jones, T. S., & Kmitta, D. (2002). *School conflict management: Evaluating your Conflict Resolution Education Program*. Ohio Commission on Dispute Resolution & Conflict Management, Columbus, OH.

Johnson, P. W., & Johnson, R.T (1994). Constructive conflicts in the school, *Journal of Social Issues*, 50: 117–137.

Kann, L., McManus, T., Harris, W., Shanklin, S., Flint, K., Hawkins, J., . . . Zaza, S. (2016). Youth risk behavior surveillance – United States, 2015. *Morbidity and Mortality Weekly Report: Surveillance Summaries, 65*(6): 1–174. DOI:10.2307/24805802

Katsh, E., & Rabinovich-Einy, O. (2017). *Digital Justice – Technology and the Internet of Disputes*. Oxford: Oxford University Press.

Kowalski, R., Giumetti, G., Scheroeder, A. & Lattaner, M. (2014). Bullying in the digital age: A critical review and meta-analysis of cyberbullying research among youth, *Psychology Bulletin*, 140: 1074–1108.

Lane-Garon, P.,& Richardson, T. (2003). Mediator mentors: Improving school climate, nurturing student disposition. *Conflict Resolution Quarterly, 21*(1): 47–68.

Lenhart, A., Madden, M., Macgill, A. R., & Smith, A. (2007). Teens and social media. *Pew Internet and American Life Project*. Retrieved from: https://web.archive.org/web/20080306023559/http://www.pewinternet.org/pdfs/PIP_Teens_Social_Media_Final.pdf

Mann, R., & Lev-On, A. (2015). Annual Report: The Media in Israel 2014: Agendas, Uses and Trends, *Institute for the Study of New Media, Politics and Society*, Ariel [Hebrew].

Olive, E.C. (2006). Teaching conflict resolution. *Online Journal of the International Child and Youth Care Network* (CYC-Net) – ISSN 1605-7406. ISSUE 86 March 2006. CYC online – the CYC press.

Olweus, D. (2006). Bullying at school: Knowledge base and an effective intervention program. Annals of the New York Academy of Sciences. 794: 265–276. 10.1111/j.1749-6632.1996.tb32527.x.

Palfrey, J. & Gasser U. (2008). *Born Digital – Understanding the First Generation of Digital Natives*. Basic books: New York.

Plemmons, G., Hall, M., Doupnik, S., Gay, J., Brown, C., Browning, W., Casey, R., Freundlich, K., Johnson, D.P., Lind, C., Rehm, K., Thomas, S., Williams, D. (2018). Hospitalization for suicide ideation or attempt: 2008–2015. *Pediatrics*, 141 (6)e20172426; DOI: 10.1542/peds.2017-2426. Retrieved from https://pediatrics.aappublications.org/content/141/6/e20172426

Ringrose, J., Gill, R., Livingstone, S., & Harvey, L. (2012). *A qualitative study of children, young people and 'sexting': a report prepared for the NSPCC*. National Society for the Prevention of Cruelty to Children, London, UK

Sherman, L.W., Gottfredson, D., MacKenzie, D., Eck, J., Reuter, P.,& Bushway, S. (2000). Preventing crime: What works, what doesn't, what's promising, A report to the United States Congress, Prepared for the National Institute of Justice.

Suler, J. (2004). The online disinhibition effect. *Cyberpsychology & Behavior: the Impact of the Internet, Multimedia and Virtual Reality on Behavior and Society*, *7*(3): 321–326. 10.1089/1094931041291295.

Surowiecki, J. (2005). *The Wisdom of Crowds*. New York: Random House.

Stapleton, P., Luiz, G., & Chatwin, H. (2017). Generation validation: The role of social comparison in use of Instagram among emerging adults. *Cyberpsychology, Behavior, and Social Networking*, 20: 142–149.

Statista (2018a). *Percentage of U.S. population with a social media profile from 2008 to 2018*. https://www.statista.com/statistics/273476/percentage-of-us-population-with-a-social-network-profile/

Statista (2018b). *Most famous social network sites worldwide as of October 2018, ranked by number of active users (in millions)*. Retrieved from https://www.statista.com/statistics/272014/global-social-networks-ranked-by-number-of-users/

Swant, M. (2016). Twitter says users now trust influencers nearly as much as their friends, *Adweek*, May 10. Available at: www.adweek.com/digital/twitter-says-users-now-trustinfluencers-nearly-much-their-friends-171367 (accessed 10 February 2019).

The World Economic Forum (2018). *The World Economic Forum Annual Report (2017–2018)*. https://www.weforum.org/reports/annual-report-2017-2018

Third, A., Bellerose, D., Dawkins, U., Keltie, E., & Pihl, K. (2014). Children's rights in the digital age: A download from children around the world. 38, *UNICEF, United Nations Children's FundYoung and Well Cooperative Research Centre*. ISBN: 978-0-9925966-4-4.

Yavich, R., Davidovitch, N., & Frenkel, Z. (2019). Social media and loneliness – Forever connected? *Higher Education Studies*, *9*:10–21.

Zoref, L. (2015). *Mindsharing: The Art of Crowdsourcing Everything*. Publisher: Portfolio (April 28, 2015), ISBN-10: 159184665X.

Katie Greenan

Chapter 12
Student Engagement in the Virtual Classroom: Implications for Overcoming Conflict Between Instructors and Students and Creating Collaborative Virtual Workspaces

Abstract: COVID-19 changed education and classroom culture. As a result of the pandemic, educators modified curriculum and instruction in order to create virtual courses. Virtual learning can disrupt the communication process, provide students increased anonymity, and decrease the likelihood of self-disclosure. Therefore, it can be more challenging to develop and build relationships virtually. This chapter addresses changes in classroom culture as a result of transitioning from face-to-face to virtual education in this new era. It also presents the author's interpretations of (1) previous literature and (2) her personal experiences as a result of collecting data from undergraduate students in two communication courses during the Fall 2020 Semester. Results indicated that, in addition to teaching course content, it was the educator's responsibility to inspire a communication culture that fosters self-disclosure, helps students build relationships, creates spaces for virtual conversations, and uses relatable technology.

Keywords: classroom culture, virtual education, synchronous, COVID-19, self-disclosure

The Nature of the Problem

The COVID-19 pandemic continues to transform education as teachers and students have relied predominantly on distance learning, which affects traditional classroom culture. Technology changes the way people interact and develop relationships, are influenced by others, and manage reduced social cues. According to a report released by the Comptroller's Offices of Research and Education Accountability (2014), the number of students enrolled in online courses increased from 1.6 million to 6.1 million between 2002 and 2010. According to Inside Higher Education (Lederman, 2019), 46% of educators taught online courses in 2019, up from 30% in 2013. Due to the global pandemic, most colleges and universities in the United States shut down campuses and moved to an online format from Spring 2020 through Summer 2021. This required teachers and students to quickly adapt to virtual education practices and techniques, oftentimes learning through trial-and-error. Prior to the pandemic, virtual and hybrid education were methods of instruction that educators and students could opt into,

https://doi.org/10.1515/9783110687262-013

but COVID-19 changed that. The abrupt pivot to online teaching and learning brought with it a number of challenges, often creating conflict among instructors and students, whether or not those conflicts ever surfaced or were directly addressed.

During the 2020–21 academic school year, I taught undergraduate communication courses fully online. Although my courses took a synchronous approach, cultural shifts were inevitable. The virtual environment included the same substantive course content but presented challenges to developing a collaborative classroom culture since there are fewer opportunities to build interpersonal relationships that foster student engagement, commitment, and responsibility. In traditional face-to-face instruction, I have often experienced positive and inclusive cultures, observing open communication and plentiful opportunities for students to connect with each other during class meetings. Activities and projects require students to be engaged, active participants, a great predictor of academic and social success. Additionally, students in face-to-face classrooms have an opportunity to ask questions and converse with each other before, during, and after class, which assists in creating and building community. Alternatively, virtual education creates potential conflicts between instructors and students such as a decrease in student engagement and participation. External distractions during class can also decrease communication and connection between teachers and students and/or among peers and increase anonymity, isolation, and alienation. Transitioning to virtual classrooms called on educators to quickly learn how to create supportive and inclusive class communities and navigate challenges through trial and error. All this motivated me to ask, *What can be done to overcome inherent conflict between instructors and students when trying to create an engaged community in the virtual classroom?* This chapter addresses the benefits and challenges, or potential conflicts, of navigating through online spaces by presenting empirical research about the use of technology in traditional and virtual class communities prior to COVID-19, as well as during the pandemic. I conclude the chapter with recommendations for overcoming conflict stemming from a lack of engagement based on qualitative feedback I collected from undergraduate students studying communication in this new and ever-evolving era. These recommendations also carry implications for creating more collaborative virtual workspaces more broadly.

Background

Virtual education is defined as "Distance education and training that results from the technological separation of teacher and learner which frees the student from the necessity of traveling to a fixed place, at a fixed time, to meet a fixed person, in order to be trained" (Keegan, 1995, pp.7). Virtual education is used to refer to classes that are fully offered online, using educational platforms (such as Brightspace or blackboard), virtual meeting technologies such as zoom, social media platforms, and a variety of ancillary tools including, but not limited to blogging, mobile phones, and email. Technological advances have provided educators with new opportunities to deliver and disseminate knowledge and information to students by using virtual learning strategies in the classroom. Moreover, virtual education allows educators to provide ongoing and accessible information to students to review at their convenience, while providing a quality program that meets students' needs. As the desire for more virtual education and remote work increases in post-pandemic society, the ideas for creating more collaborative online classrooms may also help employers trying to create more collaborative virtual environments for remote workers.

Literature Review

The following literature review includes three sections: a discussion of the impact of online courses on classroom culture, a discussion of student engagement and how it contributes to a positive classroom culture, and research on the use of social media in the classroom.

Classroom Culture

While new technology allows for certain freedoms, it is criticized by some who perceive reduced effectiveness in the classroom (Sherblom, 2010). Every Learner Everywhere is a network of college and technology groups that conducted two surveys in 2020. The first survey in May 2020, shortly after transitioning to a heavily online classroom format, found that only 39% of college and university educators surveyed believed remote learning was an effective teaching method (Lederman, 2020). A follow-up survey conducted in August 2020 showed the percentage jumped to 49% three months later (See Figure 12.1).

According to Sherblom (2010), the usage of technology can create more distance and eliminate nonverbal communication behaviors, reducing the amount of immediate feedback, information gathering, and learning. On the other hand, virtual education can include tools that transcend space and time and allow individuals to present a desirable self-image (i.e., posting to a discussion board rather than having to come up with an answer during a synchronous class session). As reported by Rogers (2013), The Babson Survey Research Group and Pearson Learning Solutions surveyed university and college professors about their perceptions of classroom technology. While 60% of respondents believed the efficiency and mobility of technology created better learning environments, use of technology was also seen as more distracting than helpful to students. One-half of the respondents reported that using technology in the classroom increases stress levels and two-thirds reported that it increases the number of hours

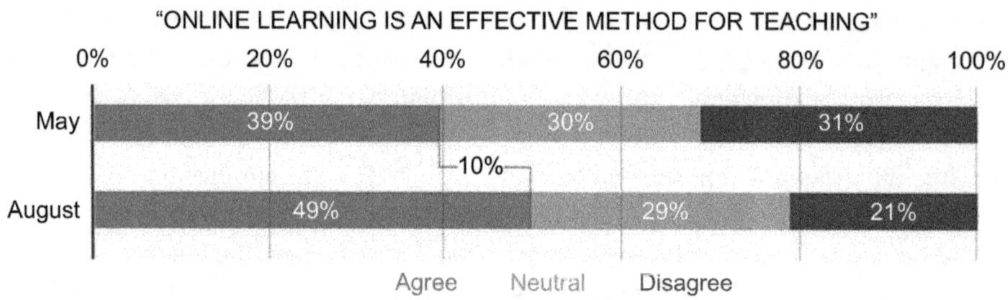

Figure 12.1: Change in Perceptions of Effectiveness of Online Learning – Survey Conducted in May and August 2020.
Source: *Inside Higher Education (2020)*

instructors devoted to each class. Furthermore, faculty members' top two concerns about virtual education included privacy issues and the integrity of the students' work. Educators were concerned individuals outside the classroom could participate in or view discussions and have the ability to assist the student with online assignments and/or course quizzes. Other respondents named deadlines and availability of resources as chief concerns related to virtual education.

According to Scheuermann (as seen in Bart, 2010), " . . . evidence indicates that online students and course facilitators overwhelmingly find considerable value in synchronous course elements" (para 6). According to Wind (2020), benefits of synchronous learning, virtual and in real time, include: the opportunity to develop community, more natural conversations among individuals, increased participation, and immediate feedback to and from students. Additionally, synchronous learning allows educators to explain miscommunication or misconceptions immediately and encourages a less hierarchically-structured environment. Alternatively, virtual synchronous class meetings can make teaching, learning, and conversing more challenging and require that all participants have high-performing technology (Wind, 2020).

Student Engagement: A Positive Classroom Culture

A positive classroom culture is one in which students can learn from professors and peers through personal exploration and discovery (Sherblom, 2010). Virtual education can provide social benefits to students by supporting an interactive community in which students engage with each other. However, scholars have argued that one of the biggest challenges of virtual education is overcoming a lack of student engagement. For example, even in synchronous classes, students may not turn on their cameras, whether due to hardware or broadband limitations or more personal reasons. Student engagement is highly correlated with active learning, and educators need to learn how to use technology effectively to engage students (Shapiro, 2013). In fact, in

2020, 71% of educators' top priority when planning the fall semester was increasing student engagement (Lederman, 2020), and this is arguably harder in the virtual environment.

Research has shown a supportive and compassionate classroom culture fosters course participation (Ho & McLeod, 2008). Moreover, classroom cultures have more influence on students' attitudes and communication styles than social status, gender, or distance (Bunz & Campbell, 2004; Park, 2008; Waldvogel, 2007). Further, social presence is " . . . an integral part of developing a positive online culture, which is influenced by conversations, activities, collaboration, familiarity, and motivation among participants . . . social presence influences self-disclosure, which affects relational development. Self-disclosure may reduce uncertainty and ambiguity in communication and increase the likelihood of building positive relationships (Greenan, 2021, paras 5–7)." Social presence is " . . . the sense of 'being together with another,'" (Biocca, Harms, & Burgoon, 2003, p. 459). It positively influences student participation and interaction, in turn, enhancing student motivation (Edwards et al., 2007). It is possible to create participative virtual environments that facilitate relationship development.

Use of Social Media in the Classroom

According to Tyma (2011), Twitter is useful inside and outside the classroom for presenting ideas and conveying communication messages. Tyma discusses how implementing Twitter in classrooms enhances student learning and academic development by increasing student involvement in large lecture halls, increasing the number of students who participate, and providing students with opportunities to convey their opinions, thoughts, and reactions in real time to the entire class including the professor, similar to a small discussion classroom. Student participation and engagement may likely increase by using social media tools and platforms purposely and deliberately during class meetings (Tyma, 2011). Tyma also argues that the use of Twitter streamlines the grading process for instructors by allowing immediate responses and feedback to questions and comments. Twitter can be used to monitor student participation and offer an alternative to traditional office hours. Tyma presents three benefits of using Twitter in the classroom: (1) it is free; (2) it provides a catalogue of conversations that students and educators can follow and monitor; and (3) students already bring technological tools with them such as laptops, iPads, and Smartphones. These points suggest that incorporating social media into class discussions and lectures is one way to increase student engagement. It might also be noted here that students already know how to use Twitter, which can be a major advantage over having to learn another platform. In some cases, social media is also directly relevant to the course; for example, students learning about media in a mass communication course would be given the opportunity to apply social networking techniques as they are learning about it.

According to Svinicki and McKeachie (2011), "There is no such thing as good teaching without good feedback" (p. 108). McKeachie points out that for feedback to be effective, students must engage with the instructor, process the feedback, and then act on it. This is consistent with Tyma's (2011) point that using technology in the classroom can serve a functional purpose in the learning process. As described above, using Twitter engages everyone via instant, real-time discussion, and interaction which allows for constant feedback between instructors, students, and even guest speakers. According to Mottet, Richmond, and McCroskey (2006), education in the United States "encourages students to interact with their instructor and fellow students as an integral part of the learning process . . . " and student feedback allows an instructor to cater to his or her needs; however, large lecture halls allow little opportunity for class discussion and interaction (pp. 51, 52). Additionally, approximately 20% of students reported being apprehensive about communicating in the classroom.

Research on student engagement demonstrates that there are challenges to engaging students even in the face-to-face classroom. During the COVID-19 pandemic, instructors, many of whom were teaching through distance education for the first time, faced the additional challenge of engaging students in a situation where they were often in a distracting environment (i.e., home with families and sometimes family obligations), faced technological barriers to participation (i.e., poor internet connections), and/or may have felt less motivated to participate in class. The goal of my teaching and learning research project was to examine my own online courses to learn how students perceived their experience with building relationships and connections in the online learning environment.

Research Process

The discussion of the research process below includes a description of data collection and analysis.

Data Collection

After receiving IRB approval and making students aware of my research plans, I collected student data during the Fall 2020 Semester over the course of 15 weeks in two undergraduate communication courses. Approximately 20 undergraduate students – 13 males and 7 females – voluntarily participated. Since class meetings were virtual, participants responded to six open-ended qualitative questions at either the beginning or end of three class meetings via zoom. Specifically, participants responded to the following questions in the zoom chat room:

1. What opportunities do you have to connect with others in the virtual classroom?
2. Why do you believe virtual education presents more, less, or about the same potential conflicts as a traditional classroom setting?
3. How have virtual classrooms changed the way you interact with peers and professors?
4. How have virtual classrooms changed the way you develop relationships with peers and professors?
5. How can virtual classrooms develop and encourage more class community?
6. How can virtual education courses promote a classroom culture that enhances student satisfaction and community?

In addition to collecting student feedback, I recorded each class meeting to review and observe student communication behaviors and interactions that included chat box conversations. Therefore, I used survey feedback, my observations from class recordings, chat box conversations, and journal notes.

Data Analysis

The same procedures were followed during data recruitment, collection, and analysis to guarantee accuracy in the research. Consistency was central during data collection and analysis to ensure credibility of the research. I ensured dependability by asking the same questions to all participants. The same procedures were applied to each participant, and research questions remained the focus throughout the process. As I reviewed class recordings and re-read my notes and student data, the following themes emerged: motivation, student engagement, and social media.

Results

The discussion of results describes my reflections on my observations and field notes followed by my reflections on the student interviews. I then present three themes that emerged from my reflections and analysis: motivation, student engagement, and social media, along with quotes from students that illustrate these themes. This section concludes with discussion of the results.

Reflections on Observations and Field Notes

Communicating virtually transformed how individuals interact in the classroom. For example, students controlled their video and audio; whereas, in a traditional classroom students continually communicated verbally and nonverbally. Hence, virtual education presents potential challenges to the formation of cultural norms as it reduces the communication of behaviors, beliefs, ideas, and values. Next, I observed student engagement and disengagement, as well as distractions that drew students' attention away from class discussions and participation, which is at the center of classroom culture. During class meetings, students shared their thoughts and ideas about virtual education with me. Although most students valued aspects of virtual education, I found that creating a cohesive class community was more difficult due to increased distractions online and at home because virtual classrooms change the level of interaction. For example, there was significantly less interpersonal communication among students due to a lack of face-to-face communication. Students stated that interactions with peers were more difficult and felt shallow in the online class as compared to a face-to-face classroom. One example of the challenge to building a unified virtual class culture occurred during a class meeting, when a student shared his screen to show the class a draft of an upcoming assignment. Instead of displaying the paper, we observed him playing a video game in which several characters were battling armed enemies. After several seconds, the student realized his faux pas and apologized repeatedly. It is unlikely the student would have played the video game in earnest in a traditional classroom setting.

Next, I observed some students tending to avoid participating in synchronous class discussions by muting their audio and video. This is a major barrier to building classroom culture since "culture is expressed in the meanings co-constructed by its participants" (Dutta, 2009, as seen in Greenan, 2021, para 6). Therefore, I used Zoom breakout rooms regularly to help students feel more comfortable. I consider virtual breakout rooms equivalent to study rooms in campus libraries in that they provide a private, more intimate environment where students can connect and interact interpersonally and in small groups with their peers.

Reflection on Student Interviews

Feedback from participants supported previous literature, as well as my observations. As a result, I grouped data into the following themes: motivation, student engagement, and social media. Names of all interviewees/participants are pseudonyms.

Motivation

I gained student responses for this theme based on survey questions 2 and 4: *Why do you believe virtual education presents more, less, or about the same potential conflicts as a traditional classroom setting?* and *How have virtual classrooms changed the way you develop relationships with peers and professors?* Participants acknowledged motivation as a major challenge with virtual education.

> It is hard to stay motivated during a virtual classroom. It seems some professors have assigned more [homework] because we are online, which also seems a bit unfair because it is hard to stay motivated while doing so much work. [During] in person classes, we can stay motivated and engaged while the teacher is at the front of the room. – Brandon, 2020

> I feel that the virtual classes offer more challenges than an in class setting. Most prominently, the lack of engagement creates an atmosphere that lacks motivation. Subsequently, this lack of motivation translates to the rest of the coursework, regardless if it is assigned in class or to be worked on individually. – Jen, 2020

Students stated that virtual class meetings impacted their participation and motivation, pointing to isolation as the primary cause:

> Interactions have declined between peers and professors . . . as our motivation declined we stop participating as much. It has made me more appreciative of one-on-one meetings with individuals though. – Terrance, 2020

> It presents more challenges for me, because I'm not built for online learning. I have to push myself 10 times harder. I'm normally an A or B student, and first semester of my freshman year I was on the dean's list, but when we went virtual last semester my grades were not good at all. – Gene

> I think virtual education is more challenging because without being in the classroom face-to-face with your professor, and learning from her/his techniques, it is harder. Being online, it is easier to slack off and not pay attention as much as you would in the classroom. I feel like it is also harder because when you are in class, the teacher can say no cell phones. But being home, and doing work, your teacher is not there to keep you on track, so we need to discipline ourselves. – Britney, 2020

Student Engagement

I gained insight from participants about student engagement based on survey questions 1 and 3: *What opportunities do you have to connect with others in the virtual classroom?* and *How has the virtual classroom changed the way you interact with peers and professors?* While students believed virtual education provided more distractions and detracted from being fully immersed in the academic environment, others acknowledged that virtual education was valuable but creating a cohesive online class community was difficult due to less team engagement.

> Connecting virtually with others during class meetings allows us to interact when necessary at any point during class at the click of a button . . . it isn't as valuable as compared to an in-person experience. I personally feel that it is less effective for morale and team engagement. Being at home takes away from being immersed in the academic environment and provides distractions . . . it needs to be blended with in person experiences or activities. – Justin, 2020

> I think continuing to be engaging . . . or encouraging participation through more one-on-one meetings would keep us active, engaged, and more willing to be part of the community. – Terrance, 2020

> It can contribute more challenges in the sense that there's significantly less interpersonal communication than [in a traditional classroom]. It's easier to miss deadlines and it can be difficult for professors to gauge how students are doing. – Nate, 2020

Social Media

Social media platforms, such as Twitter, can engage students through instant, real-time discussions and interactions. Moreover, the use of virtual tools may provide students who are more apprehensive a safe environment to communicate in large lecture halls and before an audience. Therefore, social media may enhance students' academic experiences and likely increase feedback between instructors and students. Student participants acknowledged that using social media as a teaching and learning tool can increase student engagement. Survey questions 5 and 6: *How can virtual classrooms develop and encourage more class community?* and *How can virtual education courses promote a classroom culture that enhances student satisfaction and community?* led to the excerpts below:

> We participate or ask a question without interrupting the lecture . . . [Instructors who] utilize apps get the most out of [students] and can still be engaging with the online format we are using. – Cara

> We can easily talk to people and feel less awkward, especially when the class is a really big group. – Frederick

> It allows us to talk with the other students and connect in a time where we can't connect in person. – Reign

> It can connect people from anywhere, so the digital aspect allows for some creative processes in the collaboration department. – Nate

The student responses support previous research which found that integrating social media applications into class lessons can encourage a less hierarchically-structured environment, more equal student participation, and provide more inclusive communication among all participants (Tyma, 2011).

Discussion

To achieve a supportive virtual classroom culture and reduce potential conflicts, educators can prioritize interpersonal relationships that, in turn, positively affect student engagement, attitudes, participation, and motivation. A classroom culture is likely to form at a slower rate with an absence of verbal and nonverbal communication and shared values, beliefs, and practices. To increase inclusivity and engagement in online environments, it is necessary to provide students with activities to develop and build micro communities among each other. To build a virtual classroom culture, it was important for students to interact with each other. For example, randomized breakout rooms in zoom provide ways for students to become acquainted and familiar with each other. For students who feel apprehensive in virtual environments, implementing the chat box and breakout rooms can help them feel more confident speaking in smaller groups while increasing their involvement during class; students may be more likely to share opinions, thoughts, and beliefs. Thus, these tools provide opportunities for students to connect and communicate with each other more easily and freely.

Using social media applications, which students already have experience with, are beneficial in a virtual environment for several reasons. First, they increase student participation and motivation, are relatable to students, convenient to use, and allow immediate responses and feedback to questions and comments. Moreover, most applications are free to use and provide an index of conversations that students and educators can follow and monitor. Applications like Kahoot!, podcasts, Twitter, and LinkedIn are valuable teaching and learning tools in traditional and virtual environments and can be incorporated by using the same teaching methods. For example, I created a LinkedIn assignment in which students create and build a professional profile to network with others in their respective industries. LinkedIn can be taught in any type of classroom using the same methods, and students appreciate its applicability. Additionally, in my electronic media course, students learn how to create podcasts and digital stories during virtual lab days. Students work in groups and exchange ideas and feedback while having opportunities to ask questions to me and each other.

Conclusion

As a result of COVID-19, educators had no choice but to integrate appropriate technologies into their teaching. While virtual education presents challenges, it is a useful educational tool inside and outside of the classroom. Therefore, it is beneficial for teachers to become technologically savvy in their profession as a way to connect and communicate with students in an ever-evolving technological world. Additionally, educators can identify educational goals and integrate appropriate technology after they have been established, as well as be vigilant when implementing technology in curriculum and instruction. The following recommendations can create and foster more engaged online classrooms and reduce the conflict experienced between faculty and students when they do not feel connected:

- Focus on helping students build relationships
- Create spaces for interaction, such as chat boxes and breakout rooms
- Develop structured opportunities for interaction and sharing of information and ideas
- Use technology students are familiar with (limit how much new tech they need to learn)

Furthermore, there are implications outside of academia. Since working remotely challenges the creation of a positive environment, companies and organizations can utilize the techniques above to develop a virtual workplace culture that helps employees stay engaged with the organization, decrease isolation, reduce frustration with technology, and build a cohesive climate.

A traditional classroom setting provides a structured space that encourages socialization, community, and social presence (Sherblom, 2010). Virtual learning disrupts this process since technology changes the way people communicate, verbally and nonverbally. It presents challenges since there is less interpersonal communication. There are fewer opportunities to form personal relationships with professors and peers in online classes; interactions are more difficult and can be shallow, even in breakout rooms. Transitioning to virtual classrooms calls on educators to learn about supportive and inclusive class communities, gain and reflect upon insight from students, and embrace new and innovative ways of teaching in the 21st Century.

References

Bart, M. (2010). Incorporating synchronous elements into online courses to enhance student engagement. *Faculty Focus: Higher Ed Teaching Strategies from Magna Publication*. https://www.facultyfocus.com/articles/online-education/online-student-engagement/incorporating-synchronous-elements-into-online-courses-to-enhance-student-engagement/

Bergfeld, T. (2014, January 29). *Online learning in higher education*. Retrieved from OREA | Offices of Research and Education Accountability: http://www.comptroller.tn.gov/OREA/.

Biocca, F., Harms, C., & Burgoon, J. K. (2003). Toward a more robust theory and measure of social presence: Review and suggested criteria. *Presence: Teleoperators & Virtual Environments*, *12*(5): 456–480.

Bunz, U., & Campbell, S. W. (2004). Politeness accommodation in electronic mail. *Communication Research Reports*, *21*: 1125.

Dutta, R. (2009). Excavating Second Life: Cyber-Archaeologies, heritage and virtual communities. *Journal of Material Culture*, *14*: 75–106.

Edwards, C., Edwards, A., Qing, Q., & Wahl, S.T. (2007). The influence of computer-mediated word-of-mouth communication on student perceptions of instructors and attitudes toward learning course content. *Communication Education, 56*: 255–277.

Greenan, K. A. (2021). The influence of virtual education on classroom culture. *Frontiers in Communication-Culture and Communication*. https://www.frontiersin.org/articles/10.3389/fcomm.2021.641214/full?&utm_source=Email_to_authors_&utm_medium=Email&utm_content=T1_11.5e1_author&utm_campaign=Email_publication&field=&journalName=Frontiers_in_Communication&id=641214

Ho, S. S., & McLeod, D. M. (2008). Social-psychological influences on opinion expression in face-to-face and computer-mediated communication. *Communication Research, 35*: 190–207.

Keegan, D. (1995). *Distance education technology for the new millennium: Compressed video teaching*. ZIFF Papiere. Hagen, Germany: Institute for Research into Distance Education. (Eric Document Reproduction Service No. ED 389 931).

Lederman, D. (2020). Faculty confidence in online learning grows. *Inside Higher Education*. https://www.insidehighered.com/digital-learning/article/2020/10/06/covid-era-experience-strengthens-faculty-belief-value-online

Lederman, D. (2019). Professors' slow, steady acceptance of online learning: A survey. *Inside Higher Education*. https://www.insidehighered.com/news/survey/professors-slow-steady-acceptance-online-learning-survey

Svinicki, M., & McKeachie, W. J. (2011). *Teaching tips: Strategies, research, and theory for college and university teachers* (13th Ed.). Boston: Houghton Mifflin Company.

Miller, C. (2021). Online education statistics. Educationdata.org. https://educationdata.org/online-education-statistics

Motamedi, V. (2009). The impact of technology on education: Issues and Concerns. *Malaysian Journal of Educational Technology, 9*(2): 21–25.

Mottet, T., Richmond, V., & McCroskey, J., (2006). *Handbook of instructional communication: Rhetorical and relational perspectives*. Boston: Pearson.

Park, J. (2008). Linguistic politeness and face-work in computer mediated communication, part 2: An application of the theoretical framework. *Journal of the American Society for Information Science and Technology*, 59: 2199–2209.

Rogers, M. (2013, October 21). *Wired for teaching*. Retrieved from Inside Higher Ed: https://www.insidehighered.com/news/2013/10/21/more-professors-using-social-media-teaching-tools

Shapiro, J. (2013, September 10). *3 must-knows on distance education*. Retrieved from Inside Higher Ed: http://www.insidehighered.com/views/2013/09/10/essay-three-key-facts-distance-education

Sherblom, J. C. (2010). The computer-mediated communication (CMC) classroom: A challenge of medium, presence, interaction, identity, and relationship. *Communication Education, 59*(4): 497–523.

Tyma, A. (2011). Connecting with what is out there!: Using Twitter in the large lecture. *Communication Teacher, 25*(3): 175–181.

Waldvogel, J. (2007). Greetings and closings in workplace email. *Journal of Computer Mediated Communication, 12*: 456–477.

Wind, D. K. (2020). Synchronous vs asynchronous learning: What's more effective? *Eduflow*. https://www.eduflow.com/blog/synchronous-vs-asynchronous-learning-whats-more-effective

Erica Knotts & Victoria Goodson

Chapter 13
Defining the Line: Freedom of Speech and Online Dispute Resolution Best Practices for Higher Education

Abstract: Universities have always been known for creating a thriving environment for civil discourse and conflicting beliefs, but sometimes this can contradict university policies. As universities strive to grasp the ever-changing online environment, all while exposing new layers of vulnerability and anonymity, the question arises: how can universities encourage students to express their freedom of speech while still recognizing and addressing the impact to members of the higher education community? This question has legal, ethical, policy, and philosophical implications and challenges of which we will highlight throughout this chapter. It is widely recognized that universities which provide dispute resolution options to students create conducive, positive, and thriving environments. These options can include facilitated dialogue, restorative justice, restorative practices, and mediation. In addition, these processes are not just limited to the in-person format but can also be modeled in virtual and online platforms. Within universities, the student conduct process emphasizes educational and disciplinary outcomes which tend to penalize students for using their freedom of speech if it contradicts university policy. The implementation of the dispute resolution process enables students to use their First Amendment rights so they can engage in a dialogue to understand how their beliefs and speech affect others. This chapter will serve as an examination of the best proactive and reactive dispute resolution processes for creating healthy and positive online learning communities for higher education institutions. The authors will provide real-life examples to demonstrate how these beneficial resolution outcomes can be achieved.

Keywords: Alternative Dispute Resolution, freedom of speech, higher education, student conduct, university, student rights

Introduction

The United States Constitution First amendment asserts that: “Congress shall make no law respecting an establishment of religion, or prohibiting the free exercise thereof; or abridging the freedom of speech, or of the press; or the right of the people peaceably to assemble, and to petition the Government for a redress of grievances (U.S. Const.

https://doi.org/10.1515/9783110687262-014

amend. I)." Freedom of speech really has for all intents and purposes become a colloquial term often used as a particularly defensive measure when someone's behaviors or language are called into question. There has been significant conversation in higher education regarding what constitutes freedom of speech on our campuses, as well as how to maintain and respect individual freedom while still creating a safe learning and work environment for everyone. What level of accountability or action, if any, can be taken if a constitutional right is believed to infringe upon someone else?

Defining this line can be taxing not only for students who are learning how to critically think about the world around them but also for those responsible for upholding the expectations of the institution while still remaining advocates for freedom of speech. When a person chooses to apply and enroll at a higher education institution, they are committing themselves to a pursuit of educational excellence. Public universities that are 4-year undergraduate institutions create a unique environment for students of all ages, beliefs, and backgrounds to pursue their academic degree while also legally binding students to policies that encourage and discourage certain behaviors. These policies are typically referred to as the Code of Student Conduct.

The conversation surrounding freedom of speech within higher education institutions isn't a new one, but it certainly has evolved in recent years with the increasing dependence on online platforms and communication. Most U.S. higher education institutions utilize online learning management systems, email software, online grievance reporting systems, and social media such as Facebook, Twitter, Instagram, TikTok, and YouTube to connect and communicate with the university community as well as the general population. While many universities have policies regarding freedom of speech guidelines for in-person situations, translating this to the online world has proved to be more challenging. This has become more apparent in recent years due to turbulent political environments, powerful social justice movements, as well as a devastating pandemic (COVID-19) which required a complete temporary transition to online education and communication processes for most institutions in 2020.

There are so many new ways in which individuals can express their beliefs, values, and opinions which don't require in-person communication. From virtual backgrounds, online discussion forums, to social media, the space to express oneself only seems to be increasing as well as the ability to remain somewhat anonymous. This anonymity can often lead to more confidence and aggressiveness in expressing opinions and ideas (Dawson, 2018). To meet this changing environment, online dispute resolution tactics have become increasingly important and necessary for higher education institutions to understand and implement.

Online Dispute Resolution (ODR) is an umbrella term referring to alternative dispute resolution (ADR) practices, including mediation, arbitration, facilitated dialogue (FD), and restorative justice which utilize the internet and digital communication to engage in civil discourse, resolving conflict, and creating space for educational conversations. According to Katsh (2012), ODR was first introduced in the early 1990s thanks to online business transactions occurring on websites such as eBay. With the increasing usage of the internet, online purchasing, and communications, we have seen an increase in online conflicts and disputes which are being managed through ODR systems. In 2020, with so many in-person resolution centers unable to meet due to pandemic shutdowns, many began using online video conferencing platforms such as Zoom and Google Meet to seek resolution (Elisavetsky & Marun, 2020).

In higher education, ODR practices began being introduced in the mid-1990s to start providing students with conflict resolution services and options (Law, 2013). With the increase of conflict management, alternative dispute resolution, mediation, and restorative justice courses and training, as well as the increased demand for online learning, many institutions began utilizing technology-based dispute resolution to resolve a myriad of issues and meet students where they were at. Even though most campuses still have an Office of Student Conduct or Office of the Dean of Students, the process for resolving conflict typically begins with the electronic filing of a concern or complaint which is then filtered through that office to create a strategy for resolution.

The use of ODR practices does not come without challenges to higher education. Some of these challenges include concerns surrounding access such as internet and bandwidth, confidentiality, participant follow-through, synchronicity of conversation, and extended timelines for resolution. The International Center for Online Dispute Resolution (ICODR) also highlights some of these concerns by sharing that any ODR or video conferencing practices that an organization implements should include the following five criteria: accessible, competent, confidential, fair/impartial/neutral, and secure (ICODR, 2020). Many of these challenges can be overcome in higher education institutions with adequate staff, training, resources, and support, but with the financial and budgetary constraints of most higher education institutions in recent years, these challenges have been exacerbated. Even so, many institutions, as you will read about below, have found the use of ODR practices to be a great resource for creating safe and civil conflict resolution environments.

With the increasing demand for ODR practices within higher education, the conversation shifts into best practices and skills needed to ensure successful implementation and outcomes. It is widely recognized that the way we communicate online is significantly different than our in-person interactions. Verbal and non-verbal cues, as well as emotions, can be more challenging to interpret online. This leads to more opportunities for miscommunication and heightened negative emotions which may disrupt the resolution process. Having the skills and knowledge as well as a strong electronic platform to handle miscommunication and misunderstanding is necessary to successfully resolve conflict online. This is particularly true when the conflicts or grievances include calling one's constitutional rights such as freedom of speech into question for violating university policy.

This fine line requires that ODR practitioners are trained and possess the appropriate knowledge and skills including technology management, communication tactics, balancing power differentials, as well as offering the most effective conflict management options (i.e. mediation, restorative circles, facilitated dialogue, or an educational conversation) to their parties. Recognizing the differences between these approaches as well as best practices can make the difference in creating successful and effective ODR outcomes for institutions. In higher education where defining the line between rights and policies can seem incredibly daunting, it is suggested that institutions create more space for restorative practices rather than consequence-based reactions. According to the International Institute for Restorative Practices (IIRP):

> "The IIRP distinguishes between the term's restorative practices and restorative justice. We view restorative justice as a subset of restorative practices. Restorative justice is reactive, consisting of formal or informal responses to crime and other wrongdoing after it occurs. The IIRP's definition of restorative practices also includes the use of informal and formal processes that precede wrongdoing, those that proactively build relationships and a sense of community to prevent conflict and wrongdoing". (Defining restorative, 2020)

This practice of creating conversation to bring all members of our diverse community together, whether online or in-person, can transform our interactions and higher education institutions. According to Maslow's hierarchy of needs (1943), for self-actualization and growth to occur, basic needs must first be met including safety, belongingness, and self-esteem. Working with students who come from incredibly diverse backgrounds, universities are often the place where self-actualization can be cultivated if we don't assume that students have already begun this process. If we create space to listen when conflict occurs instead of resorting to a fight or flight reaction, we are enabling our students to move up through Maslow's hierarchy and reach self-actualization. As university staff, faculty, and community partners, we can begin to understand where our student's needs are not being met which can lead to greater systemic change and support.

Similarly, according to Sanford's theory of challenge and support, individuals are more likely to develop when given a balance of challenge and support (1966). If one is challenged too much, they are likely to become frustrated and simply shut down. At the same time, if one is given too much support, they may never be pushed to critically think or create their own solutions. Restorative practices can encourage participants to work constructively and collaboratively to create solutions to their current conflicts while also enabling a skill set they can utilize in future conflicts. Alternative Dispute Resolution (ADR) approaches such as restorative justice, facilitative dialogue, and mediation directly tie into higher education as a natural bridge between university policy and freedom of speech as a way for students to proactively connect their beliefs, identities, and perspectives. If there is a breakdown of communication leading to conflict, then established processes in ADR are the preferred method for resolving these conflicts and can easily be translated to ODR platforms if deemed appropriate.

Current Institutional Practice

In addition to the Code of Student Conduct mentioned above, some institutions choose to have a freedom of speech statement which can administratively define how they define the line between student's Constitutional rights and university behavioral expectations. For example, the University of Colorado-Boulder makes the following statement on their website: "No, there is no First Amendment hate speech exception. Hate speech has no definition in case law, but it is generally understood to mean hurtful and offensive speech targeted against certain groups and individuals . . . At CU, we will make efforts to promote a culture of respect and civility, but we also recognize the constitutional boundaries that protect offensive speech (Free expression, 2021)." Another institution, North Carolina State University (NC State), shared this:

> "While NC State condemns speech of this kind, hate speech is only unprotected if it falls into one of the categories described above (e.g., 'fighting words' or 'true threats'). Although this may be difficult to understand or accept, even speech that is hateful or offensive is still likely protected by the First Amendment. However, just because there is a First Amendment right to say something, that doesn't mean it should be said. The First Amendment protects a right to say hateful things, often even when they stand in direct opposition to NC State's values of diversity, inclusion and mutual respect. However, as a campus, we must always strive to ensure an environment where all students, faculty and staff are welcomed, respected and supported, and where members of this community are tolerant of the ideas and expression of others. In addition, the First Amendment does not protect actions just because they are motivated by an individual's beliefs or opinions. Therefore, even though hate speech is protected by the First Amendment, 'hate crimes' may be regulated by North Carolina and federal criminal laws". (Free speech, 2021)

These statements can be viewed as helpful and informational for the entire campus community, in knowing how they can exercise their First Amendment rights. In addition, many institutions may choose to provide information on how the campus community can safely protest, demonstrate, and/or participate in activism activities. While these types of statements are incredibly educational and insightful, they alone do not prevent or protect institutions from being challenged. Some may interpret the freedom of speech statements from institutions, like the ones above, as asking for a legal lawsuit, while others might see it as creating clarity and being transparent (FIRE, 2021).

While this information could be viewed as helpful in community members making informed choices related to their constitutional rights, it also can be confining. Some institutions have very specific areas on their campus that are designated as "freedom of speech zones" where people (not just those affiliated with the campus community), can come to the institution to protest, demonstrate, or engage in activism. Organizations such as The Foundation for Individual Rights in Education (FIRE), proclaim that their mission is to defend and sustain the individual rights of students and faculty members at American colleges and universities. They also say that universities that have designated "free speech zones" are limiting or violating student's rights. In addition, this organization has created its own database for ranking at least 55 universities based on "What are the best schools for free speech?", and another database for rating the policies that colleges and universities have related to student freedom of speech and expression (FIRE, 2021).

To establish credibility, institutions should not *just* have a diversity and inclusion statement or even a freedom of speech policy or statement. The expectation for defining the line must come from all areas on campus, that is, all community members collaboratively working together in a fluid continuum of proactive education. In addition, creating spaces in which community members are encouraged to engage in civil discourse in reactive processes can improve understanding and build bridges.

Design, Implementation, and Outcomes of ODR

A key component of taking a whole campus approach to designing and implementing ODR processes on campus is to take a proactive and reactive approach. There are a variety of places within an institution where both proactive and reactive processes can be designed and implemented. Some of these areas are: Student Housing, Student Organizations/Clubs, Office of the Dean of Students, Social Justice and Equity Centers, Student Unions, academic classrooms, Disability Resources/Centers, Office of Equity Grievance/Bias, and Title IX Office. No matter where you choose to implement ODR, it's important that you keep in mind that the goal of facilitators, staff, faculty, community stakeholders, etc. is to work *with* students instead of *to*, or *for* them (Wachtel, 2003, 83).

Universities can choose to take a decentralized or a centralized approach in providing the ODR process, education, and resources to students. A decentralized approach would involve a plethora of departments, offices, and on-campus organizations which would offer their own internal services. A centralized approach would involve only one or two offices/departments that would be able to provide proactive and reactive services at the University. This centralized approach could be situated within the Office of the Dean of Students (sometimes synonymous with the Office of Student Conduct or Office of Community Standards). This office would be a prime conduit, as proactively they already offer student support services and reactively they are the linchpin for campus community concerns and grievances.

ODR processes can be facilitated by professional staff who have been trained in any of the following: Restorative Justice facilitators, Mediators, Negotiators, Verbal-De Escalation facilitators, Dispute Resolution practitioners, Ombudsman, etc. Your institution may choose to have employees attend professional development training where a certification or license is obtained. We must remember that it is not just housing staff, student life staff, faculty members, or financial aid staff who are encountering freedom of speech conflicts. Conflict topics can range from cultural differences, intersectionality of identities, student accounts, student accessibility, student payments, extensions or make-up assignments, etc. all of which are related to how students may choose to express themselves (verbally or nonverbally). We should also point out that it is recommended that untrained individuals should not facilitate any type of ODR processes, as unintended negative consequences or harms may result. In short, providing staff and faculty members with access to ODR professional development resources and training is essential.

The goal in a whole campus approach is to have both proactive and reactive processes in place. If an institution were to just have reactive ODR processes, then it is a never-ending stream of managing conflict after conflict. Incorporating community stakeholders (staff, faculty, campus police/public safety, etc.) into ODR processes can be of immense benefit to all parties involved, as they can encourage students to connect to various areas on campus even after the conflict is resolved.

Proactive Online Dispute Resolution Processes

It is common knowledge that typically universities offer an orientation for incoming students. These events and activities have been designed to center around relationship-building, community connection, and engagement. Often these "fun" events are not designed to connect to an individual's deeper values or the differences students have with one another.

Imagine if there were online restorative practice circle processes that occurred in which students and community stakeholders could set expectations ("the line") for students to engage in civil discourse, respectful rhetoric, and dialogue around their identity, cultural, and political beliefs? These online processes could be accessed by not just traditional students living on campus, but by the entire diverse student population. Community stakeholders within the restorative justice circle would be participating (instead of facilitating), sharing their stories, and working with the students to create expectations of communication, community standards, and how to have civil discourse about difference. In addition, peer support groups can be developed which focus on conflict resolution information/services/workshops to aid the students in their ongoing self-actualization and improved communication. It is within this space that students can ask questions, learn active listening, shared storytelling, and learn about their freedom of speech rights.

We would like to give examples of how ODR processes, education, and resources can be offered and disseminated in a mutually beneficial way for the entire campus community. We also would like to refer readers to North Carolina State University, Rutgers University-New Brunswick, University of Colorado at Boulder, and Southern

Oregon University as examples of what other institutions are doing in their campus communities. Any student, faculty, or staff names used below are fictional.

Institution Specific Proactive Suggestions

- The Restorative Justice Practices Program at Rutgers New Brunswick, is a program by which dispute resolution processes such as restorative justice circles, conferences, mediation, negotiation, and impacts panels can be facilitated. In addition, they also have proactive conflict resolution and restorative justice workshops, which can be requested of any student group, club, or organization. These workshops can be conducted in person or online. Through the online process, students have greater accessibility and availability to attend these workshops (Mission and services, 2021).
- At the University of Colorado-Boulder, the Center for Student Involvement created an online informational hub related to voting, a democratic engagement guide, and varied student activism resources. This is a great example of how educational resources and information can be used as a tool to enlighten students about their constitutional rights (ACTIVATE, 2021).
- Universities may have Bias or Equity Grievance offices, where incidents or conflicts involving hate speech, discrimination, and/or bias can be reported to. These offices are a vital part of the campus community, not only in providing ways to address these issues but also to proactively educate students on their rights and responsibilities. These offices aim to create a diverse and inclusive campus community, support civil discourse, and to give students tools to act (not react) to occurrences on campus which they may find concerning. Online workshops which inform students of their 1st Amendment rights can transform the ways in which they may use their rights responsibly (Bias impact response, 2021).
- North Carolina State University's Counseling Center has a comprehensive assortment of self-help resources for students, which include conflict management support. Health and Wellness Centers can promote events, workshops, peer support groups, self-care, etc. that focus on conflict styles, coping skills, self-reflection, tips, and tricks for self-awareness of emotions, needs, and communication (Conflict resolution, 2021).

General Proactive Suggestions

- Faculty members can be trained about circle keeping and learn basic mediation skills to create an academic course environment that is not only focused on the course material, but also building a collaborative cohort of students who can form relationships on shared expectations, needs, as well as healthy ways to address differences of values, beliefs, and culture. Oftentimes, faculty members can create discussion or working groups so that students can learn to communicate effectively and resolve conflict as it arises. Faculty members could facilitate these circle processes at the beginning of each term, in which the students and professor work together to co-create expectations for one another.

- Greek organizations often must go through a verification process to become a recognized Greek life organization affiliated with a University. Annually, there can be mandatory ODR training for all Greek Life board members and student leadership to attend. In addition, ODR workshops and processes can be available for all Greek organizations to utilize for interpersonal conflicts. Not all conflicts rise to a student conduct or policy violation level, and through proactive education, Greek members can build positive relationships that are based on shared understanding and collaborative efforts. These ODR processes or educational sessions can be instrumental for institutions' Greek Life Advisory Board or Office of Greek Life.
- Universities that have ADR academic programs and/or courses can be a tremendous resource for their campus community. ADR faculty members can provide a deep dive into ADR theory, approaches, processes in which students can apply to their own lives. Often these programs can connect with campus and community partners providing internships or work-study opportunities allowing students to engage in ADR processes both in-person and online.

Reactive Online Dispute Resolution Suggestions

The Code of Student Conduct policy that is within higher education institutions outlines community standards of behavior and expectations, some of which are delineated as being prohibited. These policies typically apply to students, regardless of whether they are on campus property or not. Many universities track and manage whether students are adhering to these standards through some sort of electronic reporting system. This system is designed so that community members including students, staff, faculty, campus public safety, etc. can report any observed concerns. Once filed, these reports are typically sent to the appropriate office (i.e. office of the dean of students) to determine the best course of action for resolution.

Specifically, in conduct cases regarding freedom of speech, many institutions have created specific policies like the ones shared above. However, these policies don't necessarily exclude or include which aspects are *acceptable* by the University. What is acceptable by the university may or may not have legal implications due to ill-defined limitations of what actions constitute violations of freedom of speech. Legally, hate speech (rude, offensive, derogatory, bias, etc.) is not prohibited speech.

These policies are often broadly worded, leaving room for subjectivity and interpretation. Traditional student conduct processes are rooted and mirrored as our own national justice systems. Universities are also mandated to have due process within a formalized tiered structure.

If a report of concern centers around potential misconduct or policy violation(s), then an investigation will be initiated and an informal or formal hearing will be held. The most common student conduct hearing formats are channeled through an administrative conference (with the hearing officer) or through a conduct hearing panel (comprising a selection of students, faculty, and staff). These formalized processes often focus on behavioral intervention and consequence-based outcomes, and can often limit opportunities for addressing contributing factors, the needs of the student, and repairing any harm that has been done.

The incorporation of ADR processes into the university's code of student conduct has been on the rise in recent years. One institution which has already begun this process is Southern Oregon University (SOU), which has updated its code of student conduct to include ADR practices as an option. In addition, SOU is in the process of creating ADR training opportunities for faculty, staff and, students and has even created new staff title positions for the hearing officer which include: "Coordinator of Student Conduct and Restorative Justice" and "Civil Expressions Facilitator." These small changes have begun to make ADR more visible within the campus and community. (Southern Oregon University, 2020). Once an institution has these ADR processes within their code of student conduct, then they can adapt their processes into an online or ODR format.

If Universities include ADR processes in their code of student conduct, they can take an educational and restorative approach as a response to freedom of speech conflicts. For example:

Students Jenna and Bridget just moved in for the Fall Term/Semester into the residential dorms. Bridget starts to decorate her side of the room with posters and pictures, while Jenna is on her phone recording a live Instagram video of her experience moving in. While Jenna is recording, she notices the comments on the stream that say "WTF" and "She is Racist!!" and "Holy Shit, what is she thinking?" Jenna looks in the background of the video and sees that her roommate put up a poster that shows the Kansas City Chiefs, depicting an athletics player dressed in indigenous regalia, saying the words "Always Savage". Jenna then confronts Bridget and says "Who the hell do you think you are? That's so offensive and racist! Take that down now or I'll message the entire floor that you're a racist!"

First Amendment rights protect both Bridget's actions to put up the poster (Freedom of Expression), and Jenna's words (Freedom of Speech). Neither of these two student's actions or words rise to the level of any University code of student conduct violation, but clearly these two students have a difference in how they express themselves and how they communicate. If ODR processes were available, a facilitated dialogue, mediation, or restorative justice circle could be a starting place for these students to address their needs and work towards a more positive relationship. Through these processes, the university is not taking any illegal steps and the students would still have an opportunity to have their voices heard. Some universities have created Bias Impact Response Teams or Student Engagement Response Teams to assist students with bridging differences.

Another example:

Rachael is the Assistant Director for Student Life and works inside the student union building. Periodically, students may contact Rachael for a meeting to discuss any concerns or issues that they may be experiencing within their student club or organization. James, a sophomore in the Hunting Club, made a drop-in appointment with Rachael. James disclosed to Rachael that they have been receiving negative comments on their Instagram and snapchat account from other known students on campus related to a recent picture they posted. James took a screenshot of the picture and comments (with student names attached), which shows James with a deer they had just killed. James was wearing camo hunting gear, and had put deer blood on their face. James had put the caption "Bagged me another one! WTG Hunting Club." Below the picture were comments from students who said "WTF you bambi killer?!", "Takes a real man to kill a defenseless animal, right!?", and "You get funded by the university to go out and kill animals? You sick F**ker!!"

James had a right to publicly post the picture and promote their student organization activities. In addition, the other students who commented did not violate freedom of speech in this scenario. In this case, James could be referred to the confidential Student Ombudsman Office to participate in an interpersonal online mediation process with the other students. All participants may voluntarily participate in any ODR process, and if the other students are known to James then there is an opportunity for a dialogue about their different values and lifestyles. The Student Ombudsman can be a great service for all the students involved and James may even feel more inclined to participate because it is a confidential service. This can give students greater peace of mind when speaking about conflicts or concerns on campus, while still being able to access ODR resources (Student Ombuds Services, 2021). In another example:

There is a controversial speaker that has been invited by a student organization to come to campus and speak in 4 days. This speaker is unable to physically be on campus, but has agreed to do a virtual Zoom meeting, where university community members may come online to see the presentation. Many staff, students, and faculty have voiced concerns through submitting reports that they are outraged that the University would allow this online event to be "approved." There also have been some minor instances of students getting into heated arguments and physical altercations within the residential halls in the days leading up to the event. The day of the event arrives, and the Zoom meeting has started. The Office of the Dean of Students has collaborated with campus partners including counseling services, housing, student life, and the multicultural centers to have online/virtual meeting rooms available at the same time as the speaker's event. Some of these meeting rooms are led by mediation and restorative justice trained student peers, while others are facilitated by trained staff members. As the event starts, any students who are seeking a safe space to talk to other community members or engage in a circle process are welcome to join one of these facilitated meeting rooms.

With the increase of online presenters, it is important for universities to have a plan of action to support students engaging in difficult conversations. In addition, there may be instances in examples such as the one above, where students may escalate their behaviors or actions which could be considered disruptive by university policy and/or violations of freedom of speech. These disruptive behaviors may include: verbal harassment that contains "true threats", students engaging in vandalism, rioting, etc.

All individuals do not have the right to violate another individual's freedom of speech. For example, if a student Zoom bombed the controversial speaker's event with a background image of Nazi flags, this is disruptive, biased, and hateful behavior but, it is still legal. Nonetheless, these actions may still have a negative impact on students even though they are protected actions. Alternatively, if the individual attempted to play loud music constantly over the speaker, preventing the speaker's right to speak, then most likely this would be considered a violation of freedom of speech. However, if the University had ODR processes, then resolving this conflict could be educational and the student could voluntarily repair the harm done to the best of their ability.

Universities in the last decade are starting to recognize that ADR processes can also be utilized as an informal resolution method within Title IX offices. Within federal guidelines, informal resolution can be a pathway or process by which students can attempt to resolve their conflicts, even those related to stalking, sexual harassment, sexual assault, sexual exploitation, and consent (Orcutt et al., 2020, 50). For example:

Jonas (he/him) is a student who just started attending the Outdoor Club. Jonas has started forming interpersonal relationships with several other students in the club and phone numbers are exchanged. One student, Elena (they/them) is one of these students who gave Jonas their contact info. Typically, these two students' text about places in the area they would like to go to or plan outdoor activities with the club. A few weeks later, Jonas started to text Elena repeatedly late at night. When Elena didn't answer Jonas's text messages within a two-day period, Jonas wrote text messages like "Why won't you answer me?" and "Guess I'm not a priority for you anymore" and "You're such a little b***h, no wonder no one wants to be in a relationship with you if you can't text them back!". Elena doesn't respond to Jonas, but is getting increasingly stressed and nervous about going to the next Outdoor Club meeting where Jonas will be attending. Despite these concerns, Elena goes to the club meeting where her friend Greg approaches her and says "Jonas has been telling other club members that you both had sex and that your obsessed with him and won't leave him alone." Elena is shocked, embarrassed, and doesn't know what to do next except to report a formal complaint to the Title IX office.

It is recommended that universities consult with their General Counsel, Administration, and Title IX office staff to research what best practices and processes work for their own institution. Not all Title IX conflicts or situations may be suitable for informal resolution. Rutgers University – New Brunswick's Title IX Policy and Grievance Procedures specifically outline how informal resolution or ODR could be a process utilized for the previously described example if the conditions below are met:

> "Informal resolution is a voluntary, remedies-based, structured interaction between or among affected Parties that balances support and accountability against a Respondent. Informal resolution is offered in various forms, but is generally designed to allow a Respondent to acknowledge harm and accept responsibility for repairing harm (to the extent possible) experienced by the Complainant and/or the University community. Informal resolution is designed to eliminate the prohibited conduct, prevent its recurrence, and remedy its effects in a manner that meets the needs of the Complainant while maintaining the safety of the campus community. Informal resolution processes aim to identify and repair harm in the community, restore wellness, and promote communication, engagement, and cooperation. Informal resolution options may include educational programs and workshops, impact statement discussions, one-on-one meetings with staff, mediation, or Restorative Practices". (Rutgers, 2020)

If only formal Title IX processes existed, then there would be limited options available to Elena. None of these formalized processes would be centered around the need to address the harms or impacts that they might have experienced if they wished to do so. If Jonas, after meeting with the Title IX Investigator: genuinely acknowledged the impact of his actions, came in good faith into an informal process to attempt to repair the harm that he caused, and wanted to accept responsibility and accountability for his actions, then it would be possible for an ODR process to occur. These informal resolutions could be in the form of online mediation, restorative justice circle, restorative justice conference, or an impact panel. Please note that the harmed party/complainant does not have to actively participate in these processes for them to occur. Harmed parties can be offered additional options such as surrogacy, in which a family member, friend, or advisor can read an impact statement to the responsible party/respondent. In addition, careful considerations and options given to the complainant within the ODR process should be considered as you would an in-person meeting: ability to be the first party to enter the virtual room, the ability to have a support person, etc. Community stakeholders such as a staff member from Victim Assistant Services could be participating in the circle process as a resource and advocate of both students. Karp and Williamson, co-chairs of the Campus PRISM Project (Promoting Restorative Initiatives for Sexual Misconduct), conduct workshops and research on how restorative approaches may provide more healing and better accountability for conflicts involving sexual or gender-based violence (Campus PRISM, 2021).

It is important to speak about building campus and community capacity to facilitate ODR processes. In addition, it's essential to get community stakeholder buy-in and train them to participate (not facilitate) in ODR processes. Community stakeholders who are trained and knowledgeable about restorative justice can be influential in supporting students, connecting them to resources, and advocating for understanding. Community stakeholders are essential to have as accomplices in pursuing ODR goals and outcomes, and are not limited to just faculty and staff within the campus community.

Conclusion

It is no surprise that higher education institutions can be challenged to define the line between university policy and freedom of speech. For institutions that are not currently engaging in ADR practices within their campus community, we urge you to consider incorporating these processes within your campus. It is also critical for institutions to successfully adapt their in-person conflict resolution practices to accommodate the ever-growing online learning community. The programs and solutions which have been shared above focus on the best practices which programs, departments, and higher education centers have been implementing when it comes to ODR. By following their lead, all higher education institutions will be empowered to embrace conflict and civil discourse effectively both online and in-person, creating space for educational conversations, additional resources, and a sense of community.

References

2020 College Free Speech Rankings FIRE. (2021). Retrieved from https://www.thefire.org/research/publications/student-surveys/2020-college-free-speech-rankings

ACTIVATE. (2021). Retrieved from https://www.colorado.edu/involvement/activate

Bias impact response. (2021). Retrieved from https://diversity.ncsu.edu/bias-impact/how-we-work/

Campus PRISM. (2021). Retrieved from https://www.sandiego.edu/soles/restorative-justice/campus-prism.php

Conflict resolution. (2021). Retrieved from https://counseling.dasa.ncsu.edu/resources/self-help-resources/conflict-resolution/

Dawson, J. (2018). Who is that? The study of anonymity and behavior. Retrieved from https://www.psychologicalscience.org/observer/who-is-that-the-study-of-anonymity-and-behavior

Defining restorative. Retrieved from https://www.iirp.edu/defining-restorative/overview

Elisavetsky, A. E., & Marun, M. V. (2020). Online dispute resolution (ODR): The great tool in times of pandemic. Retrieved from https://www.mediate.com/articles/elisavetsky-odr-pandemic.cfm

Free expression. (2021). Retrieved from https://www.colorado.edu/free-expression

Free speech. (2021). Retrieved from https://www.ncsu.edu/free-speech/

ICODR video mediation guidelines. (2020). Retrieved from https://icodr.org/wp-content/uploads/2020/03/icodrmed2.png

Katsh, E. (2012). ODR: A look at history. In M. Wahab, Online dispute resolution: theory and practice: a treatise on technology and dispute resolution (pp. 21–33). The Hague.

Law, K. M. (2013). *Best technology practices of conflict resolution specialists: A case study of online dispute resolution at united states universities* (Publication No. ED566363) [Doctoral dissertation, California State University]. ProQuest Dissertations Publishing.
Maslow, A. H. (1943). A theory of human motivation. *Psychological Review*, *50*(4), 370–396. https://doi.org/10.1037/h0054346
Mission and services. (2021). Retrieved from http://deanofstudents.rutgers.edu/restorative-justice-mission-and-services/
Orcutt, M., Petrowski, P., Karp, D., & Draper, J. (2020). Restorative justice approaches to the informal resolution of student sexual misconduct. *Journal of College and University Law*, *45*(2), 1–76.
Rutgers (2020). *Title IX Policy and Grievance Procedures* [PDF]. New Brunswick. Retrieved from https://slwordpress.rutgers.edu/compliance/wp-content/uploads/sites/42/2020/08/60-1-33-current.pdf
Sanford, N. (1966). Self and society: Social change and individual development. New York: Atherton.
Southern Oregon University (2020). *Code of Student Conduct* [PDF]. Ashland. Retrieved from https://inside.sou.edu/assets/policies/Code_of_Student_Conduct_091820.pdf
Student Ombuds Services. (2021). Retrieved from https://ombuds.dasa.ncsu.edu/
U.S. Const. amend. I.
Wachtel, T. (2003). Restorative justice in everyday life: Beyond the formal ritual. *Reclaiming Children and Youth*, *12*(2), 83–87.

Andrea Hartmann-Piraudeau

Chapter 14
Surprises and New Paths on the Journey to Developing Online Mediation Training

Abstract: The COVID-19 pandemic and its short-term impact on mediator training is the topic of this chapter. It describes the experiences of a mediation training institute in Europe (Germany) in adapting their training format during the pandemic, when on-site events were no longer possible. The new online training was observed through intensive evaluations and comparison with the on-site training. The results, which are surprising at first glance, show that participants rated the online training better than the identical face-to-face training despite initial scepticism. Hybrid formats are also included in the evaluation. The results indicate that there are advantages and disadvantages of each training format. Personal contact and coffee break conversations are missed in the online classes, while advantages to learning online included better focus on content and structure. One of the most important findings was that mediators trained online felt confident to mediate online after the training, but also indicated that they felt confident to mediate on-site. This was in contrast to those trained on-site, who felt confident to mediate on-site but were not overwhelmingly confident to mediate online. The task for the future is to combine the advantages of both formats and initial thoughts are presented here.

Keywords: mediation training, comparison, evaluation, hybrid, online, remote

Introduction

Writing this article, it feels as if the journey has already been completed and everyone has arrived at their destination. Yet when I reflect on the route and consider what happened?, how did we react?, what did we feel?, I realize that is not the case – we have not yet arrived at the "new normal." A first, major stage has been completed as we have begun to climb the mountain that suddenly appeared in front of us. We have ideas about how to continue and at the same time we have learned that more surprises await us and sometimes things turn out differently than planned. This chapter documents a first pause to reflect on the journey we have made so far.

Before February 2020, our mediation training, like most other mediation trainings in the world, was on site. We have repeatedly evaluated and adapted content, further improved training formats, and invited new lecturers with fresh perspectives into the program. We started expanding to different cities over time, developing new training languages, certifications, and alumni networks. Everything seemed

https://doi.org/10.1515/9783110687262-015

agile and adaptable, yet one thing seemed set in stone – the training always took place on site. Mediators in our training learn how to conduct mediation and apply the methods of mediation in their teams as executives, personnel managers, and managing directors. The assumption had always been that these interventions would take place on site, in their companies, studios, or offices. Of course, we were aware of online dispute resolution (ODR) and saw booths at mediation conferences promoting online mediation. Our general assessment was that this was an interesting, but not relevant, niche. Starting in 2019, we acknowledged ODR by integrating a relatively short, three-hour module into our standard mediation training called "online mediation." At the time, not all participants felt comfortable logging in from home, so an expert in online mediation came to the training and conducted the module on site through a presentation that demonstrated what online mediation might look like in practice. It was very theoretical and complicated, which was also the opinion of the participants, who reported in their evaluation after the session that it was "interesting, but not relevant."

And then everything changed.

Before I report on the experience of converting mediation training to the online format, underpinned by a quantitative and qualitative survey, I would like to briefly elaborate on who we are. Perhaps more importantly, I want to describe the mediation courses and the people who participated, who have provided the feedback and signposts throughout our journey.

Description of the Training

The Consensus Group is a mediation service and conflict consulting company in Germany.[1] With the establishment of mediation training[2] a few years ago, we reacted to an increasing demand from our clients in the business world who requested tools and techniques to deal with agile working conditions and the management of flattened teams. At first, our focus was specifically on this target group, but over the years it has expanded to include people who want to become mediators and have the goal of practicing this profession after graduation.

Mediation training is offered at a total of four locations (Stuttgart, Hamburg, Berlin, and Munich) and is usually held twice a year at all locations – at least, this was the case before COVID-19. The training is based on the specifications and standards of German Mediation Training Law. It is 120 hours. These are divided into five modules over three days. After five months the participants are certified mediators. The training group size varies from ten to fifteen participants.

1 www.consensus-group.de.

2 www.consensus-campus.de.

In this analysis, only the two locations of Stuttgart and Hamburg are considered since the composition of the trainers is identical at these two sites. There are a total of five trainers who change every weekend. On the third day of each module, a permanent trainer conducts the role plays, thus ensuring continuity.

Since COVID-19, the following new courses have been added

- Online mediation training according to the classical procedure
- Online training as an intensive course
- Hybrid training at all locations
- Classroom training at all locations.
- Online Training International

The Transition – "It Is Necessary"

New face-to-face courses were scheduled to begin starting in February 2020. COVID-19 started to call attention to the need for change, but the first module of the new courses took place on site as usual. Then the virus struck and it was forbidden to meet with more than three people in public spaces. What now? After internal consultation, we decided to do what was previously considered impossible – teach mediation online. Only the participants had to be convinced. In theory, they had the right to withdraw if the training was not carried out as planned and had already attended a module. We wanted to let them have a say, and in an effort to gain their commitment to the training we moderated a mediated discussion – a mediation on the process of the mediation training, so to speak. The participants' interests were collected and options for solutions were worked out. None of the participants considered dropping out of the training. However, two people wanted to take a break and hoped that everything would be back to normal for the next training cycle in September 2020. Interestingly, these two participants were not people who were afraid of technology, but two people from an IT environment who said they spent so many hours a day at the computer that they could not imagine attending a digital training course. All other participants were willing to take part in the experiment: they wanted to stay together in their original groups, they wanted to have a chance to revisit whether they would continue online if the situation did not change after the first online module, and they wanted a different time allocation (6 half days rather than 3 full days in one module). We were able to respond to these wishes, and we had a group that was motivated and willing to try out this format.

I would like to emphasize here that this was not an easy decision as the participants pay a lot of money for our training and had specific expectations when they enrolled. In this case, they expected to travel once a month to spend three intensive days with the group in training. Saying goodbye to this was difficult for some and agreeing to this "online experiment" was also due to lack of other opportunities.

The next module was taught online. After the training, our lecturer for the second online module learned more about zoom, using Padlet (a digital shelf) as a storage place, and more tools for online interaction: virtual whiteboards and post-it walls. The short version of the story is that the next modules were also conducted online – and even when there was a phase of relaxation of face-to-face restrictions in Germany in June, the groups retained the online format.

We have closely observed, evaluated, and assessed the trainings in order to learn as much as possible from this experience. In autumn, the next groups started and we could at least claim that we could make the shift to digital formats in case of a tightening of the COVID-19 measures. What had been a difficult emergency decision in the last course now became a marketing tool. The customers were unsettled. They were unsure about the COVID-19 infection risk as well as their personal and economic situations. They were uncertain and torn as to how they could afford to train at this time. This was reflected in the increased number of consultations and conversations with interested parties beforehand. We responded to this uncertainty and made different participation options possible. In principle, the training group stayed together from the first module to the last. With this new training, it was decided before each module whether the module could take place in person depending on the infection rate and the current virus protection laws. If we could not meet on site, the module was automatically taught online. In cases where the participants were able to meet in person according to the regulations, various precautions were taken. Minimum distance was maintained, packaged snacks were provided, chairs were placed on markers, sufficient disinfectant was used, and tests were provided as soon as possible. Nevertheless, the participants were free to choose whether they wanted to take part in person or online. For this purpose, a video transmission with a wide angle was set up in the room and the participants from home were projected onto the wall. This resulted in different formats for case simulations. There were both classic on-site simulations and hybrid simulations, for example, with one mediator online and one mediator on site. We found that it was very important for the participants to have this flexibility to decide spontaneously before the individual modules in which format they wanted to continue their learning journey. This assured flexibility and also ensured that enough participants registered,[3] even if at the beginning of the training it was unclear how the situation would develop (both globally and individually) through the end of the training five months later.

After accumulating evaluations in these formats as well as interviewing participants, we decided to offer online-only formats in addition to the flexible formats (on-site, hybrid, online). Our first online-only format was offered as a crash course. One hundred and twenty training hours within three weeks. This offer coincided with another COVID-related lockdown. The course filled up quickly, with all but one

3 Many training programs in Germany have paused their operations during this time.

of the participants in a similar situation: they all either had COVID-related short-time work, could not go to work, or had their projects put on hold or postponed. This meant time was unexpectedly created. Due to the restrictions, this time could almost only be spent at home, and our mediation training course came at the right time. In addition to the German formats, international offerings[4] were also added purely online.

Evaluation

The guiding principles of our organization prioritize the quality of our training. We engage in continuous evaluation and quality improvement. In addition to individual feedback sessions, two evaluations are carried out after each module: one on the conditions of the module content, the lecturer and the group, and a second is an evaluation of the learning progress of the participants. In addition, the instructors complete an evaluation of the individual participants after each module. The lecturers are also regularly questioned about their perception of the group, their learning progress, their commitment, and their level of knowledge. This corpus of data also allowed us to evaluate the new formats and compare them with other formats.

Overall Findings

Overall, our findings show the picture that emerges from the evaluation of the different formats over the last two years. In the evaluation forms, participants are asked what overall rating they would give at the end of each module. The scale is 1–5 (5=very good; 4=good, 3=satisfactory, 2=sufficient, 1=poor). In Table 14.1, we illustrate the assessment of all courses from February 2019 to May 2022 as an average grade (all modules were assessed and an overall grade was formed). All courses consist of 8–12 participants.

Overall, Figure 14.1 illustrates that the combined ratings for all training courses range from very good to good. The best rating of 4.71 was given for an online training. The worst rating of 4.08 was for on-site training. The average rating across all the training formats is shown in Figure 14.2.

On a very high level, the online training was rated better than the hybrid and even better than the on-site training. The on-site formats and online training were selected and booked by the participants in this form. There was the most complete consistency here in how participants sought out the training and how it was received. The

4 www.im-campus.com.

Table 14.1: Assessment of All Courses from February 2019 to May 2022.

Period	Location	Format	Average grade
February 2019–July 2019	Stuttgart	on site	4.08
March 2019–July 2019	Hamburg	on site	4.11
September 2019–February 2020	Hamburg	on site	4.32
October 2019–February 2020	Stuttgart	on site	4.35
March 2020–July 2020	Stuttgart/online	hybrid unplanned (2 modules on site, 3 modules online)	4.39
February 2020–July 2020	Hamburg/online	hybrid unplanned (2 modules on site, 3 modules online)	4.67
October 2020–March 2021	Stuttgart/online	hybrid planned (2 on-site modules, 3 online modules)	4.44
September 2021–February 2021	Hamburg/online	hybrid planned (2 on-site modules, 3 online modules)	4.38
January 2021–February 2021	online	online compact	4.54
February 2021–May 2022	online	online	4.71

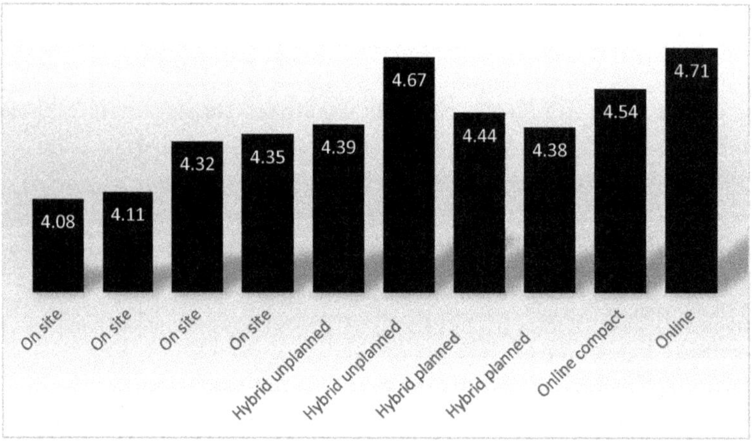

Figure 14.1: Ratings for All Training Courses across Locations and Formats.

hybrid training, however, was not booked in this format by the participants. The participants had booked an on-site training in Stuttgart or Hamburg and due to COVID this could not be carried out on site. Instead, the training was delivered in a hybrid format with two modules on site and three modules online.

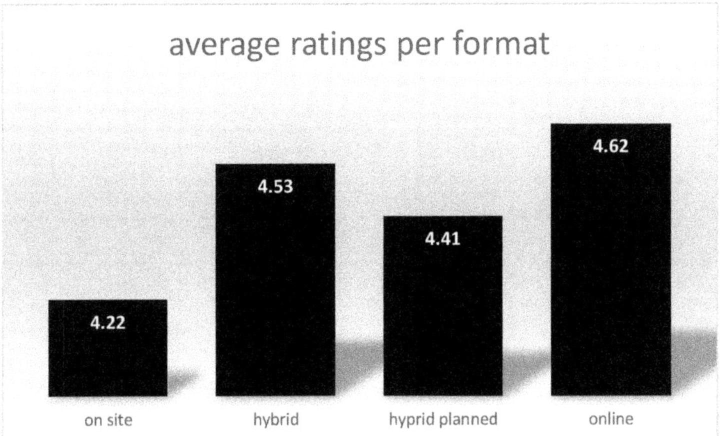

Figure 14.2: Average Ratings across All Training Locations and Formats.

The subsequent hybrid training was different. This was planned as a hybrid from the beginning. The participants were informed that, depending on the COVID-19 regulations, the modules would take place on site or online. We were very surprised to see the positive response to the unplanned hybrid training as it was the first online module ever carried out and the participants had initially reacted sceptically to the change from a face-to-face format. Despite these difficult conditions and new situations, the training was rated better than the classic on-site formats.

One hypothesis for this high acceptance could be the self-determined decision of the participants to use this format. The change from on-site teaching to online in this emergency situation was discussed in detail with the participants. The group itself decided to continue the training in this format. This could have been a commitment that led to a positive evaluation of the training, even if it was quite different from what was originally expected and booked.

The positive evaluation of the online training could also be related to the fact that the participants actively chose this format. The participants had the choice between the online training and a slightly later scheduled on-site training. The participants who chose this format therefore actively chose online and the higher ratings may reflect a preference for this format.

Since the evaluations are quite close to each other overall, it is worth taking a look at the details of the evaluation. There were two modules that were taught in all formats by the same two lecturers and were identical in structure and content, differing only in format (online/on site). These modules were each subsequently evaluated by the participants (See Table 14.2 and Figure 14.3).

The participants rated both modules in the online format approx. 0.5 points better than on site. Since the lecturers were the same in each case and the learning content was the same, there seems to be an advantage in the online format in the eyes of

Table 14.2: Comparison of Ratings of Modules 2 & 3 in Online and On-site Formats (Same Trainers and Content in Both Settings).

Period	Location	Format		Note
February 2019–July 2019	Stuttgart	on site	Module 2	3.9
			Module 3	4
March 2019–July 2019	Hamburg	on site	Module 2	4.1
			Module 3	3.9
September 2019–February 2020	Hamburg	on site	Module 2	4
			Module 3	4.1
October 2019–February 2020	Stuttgart	on site	Module 2	4.2
			Module 3	4.4
March 2020–July 2020	Stuttgart/online	online	Module 2	4.3
		online	Module 3	4.6
February 2020–July 2020	Hamburg/online	online	Module 2	4.8
		online	Module 3	4.3
October 2020– March 2021	Stuttgart/online	online	Module 2	4.3
		online	Module 3	4.5
September 2021–February 2021	Hamburg/online	on site	Module 2	4
		online	Module 3	4.4
January 2021–February 2021	online	online	Module 2	4.5
		online	Module 3	4.7
February 2021–May 2022	online	online	Module 2	4.6
		online	Module 3	4.7

the participants. For this evaluation, the participants were asked five categories of questions (see appendix).

The items assessing presentation technique, organization of material, and working atmosphere were all rated more highly in the online format. Above all, the item that read "the behavior of individual participants in the discussion seemed inappropriate" did not carry as much weight in the online format as in the on-site format. As this questionnaire was developed when there were on-site formats in January, it asked about issues that could speak to an on-site format (see below), such as the possibility of networking or movement in the room etc. It may therefore be that the design of the questionnaire was inappropriate as it may have emphasized the advantages of the online format that was taken for granted in the pre-COVID era.

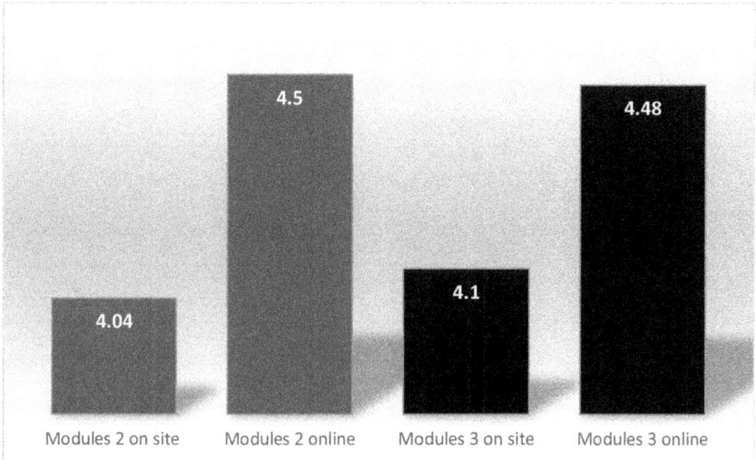

Figure 14.3: Average Ratings across Module 2 & 3 Comparing the Online and On-site Version.

Online versus On-site: Advantages

In order to learn more about the special features of the two formats from the participants, we designed additional questionnaires after the hybrid modules. These contained open questions that deal specifically with the question of where the participants see the advantages and disadvantages of the on-site and online formats. The results are listed below in Table 14.3 in order of frequency of the response. Forty participants who experienced both formats were interviewed with an open-ended questionnaire.

Table 14.3: Perceived Advantages & Disadvantages of Online & On-site Training Formats as Asked in Open-ended Questionnaires (n = 40 interview participants).

Advantages of online format	A total of 123 submissions
Better concentration (on screen, voices and faces and one's own role)	28
Better medium for theory introduction (better presentation possibilities, media mix)	22
Facial expression better to observe (in simulations)	19
Feel-good factor through your own environment	17
Better time management – no travel	17
Participants keep their speeches short (no long speeches)	8
Discussions are more balanced/ clear structures	7
Group is more disciplined (punctuality, not so many interruptions)	5

Table 14.3 (continued)

Advantages of on-site format	**A total of 53 submissions**
Personal contact, individual conversations during breaks	31
Body language is more perceptible (simulations)	14
Movement in space is possible	4
Other methods and techniques (flipchart)	2
Snacks and drinks	2

Disadvantages online format	**A total of 54 submissions**
No coffee kitchen talks (networking)	25
Sitting too long in front of the screen/ lack of physical exercise	15
Body language in simulations	10
Connection problems	2
Overstrain through technology	2

Disadvantages on-site format	**A total of 32 entries**
Travel routes/costs	15
More physically and mentally demanding	7
Less variety with pure knowledge transfer	5
Group dynamics more difficult (unequal speech shares and presence)	5

The results of the survey were discussed with the participants in the last module and further explanations have emerged from this. Overall, there were twice as many mentions of the advantages of the online format as for the on-site format. In the subsequent qualitative question -and -answer session, it became clear that on-site teaching is considered normal and the default. The participants see the greatest advantage in improved concentration in online lessons. More than half of all respondents stated that they were able to concentrate better on the lessons, the content, the exercises and also on the other participants, for example during simulations.

Participants also felt that having everything happening on their screen helped them to keep everything in view and to be attentive. It has to be said that in our training there is a "camera on'" obligation. The participants also said that by always seeing themselves and being visible so close up to everyone else, they were forced to stay focused and not get distracted. On site, on the other hand, there are some distractions, and there is always more movement in the room (someone gets up, goes to the restroom, gets a coffee, etc.), which disturbs concentration.

The second advantage mentioned was that online training provided a greater mix of media for presenting content, which was also related to improved concentration. Presentations included visual content, interactive quizzes, film clips, and group work which participants reported felt more varied than similarly applied methods in the on-site classroom. They stated, for example, that it was more pleasant to follow a presentation on their computer screen because it was closer and easier to read than, for example, content projected onto a screen in a classroom.

Almost half of the respondents also cited the more observable facial expressions of the other party in a simulation as an advantage in the online space. The participants found the conversations to be more direct and immediate and had fewer doubts about the alignment between what was said and the body language in the form of facial expressions alone. In conversation, they said they could read the others better in the online environment. The feel-good factor of being in one's own environment also played a role. Things like "preparing your own food," "your favourite brand of tea," "a comfortable chair," and wearing "more comfortable clothes" were all mentioned. There were 17 mentions of better time management. Being directly at home and not having to travel at the end of the lessons were particularly emphasized. Since the classes take place on the weekend, the topic of "still having something left of the weekend" also played a role.

A surprising issue for us, which we plan to investigate further quantitatively, is the participants' impression that everyone is more effective in the online format. For example, several participants said that there were no excessively long speaking turns, which about a quarter of the participants felt was a positive and advantageous aspect of the online format. However, when we questioned the trainers about this, they did not feel there was an observable difference in the length of individual speaking turns in the online or on-site format. The trainers did, however, perceive that the material was conveyed more quickly in online lessons because there were fewer interruptions. In on-site training, the trainers often felt that lengthy discussions had to be stopped in order to get through the program.

A final advantage of the online format was the perception of greater discipline among the group. It seems that there are not so many interruptions in the online format and the participants are more punctual. This point was particularly related to the start of classes after breaks. While in the on-site format the coffee machine conversations were often so interesting that not all of them came to an end, in the online format the participants returned on time for the restart of the lesson. This is consistent with the trainers' observations.

Moving to the advantages of on-site formats, it was precisely these coffee machine conversations and personal encounters that the participants named as the greatest advantage of the on-site formats. They stated that it was of great value to them to exchange ideas and get to know each other better during the breaks and that valuable networks could be established. In the eyes of the participants, the discussions during the breaks also led to a trusting relationship within the group and between the individuals, which provides a good basis for learning. Making mistakes, for example, or being "stupid" in one's own eyes is easier when a personal relationship and initial trust has been built up with colleagues in the course.

Body language in simulations was mentioned as the next advantage for on-site formats. Participants said that it helped them to better assess the situation when they could observe body language holistically. Movement in the space was also mentioned as an advantage of the on-site formats. Just walking to a group room, doing an exercise standing up or writing on a flip chart provides physical balance and is perceived as an advantage.

The use of the flip charts and the snacks and drinks available on-site were also mentioned as an advantage of the on-site format. The use of the flip chart was an interesting point in the discussion that followed. It seems that those who have either been working with this medium for years or who are very creative and like to express themselves visually have a greater desire and concern to include a flip chart in training and also in mediations. Those who do not have this experience are rather reluctant to write on the flipchart and prefer any digital options for making notes and visualizations.

The participants were also asked about the disadvantages of the formats. Overall, there were only half as many mentions of disadvantages compared to advantages. This discrepancy shows that the participants have a positive overall view of both formats. However, it should be noted that the question of disadvantages also reflects that often what was seen as an advantage of the on-site format is at the same time a disadvantage of the online format, and vice versa. Therefore, participants may not have answered the disadvantages question because they felt it was redundant.

It is therefore not surprising that the biggest advantage of the on-site format is also the most frequently mentioned disadvantage of the online format. The lack of coffee or break room conversations and the lack of face-to-face contact in general was perceived to make networking more difficult in the online format. The lack of movement and looking at the screen for too long were both cited as the second disadvantage. However, less than half of the respondents identified this as a disadvantage. The lack of body language in mediation simulations was also mentioned as a disadvantage of the online format. There were four mentions of connection and technology problems, and these all came from participants who do not normally work with computers and were less comfortable learning new platforms.

Online versus On-site: Disadvantages

The disadvantages of on-site teaching also reflect some (though not all) of the advantages of online teaching. Travel and costs were mentioned as advantages by 15 participants. Seven participants stated that they found on-site teaching stressful. In discussions, we learned that some participants felt they had to "behave" the whole time on-site. They perceived that they could not take a break from other participants even at lunch; whereas in the online classes, they could shut off their camera and stay quiet, creating a more relaxing space.

The final disadvantage of the on-site format discussed was about the group dynamic. There were two issues raised here (1) some participants felt overlooked during discussion sections of the training; and (2) some participants felt that individual participants dominated conversations and spoke for too long, resulting in statements such as "the discussions get too out of hand." Several of the participants perceived that being on-site invited certain participants to contribute more frequently, leading to resentment from more quiet participants. It is important to note that those participants who tended to speak more frequently did not report that they felt any less heard in the online format. Therefore, in the digital, online space everyone felt treated more equally.

Direct Comparison of Online versus On-site Training

Participants in the hybrid courses (who experienced both offline and online modules) were then asked to indicate via a sliding scale which features they preferred and in which format. Figure 14.4 illustrates how participants rated six items in terms of whether they preferred the online or on-site format. This was on a 100-point scale.

When the hybrid participants had to evaluate online and on-site aspects of the training against each other, this led to a slightly different picture. While the majority of positive mentions were previously made in the online format, the picture here is more balanced. It only becomes clear in the case of self-reflection, which the vast majority felt was more meaningful in the online format, and contact and exchange with others, where the on-site format receives a clear preference. Mediation simulations were rated as almost equally efficient on site and the online room. One can conclude from this that the advantages mentioned, such as recognizing body language on site and being able to better read the other's level of concentration and facial expressions in the online room, seem to balance each other out.

Perceptions of the Lecturers

We asked our lecturers/trainers to describe their experience with the online formats as well as their perceptions of the participants and group behavior in the online format. Several comments referred to the technology. The possibilities of interactive

The knowledge transfer in the form of presentations appealed to me more in this format

|------------------------------------x---------------|

on site 65 online

Group discussions appealed more to me in this format

|-------------------------------x-------------------|

on site 57 online

Group exercises and reflections appealed more to me in this format.

|---------------x-----------------------------------|

on site 37 online

Self-reflection exercises appealed more to me in this format.

|--x-----------|

on site 75 online

Mediation simulations appealed more to me in this format

|--------------------------x--------------------------|

on site 48 online

General exchange with other participants and lecturers appealed to me more in this format.

|--------x--|

on site 12 online

Figure 14.4: Hybrid Training Participant Responses Regarding Preference for On-Site or Online Format for Different Training Components (Numbers Reflect The Mean of All Participant Pesponses (n = 42) on a scale of 1–100).

presentations, digital blackboards and flipcharts, the functions of break-out rooms and joint synchronous work on documents were mentioned in particular.

Some comments referred to mobility and flexibility. Here, the convenience of teaching from home and not having to travel was mentioned several times. The online format was perceived as more agile and flexible in terms of time. For example, breaks were offered between the modules and work was done in more, but shorter, segments.

Other comments referred to the participants' concentration and motivation. Overall, the trainers had the impression that the participants were better able to concentrate in the online sessions. One hypothesis was that there were fewer distractions in the room and no side conversations. However, trainers observed that participants could not stay focused for as long a time in the online sessions. More breaks were necessary in the online format, but the break times were better respected here and participants returned on time. The trainers also felt that the discussions were more focused. There were not as many lengthy individual speaking turns in the online room, and both speaking time and individual contributions within the group seemed to be more evenly distributed. In terms of motivation, the trainers could see no difference between the formats.

Some comments referred to role plays. Here opinions differed. Some of the trainers found the role plays in the on-site format more instructive. Body language and discussions seemed more genuine. Others emphasized the smoother flow of the online simulations and found them more unemotional and goal-oriented. The arguments here were that facial expressions are more important than body language.

Apart from two colleagues, none of the trainers had previous experience with online teaching. However, all trainers were open to learning the new medium, at least in part due to the desire to continue teaching (and earning) in a time of limited face-to-face teaching options. The organization purchased licences for various presentation options and video platforms and a joint introduction to the platforms took place. Like the participants, the lecturers were positively surprised after initial scepticism. Above all, the learning progress and the online mediation simulations turned out to be more efficient than the team of lecturers had expected. After the first course, which was spontaneous for everyone and involved a lot of extra work, the lecturers established a new teaching routine in the online room as well. After a year of mainly online teaching, there are some on the team who would like to continue teaching online, especially if longer journeys and overnight stays can be avoided. Other colleagues are happy to be able to conduct more on-site modules again, as they find online teaching more strenuous and tiring. Everyone agreed that the training participants learned to mediate in both formats. Since this is the primary goal, both formats will be offered in the future.

Goal Achieved: "I Can Mediate"

This assessment by the teachers also corresponds to the assessment of the participants. The participants are asked at the end of the course whether they are confident to mediate. After the hybrid modules, we also introduced the question of whether participants are confident they can mediate online. Figure 14.5 illustrates the results.

On-site classroom training

Question: After the training I feel able to conduct mediations

I-- 80x ------------------------- I

does not apply applies completely

Online education

Question 1: After the training I feel able to conduct mediations

I--- 83x------------------- I

does not apply applies completely

*Question 2:*After the training I feel able to conduct online mediations independently

I-- 65x --- I

does not apply applies completely

Figure 14.5: On-site and Online Training Participants' Confidence in Mediating (measured on a 100-point scale; $n = 40$).

Figure 14.5 shows that participants in both groups felt well-equipped and able to conduct mediation. For the online group, we also asked whether they felt ready to conduct an online mediation. This was also answered in the affirmative. Unfortunately, this question has not yet been asked in the on-site training, but we strongly assume from the enquiries and discussions with the alumni that mediators who have been trained purely on site are much more reluctant to mediate online than mediators who have been trained hybrid or online. On site mediation, on the other hand, seems to have less to do with the training format. It seems that the transfer from online simulations to simulations on site requires less adjustment than the other way round. One explanation for this could be that negotiating and communicating on site is something we know and have always learned, whereas mediating and negotiating in the online space requires more effort.

In addition, I noticed an interesting observation, which has not yet been investigated in detail, as a possibility for future research. Two training groups that started in spring 2021 are training in a hybrid format. This means that some participants are attending the training purely online and the other part of the group listens to the theory online and carries out the simulations on site on the last day of each module. Both online and the on-site groups conduct a simulation of the same case in an on-site mediation and an online mediation respectively. In all six cases, the online mediation reached a result more quickly and the parties were more cheerful, relaxed, and proud of their success afterwards. The on-site simulations took significantly longer and the parties tended to complain more about the process and the results in the subsequent discussion. We have not yet been able to determine why the online medium seems to be faster and clearer in its results. Whether these simulations can also be used to draw conclusions about real mediations outside of training is also unanswered and an interesting topic to be researched further.

Implications for Future Mediation Training

In online formats, participants particularly like a good mix of presentations. Trying out different platforms and presenting them to the participants not only adds variety to the teaching of the material, but also shows the participants tools that can later be used in their mediation practice. We have compiled a library of free and fee-based tools and are actively working with them in the training. We will also use this presentation mix for classroom training in the future and, in addition to the classic on-site tools such as flip charts, moderation cards, and blackboards, we will also use and present electronic voting tools, tablets, and other digital visualization tools.

It was clear from the participants' responses that most value a known structure and adherence to it. This may be culturally different. However, we also see in our international training (in the groups there are participants from more than 15 countries) that a given structure and adherence to it provides a sense of security for the participants and is positively evaluated. This structure is perceived by the respondents in the online format as clearer and more stringent than on site. In order to improve this in the on-site training as well, we are now working with different facilitation tools and signposts that show the participants how much progress they made with the material and the program throughout the day. In the online format, it is positive that individual participants do not take up a lot of time during the sessions and that the contributions are shorter overall. This also seems to be appreciated by participants. This suggests that trainers need to facilitate a balanced distribution of participation, being sure not to allow anyone to dominate and not to overlook anyone who wants to contribute, while also not allowing the discussions to go on too long.

Social contact with the other participants and networking were mentioned as positive aspects of the on-site module. Coffee and break room conversations cannot easily be transferred to the online space, but there are numerous possibilities to create time and space for networking here as well. For example, participants are provided with virtual rooms where they can meet during the training. In addition, extra time is planned in small group discussions for networking outside of the prompted conversation. We have built breakout rooms without a specific topic and utilized playful networking tools where participants can virtually "walk" to different tables and talk, and these are very well-received by the participants.

Summary

To sum up, this spontaneous journey which we did not set out on voluntarily, provided a great wealth of knowledge. What was unthinkable in the old world is now part of a new reality: new formats of mediation training have emerged. After evaluating the interviews with our participants and the trainers and observing the interaction of the participants in the mediation training, it can be said that the online training as a new format was very well received by the participants and is equally effective in achieving the goal of becoming a mediator. This is also the case with the classical models of on-site training. Both formats have strengths and weaknesses. Knowing this gives us the opportunity to optimize the formats.

In online formats, digital presentation forms, the organization, the exercises for self-reflection and the group dynamics are rated positively. In on-site formats, the opportunities to talk to participants outside of the training, to network, to keep moving, and to better perceive the body language of others are particularly positive. The opening up of training from fully on-site to hybrid and even purely digital formats also enables the diversification of groups. Whereas the on-site room only connects participants from the immediate environment, the digital format sets no geographical limits.

Currently, mediation associations, training certification bodies, and training institutes all over the world are discussing what will be recognized in the future and how. Unfortunately, personal interests and market policy considerations play a role far too often. It would be desirable to continue this journey that has just begun and to find, test, evaluate, and further improve more new pathways instead of putting on the brakes and returning to the old formats by saying "it has always been this way."

There are initial surveys and studies[5] on how mediation practice has changed in times of COVID-19. Most active mediators assume that they will continue to mediate online more than ever, even after the end of the pandemic. Mediation training should train mediators for a professional reality and not as an end in itself to fill the coffers of training institutes. The future of mediation training lies ahead of us. Flexibility and openness to new formats and constant further development in training is what future mediators demand and deserve.

Appendix

Categories of Evaluation Questions

(Note: items marked with (*) are those that explain the biggest difference in online and on-site ratings)

Category 1: Seminar Leadership

- The seminar leaders seemed professionally competent.
- The seminar leader was able to convey the content well and in an interesting way.
- The seminar leader was sufficiently responsive to the participants (e.g. follow-up questions).
- The seminar leaders were open to suggestions and criticism.
- The behaviour of the seminar leaders contributed to a good learning climate.
- The leader seemed distant and uninvolved.

Category 2: Topic Selection

- I was interested in the individual topics.
- All essential topics were sufficiently addressed.
- The contents taught were well related to practice.
- The thematic orientation of the seminar met my expectations.
- The advance information was insufficient or misleading.

5 http://mediationblog.kluwerarbitration.com/2021/05/17/mediators-like-online-mediation-and-other-verifiable-facts/.

Category 3: Presentation of Content

- ***The presentation style was clear and varied.**
- ***The illustrative material used such as PowerPoint presentations, visualisation on the flipchart, handouts etc. contributed to a better understanding.**
- There was too much theoretical input and not enough practical exercises.
- ***The presentation of the content was clearly laid out and easy to understand**
- There were enough action-oriented and interactive elements.
- I would like to practise more on concrete case studies.
- The linguistic expression and comprehensibility fully satisfied me
- Creative methods were also used.

Category 4: Organization

- ***Due to lack of time, it was not possible to go into more detail on various topics.**
- ***There was too much of a rushed approach to some issues.**
- The thematic plan was too rigid and inflexible.
- There was enough time for questions and discussions.
- ***The schedule was essentially adhered to, changes were explained.**
- There was enough time for breaks and relaxation.

Category 5: Working Climate

- The learning atmosphere among the seminar participants was very good.
- ***The atmosphere in the group motivated to participate in the seminar.**
- Often the competence and commitment of the other participants contributed to a good working atmosphere.
- The interaction between the participants was respectful and polite.
- ***The behaviour of individual participants in the discussion was inappropriate.**
- Numerous disturbances prevented good work.

John Zeleznikow

Chapter 15
Developing User Centric Intelligent Online Dispute Resolution Systems

Abstract: Online Dispute Resolution uses the Internet to perform Alternative Dispute Resolution. Human-centered design is a methodology that begins with a fundamental concern for user experience combined with an experimental and iterative approach to developing new solutions. In this paper we examine examples of Online Dispute Resolution systems and methodologies for developing such systems. Our goal is to develop a methodology for constructing user centric intelligent Online Dispute Resolution systems. From our work on observing how Online Dispute Resolution systems are used, we believe that a truly helpful Online Dispute Resolution system should provide the following facilities: Case management, Triaging, Advisory tools, Communication tools, Decision Support tools and Drafting software. No single dispute is likely to require all six processes. But such a system would be an important starting point for expanding into a world where Artificial Intelligence is gainfully used.

Keywords: Online Dispute Resolution (ODR), user centric computing, artificial intelligence

Introduction

Lodder and Zeleznikow (2010) indicate, whilst there is no generally accepted definition of Online Dispute Resolution (ODR), *we can think of it as using the Internet to perform Alternative Dispute Resolution (ADR).* While this is a helpful working definition, it is important to note that one difficulty in providing a more precise and widely accepted definition is that ODR is many things, to many people.

ODR is often described as:

1. Technology Assisted Dispute Resolution; or
2. Technology Facilitated Dispute Resolution; or
3. Technology Based Dispute Resolution.

The one common factor in all these descriptions is the existence of a fourth party – *the* technology (Katsh & Rifkin, 2001).

https://doi.org/10.1515/9783110687262-016

The First ODR Systems

While the focus of negotiation has largely been on face-to-face processes, incorporating technology into negotiation processes has been commonplace for the last twenty years. The prime source of technology-based dispute resolution has been the telephone (Thomson, 2011), which allows people to communicate who cannot or should not be together in the same room, whether owing to geographical dislocation or to the existence of vitriolic conflict.

As Internet technology has become widespread, much attention has been directed at using information technology tools for dispute resolution. In some ways, ODR is a natural evolution of convening over the telephone. Information Technology now offers parties different levels of immediacy, interactivity, and media richness. Through some platforms, parties can choose to communicate through text; through others, they can convene in real-time video, allowing them to see each other and often, a mediator as well.

Sourdin and Zeleznikow (2020) claim that the emergence of the COVID-19 virus as a pandemic in the early months of 2020 has emphasized the importance of the development of ODR Systems. With citizens of many (if not most) communities forced into isolation, disputants are not meeting face-to-face. The justice system needs to operate in these circumstances – especially so in cases of family disputes, domestic violence, and bail applications. Systems currently in use, such as IMMEDIATION,[1] MODRON,[2] and Our Family Wizard (Lewis, 2015) only offer case management and communication. Zoom and WebEx only offer communication. None of the above systems have the decision support facilities vital to facilitate dispute resolution.

However, ODR is far more than a mere range of new communication platforms. ODR developers are seeking to create intelligent agents and robust negotiation support systems. These systems aim to assist humans in achieving better outcomes then they would themselves, even when performing to the peak of their abilities.

The decade of the 1990s saw the development of the Internet and initial proposals for ODR. Much of this work came from legal academics rather than technology developers. These academics saw the potential of ODR to resolve disputes that originated on the internet.

The decade of the 2000s saw the development of ODR for e-commerce; it was used by eBay and PayPal (Rule, 2003; Rule & Friedberg, 2005). Brett et al. (2007) investigated how the words people used in ODR affected the likelihood of settlement.

Over the past decade, we have seen the development of practical usable intelligent ODR such as Rechtwijzer in the Netherlands and UK (Smith, 2016) and the Civil Resolution Tribunal in British Columbia, Canada (Salter & Thompson, 2016).

---

1 https://www.immediation.com/ last viewed April 11, 2020.

2 https://www.modron.com/ last viewed April 11, 2020.

There has been much work on automated negotiation and agreement technologies. Agreement Technologies refer to computer systems in which autonomous software agents negotiate with one another, typically on behalf of humans, in order to come to mutually acceptable agreements (c). The vision of *Agreement Technologies* is a next-generation, open distributed system, where interactions between *computational agents* are based on the concept of *agreement*. Two key ingredients to such systems are needed: first, a normative context that defines rules of the game, or the "space" of agreements that the agents can possibly reach; and second, an interaction mechanism by means of which agreements are first established, and then enacted. Whilst automated negotiation and agreement technologies are important examples of negotiation support, they are not the focus of this article.

There has been considerable research on Artificial Intelligence at the University of Minho in Braga, Portugal. Carneiro et al. (2014) discuss their approach to intelligent ODR, while Carneiro et al. (2013) used case-based reasoning and principled negotiation in developing UMCourt which used autonomous tools to increase the effectiveness of the dispute resolution processes by increasing the amount of meaningful information that is available for the parties.

Katsh and Rabinovich-Einy (2017) investigate the use of ODR beyond e-commerce. Zeleznikow (2020) discusses the use of intelligent ODR to support self-represented litigants whilst Augar and Zeleznikow (2014) and Wilson-Evered and Zeleznikow (2021) investigate the use of intelligent ODR for family disputes.

Our Family Wizard (Lewis, 2015; Barsky, 2016) is an *electronic posting service that is a tool that can provide verifiable evidence of how parental communication takes place*. It helps separating parents engage in appropriate and civil behavior whilst assisting with developing parenting planning and maintaining a record of parent behavior. Its use is widely encouraged by U.S. Family Court judges.

The Australian Family Court system has unofficially adopted an app designed to help separated families manage daily life and hold parents accountable for their children's welfare. The app includes a shared calendar, a virtual "fridge" for children to post their certificates and artwork, as well as storage of key information such as Medicare numbers, shoe sizes, and birthday wish lists. Judges liked the app because it encourages positive communication and includes a profanity filter that tells parents who try to use bad language to go and have a cup of tea instead.[3]

Adieu Technologies offers family law advice and supports triaging and drafting plans.[4] One of its agents, Lumi, is a bot with expertise in law, mediation, and counseling . After having a confidential conversation with a client, Lumi will create

---

3 https://www.smh.com.au/technology/judges-mandate-app-for-separated-parents-20190906-p52op7.html last viewed February 18, 2020.

4 See generally Adieu, "Complete Your Financial Disclosure in a Fraction of the Time" https://www.adieu.ai/ last viewed July 27, 2020.

a step-by-step plan to help the client navigate the mediation. Amica[5] is a digital solution for Australian separating couples, which incorporates the reasoning of the Split-Up system[6] (Zeleznikow, 2004). Amica includes a machine learning algorithm that provides a suggested division of a former couple's total assets. We now discuss two widely used intelligent ODR systems.

The Rechtwijzer System

The Dutch platform Rechtwijzer (Roadmap to Justice) was designed for couples who are separating or divorcing. The aim of Rechtwijzer was to empower citizens to solve their problems by themselves or together with their partner. If necessary, it referred people to the assistance of experts. Couples paid €100 for access to Rechtwijzer, which started by asking each partner for information such as their age, income, education, whether they want the children to live with only one parent or engage in shared parenting, and then guides parents through questions about their preferences.

The platform had a diagnosis phase, an intake phase for the initiating party, and then invited the other parent to join and undertake the same intake process. Once intake was completed, the parties could start working on agreements on the topics that occur in every separation – such as future communication channels, child matters, housing, property issues (money and debts) and maintenance. The dispute resolution model was that of integrative (principled) negotiation. The process was based on interests rather than rights, but the parties were told of rules such as those for dividing property, child support and standard arrangements for visiting rights so that they could agree on the basis of informed consent. Acceptable agreements were reviewed by a neutral lawyer. The platform uses algorithms to find points of agreement, and then proposes solutions. If the proposed solutions are not accepted, then couples can employ the system to request a mediator for an additional €360, or a binding decision by an adjudicator. Rechtwijzer is voluntary and non-binding up until the point where the parties seek adjudication. Rechtwijzer had aimed to be self-financing through user contributions. This has not occurred.

---

5 https://www.amica.gov.au/ last viewed July 20, 2020.

6 SPLIT-UP is a hybrid rule based/neural network system that uses textbooks, heuristics, expert advice and cases to model that part of the Family Law Act 1975 (Australia) which deals with property division. Explanation is provided using Toulmin argument structures. Toulmin (1958) argued that that all arguments, regardless of the domain, have a structure that consists of four basic invariants: claim, data, warrant and backing. Every argument makes an assertion. The assertion of an argument stands as the claim of the argument. A mechanism is required to act as a justification for the claim, given the data. This justification is known as the warrant. The backing supports the warrant and in a legal argument is typically a reference to a statute or precedent case.

The British Columbia Civil Resolution Tribunal

The British Columbia Civil Resolution Tribunal (Salter & Thompson, 2016) is the most significant current widely available ODR system that comes closest to providing a full suite of dispute resolution services. The process commences with Solution Explorer. It diagnoses the dispute and provides legal information and tools such as customized letter templates. The template is essentially a formal, legal looking, letter of demand.

If this action does not resolve the dispute, one can then apply to the Civil Resolution Tribunal for dispute resolution. The system then directs the user to the appropriate application forms. Once the application is accepted, the user enters a secure and confidential negotiation platform, where the disputants can attempt (by themselves) to resolve their dispute.

If the parties cannot resolve the dispute, a facilitator will assist. Agreements can be turned into enforceable orders. If negotiation or facilitation does not lead to a resolution, an independent member will make a determination about the dispute.

Currently, the Civil Resolution Tribunal deals with the following categories of cases:[7]

a. **Motor vehicle injury** disputes up to $50,000
b. **Small claims** disputes up to $5,000
c. **Strata property** (condominium or owners corporation) disputes of any amount
d. **Societies and cooperative associations** disputes of any amount
e. **Shared accommodation and some housing** disputes up to $5,000

For these five domains, potential litigants can only use the Civil Resolution Tribunal. No paper-based solutions are available. Digitally disadvantaged litigants are provided with assistance in accessing the internet. One of the major reasons that the Civil Resolution Tribunal has been so successful is that British Columbia residents are mandated to use the system when dealing with issues listed in sections a-e above. Whilst such an approach may be seen as novel and discriminatory, it does ensure that the system is used, with relative ease, quickly and at minimal cost.

Classifying Online Dispute Resolution Systems

In the early years of using artificial intelligence to provide negotiation support, there was little systematic development of systems. Rather, numerous ad hoc systems were developed. The focus of these systems was upon the technology being used, rather than user needs.

7 The amounts are listed in Canadian dollars.

Thiessen and Zeleznikow's Classification for Constructing Online Dispute Resolution Systems

Thiessen and Zeleznikow (2004) observed that in 2004, Online Dispute Resolution Systems (ODR) could be classified into seven categories as indicated in Table 15.1. The systems they examined represented a wide range of approaches to dispute resolution (e.g., Artificial Intelligence, Social Psychology, and Game Theory). Jennings et al. (2001) noted that given the wide variety of possibilities for building such systems, there is no universally best approach or technique. Rather, there is an eclectic bag of methods with properties and performance characteristics that vary significantly depending on the context.

The Thiessen-Zeleznikow classification, whilst interesting, is now sixteen years old and flawed. In terms of system development, that is ancient. Information systems need to be viewed as socio-technical systems that provide information, that support decision makers, that provide behavioural support, that analyze communication processes and that are based on acceptable frameworks.

What all of the selected ODR systems in the article have in common is that they provide an alternative to litigation, providing a mechanism by which parties involved in a dispute can communicate over the Internet. Many of the illustrated systems were specifically designed to provide the best approach for a particular path to resolution.

The various categories of these systems, the techniques that these systems use, and examples of software in each of these categories are indicated in Table 15.1. In 2004, Thiessen and Zeleznikow defined information systems as systems providing information. Today, information systems are more than that, as Wu et al. (2015) describe them as socio-technical systems that provide information, support decision makers, provide behavioural support, and analyze communication processes. The *methods* listed in Table 15.1 are the techniques used to provide dispute resolution, while the *main players* were those at the time of the writing of the research. Many of these companies no longer exist and of course there are many new players.

Table 15.1: Categorization of ODR Systems.

Category	Methods	Main Players
Information Systems	Provision of information that parties can use to resolve their dispute	Scenario Builder Notgoodenough.org
Univariate blind bidding	Automation for single monetary issues	CyberSettle
Document management for negotiation	Facilitators working online and/or offline with parties making use of formal structured document management tools to help them create their contract	Negoisst

Table 15.1 (continued)

Category	Methods	Main Players
eNegotiation (or automated mediation) systems	Sophisticated optimization algorithms to generate optimal solutions for complex problems	FamilyWinner Inspire SmartSettle
Customized for negotiation or mediation of a particular type of dispute	Automated negotiation with structured forms	eBay UPI SquareTrade
General virtual mediation rooms	Human mediators working online with parties making use of mediums such as email, instant messengers, telephone, and discussion forums	ECODIR Mediation Room SquareTrade
Arbitration Systems	Human arbitrators working online with parties making use of mediums such as email, instant messengers, telephone, and discussion forums	Word & Bond

A comprehensive system encourages parties to start with negotiation. If the dispute is not settled with negotiation, the process can progress to mediation and finally recommendation or arbitration, until the dispute is resolved or failure to resolve the dispute is reported. Some systems are designed to resolve disputes that occur online while others are useful for any type of dispute, regardless of where it originated. Parties can resolve their dispute exclusively online or use a process that may also include face-to-face meetings.

Thiessen and Zeleznikow believed ODR systems face five main challenges as they attempt to present an effective medium for online dispute resolution: 1) Problem representation, 2) Preference elicitation, 3) Effective communication, 4) Neutrality provision and 5) Degree of automation.

The Thiessen and Zeleznikow model focused upon the design of information systems, rather on the needs of users. The model of Lodder and Zeleznikow is designed for neither users nor information systems designers. It integrates the research experience of the two developers of the theory.

Lodder and Zeleznikow's Three-step Classification for Constructing Negotiation Support Systems

Lodder and Zeleznikow (2005) developed a three-step model for Online Dispute Resolution based upon their Artificial Intelligence research. Their Online Dispute Resolution environment should be envisioned as a virtual space in which disputants have a variety of dispute resolution tools at their disposal. Participants can select any tool they consider appropriate for the resolution of their conflict and use the tools in any order or manner they desire. Alternatively, they can be guided through the process.

The proposed three-step model is based on a fixed order. The system proposed conforms to the following sequencing, which in their opinion produces the most effective Online Dispute Resolution environment:

1. First, the negotiation support tool should provide feedback on the likely outcome(s) of the dispute if the negotiation were to fail – i.e., give advice on the "best alternative to a negotiated agreement" (BATNA).
2. Second, the tool should attempt to resolve any existing conflicts using argumentation or dialogue techniques, similar to that provided in Lodder (2001).
3. Third, for those issues not resolved in step two, the tool should employ decision analysis techniques and compensation/trade-off strategies in order to facilitate resolution of the dispute, similar to the ideas proposed in Bellucci and Zeleznikow (2005).

Finally, if the result from step three is not acceptable to the parties, the tool should allow the parties to return to step two and repeat the process recursively until either the dispute is resolved or a stalemate occurs. A stalemate occurs when no progress is made when moving from step two to step three or vice versa. Even if a stalemate occurs, suitable forms of Alternative Dispute Resolution (such as blind bidding or arbitration) can be used on a smaller set of issues. By narrowing the issues, time and money can also be saved. Further, the disputants may feel it is no longer worth the pain of trying to achieve their initially desired goals.

In the following sections, we examine the important components of intelligent Online Dispute Resolution Systems. To do so, we introduce the concept of user centric design.

User Centric Support for Self-represented Litigants

Brown (2008) views human-centered design as a methodology that begins with a fundamental concern for user experience combined with an experimental and iterative approach to developing new solutions. Hagan (2018) investigates how court systems can be made more navigable and comprehensible to unrepresented laypeople (self-represented litigants) trying to use it to solve their family, housing, debt, employment, or other life problems. She chronicles human-centered design work to generate solutions to this fundamental challenge of access to justice. A new methodology is presented: human-centered design research that can identify key opportunity areas for interventions, user requirements for interventions, and a shortlist of vetted ideas for interventions.

We wish to enhance the Thiessen-Zeleznikow and Lodder-Zeleznikow classifications to design Intelligent Online Dispute Resolution Systems.

Galanter (2005) states that in the United States an abundance of data shows that the number of trials – federal and state, civil and criminal, jury and bench – is declining. In Galanter (2004) he provides empirical evidence that the portion of federal civil cases resolved by trial fell from 11.5 percent in 1962 to 1.8 percent in 2002, continuing a long historic decline. More startling was the 60 percent decline in the absolute number of trials since the mid-1980s. The makeup of trials shifted from a predominance of torts to a predominance of civil rights, but trials are declining in every case category. Allied to this decline in cases, is the rise of Self Represented Litigants – those disputants who are not represented by a lawyer.

Further, despite there being fewer cases being decided by trials, there is increased conflict and litigation. But this conflict is being increasingly settled via negotiation. Landsman (2009) argues that cases where disputants are not represented by lawyers pose inherent problems: they can cause delays, increase administrative costs, undermine the judges' ability to maintain impartiality, and can leave the often-unsuccessful litigant feeling as though she has been treated unfairly. He claims two broad factors may be responsible for the large volume and growth of self-represented litigants. First, multiple trends have made legal services increasingly unavailable at an affordable price. Second, American culture has long celebrated the notion of the "noble amateur." Do-it-yourself legal guides are a thriving industry, providing self-help manuals for everything from wills to divorces. Many laypeople believe that with the right guidebook they can master whatever legal challenge they face.

Zeleznikow (2020) indicates how the growing use of artificial intelligence in ODR can assist self-represented litigants.

A User Centric Approach for Constructing ODR Systems

Sourdin and Zeleznikow (2020) claim that the emergence of the COVID-19 virus as a pandemic in the early months of 2020 has emphasized the importance of the development of ODR Systems for the legal community. With citizens of many (if not most) communities forced into isolation, litigants are not meeting face-to-face. The justice system needs to operate in these circumstances – especially so in cases of family disputes and bail applications. However, the authors note that the systems currently in use, such as IMMEDIATION, MODRON and Our Family Wizard, offer limited ODR facilities, viz. case management and communication. ZOOM and TEAMS focus upon videoconferencing.

There are also other technology platforms that exist across several jurisdictions that have supported apps, as well as more sophisticated chat robots. Some of these systems have emerged from the vast complaint handling sector, where there is a greater capacity to collect demographic and other information which can assist in the development human-centered design. However, the wide variation in terms of capacity and use suggests that jurisdictional variability will continue to be a concern for courts, ADR providers and those using such services. Indeed, this concern is heightened amidst the justice sector's move to digitalization in response to COVID-19.

Similarly, disputants can suffer if they do not have the support of professional advice. Professional advice informs disputants of their BATNAs[8] and helps them focus upon interest-based solutions.

Lodder (2001) and Schoop (2010) indicate the significance of communication tools in Online Dispute Resolution. Clearly, any intelligent ODR system needs to incorporate sophisticated communication tools.

In his discussion of the GETAID system, which advises upon eligibility for Legal Aid in Victoria, Australia, Zeleznikow (2002b) indicated the importance of case management in Online Dispute Resolution. Stranieri et al. (1999) and many others discuss the significance of ODR systems providing useful advice whilst Schoop (2010) investigated providing decision support. From our empirical work investigating ODR systems (Abedi et al., 2019a; Abedi et al., 2019b; Abedi et al., 2019c), we observe that intelligent ODR systems should have the ability to conduct triaging and include document drafting software that produces agreements from negotiated plans – essentially incorporating agreement technologies.

From the work of Zeleznikow (2021) on observing how ODR systems are used, we believe that a truly helpful ODR system should provide the following facilities:

1. **Case management**: the system should allow users to enter information, ask them for appropriate data, and provide for templates to initiate the dispute.

For example, currently most clients of Victoria Legal Aid phone the organization to seek help. It is expensive, time consuming, and often inaccurate for telephonists to enter data. Mistakes are regularly made. Instead, parties should be able to initiate their conflict, enter their pertinent data, and track what is happening during the dispute. They should be kept aware of what documents are required at specific times. Because the disputing parties generally have a limited knowledge of legal processes, such support is vital.

This is especially important in the case of self-represented litigants.

2. **Triaging**: the system should make decisions, or at least give advice on how important it is to act in a timely manner and where to send the dispute. This may be particularly important in cases of domestic abuse or where there is a potential for

---

8 Fisher and Ury (1981) introduce the concept of a *BATNA* as your **B**est **a**lternative **t**o a **n**egotiated **a**greement. The reason you negotiate with someone is to produce better results than would otherwise occur. If you are unaware of what results you could obtain if the negotiations are unsuccessful, you run the risk of entering into an agreement that you would be better off rejecting; or rejecting an agreement you would be better off entering into.

children to be kidnapped. Triaging systems are vital for expediting action in high-risk cases and thus reducing potential harm.

Such systems are thus vital for protecting the interests of at-risk self-represented litigants.

3. **Advisory tools**: the system should provide tools for reality testing. Such tools could include, books, articles, reports of cases, copies of legislation and videos; there would also be calculators (such as to advise upon child support) and BATNA advisory systems (to inform disputants of the likely outcome if the dispute were to be decided by a decision-maker, e.g. judge or arbitrator). Other useful advice that could be included are copies of the relevant Acts, links to landmark cases, relevant books and reports, and videos providing useful parenting advice.

Advisory tools (as suggested by Zeleznikow (2002a) are a vital cog in supporting self-represented litigants.

An important associated question is how can we design advisory tools that self-represented litigants (or disputants without professional advisors) can gainfully use? Are the legal concepts behind the use of these tools too difficult for amateurs to understand? How do we construct suitable user interfaces for such disputants? Such research is discussed in the development of Split-Up (Stranieri et al., 1999), Rechtwizer (Smith, 2016) and the British Columbia Civil Resolution Tribunal (Salter & Thompson, 2016) systems. This issue needs to be the subject of much future research.

4. **Communication tools**: for negotiation, mediation, conciliation, or facilitation. Such tools could provide shuttle mediation if required. For many ODR providers, the provision of communication tools is their main goal. Thomson (2011) describes how Relationships Australia Queensland built a family ODR system that used Adobe Connect to emulate Australian Online Family Dispute Resolution.

Online communication tools are important for all disputants and litigants, whether they are professionally represented or not.

5. **Decision support tools:** if the disputants cannot resolve their conflict, software using game theory or artificial intelligence can be used to facilitate trade-offs. Family Winner[9] and Smartsettle[10] provide such services. Professionals (such as lawyers and

9 Family Winner (Bellucci & Zeleznikow, 2005) is a negotiation support system that asks disputants to list the items in dispute and to attach importance values to indicate how significant it is that the disputants be awarded each of the items. The system uses this information to form trade-off rules. The trade-off rules are then used to allocate issues according to a "logrolling" strategy.

10 SmartSettle (Thiessen & McMahon, 1999) is an interactive computer program developed to assist those involved in negotiating agreements among parties having conflicting objectives. It can be used during the negotiation process by opposing parties or by a professional mediator. On the basis of information provided to the program, in confidence, by each party, it can help all parties identify

mediators) can provide useful advice re trade-offs. In their absence, suitable decision support tools are vital.

Self-represented litigants are in great need of such tools as they have little experience in negotiation decision-making and are generally negotiating during a very stressful time in their life.

6. **Drafting software or Agreement Technologies**: if and once a negotiation settlement is in principle reached, the software can be used to draft suitable agreements. Research with Relationships Australia Queensland found that telephone family mediations had a success rate of 80%, but when family dispute resolution practitioners sent the disputants a parenting plan, many parents claimed that they had not agreed with the plan. Thus, ODR systems should incorporate Agreement Technologies.

Preparing drafting plans (such as parenting plans) that are acceptable to all parties is a non-trivial task. And the task is of course more difficult when one or two of the disputants/litigants do not have professional support.

No single dispute is likely to require all six processes. All ODR systems include step 4 and most include 1. The authors acknowledge that there are alternative technologies that do fulfill *other* aspects of this model, but not *all*. For example, Adieu Technologies offers family law advice (facility 3) and supports triaging and drafting plans (facilities 2 and 6).[11] Another example is Smartsettle, which provides decision support to assist negotiation (facility 5).[12] Agreement Technologies support facility 6.

The development of such a hybrid ODR system would be very significant, but costly and very time and resource consuming. Such a system would require us to construct the appropriate sub-systems 1 to 6 and ensure that all the sub-systems are capable of communicating with each other. Such a system would be an important starting point for expanding into a world where Artificial Intelligence is gainfully used.

Conclusion

The goal of Online Dispute Resolution is to use the Internet to perform Alternative Dispute Resolution. Many judicial systems are now providing Online Dispute Resolution as part of their processes. In the early years of using Artificial Intelligence to

feasible alternatives, if any exist, that should be preferred to each party's proposal. If such alternatives do not exist, the program can help parties develop counter proposals.

11 See generally: 'Complete your financial disclosure in a fraction of the time' *Adieu: Elegant Parting*, https://www.adieu.ai/ last viewed May 6, 2020.

12 See generally: 'Smartsettle' *Smartsettle: Beyond Win-Win,* https://www.smartsettle.com/about-us last viewed November 25, 2020.

provide negotiation support, there was little systematic development of systems. Rather a number of ad hoc systems were developed. The focus of these systems was upon the technology being used, rather than user needs. This can be seen in the models of Thiessen and Zeleznikow (2004) and Lodder and Zeleznikow (2005).

Human-centered design is a methodology that begins with a fundamental concern for user experience combined with an experimental and iterative approach to developing new solutions. In this paper we have described a model for constructing user centric intelligent ODR systems. Such a model integrates Case management, Triaging, Advisory tools, Communication tools, Decision support tools, and Drafting software. No single dispute is likely to require all six processes to resolve the issue at stake. However, the development of such a hybrid Online Dispute Resolution system would be a very significant important starting point for expanding into a world where Artificial Intelligence is gainfully used.

There will be many implications for business and social organizations using intelligent Online Dispute Resolution. A major benefit will be efficiency, as users will receive important information about the status of the dispute, timelines they need to meet, and documents they must provide. They will also receive useful information about potential outcomes which help anchor their negotiation offers. And they will receive advice about making trade-offs and drafting agreements.

But most importantly they will receive advice without needing to request professional support. This could be very useful in employment disputes because it might lower the intensity of the conflict and allow for the resolution of the dispute without one or more parties leaving the organization.

References

Abedi, F., Zeleznikow, J., & Bellucci, E. (2019a). Universal standards for the concept of trust in online dispute resolution systems in e-commerce disputes. *International Journal of Law and Information Technology, 27*(3): 209–237.

Abedi, F., Zeleznikow, J., & Brien, C. (2019b). Universal standards for the concept of fairness in online dispute resolution in B2C E-Disputes. *Ohio State Journal on Dispute Resolution, 34*: 357.

Abedi, F., Zeleznikow, J., & Brien, C. (2019c). Developing regulatory standards for the concept of security in online dispute resolution systems. *Computer Law & Security Review, 35*(5): 105328.

Augar, N. and Zeleznikow, J. (2014). Developing Online Support and Counseling to enhance Family Dispute Resolution in Australia. *Group Decision and Negotiation, 23*(3): 515–532

Barsky, A.E. (2016). The ethics of app-assisted family mediation. *Conflict Resolution Quarterly, 34*(1): 31–42.

Bellucci, E., & Zeleznikow, J., (2005). Developing Negotiation Decision Support Systems that support mediators: a case study of the Family_Winner system. *Artificial Intelligence and Law, 13*(2), 233–271.

Brett, J., Olekalns, M., Friedman, R., Goates, N., Anderson, C., & Lisco, C. (2007). Sticks and stones: Language, face, and online dispute resolution. *The Academy of Management Journal, 50*(1): 85–99. Retrieved March 25, 2021, from http://www.jstor.org/stable/20159842

Brown, T. (2008). Design thinking. *Harvard Business Review, 86*(6): 84.

Carneiro, D., Novais, P., Andrade, F., Zeleznikow, J., & Neves, J. (2013). Using case-based reasoning and principled negotiation to provide decision support for dispute resolution. *Knowledge and Information Systems, 36*(3): 789–826.

Carneiro, D., Novais, P., & Neves, J. (2014). *Conflict resolution and its context.* New York: Springer.

Fisher, R., & Ury, W. (1981). *Getting to Yes.* New York: Penguin Group.

Galanter, M. (2004). The vanishing trial: An examination of trials and related matters in federal and state courts. *Journal of Empirical Legal Studies, 1*(3): 459–570

Galanter, M. (2005). The hundred-year decline of trials and the thirty years war. *Stanford Law Review*, 57: 1255–1274.

Hagan, M. (2018). A Human-Centered Design approach to access to justice: Generating New prototypes and hypotheses for interventions to make courts user-friendly. *Indiana Journal of Law & Social Equality, 6*: 199.

Jennings, N.R., Faratin, P., Lomuscio, A.R., Parsons, S., Sierra, C., & Wooldridge, M., (2001). Automated negotiation: prospects, methods and challenges. *International Journal of Group Decision and Negotiation, 10*(2): 199–215.

Katsh, E.E., Katsh, M.E. and Rifkin, J., 2001. *Online dispute resolution: Resolving conflicts in cyberspace.* John Wiley & Sons, Inc., Hoboken, NJ.

Katsh, M.E. and Rabinovich-Einy, O. (2017). *Digital Justice: Technology and The Internet of Disputes.* Oxford, UK: Oxford University Press.

Landsman, S. (2009). The growing challenge of pro se litigation. *Lewis & Clark Law Review, 13*: 439.

Lodder, A., (2001). DiaLaw: On legal justification and dialogical models of argumentation. *Law and Philosophy Library, Volume 42.* Springer Science and Business Media., Dordrecht, Netherlands.

Lodder, A., & Thiessen, E. (2003). The role of artificial intelligence in online dispute resolution. In *Workshop on Online Dispute Resolution at the International Conference on Artificial Intelligence and Law, Edinburgh, UK.*

Lodder, A.R., & Zeleznikow, J. (2005). Developing an online dispute resolution environment: Dialogue tools and negotiation support systems in a three-step model. *Harvard Negotiation Law Review, 10*: 287.

Lodder, A.R., & Zeleznikow, J. (2010). *Enhanced dispute resolution through the use of information technology.* Cambridge, UK: Cambridge University Press.

Lewis, H.T.T. (2015). Helping families by maintaining a strong well-funded family court that encourages consensual peacemaking: A judicial perspective. *Family Court Review, 53*(3): 371–377. Doi http://doi.org/10.1111/fcre.12158

Ossowski, S. (2012). Agreement technologies. *Law and Philosophy Library, Volume 8.* Springer Science and Business Media., Dordrecht, Netherlands.

Rule, C. (2003). *Online dispute resolution for business: B2B, ecommerce, consumer, employment, insurance, and other commercial conflicts.* Hoboken, NJ: John Wiley & Sons.

Rule, C., & Friedberg, L. (2005). The appropriate role of dispute resolution in building trust online. *Artificial Intelligence and Law, 13*(2): 193–205.

Salter, S., & Thompson, D. (2016). Public-centered civil justice redesign: A case study of the British Columbia Civil Resolution Tribunal. *McGill Journal of Dispute Resolution 3*: 113.

Schoop, M. (2010). Support of complex electronic negotiations. In *Handbook of group decision and negotiation*, D. Mark Kilgour and C.Eden (eds.) (409–423). Dordrecht: Springer.

Smith, R. (2016). Ministry of Justice for England and Wales dives into the deep water on Online Dispute Resolution. *Dispute Resolution Magazone, 23*: 28.

Sourdin, T., & Zeleznikow, J. (2020) Courts, mediation and COVID-19. *Australian Business Law Review, 48*(2):138–158.

Stranieri, A., Zeleznikow, J., Gawler, M. and Lewis, B. (1999). A hybrid rule–neural approach for the automation of legal reasoning in the discretionary domain of family law in Australia. *Artificial Intelligence and Law, 7*(2–3):153–183.

Thiessen, E. M., & McMahon Jr, J. P. (1999). Beyond win-win in cyberspace. *Ohio State Journal on Dispute Resolution, 15*: 643.

Thiessen, E., M., & Zeleznikow, J. (2004). Technical aspects of online dispute resolution challenges and opportunities. In *Proceedings of the Third Annual Forum on Online Dispute Resolution, Melbourne, Australia* (July, 5–6).

Thomson, M. (2011). Alternative modes of delivery for family dispute resolution: The Telephone Dispute Resolution Service and the online FDR project. *Journal of Family Studies, 17*(3): 253–257.

Toulmin, S. E. (1958). *The uses of argument*. Cambridge, UK: Cambridge University Press.

Wilson-Evered, E., & Zeleznikow, J. (2021). *On-Line Family Dispute Resolution – Evidence for Creating the Ideal People and Technology Interface*. Berlin, Germany: Springer Law and Governance Series, Volume 45.

Wu, P. P. Y., Fookes, C., Pitchforth, J., & Mengersen, K. (2015). A framework for model integration and holistic modelling of socio-technical systems. *Decision Support Systems, 71*: 14–27.

Zeleznikow, J. (2002a). Using web-based legal decision support systems to improve access to justice. *Information & Communications Technology Law, 11*(1): 15–33.

Zeleznikow, J. (2002b). An Australian perspective on research and development required for the construction of applied legal decision support systems. *Artificial Intelligence and Law, 10*(4): 237–260.

Zeleznikow, J., (2004). The Split-up project: induction, context and knowledge discovery in law. *Law, Probability and Risk, 3*(2): 147–168.

Zeleznikow, J. (2020). The challenges of using Online Dispute Resolution to support self-represented litigants. *Journal of Internet Law, 23*(7): 3–14.

Zeleznikow, J. (2021). Using Artificial Intelligence to provide Intelligent Dispute Resolution Support. *Group Decision and Negotiation, 30*: 789–812. https://doi.org/10.1007/s10726-021-09734-1.

List of Figures

https://doi.org/10.1515/9783110687262-017

List of Tables

https://doi.org/10.1515/9783110687262-018

List of Contributors

Rachelly Ashwall-Yakar, PhD (Conflict Resolution, Management and Negotiation Program, Department of Interdisciplinary Studies, Bar-Ilan University). She is a Lecturer in the Conflict Resolution, Management and Negotiation Program, the Department of interdisciplinary studies at Bar-Ilan University, Israel. Her research interests include the areas of Online Dispute Resolution, Conflict Resolution Education, Diversity and Cultural Competence, Transformative Mediation and Identity-based conflicts.

John Bechara, PhD is an Assistant Professor at the Tilburg School of Social and Behavioral Sciences at Tilburg University. His research focuses on the development and consequences of social hierarchies in the intra- and inter- organizational context.

Ekaterina Bogomoletc is a PhD candidate in the Communication, Rhetoric and Digital Media program at North Carolina State University. With her industry experience in strategic communication and data analysis, she is interested in phenomena on the intersection of strategic and science communication.

William P. Bottom, PhD is the Joyce and Howard Wood Distinguished Professor in Business at Olin Business School at Washington University in St Louis. His research examines the transfer of technology from psychology and social science to policy and practice.

Melinda Burrell, PhD is a democracy and peacebuilding specialist who has spent 25 years living and working in conflict zones. She now writes, speaks, and trains on the neuroscience of communication and conflict and is a board member of the National Association for Community Mediation.

Ioana A. Cionea, PhD (University of Maryland) is an Associate Professor in the Department of Communication at the University of Oklahoma. She studies how individuals argue in their interpersonal relationships and has published in journals such as *Journal of Social and Personal Relationships* and *Journal of Intercultural Communication Research*.

Lori Dieckman is a professionally trained mediator, conflict coach, and the director of communications for NAFCM. Lori holds a BA in Psychology from the University of Northern Iowa.

Candice Edrington, PhD is currently an Assistant Professor at the University of South Carolina, Dr. Candice L. Edrington identifies herself as a scholar-activist. Her teaching and research focus on public relations, social movements, visual rhetoric, and social media. Her research is published in *the Journal of Public Interest Communications* and *Visual Communication Quarterly*.

Malaka Friedman is a PhD student in the Communication, Rhetoric and Digital Media program at North Carolina State University and the Graduate Extension Assistant for the Hill Library Makerspace. Her primary research interests have been impacted from issues her students have faced, particularly with digital literacy and access.

Victoria Goodson, M.A., Coordinator for Student Conduct and Restorative Justice at Southern Oregon University in Ashland, Oregon. Victoria also serves as a Civil Expressions Facilitator and ASSOU's Judicial Branch Advisor. Victoria holds a M.A. in Peace and Conflict Studies from the University of North Carolina at Greensboro. She also holds certifications in Mediation and Restorative Justice.

https://doi.org/10.1515/9783110687262-019

Deborah Goldstein is the Executive Director of the NC Leadership Forum at Duke University. Prior to joining NCLF, Debbie was an Executive Vice President at the Center for Responsible Lending, a national research and policy organization. She is a graduate of Brown University and Harvard Law School, and lives in Durham, NC.

Katie Greenan, PhD is an Assistant Professor of Communication at the University of Indianapolis. Greenan's research interests include interpersonal communication and relationships. She has a Graduate Certificate in Qualitative Research Methods and a Ph.D. in Educational Leadership and Policies Studies from Purdue University.

Andrea Hartmann-Piraudeau, PhD is the director of Consensus and the International Mediation Campus. She works as a mediator and university lecturer and leads international projects to establish and introduce mediation into society and court systems in Europe, Asia, and Africa. Her research interests include cross-cultural differences and the role of emotions in negotiations.

Daisung Jang, PhD (Washington University in St. Louis) is a Lecturer at the University of Queensland Business School. His research interests include negotiation, personality, emotions, and public policy organizations. He also served as a Postdoctoral Research Associate at the University of Illinois, Urbana-Champaign.

Amy Janan Johnson, PhD (Michigan State University) is a Professor in the Department of Communication at the University of Oklahoma. She conducts research on discourse-dependent families, interpersonal argument, and relationship maintenance. She has published in *Communication Monographs, Journal of Social and Personal Relationships* and *Journal of Computer-Mediated Communication.*

Yotam Keduri is an independent evaluator who has worked in the Israeli nonprofit sector for over twenty years with a focus on evaluating 'bridging' and contact-based peacebuilding programs—both cross-border programming designed to bring together Israelis and Palestinians as well as programs within Israel.

Erica Knotts, M.A., MLIS, is a Communication Instructor and Student Ombudsperson at Southern Oregon University. Knotts' academic areas of focus include crisis and health communication, conflict management, negotiation, mediation, and small group communication. Knotts holds an Interdisciplinary M.A. in Crisis, Risk and Health Communication from Southern Oregon University and a Master of Library & Information Science from Emporia State University.

D. G. Mawn, M.A., JD consults for Intuitive Synergies in Louisville, Kentucky. As President of the National Association for Community Mediation, he is the JAMS Foundation Grants Coordinator and TRUST Network Co-convener. He is also Systems Consultant for Indiana's Division of Mental Health and Addictions and Professor at George Mason University's Carter School.

Matthew Schmidt, PhD is the Director of Programs for the Laboratory for Analytic Sciences at North Carolina State University (NCSU) providing technical leadership for interdisciplinary research efforts on analytic tradecraft and tool integration. Dr. Schmidt received his Ph.D. from North Carolina State University for research on scalable subgraph detection algorithms.

Arik Segal is an international mediator and educator who specializes in the application of technologies in innovative dialogue structures. He established "Conntix" – a consultancy that focuses on conflict resolution through technology. Arik is adjunct faculty at Laudar School of Government, Diplomacy and Strategy at Reichman University (IDC Herzliya) and teaches about innovative conflict resolution and digital political campaigns.

Elizabeth L. Spradley, PhD (Texas A&M) is an Associate Professor of Communication at Stephen F. Austin State University and currently serves as the Communication Studies program coordinator. Her research focuses on narrative medicine and includes recent articles in the *Journal of Motherhood Initiative* and the *International Research Journal of Health Education.*

R. Tyler Spradley, PhD (Texas A&M) is Professor of Communication at Stephen F. Austin State University. In addition to coordinating leadership and crisis communication certificates, research focuses on high reliability, conflict, and organizational crisis communication in extreme contexts. Recent publications include *International Encyclopedia of Organizational Communication* and *Journal of Communication Pedagogy.*

Kathleen M. Vogel, PhD (Princeton University) is Professor in the School for the Future of Innovation in Society, Arizona State University. She is also Senior Global Futures Scientist, Julie Ann Wrigley Global Futures Laboratory. Vogel's research interests center around knowledge production on security and intelligence problems.

John Zeleznikow, PhD (Monash University) has conducted research and taught in Australian, US, French, Dutch, Israeli, Belgian, German, UK, Estonian, and Polish universities for forty-eight years. Over the past thirty years, Professor Zeleznikow has focused on how Artificial Intelligence can be used to enhance legal decision-making. He pioneered the use of machine learning in online dispute resolution.

Jeanne Felicity Zimmer, PhD completed her doctorate in Evaluation Studies with the supporting field of Conflict Management at the University of Minnesota, Twin Cities. She is an experienced mediator and restorative-justice facilitator, trainer, and educator, and served two terms on the NAFCM board.

About the Editors

Jessica Katz Jameson, PhD (Temple University) is a professor and department head in the Department of Communication at North Carolina State University. Her research interests include organizational conflict management, the role of emotion in mediation, and examining communication that constructs collaborative teams and organizations.

Missy F. Hannah, M.A. (University of Akron) is a social media specialist at SAS Institute where she works on the corporate social media team. Her research interests include corporate social media campaigns, social media activism, and the way those two areas intersect. She is currently a Ph.D. student in the CRDM (Communication, Rhetoric and Digital Media) program at North Carolina State University.

https://doi.org/10.1515/9783110687262-020

Index

https://doi.org/10.1515/9783110687262-021